The Rational and the Moral Order

THE PAUL CARUS LECTURES

PUBLISHED IN MEMORY OF

PAUL CARUS
1852–1919

EDITOR OF
THE OPEN COURT
AND
THE MONIST
FROM
1888 TO 1919

THE PAUL CARUS LECTURE SERIES 18

The Rational and the Moral Order

The Social Roots of Reason and Morality

KURT BAIER

OPEN COURT

Chicago and La Salle, Illinois

OPEN COURT and the above logo are registered in the U.S. Patent and Trademark Office.

© 1995 by Open Court Publishing Company

First printing 1995

Printed and bound in the United States of America.

Library of Congress Cataloging-in-Publication Data
Baier, Kurt.
    The rational and the moral order : the social roots of reason and morality / Kurt Baier.
       p.   cm.— (The Paul Carus lectures ; 18th ser.)
    Includes bibliographical references and index.
    ISBN 0-8126-9263-2. — ISBN 0-8126-9264-0 (pbk.)
    1. Social sciences and ethics. 2. Reason. I. Title.
II. Series.
BJ51.B35 1944
171′.2—dc20
                                    94-38462
                                        CIP

CONTENTS

CONTENTS ix

BOOK TWO: THE MORAL ORDER

CONTENTS

PREFACE

This book is intended primarily for those who believe in the great practical importance of distinguishing correctly between right and wrong, although they themselves are somewhat unclear about how to do so and although they suspect that the practical benefits of people doing what they think right can be reaped only if the distinction is drawn correctly. The most general thesis of this book is that uncertainties and disagreements about these matters can be satisfactorily settled only by providing an accurate acccount of what moralities are, both those of individuals and of societies, as well as of the relation between these two types of morality. In providing such an account, this book builds on three ideas that may be formulated, roughly, as follows: a person can have a morality only if she grows up in a society constituting a moral order, that is, a society with certain institutions and practices, including moral education, criticism, and reform; a person's morality consists primarily in dispositions to conform her behavior to directives she believes to be such that, by the best principles of justification, she would always be justified in following them and never justified in not doing so; what makes them such directives, is that they pass some test of acceptability, in my view that of practical reason.

Given these basic ideas, understanding what moralities are also calls for a theory of practical reason which exhibits them as generating the best principles of practical justification and, if that requires it, a theory of reason in general and of its relation to the particular kind that is practical reason. Accordingly, Book One begins with a relatively brief sketch of reason in general, and then proceeds to a more detailed account of practical reason, in which a crucial distinction is drawn between "self-anchored" (including prudential) and "society-anchored" (including legal) reasons. Part One of Book Two provides, at the highest level of generality, a theory of moralities which construes moral reasons as society-anchored. Part Two of Book Two attempts to show what more is needed if a morality specified at such a high level of generality is to be usable for deriving answers to specific moral questions in concrete situations. Accordingly, Part Two is divided between an account (in chapter 8) of the concepts and terms employed by people growing up in English-speaking cultures to formulate their moral judgments, and an account (in chapter 9) of the way—at any rate by my lights—those in this society who accept my theory could answer certain highly specific moral questions about whether or not to bring about or to prevent someone's death, and what moral judgment to pass on someone who had done one or other of these two things.

In presenting my theory of moralities and their justification through practical reason, I develop my account in as simple and direct a way as I can, adverting to other accounts only where this seemed a helpful expository device. I have not sought to make my own views more convincing by attempts to refute the most widely accepted rival accounts. Some readers may find this neglect of the numerous attractive alternatives a weakness or at any rate a disappointment. However, I hope that, by presenting my theses in this self-contained way, my book will be accessible to a wide audience including, besides professional philosophers, graduates, and undergraduates in philosophy, also others who are interested in a reason-based way of dealing with acute moral problems but whose familiarity with moral philosophy is limited.

Some readers of this Preface may want to know why I offer yet another book on ethics at a time when the ever-growing avalanche of excellent new publications on this subject is bound quickly to outdate and then to bury it? I offer it now, not because I flatter myself that it will escape this common fate, but partly because, even in its present far from perfect form, it can, I think, advance the reader's comprehension of the nature and aim of the moral enterprise and of why everyone's appropriate and full participation in it is so important, and partly because I know that, at this point, further revision is not likely to bring significant further improvement.

Readers should note that citations of the publications quoted or referred to in the text are placed at the foot of the page on which the reference occurs, and that discussions of a number of intricate issues which, though helpful, are not essential to following the argument in the text, have been relegated to notes collected in an Appendix. Notes are indicated in the text by an asterisk—or if there is more than one note relating to the same page, by the appropriate number of asterisks.

ACKNOWLEDGMENTS

Any author who has brooded on his brainchild as long as I have, is likely to have received some help along the way. In my case, all of the three main kinds—intellectual stimulation and challenge, release from duties unrelated to research, and financial assistance—were provided in generous amounts, and I am deeply grateful to the many providers. I incurred the first major intellectual debts relevant to this book while the Philosophy Department of the University of Pittsburgh held a research grant to investigate the impact of technological change on American values. The result of this investigation was a book edited by Nicholas Rescher and myself, entitled *Values and the Future*. My view of valuing, value, values, and the good were decisively influenced by my regular discussions with Nicholas Rescher, Jerome Schneewind, and David Braybrooke.

I also owe a great debt of gratitude to the Rockefeller Foundation and the National Humanities from whom I received research grants in 1979/80 and to the University of Pittsburgh and its Philosophy Department who granted me study leave. This gave me nine months of ideal conditions for research, during which I restructured and streamlined the design of a book I had planned earlier, and solved several problems that had delayed progress, among them the relation between reasons and motives, between pleasure, self-interest, happiness, fulfillment, goodness, the good, and between moral and prudential reasons. I was greatly helped by my daily lunch-time discussions with the Fellows at the Institute, and with several philosophers located in the area. My greatest debts are to the late David Falk, Martin Golding, Tom Hill, Tom Reagan, and Paul Ziff.

Although, at the end of that fruitful and happy period, the book was not quite ready for publication, the draft contained several relatively self-contained ideas that were accepted for publication. Some of these are listed in the bibliography at the end of this book.

I owe a further similar debt to the American Philosophical Association that invited me to give the Carus Lectures which I delivered in March 1990 in New Orleans, and to the Open Court Publishing Company for publishing them in this expanded form. I wish to express my appreciation to all who made this possible, especially the editor, Kerri Mommer, and her team of assistants.

I have also been very fortunate in receiving extensive help from present and former colleagues and visitors at the University of Pittsburgh—too many to list all of them—but I would be remiss not to mention the exceptional and sustained interactions as a result of which I came to see the errors in some of my views or was enabled to develop an idea that owed as much to the others' input as to mine. Of such discussions over extended periods of time relating to topics covered in this book, I remember three as particularly important: one with my colleague David Gauthier (on rationality and its relation to preferences and to value); one, in weekly meetings in which we critically examined each other's work in progress, with my former colleague Shelly Kagan (on the supposed incoherence of commonsense morality and the presumed plausibility of the principle of utility as an obligatory supreme practical principle); and one with a visitor to my Department, Bruce Russell (on ethical intuitionism and on whether killing is worse than letting die). More recently, I benefited from critical comments on the original version of my three Carus Lectures by Robert Audi and from Paul Hurley's extensive comments on an earlier version of Book One.

I have had similarly extended and illuminating discussions with a good many of the graduate students whose Ph.D. dissertations I had, or now have, the privilege of directing and from which, I am sure, I learned as much as or more than they did from my comments. They prominently include, in chronological order, Stephen Darwall, James Sterba, Laurence Thomas, Ted Benditt, Maggie Cohen, Michael Luey, Christopher McMahon, Paul Hurley, Jonathan Mandle, Dale Miller, and Claire Finkelstein. My views have also been strongly influenced by the explicit or implicit critiques of my views in the published work of some of them, e.g., in Darwall's *Impartial Reason*, Sterba's "Justifying Morality: The Right and the Wrong Way," and Thomas's *Living Morally*. I am also deeply indebted to Thomas for organizing, editing, and writing "A Tribute" for a Festschrift in my honor, and to all its distinguished contributors.

I incurred yet another massive debt of all three kinds through a Departmental Colloquium in my honor, on the topic "Reason and Morality" held at Pittsburgh, April 10–11, 1993. It was conceived and planned in 1991 by Rudolph Weingartner, at that time Chair of the Philosophy Department, in consultation with the departmental faculty and Peter Koehler, Dean of the Faculty of Arts and Sciences. I am expecially grateful to these two initiators, to my colleagues Robert Brandom and Richard Gale who did most of the spade work, and to the distinguished philosophers (Stephen Darwall, David Gauthier, Allan Gibbard, Jean Hampton, Shelly Kagan, Peter Railton, Joseph Raz, Thomas Scanlon, Jerome Schneewind, Laurence Thomas, and Judith Jarvis Thomson) whose papers are to appear in a companion volume to this book (forthcoming from Open Court). To all of the many participants in the Colloquium and to the contributors to the companion volume, I hereby express my heartfelt gratitude. I only regret that I am not free to show it by incorporating in the present version of my book, the many lessons I have learnt from them. I shall, however, have an opportunity to comment briefly, in this companion volume, on some of the doubts and objections raised.

There is, finally, a debt, as much of the heart as of the intellect, piled up over more than thirty years and still growing, which is owed to a very special philosopher, Annette Baier. In this case, the beneficial influence has been exerted not merely by one conversation or discussion, or a series of them, on one particular topic or a range of them; it is unceasing and all-encompassing; it is not just a steady drip that hollows the stone, but a swift-flowing stream that shapes it on all sides and, when swollen, turns it over and around so that all its sides are eventually licked into shape.

I have left to the very end debts of a fourth category—production of the book—because most of them are incurred at the very end. But not all. One person, Collie Henderson, has been involved in it for a very long time indeed. She flawlessly typed the innumeraable versions of this book, often from manuscripts written by me in a hand that sometimes even I cannot decipher. She automatically corrects the punctuation, the hyphenation, and the spelling, makes sense of, and supplies the verb for, my sometimes verbless sentences and, while she does not insist on reformulating awkward sentences, she draws attention to them and suggests improvements. I thank her most warmly for the special effort and care with which she has discharged her ofter very demanding tasks.

I am also deeply indebted to Dale Miller who took time off from writing about Mill to bring order into the chaos that were my footnotes. His ingenuity and perseverance succeeded in locating the many elusive references which I had jotted down from memory, often incompletely and wrongly. He also helped me with the tedious job of proofreading. The responsibility for any omissions and errors in both these tasks remains, alas, entirely mine.

Three Problems for Ethical Theory

Every now and then, there arise in a given domain serious doubts and disagreements about the beliefs that have been held unquestioned for a long time; when attempts are made to put these doubts to rest there also arises disagreement about how to get at the truth. If the issues are thought to be important, systematic investigations get started and, as in the case of astronomy, optics, or mechanics, fruitful methods are found and researchers build up a solid body of knowledge that is further enlarged and made more productive as the inquiry continues and advances. The striking successes in such disciplines lend prestige to their practitioners and authority to their findings. The public at large is satisfied that the labor and other resources expended on its behalf have conferred great benefits and may well continue to do so.

Similar expectations seem to underlie the continuing and expanding inquiries in ethics. But, although it is one of the oldest disciplines, by most assessments ethics has not been a very successful one.[1] While some philosophical subjects, such as logic, have made remarkable strides in improving the precision and trustworthiness of the best claims that can be made in their domains, this cannot be said about ethics. The question naturally arises why this should be so, particularly in view of its venerable age and the generally proclaimed importance of its subject matter. Why, we want to ask, is ethics still only a branch of philosophy, as natural philosophy used to be before it became physics? Why must it still try to be a first-order discipline like physics as well as a second-order one like philosophy of physics? Why must it still attempt to give answers to its ground-level questions and also deal with specifically philosophical

---

[1] On the lack of progress in ethics, see John Rawls, *A Theory of Justice* [hereafter *TJ*] (Cambridge, Mass.: Harvard University Press, 1971), 52; Bernard Williams, *Ethics and the Limits of Philosophy* (Cambridge, Mass.: Harvard University Press, 1985), preface VII, 17; Derek Parfit, *Reasons and Persons* (London: Oxford University Press, 1984), 453.

questions arising out of these answers? Why has there not yet developed a separate discipline in its own right, relying on its own tailor-made method, its own basic principles, and its own securely established results?

Of course, philosophers have tried again and again to put ethics on such solid foundations, to enable it to progress, like other successful systematic inquiries, on the road to knowledge, agreement, and authority. Alas, only minor successes, it is generally agreed, have so far crowned these efforts. Not only do philosophers still disagree on what one ought or ought not to do or be or feel, but they disagree on or are in serious doubt about how such disagreements should be resolved; indeed some are not even sure that there can be *any* generally acceptable method for resolving them, or that philosophers or indeed anyone should continue to devote their time to finding one.

Some think that the subject matter of ethics is incurably contentious and that it is a mistake to hope for a breakthrough in understanding or in method that could lead to an authoritative resolution of the disagreements or doubts.[2] But if they are right in this pessimistic assessment, what is it about the subject matter of ethics that makes these disagreements so intractable? The most widely held view would seem to be that it is the evaluative or normative character of the disagreements which, because not empirical or factual, are incapable of objective resolution, and so must remain forever in contention. But this can hardly be the whole explanation since other normative disciplines have done very well. I have already mentioned one, logic, when conceived as the inquiry into how we ought and how we ought not to argue. And, perhaps more surprisingly, we could also list all the natural sciences if we include in ethics what has been called "the ethics of belief,"[3] the inquiry into what we should and what we should not believe, including scientific beliefs. For few would challenge the claim that many sciences have not merely given us what are currently the best available beliefs in the domains they investigate, but also that these beliefs are vastly superior to prescientific ones and are in any case very highly reliable and practically serviceable by the most demanding standards.

Others attribute ethics' backwardness to external impediments erected to block its progress when it inquires into what is the best, the most desirable, the most worthwhile life. For, it is suspected, the better that life becomes for some, the worse it tends to be for others. Not surprising, then,

---

[2] Bernard Williams, *Ethics and the Limits of Philosophy*, 132–55.

[3] W. K. Clifford, "The Ethics of Belief," *The Ethics of Belief and Other Essays*, ed. Leslie Stephen and Sir Frederick Pollock (London: Watts, 1947), 70–96.

that those whom the prevailing social conditions have enabled to lead the good life, as they conceive it, are likely to oppose anything that could rock the boat in which they have found such a comfortable perch. Hence they are likely to oppose not only the efforts of the less favored who try to improve their social conditions, but also of those who inquire into how such a change can best be done and try to disseminate their recipes. Supporters of this view also remind us that progress in any discipline tends to be expensive, and why would those with the necessary resources expend them on an inquiry which, at best, is unlikely to improve their position and, at worst, may well undermine it? Are they not much more likely to finance the purveyors of those established convictions which help to perpetuate their privileges?

I do not wish to belittle the force of these arguments, but they can hardly be the most important part of the story. For, in the first place, in many countries including ours, the current climate for research in ethics is not unfavorable, let alone oppressive. Books, journals, and conferences on ethics proliferate at an astonishing rate, and so-called applied ethics is thriving even in areas such as medical and business ethics in which entrenched establishments might well feel threatened. In the second place, it cannot be overlooked that there are very considerable obstacles internal to the inquiry which must first be overcome if there is to be the sort of progress we have seen in the natural sciences. Of course, if they can be overcome—and this is a big "if"—and if the inquiry one day really takes wing and if its findings seriously threaten the privileged and powerful, researchers may well encounter the political obstacles mentioned earlier. But as things are in ethics now, we can ignore this worry for the moment.

What, then, are these internal difficulties? The most important belong to two major categories. The first comprises those that concern the nature of morality, its place in ethics as a whole, and its relation to rationality. The second includes those that arise out of accounts of the role that experience can play in confirming and disconfirming moral judgments and ethical theories. In this book I shall be concerned only with the first category—in my opinion by far the easier and the philosophically more tractable.

First, then, a few words about the subject matter of ethics, the philosophical discipline. In its widest (though not widely used) sense it is the inquiry into the evaluative and normative. As I mentioned, ethics in this widest sense includes the ethics of belief. In a somewhat narrower sense, employed for instance by Henry Sidgwick in his great work, *The Methods of Ethics*, it is synonymous with 'practical philosophy.' In this sense, ethics is the inquiry into what it is according to reason, and what it is contrary to it, for a given person to aim at or do in particular circumstances or in her life as a whole. We can call this the inquiry into *the rational life*.

We can also think of ethics as the inquiry into *the good life*. It then asks what is the good or the best life to lead for anyone or for persons of various kinds or for such persons in a variety of circumstances. It also asks whether the best life for such persons is better than the best for persons of other kinds or in other circumstances—thus Aristotle appears to have thought the philosopher's life of contemplation better than that of any other kind[4] and so also inquires into whether one could and should try suitably to transform the kind of person one currently is to make oneself capable of leading a superior life.

Finally, ethics may be thought of as the study of *the moral life*. Its central questions then are how we tell in what respects someone's life, her character, and her actions are in accordance with morality, and in what respects are contrary to it.

Section 1.   The Rationality Problem

The first problem arises in its most acute form if, as many now hold, these three types of life do not necessarily or actually always coincide.[5] For in that case, whenever the moral life diverges from either or both the rational and the good life, it seems we need to find out which is the most choiceworthy, but we cannot see how. At the same time, it seems impossible to give up any one of the convictions that give rise to the problem.

The first of these convictions is that we cannot rationally justify our conduct unless it is for our good, which we naturally identify with our happiness. In Bishop Butler's famous words: "Let it be allowed, though virtue or moral rectitude does indeed consist in affection to and pursuit of what is right and good as such, yet that, when we sit down in a cool hour, we can neither justify to ourselves this or any other pursuit till we are convinced that it will be for our happiness, or at least not against it."[6]

---

[4] Aristotle, *Nicomachean Ethics*, ed. Terence Irwin (Indianapolis, Ind.: Hackett Publishing Co., 1985) 284–87 [1177a10–1178a5]. For a sophisticated interpretation of Aristotle's overall view see Richard Kraut, *Aristotle on the Human Good* (Princeton, N.J.: Princeton University Press, 1989), especially chapter 1.

[5] Thomas Nagel, *The View from Nowhere* (New York: Oxford University Press, 1986), 189–207.

[6] Joseph Butler, *The Works of Joseph Butler*, vol. 2, ed. W. E. Gladstone (London: Oxford

The second conviction is that the moral life cannot be choiceworthy unless it is rational to lead it. If the precepts of morality were contrary to our good, and so contrary to reason, then the moral life would be worthless—or as Hobbes puts it in a splendid passage in *Leviathan:* "The Kingdom of God is gotten by violence: but what if it could be gotten by unjust violence? were it against Reason so to get it, when it is impossible to receive hurt by it? and if it be not against Reason, it is not against Justice: *or else Justice is not to be approved for good."*[7]

The third conviction is that, unlike the conditional requirements of reason which are counsels of prudence or self-interest, the unconditional requirements of duty, the dictates of morality, do not necessarily, and often do not in fact, promote our ends, our happiness, or our good. Nevertheless, only a will that is set on fulfilling these requirements has moral, that is, unconditional, that is, the highest worth. As Kant says: "Nothing can be taken as good without qualification except a good will . . . [it] is good in itself . . . [and] is to be esteemed beyond comparison and for higher than anything it could ever bring about merely in order to favor some inclination or, if you like, the sum total of inclination," [that is, happiness].[8] But the good will is the will to do one's duty for duty's sake. Thus satisfying the moral requirement which has the highest worth and makes us deserving of happiness may well actually makes us unhappy.

If these three plausible theses are sound, then leading the moral life may sometimes make one unhappy, in which case it is contrary to reason and so worthless, and so not choiceworthy. But leading the moral life also is an unconditional requirement of reason, the disposition to comply with which alone has moral, and so the absolutely highest, worth and so is eminently choiceworthy. It seems, therefore, that the rational, the good, and the moral life may well, perhaps are bound to, come into conflict with one another, and that we must sometimes subordinate the demands of at least one of them, but that there is no appropriate supreme point of view from which to make the choice. Consistency, it would seem, requires us to give up one or other of these theses but we can find no adequate reason for giving up one rather than another.

Philosophers have favored one or other of three different escapes from

---

University Press, 1897), 173. Sermon XI at the Rolls Chapel, section 21.

[7] Thomas Hobbes, *Leviathan* (1951; reprint, New York: Penguin Books, 1984), chapter 15, 203, my emphasis.

[8] Immanuel Kant, *Groundwork of the Metaphysics of Morals,* in *The Moral Law,* tr. H. J. Paton (London: Hutchinson University Library, 1961), 61f.; [393/4].

this problem. The ancient Greek approach (widely followed until Kant) regarded it as one of the main tasks of ethics to prove that there is no real conflict between these three types of life. In that view, it is the ethicist's primary task to characterize the three types of life in such a way that both the rational and the moral life are seen to be capable of being smoothly accommodated within the good life. In this view, the invidious choice simply never does or can arise.

The second major approach concedes the possibility or likelihood of divergence and takes rationality to be the ultimate criterion of choice-worthiness. It comprises three versions. One argues that the rational thing to do when the happy (or good) and the moral life conflict, is to choose the happy rather than the moral life. Although Butler's famous dictum, quoted a few paragraphs ago, appears to favor this view, he himself also appears to hold the converse position. In fact, it seems that no great moral philosopher has unequivocally adopted this "low appraisal" of morality, though some of the Greek sophists, such as Thrasymachus, clearly embraced it. The second version (for instance, Hobbes and Kant) argues that, on the contrary, it is rational to choose the moral rather than the happy life, when there is or appears to be a conflict between them, since the moral life is a part (although they disagree on exactly what part) of the rational life. In this second version, then, it can never be rational to be immoral. The third version argues that it is equally rational to choose either the happy or the moral life. In this third version, it can be in accordance with reason to choose what is wrong but equally so to choose what makes one unhappy; however, neither can be rationally required.[9] The third major approach holds that reason requires one to choose the good life even when that conflicts with morality, but argues that the ultimate criterion of choiceworthiness is morality rather than rationality, or (perhaps) that at this point the notion of choiceworthiness loses its grip.[10]

There is no general agreement about which of these escapes is the best. In my view, philosophers have done much better at showing the inadequacy of the versions they oppose than in demonstrating the superiority of the version they favor. It seems that all these resolutions are arbitrary. Each simply demotes one or other of the factors that give rise to the

---

[9] Henry Sidgwick, *The Methods of Ethics*, [hereafter *ME*] 7th ed. (London: Macmillan, 1907), 506–9.

[10] For example, see Philippa Foot, "Morality as a System of Hypothetical Imperatives," *The Philosophical Review* 81 (1972). Reprinted in *Virtues and Vices* (Berkeley, Calif.: University of California Press, 1978), 157–67.

problem, but none shows convincingly why this factor, rather than one of the other two, should be singled out for demotion.

Section 2.   The Motivation Problem

Another closely related problem concerns the relation of reason to motivation. If reason is to have any practical significance, if we often, perhaps always, can do what we know or believe we have compelling reason to do, then, it seems, reason must be able to motivate us to act accordingly. Furthermore, if, as conventional wisdom and many philosophers appear to hold, moral considerations are practical reasons, then it seems reason must always be able to motivate normal people in normal circumstances, for otherwise they cannot be held responsible for their immoral conduct. That is to say, reason must be able to move *us* (or *we* must be able) to act as it tells us morality requires. We know, of course, that people often yield to temptation and to threats when it is contrary to reason and to morality to do so, but that, it is widely believed, is not because reason lacked the power so to motivate them, but only because they did not make the necessary effort.

In any case, it seems, at least the following must (always, or at least in certain suitable circumstances?) be true: that when we believe we have compelling reason to deliberate before we act, we can and (always, etc.?) do deliberate and, having deliberated, can and do act in accordance with the outcome of our deliberation. But how can this be true? Is reason a faculty that both tells us what is in accordance with reason, and then inclines us to do so? Or does reason merely tell us how to attain that for which we have by "extrarational" forces become motivated to aim? Can something be a reason for someone to do something without its actually motivating him to do so; or is being a motivator a necessary condition of being a reason for that person?

There are two major types of "solution" to this motivation problem, according to their account of the origin of the power of reason to motivate. The first, following one line of thought in Hume's writings, holds that reason is wholly inert and is therefore by itself incapable of moving us to action; thus, in his famous words, it is and ought only to be the slave of the passions.[11] On this view, what motivates us, that is, inclines us, to change the ends we are currently pursuing (whether the pursuit involves resting or

---

[11] David Hume, *A Treatise of Human Nature*, eds. L. A. Selby-Bigge and P. H. Nidditch, 2nd ed. (Oxford: Oxford University Press, 1978), 415.

chasing after something) is our passions, not reason itself, for reason itself cannot determine what ends to pursue, but at most *how* to attain ends one has in other ways come to desire. Call this view "Instrumentalism." It tells us that reason is a power whose only practical function is to discover the necessary or best means to our ends. Instrumentalism solves the motivation problem by embracing the view that motivation "comes from sources outside reason itself." A major problem for this view is to find a reconciliation between what reason appears to tell us to do and what we are motivated to do, as when it appears to tell us to adopt a new end, for example, to give up smoking when we want to smoke.

The other approach, following one line of thought in Kant's writings, ascribes to reason not only the function and power allowed by Instrumentalism, but also the further function and power denied by it, namely, that of telling us what ends to pursue or not to pursue. Call this second approach, for lack of a better term, "Anti-Instrumentalism." It denies the Instrumentalist claim that reason cannot critically examine and determine our "ultimate" ends (that is, those that are not merely intermediate ends which could be so examined by reference to further and more nearly ultimate ones; Aristotle thought of "eudaimonia," Hume of pleasure, as such an ultimate end). Most Anti-Instrumentalists are, therefore, driven to embrace the view that reason is a faculty or power with its own motivational resources. Kant, for instance, claims that "respect (Achtung) for the law" is such an intrarational motivating power.[12]

A brief look at a few popular versions of Instrumentalism and Anti-Instrumentalism should convince us that neither approach gives a satisfactory solution of the motivation problem. Take first what I call "the Sidgwickian variant" of Instrumentalism.[13] Although generally in the

---

[12] The distinction between what I call (1) "Intrinsicalism" versus "Extrinsicalism" should be kept apart from the one already mentioned, namely, (2) "Instrumentalism" versus "Anti-Instrumentalism," and from a further one, (3) "Internalism" versus "Externalism." As we have seen, the first concerns *the source* of the power to motivate us as reason tell us to; the second concerns the powers and function of reason. As originally defined by Frankena [William K. Frankena, "Obligation and Motivation in Recent Moral Philosophy," *Essays in Moral Philosophy*, ed. A. I. Melden (Seattle, Wash.: University of Washington Press, 1958), 40–41; Frankena attributes the distinction to David Falk, "'Ought' and Motivation," *Proceedings of The Aristotelian Society* XLVIII (1947–48), 137], the distinction in the third concerns the question of whether or not something can be a reason for someone to do something independently of whether her knowing or believing that it is a reason for her to do that thing motivates her to do it. It would seem, then, that one can be an Internalist or an Externalist independently of which side one comes down on in the Intrinsicalist/Extrinsicalist debate, but it may be hard or impossible consistently to combine Anti-Instrumentalism with Extrinsicalism.

[13] Sidgwick, ME, chapters 3, 9, especially iiif.

spirit of the anti-rationalist strand in Hume, Sidgwick attempts to avoid the paradoxical implications of that conception by tightening the connection between our normative judgments and the deliberations whose conclusions they are. He holds (1) that the work of practical reason involves, first, deliberation about what to do, by surveying and weighing the relevant pros and cons (let us call that "the reflective task") and, second, action in accordance with the outcome of deliberation (call that "the executive task"); and he holds (2) that action in accordance with reason is action in accordance with the outcome of such deliberation, which he construes as acting the way *one is inclined to act* after one has fully surveyed and adequately attended to the relevant consequences of all the alternatives open to one.

This is an account, prima facie not implausible, of how we are to understand talk of "what reason requires and permits," or of how we come "to hear the voice of reason" or to grasp "the dictates of reason as written on the hearts of man." This account of practical deliberation and its outcome also appears to dispose of the motivation problem or at least to make it less intractable than it at first appears.

These and other strengths have made this model widely popular. Nevertheless, there are several difficulties which appear to make it unacceptable. Here are two. The first is that while it does indeed dispose of the motivation problem at what it turns into its most salient point, the problem reappears at a point further back in the process of arriving at a judgment of what we ought to do. On the commonsense account of deliberation, the most salient point is the completion of the reflective task which then poses the practical task for us. On the Sidgwickian variant, that point ceases to be salient. What rises to become salient are the (hidden?) factors that determine whether or not what we are going to do about a particular matter is determined by a practical judgment and the deliberation generating it. Suppose it does not occur to you to deliberate, or you do not feel like deliberating about whether to give to a certain charity, but, instead, you follow your unreflective inclination not to give. Suppose, also, that if you had deliberated about whether to give, you would have formed the judgment that you should give and with it (ipso facto) the inclination to give. Does this (counterfactual conditional) fact show that it was not contrary to reason for you not to give to that charity? On the one hand, it seems so, for it seems not to be the case that what you actually did was contrary to your judgment of what you ought to do, since you did not arrive at such a judgment; however, does it not, for the same reason, also seem not to be the case that it was *not* contrary to it, for if it is not contrary to it, it is in accordance with it, but how can it be in accordance with a judgment you did not make? On the other hand, why discount the judgment you would have arrived at if, contrary to fact, you had deliberated? Presumably, we must attach some weight to the outcome of deliberation irrespective of whether or not it actually occurred. Otherwise why not always save time and energy by not deliberating?

Someone might suggest that the judgment (i.e., about whether or not we ought to give) which we would have arrived at if we had deliberated about it should determine whether or not we ought to give if and only if, had we deliberated about whether or not to deliberate about whether we ought to give, we would have decided to deliberate about whether to give. But that appears to create a vicious infinite regress, for it seems we would have to say that the outcome of our counterfactual deliberation counts if and only if, supposing (counterfactually) we had deliberated about whether to deliberate about whether to deliberate about whether to give, then we would have decided that we should so deliberate. But then, since we had not so deliberated, the regress continues, and so forth without end. If counterfactual deliberation at the first level has no weight, then presumably it can have no weight at the second or any higher level either.

Finally, might not a person reason as follows? If I deliberate about whether to give to charity, I might come to the conclusion that I should give, but I now do not want to. Why should I risk deliberating if, were I not to deliberate, I would not want to and would not give and so be better off? And so it goes at each stage of the deliberation. It seems, then, on the basis of this construal of deliberation and the practical judgment arising out of it, that we might well be better off not to deliberate but to act on impulse.

The question then is whether or not to take into account the counterfactual judgments resulting from counterfactual deliberations. If we say *no*, then that might well incline us not to deliberate in order not to arrive at decisions we currently do not like. But that seems contrary to the point of deliberating in the first place. But if we say *yes*, then the motivation problem arises again. For we then seem to have a conflict between what reason tells us to do and what we are motivated to do.

The second problem concerns another peculiarity of the Sidgwickian account of deliberation. Compare it with the commonsense account of reflecting on whether or not to believe something. Suppose you have received an anonymous letter telling you that your neighbors are plotting to kill you. Would you conduct your reflection in the way suggested by the Sidgwickian model? Would you not rather try to discover as much as possible of the *relevant evidence*, and would you not believe whatever the best evidence points to, or if that goes against the grain, at least try to? You may, for instance (taking another example), find it hard or impossible to believe that Jack is not your son even though the relevant blood groups constitute conclusive evidence that he is not. In any case, would not others—and normally you yourself also—agree that your belief is in accordance with reason if and only if it is warranted by the evidence (or at least not in conflict with it)? If you believe that Jack is your son even though you know about those blood groups and believe for good reasons that this constitutes conclusive evidence against his being your son, then there would be general agreement that your belief is irrational because flying in the face of what is, and what you purport to believe is, conclusive evidence.

The Sidgwickian variant thus implies that being in accordance with reason is a very different matter in the case of action from what it is in the case of belief. On Sidgwick's account, action in accordance with reason is *action from adequately informed inclination*, whereas belief in accordance with reason is *belief in accordance with the best evidence, whatever one's adequately informed inclination to believe*. Thus, in reflecting about what to believe, we draw a clear distinction between what further things our belief that certain things are facts inclines us to believe, and what further beliefs are warranted by these facts. Thus, the explanation of why, on the Sidgwickian variant, the motivation problem seems to have been solved, is simply that this version so conceives of practical deliberation that such a problem cannot arise at the point at which we ordinarily think it can and does arise. For that variant so conceives practical deliberation that its conclusion, as in Aristotle's practical syllogism, is what the person is overall inclined to do. There is no logical gap between the completion of the reflective and the executive task. This raises the further question of whether we can accept such a significant revision of our conception of rational deliberation and of the practical judgments telling us what it is in accordance with, what contrary to reason to do, especially because it appears that so conceived we may do better to avoid deliberation and that even this way of deliberating does not really solve the motivation problem but merely shifts its locus.

Consider, then, two further implications of this variant. Note, first, that it makes any and every fact capable of affecting one's inclination, relevant to what one should do, but that it would be hard or impossible to know, before actually deliberating about them, whether all or even most facts of one's situation would or would not affect what one was disposed to do. Hence it becomes difficult or impossible to make sure that one has adequately attended to *all* the relevant facts and that the relevance of a fact has not changed while one attended to others. With luck, the same facts will be relevant to the same practical question every time one attends to them, but they are not likely to exert the same influence every time or even to pull in the same direction. The resulting inclination may even be different depending on the order in which one reviews the facts and on how thoroughly and imaginatively one attends to each of them. Attending to some of them may itself be a motivational problem (try adequately attending to all the relevant facts when you need a fix, or when the burglar comes at you with a gun, or when your love has stripped for action), and attending to all of them simultaneously may be impossible. For these reasons, it would be difficult if not impossible to know at what point one has completed one's deliberation and so what one should do on a particular occasion. This further confirms the conclusion that deliberation so conceived is a waste of time and energy.

A second disturbing corollary is that the practical judgment resulting from deliberation, instead of being a verbal guide to action, is transformed into a further causal factor, jostling others. When I deliberate in this fashion about whether to give up smoking, I reflect on the consequences both of smoking and of giving it up; I identify the "relevant" facts and carefully and imaginatively attend to all of them. Of course, while I do all this, I am still strongly inclined to smoke; indeed, I am now desperate for a cigarette. However, the facts I have examined may have led me to the judgment that it would be contrary to reason to go on smoking and that I should give it up. On the Sidgwickian model, the content of this judgment has no special guiding role. It does not formulate the conclusion of my reflective task thereby setting my executive task; it is simply another causal factor. If I follow my inclination after (somehow) finishing my deliberation, then there is no question of whether or not my action was (or at least was in accordance with my judgment of what was) in accordance with reason. If my overall inclination after deliberation is to go on smoking, then for me to do so *is* in accordance with reason, even if my judgment was that I should give it up. Thus, it appears that Sidgwickian deliberation is not a surveying, weighing, and computing of the relevant reasons, but is, at worst, like Hobbes's,[14] a determining of the last appetite in deliberation and, at best, a determining of what one *really wants,* in one sense of this expression. It does not allow the question we surely can ask, namely, whether we ought to do what in this sense we "really" want to do. I may well, in this sense, really want to smoke a cigarette even when I judge that it would be best not to and that therefore it would be contrary to reason to smoke and that therefore I should not smoke.

---

[14] Hobbes, *Leviathan,* 126–28.

It seems, then, that what is wrong with the Sidgwickian variant is its lack of an objective procedure or canon of reasoning—analogous to that in thinking about what to believe—one that regiments the deliberation and leads to conclusions that, when formulated, can *guide* action, that is, can tell us what to do before we know what is our dominant inclination after deliberating. Thus, if reasons for action are like reasons for believing, then it seems a mistake to make "informed inclination" the necessary *and sufficient* condition of action according to reason.

Consider, then, another variant which adds as a further necessary condition an independent procedure for conducting a practical deliberation but retains what seemed promising in the Sidgwickian variant, namely, that the conclusion of a person's practical deliberation cannot constitute a compelling practical reason for her to do a certain thing unless it also has the ability to motivate her accordingly. The problem with this is that such a compromise simply raises anew the old motivation problem. For if the procedure is genuinely independent of our motivations, then the conclusion of our deliberation may conflict with our final overall inclination, as indeed is frequently the case.

Turn, then, to an Anti-Instrumentalist account along what many would consider roughly (or very roughly) Kantian lines. Suppose that in deliberation we follow a procedure that is genuinely independent of our "extrarational" motivation and that reason has its own motivational resources, that is, dispositions to act in accordance with whatever we find to be the conclusion of our practical deliberation. Suppose, further, that this motivation is sufficiently strong to overcome even the strongest extrarational motivations, and that the procedure consists in applying a test of formal universalizability to tentative maxims drawn from the ends determined by our desires and from our knowledge of the means for attaining them. Unlike the Sidgwickian variant, this model allows, indeed stresses, conflicts between our final overall inclinations and the maxims we arrive at when the tentative ones have been purified by this test of universalizability. It solves the motivation problem by the claim that reason has its own motivational resources—say, a deep respect for the practical judgments based on universalizable maxims—which are always sufficient to overcome the motives generated by our desires.

It seems, however, that every account of such an Anti-Instrumentalist and Intrarationalist type faces two serious problems about the nature and powers of reason. The first concerns the nature of the (mental) powers on account of which we tell whether something is a reason for someone to do something and how it can be that such recognition of something as a reason, ipso facto or by some mental procedure, "mobilizes" the required intrarational motivation to conform to the practical judgment which is the conclusion of practical deliberation. The second concerns the relation between the aims of reason and our overall motivation.

Concerning the first point, it seems impossible to give an account of reason which can make sense of the claim that it has and can mobilize the motivational resources required to overcome extrarational motivation. This type of theory needs, first, to dispose of the view that reason is wholly inert and therefore is and ought only to be the slave of the passions. It also needs to show that reason is the sort of thing which has motivational powers that come into play whenever (and only when?) we form practical judgments. Furthermore, it needs to provide an explanation of what it is for reason actually to *have* motivational power which, however, does not actually *come into play* when, for instance, a weak-willed person arrives at a judgment of what it is in accordance with reason to do, but which she (or her reason) does not (but could have) mobilize to overcome those motivational forces by which she (or it) actually was moved. And finally, this type of theory must be able to distinguish the cases, if there are any, in which reason or its owner could have mobilized such motivational resources (though it or she in fact did not) from those other cases, if there are any, in which reason or its owner did not have such additional resources or was unable to mobilize them. This last point is particularly important for those many thinkers who hold the deeply entrenched commonsense view that genuine moral considerations are paramount practical reasons which can and often do come into conflict with nonmoral and extrarational motivations, but that we always, or at any rate often, could have mobilized our intrarational motivational resources to overcome those extrarational motives which on some occasions actually won the day.

The second point concerns a quite different difficulty, namely, why one should follow the dictates of reason so conceived, that is, tied to this deliberation procedure and having the powers ascribed to it by this (very roughly) Kantian conception. In instrumental theories, reason is conceived as the ability to tell us the means to our ultimate ends, while the question of why we should aim at such an ultimate end does not or cannot arise. Thus, we are not inclined to ask, perhaps cannot sensibly ask, "Why go for pleasure, happiness, flourishing, self-realization, preference-satisfaction, the good, and so on?" This is not merely the question of what ends, as a matter of empirical fact or of psychological necessity, we all aim at. Rather, it is the question, "What ends are such that we cannot sensibly ask why people want to aim at these things on their own account?, or even, What ends are such that we cannot sensibly ask why people *should not* fail to aim at them on their own account?" About ends of this sort we are inclined to think that we all *in fact* do aim at them or at least that, if we do not, we would like to be persons who do, and we regret not being such persons. We think of such ends as in some way at least universally acceptable or even universally regarded as desirable, truly worthwhile or ideal. We feel that we are not misguided, deceived, or in for disappointment or regret, if we do aim at them, or even that we are on the wrong track if we do not.

The problem with a theory of reason such as the roughly Kantian one we are now considering is that it rejects any connection between reason and such other commonly recognized "ultimate ends." It has therefore cut reason off from those undeniable sources of motivation which, if conceived of as internal to reason, are not embarrassed by the question, "But why go for that?" It seems plausible to regard happiness or flourishing or fulfillment as such ultimate ends. But our roughly Kantian conception of reason rejects the idea that reason tells us the best means to happiness or any other such ordinary ultimate end. It replaces it with the idea that the ultimate end is to become deserving of happiness by acting in accordance with principles of reason, that is, roughly, universalizable maxims. But it is much less plausible to think of this as an ultimate aim, in the sense that it is incapable of being embarrassed by the question, "Why go for that?"

This leaves us with a difficult choice. Should we impose on deliberation a procedure, method, or canon, according to which the content and weight of practical reasons do not necessarily coincide with "motivating facts," thus yielding an outcome independent of and possibly in conflict with our overall inclination after deliberation? Or should we simply bring what we already know to be motivating facts to bear on our inclinations so that on its completion the outcome, our "conclusion," is necessarily in agreement with our overall inclination but therefore possibly in conflict with what we ourselves may judge to be the balance of reasons?

In the former case, we confront the seemingly insuperable problem of finding a method that satisfies two conditions: that practical judgments rest on *a method* and on inputs such that we have no difficulty with the question, "Why comply with its all-things-considered judgments?"; and that, in cases of conflict with our overall inclination, these judgments always generate adequate motivation to overcome our extrarational motivation.

In the latter case we face two different problems. One is to give an account of deliberation that does not turn it into an impossibility or a waste of effort. The other is to show why practical, unlike cognitive, deliberation need not, if it is to avoid being a waste of time, follow a procedure that issues in a judgment recommending behavior which is superior to doing merely what one "really" wants to do and which, when different from that, can set us a genuine executive task, namely, to generate the motivation necessary for acting in accordance with that judgment rather than with what we really want to do.

Section 3.   Morality and Sanctions

A third such internal problem concerns the role of sanctions. It arises out of our conviction that societies are morally justified, perhaps required, to impose sanctions on moral wrongs. Some have held that only unlawful actions but not morally wrong ones may be punished, but others have doubted that. Some have doubted it on the grounds that even unlawful actions are rightly punished only if they are also morally wrong, others on the ground that even general moral disapproval or the pangs of a person's own conscience constitute punishment. In any case, it appears to be generally thought that at least these so-called *moral* sanctions are appropriate in response to immoral action.

The problem remains that although it seems plausible and generally accepted that immorality should be sanctioned, it does not seem plausible or generally accepted that irrationality should be. Are we then wrong in thinking that these different responses to immorality and irrationality are appropriate, or is there really a fundamental difference between immorality and irrationality which explains and justifies these different responses? What might the difference be? Is it perhaps that the requirements of morality are different from those of reason? There certainly appear to be things, such as making a detour to avoid crossing the path of a black cat, or to risk virtually certain death to climb a difficult mountain in a snowstorm, which are irrational but not for that reason alone immoral; conversely, there appear to be things, such as bribing a foreign official to land a profitable contract, which are immoral but not for that reason alone irrational, as when one has every reason to expect that the bribery will not be discovered or, if discovered, will not be costlier than not getting the contract. It seems true, then, that moral considerations are not necessarily reasons and reasons not necessarily moral considerations. But if not, it would seem that sanctions in support of moral precepts are not, or at least not on their own account, rationally justified, since people would not have reason to comply with them as such. For, what reason could they be given for being pressured into doing what they have no reason to do? If someone else saw reason for them to be so pressured, this surely would only lend credence to views, such as those of Thrasymachus and Marx, according to which moralities are systems of principles and precepts that have been fraudulently imposed by a ruling class, for its own advantage, on a ruled class. Such a conception of morality would indeed explain "the need" (that is, the need of the ruling class) for sanctions, but it would also seem to show that, although the imposition of such sanctions could be rationally justified to the ruling class, it could not be so justified to the ruled class. But that is precisely our earlier difficulty, that such sanctions cannot be rationally justified, at least not to everyone on whom they are to be imposed.

Was it perhaps a mistake in the first place to think that there can be no rationally justifiable sanctions on irrational behavior? Does not the epithet "irrational" carry an evaluative thrust much as do "unwise," "imprudent," "foolish," "reckless," and the like, and do not these in turn resemble "wicked," "wrongful," "immoral," and so on, in expressing a negative reaction to the things to which they are ascribed? Do they not then, themselves, constitute a comparable pressure against the behavior to which they apply and so a kind of rational sanction comparable to the so-called moral sanction?

But there are significant differences between different types of sanction. For our purposes here we should distinguish three kinds: self-protective, choice-weighting, and corrective. In calling something imprudent or unwise or reckless or foolish or generally irrational, we indicate that we think it is the type which justifies self-protective pressure, the kind appropriate for behavior which, though it tends to be detrimental primarily to the agent himself, also tends to be indirectly detrimental to those associated with him in certain joint enterprises. It would therefore be prudent to take such measures as would protect oneself from such indirect detriment. Thus, if one tells people that someone is imprudent or irrational, it helps to build up a certain reputation which discourages others from entering into certain joint enterprises with that person. In this indirect way it puts some pressure on him to change his ways.

Choice-weighting pressures, by contrast, are those that make something more or less preferable (or dispreferable) for someone than it otherwise would be, whether or not it is the purpose or function of the pressure to bring about choices in that direction. The imposition of an import duty on foreign cars usually has that aim and that effect; the imposition of a cigarette tax may not—for its aim may be to increase revenue which is of course less likely to be achieved if consumption is thereby reduced. Note, however, that even where the aim is a change in behavior patterns, the pressure is such as to leave agents *free* to ignore it; it remains legally and morally permissible for them to choose as before. However, the choice itself, we may say, will no longer be a free one since it is now artificially weighted—it can no longer be made simply on the merits of the alternatives themselves. That people are free to ignore the weighting then means, among other things, that ignoring it is a legitimate, permissible option, and therefore punishing them for ignoring the weighting would not be justifiable.

The third type, corrective pressure, is such as to leave the agent no legitimate option but to choose a certain course. It implies that he can legitimately be prevented from doing a certain thing or compelled to do the opposite or threatened with penalties if he does not do it or made to pay compensation to someone if he has done it. But not only that, for corrective pressure is designed not merely to undo—or to compensate some for others' doing—something to which such pressure is justifiably attached. Those to whom such pressure is being applied are not merely made to "pay their debt to society" (as punishment is often misleadingly characterized), like someone who has bought cigarettes carrying an excise tax and so is paying for his (conceivably unobjectionable) self-indulgence, but these pressures are applied with a view to changing the agent's pattern of behavior, to *remotivate* him. This is the most important difference between corrective and the other kinds of sanction. It is what makes corrective sanction the most intrusive and for this reason the prima facie most objectionable.

It would seem, then, that when we think that sanctions cannot justifiably be imposed for irrationality, what we have in mind are corrective, but not self-protective sanctions. Hence, even if it is a fact that all valid moral considerations are valid practical reasons, this would not explain or justify the belief that there is rational justification for the imposition of corrective sanctions on moral wrongs. For although we appear to think that the imposition of self-protective, perhaps even of choice-weighting pressures against irrationality is justified, we also appear to think that the imposition of corrective sanctions on irrationality is unjustified. We tend to think it solely *our own business* whether we are rational or irrational, but not whether we are moral or immoral. The question, therefore, remains, whether moral considerations are reasons and if so, what it is about moral reasons that distinguishes them from others, such as those of prudence, that would justify the imposition of corrective pressure on immorality but not on imprudence.

It may perhaps be thought that views, such as those of the classical Legal Positivists,[15] have pinpointed that difference. For they held that moral obligation and duty are to be explicated in terms of the existence of such corrective social sanctions on certain types of behavior (though, of course, they did not use this terminology). That will not help, however, for even the severest sanctions threatened by a bank robber are only choice-weighting, not corrective; to explicate obligation it is insufficient to show that such sanctions exist, rather their existence must itself be justified, both on its own account and on account of what the sanctions are imposed for. For we do not think it wrong not to meet the demands of the bank robber, but we do think it wrong to break our obligations. Conversely, it appears we think it wrong to kill or to break our contracts even though no effective corrective sanction exists. Furthermore, it seems, we think not only that the imposition of such corrective sanctions would be rationally and morally justified, that is, permissible, but also that they rationally and morally ought to be imposed by society, that it would be impermissible not to impose them.

J. S. Mill recognized this when he explained (in chapter 5 of his *Utilitarianism*) that for something to be an obligation of someone to do something in a given situation, there has to be a suitable justification (for Mill, a utilitarian one) not only for that person's doing that thing, but also for imposing a suitable sanction on those not doing it. But one may well have doubts about this account: do we not need an explanation of what it is about the moral wrongness (or the moral requiredness) of some conduct which, unlike its foolishness, morally justifies and perhaps requires its being supported by corrective rather than merely self-protective or choice-weighting pressures? Would we really have an obligation not to be foolish if the imposition of corrective pressures were justifiable on utilitarian grounds? Must not the imposition of a suitable corrective sanction be justified by a prior substantiation of the claim that the action on which it is to be imposed is wrong or is a duty? And does not that mean that the action's being wrong (or a duty), cannot *consist* in its (or its

---

[15] Thus, John Austin writes that "Of the duties imposed by positive moral rules . . . we may say . . . that they are sanctioned or enforced morally." *The Province of Jurisprudence Determined Etc.*, ed. H. L. A. Hart (London: Weidenfeld and Nicolson, 1954), 158. See also Jeremy Bentham, *A Fragment on Government*, ed. J. H. Burns and H. L. A. Hart (Cambridge, UK: Cambridge University Press, 1988), 108–10n. "[W]ithout the notion of punishment no notion can we have of either right or duty. . . . One may conceive three sorts of duties: political, moral, and religious, correspondent to the three sorts of sanctions by which they are enforced . . . Moral duty is created by various mortifications resulting from the ill-will of . . . the community in general."

omission's) not being justified, together with the (utilitarian) justifiability of its being suitably sanctioned?[16]

It seems clear, at least to me, that ethics is unlikely to advance unless at least these three internal problems can be solved or dissolved. We must know whether or not moral considerations are a species of reasons, whether and if so why corrective sanctions should be attached to wrong-doing and other immoralities, and what the relation is between on the one hand moral reasons—and practical reasons generally—and on the other hand motivation. But for this we need a clearer account of moral and practical as well as other kinds of reasons and of the power of faculty we call Reason, often with a capital R. My thesis is that the two factors that have contributed most to the problems I have sketched are the widespread misconceptions of Reason and of Morality. It seems to me that, although a good many now suspect that Morality has been seriously misconceived throughout the long history of ethics, far fewer appear to harbor such suspicions about Reason. Be that as it may, I shall in Book One give an account of Reason and of the various types of reasons, and so prepare the ground for the solution of the motivation problem. In Book Two, I examine the concept of Morality thereby enabling us, among other things, to see that moral considerations are genuine practical reasons which may conflict with other kinds of practical reasons but can defeat them. It will also enable us to see why there should be corrective sanctions of a certain kind for wrong-doing and other kinds of immorality. Finally, in chapter 9, I shall use the results gained earlier for the purpose of shedding light on a few currently much-discussed moral problems, such as whether it is worse to kill than to let die. I hope, in that part, to convince the reader that my clarifications of Reason and Morality and the relation between them put us in a better position to settle such moral problems and to regard a problem thus settled as solved.

---

[16] In my paper on "Moral Obligation," (*American Philosophical Quarterly* 3 [July 1966]: 1–17) where I embraced a view not sufficiently distinguished from that of J. S. Mill in his *Utilitarianism* (see *Utilitarianism, Essays on Ethics, Religion, and Society: Collected Works of John Stuart Mill*, vol. 10, ed. J. M. Robson [Toronto: University of Toronto Press, 1969], 246 [chapter 5, paragraph 14], I may reasonably be judged open to this objection. For my present view which, I hope not to be open to it, see chapter 8, especially sections 4 and 5.3.

Book One

The Order of Reason

PART ONE:
A THEORY
OF REASON

CHAPTER ONE

The Concept of Reason

Section 1. The Right Conception of the Concept of Reason[1]

Is reason a faculty like sight enabling us to become aware of or know things, and, if so, what things? Or is it a power like intelligence that enables us to do or learn to do things, and, if so, what things? What is the relation between reason, rationality, reasonableness, reasons, and reasoning? Do we know a priori what is rational, what is irrational, or do we know it a posteriori by some kind of perception or observation, some inner or nonsensory sense, or can we know it in either way? Is reasoning the same as inferring, and inferring the same as deducing, or are there types of "sound" reasoning in which the conclusion does not "follow logically," that is, with logical necessity, from the premises? Does reason have the power to move us to action or is it wholly inert? Can reason tell us what ends to pursue or can it only tell us the appropriate means to ends determined in other ways?

Philosophers (and, no doubt, writers in other disciplines) appear to disagree on these and other questions, but it is not always clear whether these are substantive or merely verbal disagreements. Could it be that some or all of their disagreements would dissolve if they discovered that they have used the word "reason" in different ways or that they operate with different conceptions of reason or of the concept of reason? Suppose, then, you discover that something is required by reason according to one conception of it, but forbidden by another. Will you not want to insist that this discovery does not dispose of the problem? Will you not want to ask whether reason *really* requires or really forbids it, and so wonder which of these two conceptions is the right one, which of them you ought to adopt, if indeed either of them? And can it be, once more, your reason that answers these questions, and if not your reason, what else?

---

[1] Cf. Alasdair MacIntyre, *Whose Justice? Which Rationality?* (Notre Dame, Ind.: University of Notre Dame Press, 1988).

It appears there are several competing conceptions of the concept of reason, but can there be more than one concept? If there is only one, how is this to be interpreted? Is it as with Jekyll and Hyde: there seem to be two persons but when all the evidence is in, the only possible or plausible conclusion is that there is only one, though one with two distinct personalities? Or is it more like the case of the supreme commander of an army where there could be, as with Roman consuls, two (or more) in "supreme command," but where that would be a rather unwise arrangement? Or is it like neither of these?

How then should we regard these different conceptions of the concept? Are they competing attempts to get that concept right—as philosophers appear to have assumed in giving rival accounts of the concept of mind or the concept of cause—and is there, then, only one right conception of it, all rival ones being *mis*conceptions? Or are these different conceptions best regarded as competing blueprints, alternative "mock-ups" intended to supersede the now surpassed earlier proposals including the one (if indeed there is only one) that is embedded in our common practice?

These two rival construals of the various rival conceptions of the concept of reason proposed by philosophers have different implications about what needs doing in the face of such diversity. Both would seem to imply that it would be best if we all embraced the same conception, but they imply this for different reasons. On the first construal, most or all of us already handle, in the appropriate way, the family of expressions that belong to or make up the concept of reason, but we may get confused when we try to spell out how we do it; just as, according to St. Augustine, we know quite well what time is, at least in the sense that we can understand and answer the various questions involving time—for instance, *when* Rosalind was born or whether she was born *before* or *after* Jedediah or *how long* their mother was in labor, and so on—but we become confused when we stand back from our practice, linguistic and non-linguistic, and try to describe, explain, and justify it. On this version, the right conception of the concept is the one that *correctly describes our practice*, including the way we in fact use the terms comprised by the concept, and whose justification rests on a correct description of the way we (all) use the terms "in" or "of" or "belonging to" the concept, for that is what we are aiming at when we try to select the right conception of the concept.

On the second version, our practice cannot, or is not likely to, be perfect (even if it is uniform) until we, the practitioners, have the right conception; for it is our conception of the concept which inevitably guides our practice, and if the practice is to be satisfactory, it must be guided by what is, on the basis of the appropriate criteria, the right conception. Thus, even if we have and there is only one concept of reason (that is, we all use these terms in the same way), and even if we have (on the first version) the right conception of *it*, there is still the question of whether we should continue with this entrenched practice or change it to conform with one or other improved model of it.

Of course, establishing such superiority, indeed even setting out exactly what would make a practice superior to another and why it would be superior, is a difficult task, especially when the concept is as complex and fundamental as that of reason. It would seem, then, that whether one single concept is (or several are) now established in our culture or in all cultures, getting it (or them) right would be a useful, if not a necessary, first step. I hope the remarks that follow will make it clearer to what extent there really is only one established concept of reason and, if so, to what extent it is necessary to go beyond it, either because nothing is firmly established on certain important matters ostensibly covered by the concept, or because what is so established is unsatisfactory.

Recently, some philosophers have drawn a further distinction between the concept of something, say justice or law, and a conception of it. This third distinction construes both as normative principles more or less abstractly formulated. Thus, Rawls notes that

> "it is natural to think of the concept of justice as distinct from the conceptions of justice and as being specified by the role which these different sets of principles, these different conceptions, have in common. Those who hold different conceptions of justice can, then, still agree that institutions are just when no arbitrary distinctions are made between persons in the assigning of basic rights and duties and when the rules determine a proper balance between competing claims to the advantages of social life. Men can agree to this description of just institutions since the notions of an arbitrary distinction and of a proper balance, which are included in the concept of justice, are left open for each to interpret according to the principles of justice that he accepts."[2]

And Ronald Dworkin says:

> "The law of a community . . . is the scheme of rights and responsibilities that meet that complex standard: they license coercion because they flow from past decisions of the right sort. . . . Conceptions of law refine the

---

[2] Rawls, *TJ*, 5.

initial, uncontroversial interpretation I just suggested provides our concept of law."[3]

The third construal differs from the first two in that disagreement on a conception is compatible with agreement on the concept. It implies a distinction between a conception of the concept X and a conception of X. If one rejects someone's conception of, say, justice or law, in this third sense, one does not imply that it presupposes an unsound conception of the concept of justice or law, as it would be on the first two construals. One normally rejects it on account of the unsoundness of the way it "interprets" or "refines," that is, renders more specific, the highly abstract and agreed-upon principle enshrined in the concept.

This last construal does not seem to make sense for apparently nonevaluative and nonnormative concepts such as those of mind, space, or time. But since the concept of reason, like those of justice and law, is evaluative/normative in that it includes evaluative/normative opposites, such as rational/irrational, reasonable/unreasonable, and, as we shall see, many others, we must pay attention to this construal also. However, we can, at any rate, stay at the very high level of abstraction appropriate for the concept of reason, since we need not in this book descend to *all* the contentious areas in which we distinguish between rationality/irrationality, and the other pairs of normative opposites. Indeed, we shall see that a careful scrutiny of the concept of reason will allow us to survey its scope at a high level of abstraction and noncontentiousness. Later on in our investigation, we can descend to more specific and contested formulations in the areas of our prime concern, the practical in general and the moral in particular.

Section 2.   Reason in Philosophy and Common Sense

In philosophy, reason has long occupied a special place of honor and authority. Many philosophers have regarded reason as their chief instrument of research and their supreme court of appeal. Most have claimed to rely on reason, not on perception or public opinion or revelation, let alone on feeling, to support or refute philosophical theories.

This high esteem is not, by any means, confined to philosophy but

---

[3] Ronald Dworkin, *Law's Empire* (Cambridge, Mass.: Harvard University Press, 1986), 93f.

seems deeply embedded in our culture. Conventional wisdom treats reason as humanity's distinctive power and glory. It is on account of it, that we have—perhaps overoptimistically—called our species "homo sapiens." Other creatures may have wings or claws or sharper eyes, but none, it is generally believed, have this unique power of reason, not even a weak or low variety of it. We alone have science, morality, and philosophy, and through them, wisdom, for we alone are rational.

Thus, not only do philosophers believe in the reign of reason, but in most or all Western civilizations, not only in our culture, anything that anyone believes, feels, or does can be judged rational or irrational, reasonable or unreasonable, required by, in accordance with, or contrary to reason. It is assumed that most people respect this standard and will want to guide themselves by it. At any rate we are all liable and quite likely to be judged by it. People who cannot or do not are looked down on as fools, lacking self-mastery, or worse.

The knowledge of what reason counsels, requires, forbids, or permits, is thus believed practically important. If we are concerned to make the most of our lives, we should heed the voice of reason. We can justify our performance—what we believe, feel, or do—to ourselves and to others if but only if we guide ourselves as best we can in accordance with reason. The dictates and counsels of reason provide a basis from which to criticize ourselves and others, as well as to justify ourselves to ourselves and to others. If we follow reason, we are "rationally" justified and need not feel that we failed in ways for which we must reproach ourselves or accept the reproaches of others.*

This justificatory implication of something being in accordance with reason, the liability to criticism from others and oneself for going against reason, and the opportunity of being immune from such criticism by conforming with it have important practical consequences. To the extent that the idea of rationality and the standard of reason are respected, people will voluntarily guide themselves by them and will evaluate one another by this standard, thereby exerting some pressure on one another to heed the guidelines of reason. But it should be noted that our idea of reason implies that people will themselves want to follow its directives not only in order to avoid the criticism of others, but also and mainly because they will recognize the merit of that criticism, will themselves regret being open to it, and will want to perform in ways not thus exposed. It is generally assumed that this merit of following reason is that it leads to what, if only we reflected about the matter, we would want to do anyway. Common sense thinks of the voice of reason as having universal appeal to us as rational beings.

I need not dwell on the importance of this justificatory function. Clearly, if at all possible, it would be helpful to have guidelines of that kind accessible to us. Clearly, it would be desirable to have social and personal arrangements we could recognize as rationally justified, that is, such that, whether we like them or not on their own account, we can see the merit of having and conforming to them. To be wholly satisfactory, a conception of reason should, therefore, if at all possible, do two connected things. It should tell us how to identify "the voice of reason"—what reason tells us— and it should at the same time show that heeding that voice (so identified) has the merit, ignoring it the demerit, which we attribute to it. Of course, it is conceivable that no account, including the currently accepted one, of what the "power" of reason is and what the voice of reason therefore can and does tell us is capable of explaining the presumed merit of heeding it. Proving this impossibility would amount to a justified toppling of reason from its present place of honor and authority in our conventional wisdom. However, such a dethronement is a bigger task than merely the demonstration that a particular conception of the power of reason is thus deficient. For that would still leave us free to argue that this particular conception is a misconception or a flawed conception. After all, we are not tied to a particular conception of the power(s) of reason as we are to the powers of some of our other faculties, such as sight or hearing. What powers to assign to reason is not a straightforwardly empirical matter based primarily on an examination of the relevant organ.

Section 3.   The Dominant Conception

What then is the currently dominant conception of the faculty of reason and its powers? It seems clear that there is no single such conception accepted in all the disciplines and contexts in which reason is invoked. But it seems there is a conception—I call it, with some exaggeration, "the dominant conception"—which has been preeminent in the thinking of philosophers and has also been influential in other domains. It is modeled on our highly sophisticated and formally regimented thinking in mathematical and logical proofs. It construes reason (and rationality in one sense of that term) as an individual power, faculty, or ability, like sight or intelligence, whose exercise involves a kind of nonsensory grasp of logical relations (entailments)—and the imaginative conjoining of these and other insights in chains of reasoning, arguments, inferences, and deductions—adding up to proofs of important theorems.

Reasons, the links in these chains, are thought of as known propositions entailing others for which they are reasons. For example, "The sum of the internal angles of a triangle is 180°. Therefore this angle is 60° because each of the other two angles is also 60°." Here the subclause beginning with "because" would be construed as the reason for the conclusion, that this angle is 60°.[4] It should, however, be noted that the dominant conception sees no barrier to reason's "seeing" such relations between cause and effect, or between facts and what is to be done.

The dominant conception also allows a second, evaluative sense of "rationality," by which it means an excellence of beings endowed with the power of reason (rationality in the first sense), an excellence which is demonstrated in the skillful use of that power. It then naturally construes the ideal of rationality as the highest degree of that excellence, that is, flawless consistency and perhaps, as well, supreme ingenuity in the construction of chains of reasoning.

Section 4. Hume's Demotion of Reason in Practice

As has been widely noted, Hume credited reason with the same powers that were traditionally ascribed to it, but restricted their range. Like that tradition, he allowed it those powers needed to establish truth and falsehood, but from this he derived conclusions that greatly reduced the contribution of reason in the field of practice. Since, in his view, truth and falsehood apply only to representations of "original existences" (such as events, states of the world, and actions), reason can make no practical judgments, no judgments about what people ought to do or what courses of action they ought to pursue, and the like. Judgments about original existences including actions can be true or false only if they are representations (or misrepresentations) of them; but in that case they are not truly practical for they can claim only that someone *was, is, will be,* or *under certain conditions would be* doing something, not that he *ought* to do it. To be truly practical, to be genuine ought-judgments, they would somehow have to generate or lead to the actions concerning which they are judgments. But then they cannot be representations, hence they cannot be true or false, and so cannot be the product of reason alone.

---

[4] The *Oxford English Dictionary* (vol. 8 [Oxford: Oxford University Press, 1933], 211) quotes from Whately's Logic (i, 2) "A premiss placed after its conclusion is called The Reason of it, and is introduced by one of those conjunctions which are called causal. The Major premiss is often called the Principle, and the word Reason is then confined to the Minor."

Hume made a further claim about reason that shocked many of his readers: that reason is wholly inert and cannot by itself alone move us to action, as it would have to do if it were to be truly practical.[5] Thus, even if reason were not confined to asserting what purports to be representations of original existences, but could make sound judgments about what to do, such judgments, to be of any practical use, would have to be able to move us to action. But this is impossible since as products of reason they are wholly inert and so cannot by themselves move us to action. Hence, even if *per impossibile* reason were applicable to practice, as it is not, it would still be of no practical use since it could not lead us to act as its judgments would then tell us.

Despite strong statements—such as it not being contrary to reason to prefer the destruction of the whole world to the scratching of one's finger and to act according to this preference—Hume allows[6] that one can act according or contrary to reason when one employs reason as "the slave of the passions." One does this in two different situations. The first hinges on what one takes to be an adequate means to one's own end determined by one's passions. One acts according to reason if one does what one believes is an adequate means to an end so acquired, and contrary to reason if one does not act in this way. The second hinges on beliefs about facts which indirectly determine one's action. One acts contrary to reason if one labors under some misapprehension of fact such that if one had not so labored, one's passions would have determined a different end or one would have had a different belief about what was an adequate means to one's end; one acts according to reason if one does not labor under such a misapprehension. However, in the absence of factual beliefs relevant in this way to one's ends, the determination of an end can be neither in accordance with nor contrary to reason.* This is not the place to examine whether Hume himself accepted or lampooned this conception of reason whose disturbing (and in the opinion of some, paradoxical) implications he lovingly elaborated. In any case, as I shall argue shortly, this conception is open to such serious objections that we should attempt to replace it by a more satisfactory one.

The dominant conception, as we noted, distinguishes between what is often called theoretical and practical reason. Hume's reflections have persuaded many that this conception can provide reason with only a very subordinate or instrumental function. It can ground Kantian hypothetical

---

[5] Hume, *Treatise*, 458.

[6] Hume, *Treatise*, 416.

imperatives but must leave to desires the end-setting role Kant and common sense assign to reason.

Not surprisingly, in light of the great successes in the natural sciences, Hume's skeptical reflections about the powers of theoretical reason in matters of empirical fact, as opposed to relations of ideas, are usually waved aside as a typical philosopher's conundrum—clever but surely flawed somehow, even if one cannot say exactly how—yet not a serious roadblock in the path of further scientific advances. At the same time, there is generally felt to be less cause for optimism in the domain of practice. Ethics has scored no comparable triumphs and Hume's boosting of the passions at the expense of practical reason has seemed an attractive move because it could attribute the persistent lack of progress to misguided reliance on reason and it could hold out at least some hope for greater success through reliance on other mental faculties.

But this bifurcation of reason into theoretical and practical and the acceptance of a good deal of the dominant conception in the theoretical domain and its rejection in the practical is not a satisfactory solution. Quite apart from the undesirability of such a division in the nature of reason, a closer examination of the dominant conception's account of the working of theoretical reason even in the domain of the relation of ideas where it is most plausible is far from satisfactory.

Section 5. The Dominant Conception of Theoretical Reason[7]

To begin with, we must note an ambiguity in the distinction between theoretical (or speculative) and practical reason. We may distinguish on the basis of the kind of subject matter, whether reason is employed in the field of, on the one hand, theories, hypotheses, beliefs, and perhaps also events, facts, or states of affairs, or on the other hand, actions, intentions, decisions, choices, and the like; call this the "topic sense" of the distinction. Alternatively, the distinction may be based on the mode of reasoning, whether reason is employed in theorizing, explaining, proving, predicting, and the like, or in deliberating, deciding, choosing, trying to "perform" in a certain way—to do, feel, believe, or aim at something; call

---

[7] I here incorporate some points developed more fully in my "The Social Source of Reason," presidential address, APA Eastern Division, 1977, *Proceedings and Addresses of the American Philosophical Association* 51, no. 6 (August 1978): 707–33.

this the "activity sense" of the distinction. Hence when reason is employed in telling us what to believe, this is theoretical reason in the topic sense because belief is a theoretical, not a practical topic; but it is practical reason in the activity sense because in deliberating about what to believe, the relevant judgment of reason concerns a "performance," what we are to believe. Moreover, this distinction, apart from being ambiguous, also leaves it unclear how we are to classify certain employments of reason. If I investigate the curative powers of a new drug, is this theoretical or practical in the topic sense? If I explain what someone did in terms of his reasons for doing it, is this theoretical or practical in the activity sense?

Consider, then, Hume's notorious question, whether one can reason from fact to action, and the frequently adopted view that one cannot. That conclusion may be thought to rest on two premises taken from the dominant conception, namely, that reasons for something are true or known propositions *entailing that for which they are reasons,* and that reasoning, the wielding of such reasons, is inferring or deducing from factual beliefs, that for which they are reasons. From these two premises one can then derive the conclusion that there can be no such thing as genuine practical reasoning, because such reasoning would have to infer something, namely, actions, to which it is not possible to make inferences.

Why not? Well, how could it be possible if practical reasoning really is inferring something "practical," such as an action, decision, or intention? Surely, these things have the wrong conceptual status to be something concluded, deduced, or inferred. For in order to be a conclusion, something must be capable of being said or asserted. But actions, decisions, and intentions are not thus capable. Of course, one can conclude, deduce, or infer *that* one will, or that one intends to, take an umbrella, but would not this be an instance of theoretical rather than practical reasoning? The reasons appear not to be practical, not reasons *to* take, or *to* form the intention to take an umbrella, rather, they are theoretical reasons, reasons in support of the (possible) fact *that* one will, or that one intends to, take one. That I have taken the cover off my umbrella may be for someone else a reason in support of the (possible) fact *that* I shall take it with me on my walk, but it is not a practical reason for me *to* take it.

Plausible though it is, this line of reasoning presents us with an awkward dilemma concerning the nature of reasons for something: are doings, intendings, inferrings, concludings, and thinkings the sorts of thing for which there can be reasons? If the dominant conception implies that the answer is no because they are not the sorts of things that can be inferred or concluded, since they cannot be entailed by facts, then indeed there can be no reasons for doings and intendings, no practical reasons;

but by the same token there also can be no reasons for thinkings or concludings, which would seem to eliminate a large and important class of theoretical reasons as well. But surely this is quite implausible. It would mean that guiding our thinking and reasoning, or at least formulating what actually guides our reasoning, is not an important function of logic. We should have to deny that even what we normally regard as the strongest reason in support of q, namely, that p and that p entails q, are together a reason *for thinking* that q, since nothing can be a reason for thinking anything.[8]

If, however, we grasp the other horn of the dilemma, that there can be reasons for thinkings and the like, then reasons and reasoning cannot be what the dominant conception says they are, namely, facts that entail what they are reasons for. For then the impossibility of *inferring* them also has no bearing on the possibility of practical reasoning, for then that uninferribility cannot make it impossible to give reasons for deciding, acting, and so on, any more than it is for thinking, even though one cannot infer these things.

If these reflections are sound, as I think they are, then we must also reject another contention, which has achieved the status of a dogma among some recent admirers of Hume (though they may admire him for a view he did not himself embrace),[9] namely, that there can be no (practical) reasoning from facts to practical judgments, that is, judgments of the form "Jones ought to do A," because there is a "logical gap" between "is" and "ought" and because one cannot reason across a logical gap. But if facts can be reasons for thinkings, then one can reason across a logical gap, since then one can reason from facts to what is not entailed by them. Thus, even if there are no entailments between "is" and "ought," this would not show that facts cannot be reasons for ought-judgments.[10]

It is, in any case, easy to see that reasons for or against something cannot be defined as facts entailing or inconsistent with it. That I have a warm coat and that that entails that I have a coat, can prove, that is, can be a "probative" reason for thinking, that I have a coat, but it cannot be the reason for (explanation of) my having a coat, or a reason (justification) for

---

[8] There can, of course, be an explanatory reason for someone's thinking something, the reason why he, rightly or wrongly, thought it. That there was a thick fog may be the (explanatory) reason for someone's (wrongly) thinking that there was no water in the gorge.

[9] Hume, *Treatise*, 469–70. See also R. M. Hare, *The Language of Morals* (Oxford: Oxford University Press, 1952), 27–31.

[10] I have examined these matters in greater detail in my paper, "Reason and Experience," *Noûs* 7, no. 1 (March 1973): 56–67, esp. 63–64, and in my presidential address, "The Social Source of Reason."

(or rational claim by) me to have one. And once we see this, it should also be clear that what is entailed by some fact cannot be the same as what that fact is a reason for.

The dominant conception thus appears to be guilty of three mistakes. It misidentifies what reasons are reasons for, it wrongly identifies reasons with the bases of reasons, and it is committed to a mistaken view of what the basis or ground of all reasons must be. Although some facts are reasons for believing other facts *because* they entail them, the entailment is only the basis or ground of the reason, not the reason itself, and there are other bases of a fact being a reason.

The dominant conception construes all kinds of reasons as logical or deductive ones. But these are only a subclass of conclusive reasons which in turn is only a subclass of reasons. Another subclass of conclusive reasons is based on conclusive evidence. Thus, the fact that Jones's fingerprints were on a certain gun is conclusive evidence that Jones actually held that gun. But, not all evidence is conclusive, yet even inconclusive evidence can be the basis of a more or less weighty reason—i.e., warrant or rational justification—for believing that for which it is evidence. Once we distinguish between reasons and their bases, we need no longer deny the existence of reasons for actions and choices, on the grounds that facts cannot entail these things or that such reasons cannot be based on entailment. Once we accept this point, we have abandoned the dominant conception of reason.

Section 6.   A Fresh Start

Let us then attempt to sketch a conception of reason which does justice—or at least comes closer to doing justice than does the dominant conception—to our concept of reason, assuming for the moment that we have one coherent such concept and that it is at least promising enough to become clear about it even if it turns out to need modifications in some respects and greater specificity than its established doctrines and principles can provide.

I take it for granted that the concept of reason comprises not only the word *reason* itself, but a sizable family of expressions, and that only some of them wear their consanguinity with reason on their linguistic sleeve. I also assume it granted that those that do—for instance, reasons, rationality, reasonableness, reasoning, accordance with reason, and having reasons—are members of that family, and that others, which are not so obviously blood-relations—for instance, consistency, coherence, deduction, validity, implication, entailment, proof—are nevertheless generally accepted as such family members. Finally, there appear to be some—for instance, explanation, understanding, induction, evidence, inference, derivation, justification—whose membership, though plausible, may yet be called into question. A fuller understanding of the first two groups will help us decide which of those in the third group, if any, belong to the concept and explain why those that do not may yet seem to do so.

There appear to be three main questions which the most widely accepted rival conceptions of the concept of reason attempt to answer. (1) What are the capacities, powers, and abilities, if any, that constitute a being's having Reason, its being a rational being? (2) What sort of thing do rational beings try to accomplish when exercising these abilities? (3) In what ways and by what standards do we appraise such exercises? It seems clear that the merit of rival conceptions will have to be determined on the basis of the merit of the answers to these questions, and that that merit will have to be judged by criteria developed from the meaning and use of the various expressions belonging to the concept and on the relation between them.

I shall not attempt to tackle these questions head-on or in that order. It will be more profitable to begin by exploring the meaning and use of the various notions comprised in the concept that naturally occur in a discussion of some of the more widely received rival conceptions. At the same time, it is only fair to warn the reader at the outset that, as my main interest in this book is morality, I think I justifiably can, as in any case for obvious reasons I must, ignore certain parts of the concept of reason altogether or treat them in a merely cursory way, and that some of the things I shall say about the concept as a whole may be more apposite to the parts of the concept of special importance to ethics and less so to other parts (such as the role of reason in mathematics, logic, or physics) that are peripheral to our concerns here.

Section 7.   Rationality

What do we say about a being when we ascribe rationality to it, when we say that it is a rational being or that it possesses Reason—or do only philosophers say this sort of thing? There appear to be four different senses: a capacity, an ability, a tendency, and an evaluative sense. Unlike a cat, a baby (we think) is a rational being, in the sense of having a certain capacity which, probably, few if any other species possess. It is, nevertheless, still prerational, has not yet reached the age of reason, and is not yet "fully rational," the way a normal adult is. Thus, a (merely) "capacity-rational" being, such as a (normal) baby, must still acquire a certain complex ability before it is able to do things which can then be evaluated as rational or irrational, reasonable or unreasonable, and the like. Finally, we may deny that something would be a rational being even if it were capacity- and ability-rational but had no tendency to do what is rational rather than what is irrational.

The four different senses of "rationality" can be distinguished by the four corresponding opposites. We can speak of the nonrationality of a being if it lacks rationality in the capacity sense; of its prerationality if it (as yet) lacks rationality in the ability sense—what I called "full rationality"; of its irrationality if it falls below the minimal standard of acceptability for conformity with reason, whether in the performance of its reflective or its executive task;[11] and of its arationality if, though a capacity-rational and fully rational being, it entirely lacks such a tendency—although the existence of such arational beings seems more dubious still than that of (analogous) "amoral" ones. It would seem, then, that those who have the ability to determine what would be rational and what would be irrational, will also normally *incline* to being rational rather than irrational. There must then be something about rationality that appeals to us, that inclines us towards it, and something about irrationality that inclines us away from it. At the same time it seems that irrationality is not only not impossible but that it occurs not infrequently.

There is thus a nuclear sense of "rationality," namely, the ability sense--"full rationality" as I have called it or "having reached the age of reason," as it is often called—in terms of which the others can be explicated. Rationality in the capacity sense is the capacity to acquire full rationality; in the evaluative senses—minimal and perfect (or ideal)—rationality is the exercise of that ability up to either of these standards; in the tendency sense, rationality is the tendency of a fully rational person to exercise that ability at least up to the minimal standard. What, then, can this capacity and this ability be, the possession of which inclines one both to exercise the ability and to do so in order to reach one of its possible evaluative outcomes (rationality) rather than the opposite (irrationality)? Some have conceived of this capacity and ability as quasi-perceptual, as something like Plato's "eye of the soul," or as some inner ear that enables us to hear "the voice of reason." However, if reason is indeed a cognitive

---

[11] For the definition of this term see above, introduction, p. 9.

faculty, our other beliefs about it strongly suggest that it is not a perceptual one, such as sight or hearing, even when what it cognizes is—implausibly —supposed to be words, the words spoken by the voice of reason or perhaps written by reason on the hearts of humans. We do not think of reason as tied to a special organ, the way sight and hearing are to our eyes and ears, whose powers of discrimination can be improved by gadgets, such as eyeglasses or hearing aids. Nor do we conceive of it as a faculty of observation, that is, a sensitivity to sensory stimuli that enable us to discriminate the characters or properties of things in the world by which we distinguish and identify them or confirm and disconfirm hunches about how they tend to behave.[12]

Section 8.   Evaluation from the Rational Point of View

If reason (the ability we have when we are fully rational) is a cognitive faculty, then intelligence would seem to be a better model than perception. For it would better accommodate the uses of so-called "practical" (as opposed to so-called "theoretical" or "speculative") reason and of the evaluative/normative terms from the reason family, such as "rationality/ irrationality," which are hard to fit into the perceptual model.

Certainly, both rationality and intelligence can be used to evaluate the way in which beings capable of having desires and ends tackle the task of satisfying a given desire or attaining a given end. Rationality in the evaluative sense could then be construed simply as a very high, irrationality as a very low, degree of intelligence. Recall the impressive performance of Koehler's ape: when he found that either of the two sticks in his cage was too short to reach a bunch of bananas dangling temptingly on a branch nearby, he sat down and "pondered" for a while, much as humans would do, and then, suddenly, "hit on the idea" of putting the two sticks together to extend his reach. This ape would be judged more intelligent than his mate who, let's say, having unsuccessfully tried each of the sticks separately, does not even sit down to ponder, let alone hit on any useful idea, but gives up despondently. Should we then ascribe rationality to Koehler's ape but not to his unsuccessful mate, perhaps on account of the fact that in pondering and hitting on a useful idea, he demonstrates not

---

[12] For a stipulative answer to the question of what are the powers or functions of reason, see e.g., C. D. Broad, *Five Types of Ethical Theory* (London: Kegan Paul, 1944), 105f.

only a greater degree of intelligence than she does but also a higher "level" of intelligence than, say, a cat trying to find a way out of a so-called puzzle box by random trial and error and that by "rationality" we mean that higher level of intelligence?

No doubt, if we could ascribe rationality/irrationality in the evaluative sense to Koehler's ape, we could—indeed it seems we would have to—ascribe also capacity rationality and full rationality to him since, it would appear, evaluative rationality/irrationality presupposes the other two. We think of a cat as a nonrational being, not because someone has, perhaps by examining its brain or whatever, detected that it lacks that capacity. Rather, we think of it as nonrational because there is nothing in its behavior on account of which the evaluation rational/irrational seems to be warranted. Similarly with the human baby: we have no empirical evidence, (say, physiological or neurological) to show that it possesses rationality in the capacity or ability sense whereas the ape does not; nor is there (as yet) anything in its behavior that warrants the evaluation rational/irrational. Rather, we expect that probably there will eventually be such behavioral evidence because we know that normal babies under normal circumstances eventually become fully rational, and because there seems to be nothing abnormal about this baby and about the circumstances in which it will grow up. Thus, our primary criteria on the basis of which we ascribe rationality in the capacity and ability senses appear to be extracted from the fact that an adult being's behavior is such as to warrant the evaluation rational/irrational. The further derived criteria of capacity and full rationality are justified by the fact that this sort of behavior is not present at birth, but only at a point relatively late in a child's development.

By contrast, there is simply nothing in the behavior of Koehler's (normal adult) ape that we think warrants the evaluation rational/ irrational nor in that of his (equally normal adult) mate. Thus, what the (capacity-rational) baby acquires as it gets closer and closer to the ability to engage in the sort of behavior that can be rational or irrational, cannot simply be greater intelligence. For as far as intelligence is concerned, both the ape and the baby act more or less intelligently on different occasions, and both can be judged on average to be more or less intelligent than other members of their species, and normal adult human beings can be judged more intelligent than normal adult apes, but there is nothing in the development of apes that is comparable to a baby's becoming "fully rational," that is, acquiring a new ability whose exercises can be evaluated as rational/irrational long after they have come to act more or less intelligently. Intelligence/unintelligence (or stupidity) differ significantly from rationality/irrationality. While both pairs evaluate particular performances of a person, or a range of performances of a person, the latter pair presupposes an empirically acquired ability at a certain level of excellence, but the former does not. To be irrational, a being must have a certain capacity (capacity rationality) and must have acquired an ability at a certain level of excellence (full rationality). To be unintelligent (or stupid), a being needs only a certain capacity (to learn by and from experience; apparently not possessed by insects, which therefore cannot be more or less intelligent than other members of their species), but no development of this capacity up to a certain level of excellence; an unintelligent dog is not one that has an acquired ability which it sometimes exercises well, sometimes poorly.

It will help to say more clearly wherein the exercises of a being's full rationality consist. They consist in its "performances" (its beliefs, feelings, or actions), on account of the character of which we evaluate them as either rational or irrational. It seems obvious to me that an exercise of this ability must in the first place consist in the linguistic formulation of the kinds of performance in which reason permits or does not permit its possessor or others to engage, in a variety of circumstances. This explains why one can be rational/irrational only if one is already fully rational, because that involves the ability to tell what reason does and what it does not permit, what is according to and what contrary to reason. That is why one is judged rational/irrational—but not intelligent/stupid—on the basis of one's exercise of one's full rationality, that is, how well one did in judging what is according to and what is contrary to reason, and how well one "performed" in light of that result, that is, how well one conformed one's belief, feeling, or action to that judgment.

These and other points will become clearer if we look more closely at rationality/irrationality and some of the other pairs of evaluative terms from the concept of reason, such as reasonable/unreasonable, coherent/incoherent, consistent/inconsistent, logical/illogical, according/contrary to reason. For we use them in various judgments of people's exercises of that basic ability, "full rationality," which we think all normal human adults have acquired and whose exercises are what having reason enables them to do, namely, to make clear to themselves and others what reason requires or permits or forbids on particular occasions.

It seems clear that, when applied to particular exercises of full rationality, the most frequently discussed opposites from this group, namely, rationality and irrationality, are, strictly speaking, contradictories. In other words, in exercising that ability, we arrive at a judgment to the effect that something is (was, will be, would be, would have been) rational or irrational. As already indicated, I call the subject matter of such judgments a "performance," for example, an action (cutting off one's nose to spite one's face), a belief (that the earth is flat), or an emotion (occurrent fear of a gun one knows to be unloaded). Any such performance which can be either rational or irrational (as, for instance, the pupillar reflex or one's heartbeat cannot be), must be one or other and cannot be both; any that is not irrational cannot fail to be rational and, conversely, any that is not rational cannot fail to be irrational.

Like perfection, rationality is incapable of degrees (at least when used to judge performances);[13] a performance can only be more or less nearly perfect or rational than another. In contrast, its contradictory, irrationality, is, like imperfection, capable of degrees. Any performance that falls more or less short of rationality is more or less irrational. Thus, (evaluative) rationality borders without gap on irrationality, as perfection borders on imperfection.

However, this does not mean that, like perfection, rationality (in the evaluative sense) marks a high achievement in the exercise of full rationality (though no doubt we may consider full rationality a great asset of the species by comparison with the assets available to members of other, nonrational species), let alone the highest possible in the various "skills of reason." Rationality is merely the absence of irrationality, the latter a truly blatant sort of violation of the requirements of reason. Rationality/irrationality is thus an evaluative pair like pass/fail, which is used to weed out the (normally few) hopeless cases, whereas perfection crowns the (normally few if indeed any) flawless ones who have performed in a way that cannot be improved upon.

Section 9.   Other Evaluative Terms from the Concept of Reason

A brief glance at the role of some of the other pairs of evaluative terms will help to clarify this further. Suppose, for instance, I assert something that amounts to a *contradiction*, then I am guilty of an *inconsistency* and therefore of a performance that is *contrary to reason*. However, not every inconsistency, hence not every contrariety to reason, amounts necessarily to an *irrationality*. Thus, one need not be guilty of an irrationality just because one's claims commit one to an inconsistency (as, e.g., Sidgwick

---

[13] I leave open the question of whether, unlike performances, persons can be more or less *rational* than others, since more or fewer performances of theirs than of others may be rational or more nearly rational.

does when he claims that in a choice between promoting one's own greatest good and that of the greatest number, either is rational, *and* that only the choice of the greatest good of the greatest number is rational). Asserting what amounts to an inconsistency need not be a flagrant violation of reason, a flying in its face, an irrationality. Indeed, it may take some cleverness to discover that the claims one originally made, perhaps on different occasions and in different words, can be shown to commit one to views logically equivalent to differently formulated views that are *obviously* inconsistent ones. Again, certain inconsistencies, such as those in the testimony of an accused criminal, may be far from irrational, since he wants to be acquitted and needs the jury to believe that he is innocent and so may have to convince them of the truth of each of two inconsistent claims about the facts; thus, he cannot avoid making inconsistent claims, but at best can formulate them in ways designed to conceal the inconsistency from the court. Thus, a contrariety to reason may not be blatant or flagrant enough to amount to an irrationality.

Consider, then, a contrariety to reason which really does amount to an irrationality, say, Moore's famous paradox: "I went to the pictures last Tuesday, but I don't believe I did."[14] Although this proposition does not involve a contradiction, for it could conceivably be true, still, seriously asserting it would be absurd, and so irrational. For any competent speaker would know that (even if she cannot say why) she cannot, without absurdity, assert something and in the same breath deny that she believes it. Thus, asserting Moore's proposition is not merely contrary to reason but, since it is quite obviously so, it is a flagrant (not an understandably overlooked or intelligently chosen) violation of the canons of reason, and so is an irrationality.

Although for our purposes here we do not need to do so, can we say why it is absurd? Perhaps the following is an adequate explanation (although there may be other and better ones). Clearly, it is contrary to reason (at least other things being equal) to assert p if one does not believe p. For either one believes that p is adequately warranted or one does not. If the former, then it is contrary to reason not to believe p, as one claims one does. If the latter, then it is contrary to reason to assert p, as one does. But, of course, this need not be irrational since lying is an example of this and lying may be in one's best interest, telling the truth to one's detriment, and that would seem to be an excellent reason in favor of lying and against telling the truth. However, the very thing that saves the contrariety to

---

[14] G. E. Moore, "A Reply to My Critics," *The Philosophy of G. E. Moore*, 3rd ed., Library of Living Philosophers, vol. 4, ed. Paul A. Schilpp (La Salle, Ill.: Open Court, 1968), 543.

reason involved in lying from being irrational is lost if one does not keep one's disbelief to oneself. To assert that one does not believe what one has just asserted is to discredit oneself as an asserter and so defeats an important purpose of any serious assertion, namely, to be believed by one's interlocutor. But it is absurd to do (in this case, *say*) something which so obviously defeats one's purpose in doing (saying) it so that no normal adult can fail to see it.

This example illustrates several important aspects of the structure of the concept of reason. The first is that we must distinguish between whether or not a performance of a certain sort is in accordance with reason and how serious is a person's failure to perform in accordance with it. Thus, a person's performance may be contrary to reason in some respects, as in the case of our liar, namely, insofar as he asserts something he himself for good reason does not believe, but it may also be in accordance with reason in other respects, namely, insofar as he thinks for good reason that it would be in his best interest if someone else were to believe it and contrary to it if that person were not. Even if, as we may assume, the lying assertion is, all things considered, contrary to reason, it does not amount to a gross noncompliance for which the severe stricture—irrationality— would be appropriate.

A further important point (though here not strictly pertinent) is that if, as I shall argue in Book Two, immorality is necessarily contrary to reason, it may yet not be irrational. For one may have excellent (but not sufficient) reasons for being immoral, just as one may have excellent (though not sufficient) reasons for acting contrary to other kinds of reason. Of course, there is still an important difference between irrationality and immorality: one could not have excellent reasons to act irrationally since, if one had such reasons, one would not be acting irrationally but at worst contrary to reason; by contrast, one could well have excellent reasons for acting immorally, as when one offers a government official a bribe to land a profitable contract that would otherwise go to a competitor.

The third point is that we must distinguish between two types of accordance with/contrariety to reason, often called, respectively, "other things equal" (or "pro tanto," or "prima facie," or "as such") and "all things considered" (or "overall," or "in the final analysis," or "sans phrase") depending on how much is taken into account. In my liar example, our generally accepted views would allow that the liar's performance is contrary to reason on two counts: (1) it is a case of asserting something the asserter does not believe, and (2) it is a lie, that is, a noncompliance with a moral requirement, which is often construed as a requirement of a certain sort of (i.e., moral) reason. However, at the same time, the behavior may (usually will) also be something at least in accordance with, that is, permitted by another sort of (i.e., prudential) reason, or even required by it, because it is something doing which is in the doer's best interest, whereas not doing it is to his detriment.

Suppose, for argument's sake, that our liar's behavior does not have any further characteristic on account of which it would be according/contrary to reason, other things equal. Then there are two opposing requirements of reason arising out of the characteristics of our liar's behavior: on the one hand, that he not behave in this way since, being a case of asserting something which for good reason he does not believe and also a case of lying, it is, other things equal, contrary to reason, and on the other hand, that he behave in this way since, being (let us assume) a case of averting something to his detriment, it is, other things equal, in accordance with reason. However, these two opposing requirements of reason would normally be regarded as "merely" prima facie ones and so would still have to be compounded into a single overall, all-things-considered, final judgment which resolves the prima facie conflict. To do this, we first need to rank these requirements according to their normative force. We must determine whether the first two prima facie prohibitions by reason, together, "defeat" the third requirement (or permission) by reason. If they do, then reason requires, all things considered, that our liar not perform in the way in which he has performed; if they do not, then reason permits (or possibly even requires) that he perform in this way.

Section 10.   The Typology of Reason

It is time now for a more thorough examination of another term from the reason family: "a reason" and its plural, "reasons." When, in section 4 and section 5, I spoke of a certain fact, say, that a "performance," such as someone's believing or doing something, possessed certain characteristics (e.g., being self-contradictory or self-defeating), as constituting a reason, other things equal, against this performance, I could also have said that it "counted against" or was "unfavorably relevant to" the performance, or that it was, other things equal, "contrary to reason." This is the minimal content of what we may call a reason-statement, that is, a statement of the form that something is a reason for or against something. Plainly there are many different types of such reason-statements, depending on the various sorts of thing to which reasons can be favorably or unfavorably relevant and the various other dimensions in respect of which reasons can differ from one another.[15]

There are, of course, many ways in which we can classify reasons, but for our purposes it is important to find one that illuminates the ways in which we specify exactly what is said by the different types of reasons the classification distinguishes. The typology I shall sketch in this chapter—following our current practices as closely as I can—seems well designed to provide this illumination. I have already suggested that there are certain types of activity—I called them "activities of reason" because in them reasons play a crucial role—with certain important high-level aims, such as (greater) certainty (when we attempt to prove or give evidential support for something), truth (when we reflect about what to believe), understanding (when we try to explain something), the good (when we deliberate about what to do), and appropriateness (when we reflect about our attitudes and feelings concerning something).

We already noted some of the flaws of the traditional division into the theoretical (or speculative) and the practical employment of reason. I think we can remedy these flaws by working with another classification, which distinguishes four types of reason: (1) explanatory reasons, reasons *why*, as in "the reason why the bottle burst"; (2) fact-linking reasons, reasons *that*, as in "a reason that John is not the father of Jill's son, Jack"; (3) directive reasons, reasons *to*, as in "a reason to believe that John is the father of Jill's son, Jack"; and (4) directive explanatory reasons, "reasons *for which*," as in "the reason for which he subscribed." For our purposes, directive reasons are the most important. There are several subclasses of this type: those I call cognitive, such as reasons to believe, think, assume, suspect, expect something, and so on; those I call practical, such as reasons to act, do, want, wish something, and so on; those I call affective, such as reasons to fear, grieve, rejoice, be angry, and so on; and those I call evaluative, such as reasons to value, cherish, treasure something. Our main task will be to get clear about the differences and similarities between practical and cognitive reasons (which are obscured by the traditional distinction between theoretical and practical reasons), and those between directive explanatory and nondirective explanatory reasons, and those between directive explanatory and nonexplanatory directive reasons. I postpone this task to the next chapter.

At this point, I want to draw attention to a deeper dichotomy which

---

[15] For further details, see chapter 2, section 1, pp. 70–77.

may well underlie the traditional distinction between theoretical and practical reason. That deeper dichotomy relates to two importantly different attitudes toward, or aims in respect of, different aspects of the world of which we are a part. One is wishing simply to take cognizance of what (i.e., of the fact that this or that) was, is, will be, or would under certain conditions be the case, of what has happened, is happening, will happen, or would happen under certain conditions, or of what states various things were, are, will, or would be in, or what states of affairs did, do, will, or would in certain circumstances prevail, and so on. The other quite different attitude or disposition is one of wishing to intervene in the course of events so as to bring about (or prevent) the coming about of certain things, which otherwise would not (or would) come about. Note that whereas it is wholly inappropriate, indeed irrational, to adopt the interventionist attitude toward those aspects of the world which we know or should know we cannot directly or indirectly deflect from their "natural" course, it may be perfectly natural to wish merely to take cognizance of what that natural course is, will, or would be, even if we could deflect it by suitable intervention.

This dichotomy does not mesh neatly with the four types of reason I mentioned earlier, but these two classifications usefully complement each other: some practical reasons clearly fall in the interventionist category, but not all do, though, because some doings are done for their own sakes and not in order to bring about or prevent some happening or state or state of affairs, or to maintain one. Other directive reasons, e.g., cognitive ones, may fall into both categories. In telling us to believe something, that is, normally, to believe it *true*, they tell us to believe something there is to take cognizance of.[16] In this, they overlap with fact-linking reasons which are facts that constitute more or less weighty evidence for what there is to take cognizance of. But unlike fact-linking reasons which altogether abstract from appropriate human responses to what there is, cognitive reasons tell us *what to believe there is* to take cognizance of. They direct us to believe something, that is, to "perform" in a certain way, but the ground on which they so direct us is the same as in the corresponding fact-linking reason which only tells us that, in view of the fact that constitutes the reason, there is a certain greater or lesser chance that there is a certain thing, but remain silent about whether or not to believe there is that thing. Thus, if R_1 is a fact-linking reason, say, the fact that the fact that something is a cube

---

[16] For further details, see chapter 1, p. 46f.; see also book 2, chapter 8, section 2, and chapter 9, section 3.1.

entails that it has twelve edges, then R_1 tells us that it is certain that if a certain thing, say, a lump of sugar is a cube, then it has twelve edges. But then this same fact which constitutes the fact-linking reason R_1 also constitutes a cognitive reason, a reason *to* believe that that lump of sugar has twelve edges.

Five points should be noted. The first is that not all fact-linking reasons have the same "force," as I shall call it. Not all such reasons are based on entailments, not even all conclusive reasons are. The fact that a woman, her child, and a man, belong to certain blood groups constitutes a conclusive fact-linking reason that he is not the father of her child; however, this is not an entailment but a causal connection or rather, lack of one. And some such reasons (say, that the man was in prison during the tenth and ninth months prior to the child's birth) are not conclusive, but support the fact to which they are favorably relevant only with a certain probabilistic force, making it only more or less probable, that he is not the father of her child.

The second is that although such evidential relations as are involved in what I call fact-linking reasons arguably cannot hold between the facts that constitute cognitive reasons and what they are such reasons for, they can be the grounds of such reasons and, if they are adequate grounds (as they surely are when the evidential relationship is logically or causally conclusive), then what they are grounds of are adequate cognitive (i.e., directive) reasons.

The third point concerns the difference between "fact-linking" and "directive" reasons: that whereas the former are favorably or unfavorably relevant to facts, the latter are not. Bear in mind, though, that I here use "fact" to mean only what might be called "constative fact,"[17] such as that John is Jack's father or that anything that is a cube has twelve edges, that is, something that can be *truly or falsely* asserted in a that-clause, though not everything that can be so asserted is a constative fact in my sense. It seems that the expression "to believe" or "to act" used in formulating cognitive or practical reasons can be correctly expanded into a that-clause, e.g., "that so-and-so *is to* believe or do such-and-such," and that these are not intended as stating constative facts. I shall have more to say about these matters in Book Two.[18]

The fourth point is that this throws light on Hume's notorious

---

[17] Here I follow J. L. Austin, *How to Do Things With Words* (London: Oxford University Press, 1962), 3.

[18] Book 2, chapter 8, sections 1 and 2.

question, whether one can soundly reason from "is" to "ought" and on what many philosophers have embraced as the right answer, namely, that one cannot. It seems clear that we can take "is" to refer to constative facts and "ought" to cases such as those in which someone knows a fact and knows that it constitutes a conclusive or an all-things-considered reason for him to believe a certain thing, e.g., the fact that if a lump of sugar is a cube, then it necessarily has twelve edges. For if he knows this fact about the lump of sugar and knows that it entails that the lump has twelve edges, then he also ought to know that he ought to believe that it has twelve edges, since he ought to know that it must be true that it has twelve edges, and that believing it means believing it to be true. Thus, the fact—I assume for the moment that it is a fact—that there can be no entailment between the fact that constitutes the cognitive reason and what it is a reason for, namely, *to believe* something, is not an obstacle to reasoning soundly from "is" to "ought" since cognitive reasons are designed to enable us to reason precisely in this way. And they are based on the same sorts of grounds on which the standard arguments employing (constative) fact-linking reasons are based.

Finally, it is worth noting that what I have called fact-linking reasons, which are the stock in trade of traditional accounts of what reasons are, seem not to be related with Reason, at least not in any obvious ways. Of course, from p, and p entails q, we can validly infer q, and in the fact that p, and that p entails q, we have a reason *to* infer (and so *to* believe) q. But Reason does not seem to come into the picture until we relevantly "perform" one way or another, say by inferring or believing something; until, in other words, we perform according or contrary to some directive reason. Entailments and other evidential relations seem to connect with reason only as the grounds of directive reasons intended to guide our various performances which therefore can be in accordance with or contrary to reason. The fact that p entails q does not seem to have a closer connection with reason than fact that p.

Consider then the third type of reason I have mentioned: explanatory reasons, reasons why, and the corresponding reason-statement, e.g., the fact that the air temperature dropped to 20°F and that the milk froze and expanded is the reason (explanation) why the milk bottle burst. The corresponding reason-statement is of the form, the fact F_1 is an explanatory reason, R_1, if and only if, when it fills a place in a suitable explanation schema, S, it explains an explanandum fact, F_2, that is, a fact calling for explanation. Not every fact calls for explanation. Given our knowledge of the way the world works, we cannot hope to find an explanation schema for facts such as that each of three brothers died a natural death on his birthday in the same year.[19] That something calls for explanation implies that there is already an empirically discovered "normal" or "natural" pattern of behavior and some known cases in which something has deflected something from that pattern, as when a pregnant woman miscarries or when her babies are conjoined twins, and so on. We should keep apart two different ways in which our knowledge enlarges our understanding. One is the discovery of phenomena, that is, of general event-patterns by subsumptions under which we can understand what is going on as normal and so not as calling for further explanation. The other is the discovery of some events that do not follow the pattern which events of that kind normally follow, thus calling for further explanation and giving that explanation by stating that deflecting factor.[20]

The growth of our knowledge thus makes possible a parallel growth of our understanding. We are able to find more accurate patterns of behavior and a fuller account of factors deflecting things from their normal (or natural) pattern. The move from the Aristotelian to the Newtonian (explanatory) theory of motion is both a move from one pattern of normal behavior (rest on the surface of the earth and motion towards it) to another (motion at uniform velocity) and a change in the conception of the forces that deflect things from their normal pattern (speed of movement in proportion to weight versus acceleration of movement in accordance with the magnitude of the forces including the force of gravity impressed on the mass of the moving bodies). The two theories embrace different normal behavior patterns (natural motion) as not calling for (further) explanation and give different accounts of the factors that deflect things from natural motion. Each theory of motion enables us to understand the behavior the theory defines as motion, either as natural (and so not calling for further explanation) or as due to the impact of a force. Thus an explanatory reason is a fact which shows the motion to be explained as either natural motion and so not in need of (further) explanation or as motion due to the impact of a deflecting force. The "strange fact" of the three brothers dying on their birthdays is not an instance of a phenomenon of a recognizable type, as are the phenomena of bodily motion, or optical or electrical phenomena, other instances of which can be recognized, and regular patterns discovered and captured in more precise descriptions. We do not believe in "natural" death-dates relative to birth-dates, under which the case of the

---

[19] I owe this example to Stephen Toulmin.

[20] For further discussion of these and other related points, see below chapter 2, pp. 63–84.

three brothers can be subsumed or from which some suspected hidden force has deflected them. Therefore this fact, though strange in the sense of rare, does not call for explanation, and so none need or could be given.

Of course, there are many types of explananda and many explanatory schemata (theories), some better than others—by criteria we need not go into here. (We shall, however, have to return to various types of explanation of human behavior in chapter 3.) What it is important to note here is that when we seek or accept such an explanation of something, our attitude is one of wishing to take cognizance, not to intervene. We are in the role of puzzled or partly ignorant observers, not of agents. We are after knowledge or at least true belief, but of a certain systematic sort, for instance a pattern of "natural" behavior and "forces" that deflect from it. When we have this systematized information, our puzzlement or ignorance is removed, and so we understand.

An examination of what makes explanatory reasons sound or unsound, or in other ways better or worse, and what sort of performance, if any, can count as according or contrary to reason would take us very far afield, quite apart from requiring kinds of expertise I do not possess. Hence I shall not pursue this topic any further.

Section 11. Why Follow Reason?

Earlier in this chapter (section 4, pp. 29–31), I gave an account, in terms of accordance with/contrariety to reason, of the various things that are sometimes called dictates or prohibitions or permissions and so on, of reason. We must now note what may be regarded as the most general such requirement, namely, that one always do what is in accordance with reason, never what is contrary to it. However, this most general requirement cannot be explicated in the same way, for it is the requirement that we respect the specific requirements of reason, that is, the specifications of what is according and what is contrary to reason. But these specifications could not amount to requirements of reason unless there also were this most general requirement, namely, the requirement that one conform to all the (correct or sound) specifications that apply to one of what is in accordance with reason. For in the absence of this general requirement, the distinction between being according or contrary to reason has no more "directive" or "normative" force than the distinction between fitting or not fitting some description, such as, being in the dining room or having breakfast. It would simply tell us a (constative) fact about an actual or possible performance, say, a belief, an action, or a feeling. We have not yet made clear why these facts, that performing in one way is according to reason, and performing in another contrary to it, are a requirement and so *should* always incline us to perform in the former *rather than* the latter way. It is, of course, this most general requirement that generates the notorious question, "Why follow reason?", and its more popular moral analogue, "Why be moral?" At this point, it will be best if I briefly discuss the former question, but postpone the latter to Book Two (chapter 7, section 7).

We may hope to dodge the sting of "Why follow reason?" by construing the specific requirements of reason as those that do not stand in need of any justification since they are the requirements of something which, it is not implausible to maintain, is the ultimate justifier in our culture; or, if that is doubted, which surely has long played that role in philosophical contexts. And it will hardly be doubted that the existence of such a universal justifier would be desirable, especially in interpersonal relations where it would function as an alternative to force and fraud. But this move puts off the moment of truth even in philosophy only to the point where the specific requirements of reason are spelled out, or (to put it in the way suggested in this chapter, section 1), when we descend to our conception of accordance with and contrariety to reason. For then, those who are willing to acknowledge reason as the ultimate justifier may simply deny that a given sentence correctly "spells out" a specific requirement of reason. Thus, even if sound, the conventional or linguistic point that reason *is* the ultimate justifier takes us at most a very short distance, unless we can offer a convincing account of why *the method* by which the more specific requirements of reason have been derived deserves to be recognized as one that yields only requirements which are (rationally) justified, why the requirements alleged to be those of reason really are such, and why, in other words, the benefits of being justified should be dependent on conformity with the outcome of that method.

On my view, there is a substantive answer to "Why follow reason?" and it is quite simple: following reason is the best available way to attain certain very general ends which, at least when we think about it, we all, at least normally, want to attain, such as discovering true rather than false answers to questions about matters that are important to us. It is the best method because it consists in following certain general guidelines made available to us by our culture for the purpose of enabling us to guide ourselves in our attempts to find answers to such important questions. Of course, these guidelines are not infallible, but they are at least the best starting points we have because, being general, they have been used by large numbers over a long time and so have been exposed to the most widespread critical probing and testing that can be organized. We may, of course, sometimes be able to discover flaws in these guidelines; in such cases, following reason means suitably departing from them. But in the normal absence of such superior knowledge we stand the best chance of success if we follow them. (For additional remarks, see below.)

Thus, these publicly available guidelines are not themselves the (infallible) guidelines for attaining these important ends, but merely what a culture has worked out to be the closest attainable approximation to them it could produce. But their generality, their public availability, and their widespread employment and revision, generation after generation, give them a high likelihood that more errors have been eliminated than any single individual among us could eliminate by his own efforts, and therefore are normally our best bet. Of course, a detached comparison between the methods of different cultures may yield still better results. This seems to me the sound basis of the widespread conviction that reason is tied to universality.

Unlike intelligence, reason thus involves a division of labor between society and the individual. One cannot become fully rational (as I have called it) except in the context of a social order that is also *an order of reason*, that is, one which develops, makes publicly available, tries to improve, and educates its members so as to be able to apply, these guidelines for solving frequently recurring problems of certain kinds when they arise.

If this is correct, it brings to light one reason why the performance of Koehler's ape, despite his high degree and level of intelligence, cannot be said to be either rational or irrational: he is not a member of an order of reason and so could not, even if he had the other required abilities, take advantage of the socially provided "machinery" needed to reflect in a regimented way about which of the alternative performances open to him is according, which contrary to reason, and then to perform according rather than contrary to it. A being's performances cannot be judged rational or irrational until he *and his "fellows"* have available to them this sort of apparatus for determining what, in a particular situation, it is according and what contrary to reason for a particular individual, whether himself or others, to perform.

Thus, degree of accordance with reason does not, like degree of intelligence, rank the novelty, ingenuity, efficacy, or efficiency of someone's solutions to a "how-to" question or problem. Rather, it assesses someone's performance in two rather special tasks which, in the Introduction, I have called the "reflective" and the "executive" tasks, respectively. They are the tasks, first of determining what is according, what contrary to reason, and then of performing according rather than contrary to it. Performing these tasks consists in following a more or less regimented procedure, essentially of identifying those of the publicly available general guidelines that are relevant and applying them to the case in hand. Insofar as there is scope for novelty or ingenuity at all, it typically is displayed in the reflective task by overcoming the difficulties of applying a general guideline to a case to which it does not neatly apply; it is the sort of novelty and ingenuity displayed by a judge. Although the kind of imagination, intelligence, or ingenuity we give high marks to in the case of Koehler's ape, can also be displayed in the domain of reason, it is at a level of much greater generality and sophistication, as when someone, say, a scientist attempts to improve these publicly available guidelines and so propounds a new and better theory, or when a legal reformer advocates a new and better law. But this is not a matter of rationality, reasonableness, or accordance with reasons or a high degree of these things. It is an improvement of the general guidelines we rely on in performing the normally more pedestrian task of performing according to reason.

More importantly, it should also be clear by now that (and why) it is a mistake to conceive of rationality in the evaluative sense as the central notion in the concept of reason and to try and elucidate the concept by a reductive definition of that idea in terms of the maximization of some extrarational good such as pleasure, happiness, or preference-satisfaction.[21] This would be too short a path from the nonrational to the evaluatively rational.

One important reason for this mistake is, as I argued, that contrary to a common belief, the basic notion in the concept of reason is not "rationality/irrationality." For that appraisal is made on the basis of how well or poorly a fully rational being has discharged his reflective and executive tasks on a particular occasion, that is, how well or poorly he has judged what is according, what contrary to reason, and on whether or not he has performed accordingly. A still more important reason, I should add, is that even the more generic evaluative notion of accordance with/ contrariety to reason cannot be captured by such a reductive definition. For what is according, what contrary to reason must be determined by a process of regimented thinking in which the appropriate use of the relevant reasons is essential. Thus, the truly basic notion in the concept is that of *a reason*, and that, in turn, hinges on the various activities of reason

---

[21] For example, David Gauthier identifies rationality, in *Morals by Agreement*, with "utility-maximization at the level of dispositions to choose" (Oxford: Oxford University Press, 1986), 182.

with their various aims and the publicly available general guidelines developed by the culture of one's society.

Section 12.   The Concept of Reason

I can now briefly summarize my answers to the three questions raised in chapter 1. The first question, it may be remembered, was, "What are the capacities, powers, and abilities involved in having reason, in being a rational being?" The answer is that we cannot (at least, as yet) say, in any physiological, neurological, or other precise empirical terminology, wherein that capacity consists, on account of which we are rational beings. All we can do, at this stage of our knowledge, is to explain it in terms of the characteristic ability of those capacity-rational beings who have become "fully rational." We can say (only rather uninformatively) that the capacity consists in whatever suffices for a being, in the normal course of growing up into a normal adult in a society that is an order of reason, to become fully rational; and full rationality consists in the ability to perform the various activities of reason, involving the use of the various appropriate types of reasons in accordance with the relevant procedures of reasoning. I have emphasized, in particular, the ability relevant to all kinds of directive reasons, namely, to perform the reflective and the executive tasks, as I have called them.

Question 2, it will be remembered, was, "What sort of thing do rational beings try to accomplish when exercising these abilities?" The answer is that each type of activity of reason has its own important end: proving aims at certainty, explaining at understanding, thinking about what to believe at truth, and so on. In each case, the performer aims at the germane task and uses the germane reasons, that is, those designed to give him the best chance to attain that end. On the view here advanced, what a fully rational person uses when engaging in an activity of reason are not necessarily facts singled out by the best possible guidelines but only facts singled out by the guidelines the society's best efforts managed to produce—they may be superseded the next day by what the best judges in the society consider superior ones. Thus, a fully rational being may, and perhaps should, know that these guidelines *may* not be the best to rely on, but, given the superiority of the powers of a society over those of an individual, to arrive at helpful guidelines, he would, nevertheless, be best advised to follow them except of course when he happens to be in a good position himself to improve on them. Thus, rationality, reasonableness, and even accordance with reason belong with warranted assertibility or justifiability rather than with truth or knowledge. They credit someone with having used the best available methods for attaining the end of one or other activity of reason, rather than with being successful in attaining it.

Question 3 was, "In what ways and by what standards do we appraise such exercises?" The answer is that we examine a person's performance in light of the best judgment given the best available resources (i.e., the best scientific theories, the wisdom of hindsight, and so on) about the sort of case to which his performance was directed (e.g., how well he explained, proved, or deliberated about something) and see whether his performance matches, or to what extent it falls short of, that best judgment. This sort of comparison is what we have in mind when we say that his performance was in accordance with or contrary to reason. Of course, we may also wish to evaluate a performance in light of the special circumstances in which it was performed. Judgments of this kind are made in terms of rationality/ irrationality or reasonableness/unreasonableness, and the like.

My general account of the content of reasons, it will be clear by now, is a version of Instrumentalism, but with a number of important modifications. In my view, Reason is best thought of, not as an individual psychological power analogous to sight or intelligence, but rather as a whole range of capacities and acquired abilities whose use presupposes the availability of generally available and generally learned or even taught methods—involving what we call reasons and their appropriate combinations—for attaining certain specific high-level ends, such as certainty, understanding, the best belief, and so on. A second modification is the diversity of these high-level ends for the attainment of which reasons are instrumental. As a consequence, as we shall see in the following chapters, the reasons employed in attaining these various high-level ends are used in importantly different ways that need to be kept apart. A third modification is that unlike its standard form, which fits primarily practical reasons, this form of Instrumentalism fits all types.

We can now add a word about the concept of reason as a whole. We can say that the central idea is that of *a society having the concept* or, as I have put it, *being an order of reason*. It is only if a society is such an order that an individual born into it can and will acquire the skills necessary for him to engage in the various activities of reason and the tendency to engage in them and to act according rather than contrary to the relevant publicly available guidelines. For this to be possible, the society must do its part to maintain the practices (or the enterprise) of reason, that is, see to it, through its educational practices, that the relevant guidelines are publicly available and that individuals come to appreciate that following them affords the best chance of attaining those important ends, at which the activities of reason aim. Such societies will also tend to set aside an adequate part of their resources for the continued improvement of these guidelines, as by adequately supporting scientific research and teaching, and the like.

The ideal of individual rationality is thus primarily a procedural rather than an outcome ideal, although not a purely procedural one since the procedure, the method of the relevant activity of reason, is based on beliefs about its efficacy in producing the desired outcome, and changes along with changes in beliefs about what is such an efficacious procedure. In other words, a person does not fall short of the ideal simply because the conclusion of her reasoning turns out not to have reached the ultimate goal that she was seeking—truth, understanding, the good, and so on. It is therefore, as I said, closer to "warranted assertibility" than to truth, closer to justified belief than to knowledge.

Of course, "Reason" can also be the name of an individual capacity or ability, but it is not one we can identify by studying a distinct seat or organ, as we can in the case of sight or hearing. It is, rather, a composite of capacities, including intelligence and language, which together can give rise to the central ability, which I have called full rationality, but only if an individual with these capacities grows up in an order of reason. Even with all these capacities an individual cannot "hear the voice of reason" in answer to her particular question unless she has learned, by her own reasoning, her own regimented thinking, to generate reason's overall judgment of what "performance" would on this occasion be in accordance with reason.

CHAPTER TWO

The Form of Directive Reasons

Section 1. Introduction

In chapter 1, I argued that an individual's "life of reason" consists, not in the exercise of an individual faculty or power, Reason, whose outstanding asset is the innate ability of seeing logically necessary connections between entities so connected and to infer from the existence of one such entity to that of another with which it is thus necessarily connected, but rather in that of playing the various roles which a society, by virtue of being an order of reason, enables, encourages, or requires its members to play. The primary role is that of the rational agent engaged in one or other of the activities of reason, such as proving, explaining, and deliberating. The main point I emphasized was that the individual's ability to engage in any of the activities of reason presupposes membership in an order of reason and the division of labor between society and individual that this implies. The most obvious tasks for the society are three: the training of the new generations in the publicly available guidelines on which individuals' particular performances of the activities depend; the organization of the improvement where possible and desirable of these guidelines; and the application of the appropriate social pressures on members to perform in accordance with these guidelines. For reasons that will become clearer later, especially in Book Two, this second task is especially important in the area of practical reasons.

In this chapter, I shall examine mainly the guidelines on which directive reasons hinge, and what I shall call "the form" of reasons themselves and of reason-statements, that is, statements in which something is claimed to be a directive reason, a reason *to.* . . . Although our prime concern is practical reasons, I shall often illustrate a point by a cognitive reason because it is often easier to find uncontested specimens of cognitive than of practical reasons. There are also secondary roles, such as appraising the performances by others of these activities, either in one's mind or to their faces or behind their backs, applying the appropriate sanctions, critically examining, and, where one can, suggesting or advocating certain improvements in the publicly available guidelines on whose merit depends the rational agent's ability to attain the end of the activity of reason in which she engages.

Concerning these guidelines, it is perhaps worth emphasizing that in order to be able to take advantage of them, it is neither necessary nor sufficient to be able to recite them. It is not necessary because one may learn a guideline by being shown how to do something or when not to do it. It is not sufficient, for one must also be able to recognize which of them are applicable to which of the various concrete situations in which one may find oneself and, when several are applicable, to compound them into an overall directive judgment. Where they have been put in words, they must be so formulated that properly socialized adults will recognize which aspects of the situations they find themselves in will constitute directive reasons to "perform" (that is, believe, act, feel, and so on) in certain specific ways rather than in others open to them. The guidelines must also be understood to purport to be so designed that those who conform to them stand to "perform" better than those who follow their unreflective inclinations or than those who do their reflecting in ways not regimented by the guidelines. They also purport to be so designed that following them offers a better chance of arriving at overall directive judgments that are consistent with one another, are formulated with adequate precision and empirically sound than the chance they would have if their "performances" were based on unreflective inclination or on reflection not thus regimented. I take it to be uncontroversial that in some areas of cognitive reasoning, such as logic and the natural sciences, spectacular successes have been scored in the design of the basis for such guidelines.

It will bear repeating that not all reasons are based on necessary truths, that not all are logical or deductive reasons. Such reasons cannot compete and conflict with one another. If a certain lump of sugar is a cube, then this is a deductive reason to think it has twelve edges. There is no possibility that we should discover another fact which is a reason to think that this lump has no edges or has fewer or more than twelve. Such reasons are logically, and so necessarily, conclusive and necessarily noncompeting.

There are—it surely will surprise no one—other types of reasons, facts that constitute reasons for something that can come into conflict with other facts that are reasons against that thing. They are sometimes called reasons "other things equal," "pro tanto," "presumptive," or "defeasible," and most often, following W. D. Ross, "prima facie." The term Ross chose is, however, ambiguous; it sometimes means the same as the first four, but sometimes it means "apparent" or "seeming," something that at first sight appears or seems to be a reason but on closer inspection may turn out not to be one at all. Something may be such a merely apparent reason because it may only appear to be but not be a fact as when, because the check bore the date of April 15, it seemed to have been signed on April 15, but in fact was not, as became clear when several of the checks with lower check numbers were found to bear later dates; or because though it was signed on that day, that fact is not a conclusive reason to think that this check was paid on time because it was signed so late on the 15th that the letter in which it was sent did not, as it should, bear the postmark of April 15. In this case, then, there is no clash between two competing reasons, but only the unmasking of a single false appearance, the reduction of an apparent single reason to no reason at all.[1]

The first four expressions (other things equal, and so on) on the one hand, and Ross's typical use of prima facie, on the other, work rather differently. As already indicated, the former imply the possibility that in a case under consideration, reflection may bring to light not only the reason already in hand but also additional relevant ones, some or all of which may be in conflict with it. The outcome will then depend on the resultant *force*, of the reason *all things considered, sans phrase,* or *overall*. We shall shortly look more closely at this metaphor taken from the compounding of a multiplicity of mechanical forces into a resultant overall force in Newtonian mechanics.

In many of these cases, there may be difficulties in bringing to light all the relevant competing reasons. There may then be guidelines about who has the "burden of proof." A person acts in accordance with reason if he acts in accordance with the overall balance of the competing reasons he has unearthed even though they were not all the relevant ones, but only if he has discharged the relevant burden of proof, that is, has made the effort required by that burden. Quite often, especially when there is a disagreement between two people about what are the relevant reasons, the burden of proof may shift from the person who has produced the first reason, usually the one that favors him, to the other person in whose interest it is to rebut or override the reason brought to light by the first. If Jill claims that

---

[1] For a more detailed account of my views, see my review of Mortimer R. and Sanford H. Kadish, *Discretion to Disobey: A Study of Lawful Departure from Legal Rules* in the *University of Pennsylvania Law Review* 124 (1975):577–80. For somewhat different views see Shelly Kagan, *The Limits of Morality* (Oxford: Oxford University Press, 1989), 16–17; Jonathan Dancy, *Moral Reasons* (Oxford: Blackwell, 1993):92–100; Kent Greenwalt, *Conflicts of Law and Morality* (New York: Oxford University Press, 1989), 101–3; M.B.E. Smith, "Is There a Prima Facie Obligation to Obey the Law?" *Yale Law Journal* 82, no. 5 (April 1973): 950–76.

Jack must pay her $1,000 on Thursday because she lent him that amount on condition that he pay it back no later than that, then the burden of proof may be on Jack to show that there is another competing reason that defeats Jill's reason and therefore shows—unless in turn defeated by a further relevant reason—that Jack need not pay that amount by that date.

We can say that, unlike a deductive reason, such a nondeductive one does not rely on an entailment or implication but on what may be called a *presumptive implication,* that is, an implication that is defeasible, one that can be defeated by a competing reason of greater force. However, subject to the guidelines about the burden of proof, it may be according to reason to act on the balance of the few known such reasons even if other stronger competing reasons may still come to light later. Are only practical reasons presumptive in the sense of having such presumptive implications? Clearly not; the cognitive ones, for instance, are so too. It would seem that scientific laws, for example, typically generate only presumptive implications.[2] The law of gravity does not imply that in ordinary circumstances feathers drop with the same acceleration as stones; or that relative to certain evidence (say, an anticyclone stationary over our area for the last two days) making it virtually certain that the sun will shine tomorrow, is compatible with the fact that relative to other evidence (say, a depression approaching from the West), there is only a fifty-fifty chance of sunshine tomorrow.

We may think, however, that presumptive implication is only second best to entailment and we may, therefore, try to convert the former into the latter. This may seem easy since, when we know what "possible facts" can defeat a presumptive implication and know which of such possible facts are "actual" and which are not, then we also know what conclusion we can deduce from the various premises that constitute conflicting presumptive pros and cons. However, although in some such way we can perhaps spread an ever tighter net of scientific laws over the world revealed to us by our observations, yet, as they extend further and further into the distant parts of the cosmos and into the structure of matter, we may continually have to redraw the boundary conditions within which these laws hold and to modify the laws when we discover the impact on them of further changes in the boundary conditions. As long as this process continues, we cannot complete the list of defeating conditions, since new such condi-

---

[2] The claim that they enable us to make only "predictions," not "prophecy"—that is, predictions in the ordinary sense—is another way of saying the same thing. Cf. Karl R. Popper, *Conjectures and Refutations* (London: Routledge and Kegan Paul, 1963), 339–40.

tions emerge as we learn more about the world, and so we cannot effectively turn presumptive implications into unconditional ones.

In any case, this wish so to transform presumptive implications ignores the real need for them, namely, the need to explain events as due to the impact of a multiplicity of forces or causal factors, each of which makes a specific contribution to the force resulting from their combination in the particular case. Conversely, we can often predict what will happen once we know what forces are at work and what impact each of them would make in the absence of the others. Similarly, it would be useful to know what conclusion we can draw from a given fact, quite irrespective of whether or not there are other possible facts which, if actual, would defeat this conclusion. We may, for instance, want to know whether the fact that taxation and interest rates are being lowered presumptively implies that productivity will increase, supposing everything else remained the same; and we may want to have such information even if we do not yet know exactly what these other things are and whether, say, the fact that military spending is being held at the present level, is one of these limiting conditions or whether productivity will rise irrespective of whether military spending is increased or decreased.

In these cases, our interest is not in what we can *deduce* from these facts. Rather, we want to know what "pull" certain conditions or factors or forces exert on certain events or states of affairs under certain other specified or "normal" (but unknown) conditions. We are primarily interested in the forces which, in the absence of other competing ones, will under such conditions bring about certain outcomes—some wanted, some unwanted—so that we can manipulate them so as to bring about the wanted or to prevent the unwanted. For this purpose, presumptive implication may be perfectly adequate, especially where unknown boundary conditions are fairly stable or at least do not often change unexpectedly.

Since reasoning involves the use of reasons, it could not get far, if it can get off the ground at all, without generally available and generally applicable guidelines, so that people can apply them to their particular problem cases and so continually test them by their use. Even an individual a thousand times more intelligent and productive than, say, Aristotle, could not have developed, solely by his own thinking, the advances made by generation after generation of logicians and laymen. And this applies even more to the guidelines developed by the various cooperative and cumulative disciplines, above all the empirical sciences.

It seems fair to say that for a long time now logicians have understood very well the sort of arguments that are studied in deductive logic, and also the cognitive reasoning based on it. From its premises we can move to the conclusion without needing to expect competing implications of other premises and to compound such conflicting implications into a final conclusion. But it seems we do not equally well understand that other large realm of reasoning, in which reasons are not conclusive *ab initio*, but where we have to work with defeasible (other-things-equal, pro tanto, etc.) reasons which do compete with others and where we do need to compound these competing reasons into a final all-things-considered one.

One thing to bear in mind in the following discussion is the division of labor I mentioned between society and individuals and the connection the individual must make between the guidelines provided by society and the solution to his question or problem. For this purpose he must identify and then apply the relevant guideline(s) to his case, and if more than one is relevant, combine them into an overall judgment. As we shall see, the guidelines must satisfy two opposing demands: that they be sufficiently general, or else they will not apply to a sufficient number of cases so that the individual has to master too many of them; and they must be sufficiently specific or else they will not provide the guidance they are supposed to give.

The task for society thus is a rather difficult one, perhaps just as difficult as that for the more advanced sciences. For what society must produce are guidelines for general self-guidance, so not only must there not be too many but they must be simple enough for everyone to understand and follow or else rely, as we must in law, on the help of experts which would, for obvious reasons, be a great drawback. Furthermore, society must provide generally applicable guidelines which when applied by a user to his problem yield relevant reasons—in many cases reasons that are merely pro tanto and so compete and conflict with others—which he must combine in an overall, all-things-considered, directive judgment of what to believe, do, feel, and so on. But this makes a very strong demand on those constructing the guidelines: they must be generally applicable whatever may be, in varying circumstances, the other guidelines also applicable to the case in hand. What counts for the individual is the final reason, but he must construct that out of a number of elements of a fixed or at least somehow determinable magnitude into an overall compound which gives him the "right" directive. Truly a tall order.

Let us therefore take a somewhat closer look at the form of directive reasons and the corresponding reason-statements, those that say of something that it is or would be a directive reason with certain characteristics.

Section 2.   The Dimensions of Directive Reason-Statements

I shall take as the canonical form the complete reason-statement, that is, the statement that fills in all the dimensions of the reason. In what follows I characterize as best I can each of the dimensions of such directive reasons. Bear in mind that, as in a statute of law so also in a guideline, types of fact, events, situations, states of affairs, and so on, are said to be connected with some "target," something to be believed, done, felt, and so on, whereas in a concrete case it is the token fact, event, etc., which, having been subsumed under the type, becomes the subject of the reason-statement. In what follows, I shall normally be talking about concrete directive reasons, the directive reasons there are for someone, or that he has, in a concrete situation. I begin with:

2.1.   The Constituent: That Which Constitutes the Reason, That Which the Reason-Statement Is About

It seems unclear, at first sight, whether the constituent *is* a fact or is something that someone who has a reason or acts for a reason *believes to be* a fact. On the one hand, it seems, my reason for shooting someone must have been my belief that she was attacking me, not the fact that she was, since in fact she was not attacking me. On the other hand, it seems, I could not have had that reason to shoot her if it is not a fact that she attacked me. Must we choose between these alternatives? Or are there perhaps two different senses of "reason"? Neither. Whether the constituent is a fact or a belief depends on the context in which the reason-statement is made.

2.1.1   The Context of Explanation

Suppose Jones calls her husband to tell him she will be late for dinner. The reason-statement that her reason for phoning is that she will be late is a reason-statement in an explanatory context. This explanation of her phone call is a reason-explanation since she takes the fact that she will be late to be a (directive) reason to call him and since that belief is the (explanatory) reason why she calls him. If she would have called him anyway or if she called only because she wanted him to tell their neighbors, who have no telephone, that they would be unable to come for their regular game of bridge, then though being late for dinner is a reason to call and she believes that it is, it was not *her* reason for calling him. Similarly, had she not believed that being late *is* a reason to call—suppose she thinks it is absurd to make a fuss about not calling when one is late, but knows her husband would make a fuss and wants to avoid that—then her reason for calling is not that she will be late, but that she wants to avoid the fuss, a consideration she does regard as a reason.

Jones has two beliefs, that she will be late and that this is a reason for her to call her husband. Both beliefs are required for the special kind of explanation of why she phoned, which is often called a reason-explanation, one in terms of the agent's reason. The explanatory reason really is a belief of the agent, but it presupposes, rightly or wrongly, that something is a practical reason whose constituent is a fact. Thus, in explanatory contexts, "she had a reason" or "she acted for a reason" refers (obliquely) to a (supposed) directive reason for her to perform as she did. It also implies that her belief in this directive reason was an explanatory (operative, effectively motivating) reason; in other words, that her belief that she had a directive reason to perform in this way actually moved her to perform as the supposed directive reason directed her to perform. In this context, therefore, one cannot have a reason without being motivated accordingly, but one may *have* (or have had) *a reason* for performing in a certain way without there actually *being* (or having been) *a reason* for one to perform in this way.[3]

"She had a reason for doing what she did" thus explains through an explanatory schema involving "ideal" behavior, that is, the *agent's correct* performance of her reflective and executive tasks. If she performs both of them correctly, then the explanation is complete. By contrast, failure in either task requires a further (often, causal) explanation of why she failed. Of course, there could be such a causal explanation also of the cases of success (just as there could be a causal explanation of why the dinner plates do not fall through the dinner table, although normally this would not call for explanation). But in the case of correct performance of the two tasks it would not be needed as a completion of the reason-explanation. In that context, that fact, correct performance (or plates not falling through the table), normally does not call for a further supplementary explanation. In that context, asking for such a further causal explanation of why a person has acted in accordance with a reason, suggests (if it does not imply) that the reason-explanation offered is not the *complete,* or even *the real,* explanation of why she acted that way. But in some other, wider, more theoretical context, this need not be implied by asking for and giving such a further causal explanation, for in that other context one may set out to

---

[3] But for a slight modification of this point, see chapter 3, section 3, especially p. 109.

explain how it is that, *normally,* people do act for reasons, that is, from motives deriving from the belief that a certain fact is a reason to do something. I return to this topic in chapter 3.

2.1.2. The Context of Justification

In this context, the normative standards of *having an (adequate) reason* are more stringent than in an explanatory one. For here we are interested not merely in what actually moved the person irrespective of how closely she came to the ideal model, but in whether or not she did what could reasonably be expected of her in both the reflective and executive tasks. Although, even in this context, having adequate reason does not require that what one took to be facts and reasons really were, but neither is it enough, as it is in explanatory contexts, that one should actually have believed they were. Rather, it is necessary that one's performance in both tasks (the reflective and the executive) should come up to a certain standard of excellence.

It would seem that in justifying our performance, whether to ourselves or to others, this standard requires us to follow the generally recognized guidelines where we can, or where we lack the expertise to do so, to follow the advice of recognized experts. Where we ourselves are such experts, we can also be expected to make efforts to find and act in accordance with improvements in these guidelines where we think them deficient. The right standard will also require or allow weighing the benefits of such improvements against the costs of finding them.

Thus, in this context also, but for different reasons, one can *have* a reason for doing something when in fact *there is* no reason for one to do it; conversely, there may be a reason for us to do something when we do not have a reason for doing it, because we cannot in reason be expected to know the fact that is the reason for us, or to know that it is such a reason.[4]

2.1.3. The Context of Deliberation

The most stringent conditions of actually having a reason are those applicable in this context, for here our aim is to find out what there actually is reason for us to do (believe, feel, and so on). Here *we have* a reason for something if and only if *there really is* a reason for us to perform in the way the supposed reason directs us to. In this context, the gap between there being and one having a reason vanishes. Of course, our

---

[4] Russell Grice, *The Grounds of Moral Judgment* (London: Cambridge University Press, 1967), 20.

deliberations may yield only what we have reason to take to be reasons, or even only what we in fact, though without good reasons, think are reasons (but then what we got is not what we were looking for). When we later discover that what we took to be was not a reason, then we must admit that, contrary to what we thought with whatever justification, we did not after all have a reason for what we did. It would be wrong to think that we must make the same admission in the other two contexts.*

Clearly, the primary context for practical reasons is that of deliberation. It is also for that context that our practical guidelines are primarily intended. They are meant to connect, for all or some of us, certain types of situations with one of the several alternatives open to us in them. It is part of our conventional wisdom that the fact that one has a headache is a reason for anyone to take a headache pill; but only for those with an especially sensitive stomach is there reason to take a Bufferin rather than an ordinary aspirin (supposing that the Bufferin ads can be trusted—a big "if," of course; one of the obstacles to sound practical reasoning is the profitability of spreading unsound guidelines).

Thus, in the context of deliberation, both having and there being a reason are equally closely tied to truth, for here neither is tied to the relative favorableness of the person's epistemic position. If there was no reason for him to do it, then he had none. By contrast, in the other two contexts, that personal position is taken into account when we judge whether the person had a reason. He may have had one even if there was none and conversely, he may not have had one though there was one.**

2.2.   The Target

What I call the target of directive reasons, including of course practical ones, is what they are reasons for or against, what they favor or disfavor, what they direct us to "perform"; a cognitive reason, to believe something, a practical one, to do something, and so on. The target—what the reason directs us to perform—is tied to the constituent by way of a directive. The target thus is the performance—the believing, acting, feeling, and so on, to which the reason-statement tells us the constituent is favorably or unfavorably relevant. Since directive reasons are favorably or unfavorably relevant to something, e.g., believings, actings, feelings, treasurings, and the like, over which we have a measure of control, they favor or disfavor performances which we could directly or indirectly bring about.

For example, the fact that this is a cube is a (cognitive) reason for anyone *to believe* that it has (rather than to disbelieve or doubt that it has, or to believe that it does not have) twelve edges; its target is believing that it has (rather than disbelieving or doubting that it has, or believing that it does not have) twelve edges. Again, the fact that it is, in the present circumstances, imprudent for me to buy junk bonds is a (practical) reason for me *not to buy* (rather than to buy or in other ways acquire) junk bonds; its target is not buying (rather than buying) junk bonds. Again, the fact that a certain gun is not loaded is a reason for those at whom it is pointed not to be (rather than to be) frightened; its target is not being (rather than being) frightened.

Well, then, what is the target in the case of directive reasons? It will be best to examine this in light of a comparison between what I have called fact-linking reason and two subclasses of directive reasons, cognitive and practical ones.

As we have seen (in chapter 1), the target of fact-linking reasons is always a constative fact, something that can be true or false, hence something that can be entailed by the constituent of the reason, as in our example of the cubic lump of sugar. In that case the fact that constituted the fact-linking reason under review, namely, that a certain lump of sugar is a cube, is such a reason whose target—for which it is a reason—is the fact entailed by the reason, namely, that it has twelve edges. In this case it is clear that the relations between constituent and target are epistemic relations, including entailments. And it is clear that *the ground,* on which the fact that the lump of sugar is a cube is such a reason, is that it entails the target.

Moving to the corresponding cognitive reason, we see that here the target cannot be a constative fact. For the target is "*to believe* that the lump of sugar has twelve edges." But there appear to be only two constative facts that are plausible candidates: "that the lump has twelve edges" or "that the person in question believes that the lump has twelve edges." But the first is the target of the original fact-linking reason, and the second is the target of another fact-linking reason, one that is concerned with taking cognizance of a fact concerning a belief of the person in question about the lump of sugar, namely, that it has twelve edges. But that is not the sort of thing which is the target of a directive reason. The fact that he believes this may show that he has satisfactorily discharged the executive task, if he has first completed the reflective task of arriving at the judgment that this is what he is to believe and then came to believe it *because* that was the judgment that emerged from his effort to discharge the reflective task. The target of the cognitive reason, what it is for, is formulated with the words "to believe." I suggested earlier that this can plausibly be read as short for a directive capable of being expressed in a "that clause," "that *he is to believe* that the lump has twelve edges." At any rate, even if it is the formulation of a fact, it is not a constative fact, but something *to be* accomplished. It formulates *the executive task;* to make a part of the world, in this case his own belief state, conform to the judgment that completes the reflective task. Here the direction of fit between the world-describing or world-depicting component of the sentence is the opposite of that in a description or a statement of constative fact.

Many, but of course not all sentences containing such a world-depicting component can formulate directives. "There will be an eclipse of the sun tomorrow" has such a component, but it cannot be used as a directive because it is not the sort that can be followed or not followed. "The procession will enter the town hall at 10 A.M." can be used or interpreted as either. Spectators who read it in a program of the festivities will read it as a statement of constative fact, the leaders of the procession as a directive.[5]

As I use the term here, "directive" is not a grammatical term like "indicative" or "imperative," but is a certain use or interpretation of sentences of various grammatical forms. As we just saw, indicatives can be used and in some contexts naturally interpreted as directives. So, of course, can imperatives. Commands, orders, pleas, exhortations, requests, appeals, advice, rules, norms, instructions, are names of different classes of directives. It is important to note that whereas in a constative, the conformity of its depictive (or representative) element to what it purports to depict (or represent) is its most important merit (truth), in a directive, that conformity (often called "being satisfied") is sometimes a merit of the person satisfying it, but by no means always (as when he follows bad advice or obeys an iniquitous law) and is never a merit of the directive itself. What constitutes the merit of a directive depends on what are the legitimate ends of the enterprise of which it is a part. In the case of the directives which are the targets of cognitive reasons, that aim is normally the truth, in the sense of acquiring true rather than false beliefs. Thus, the directives which constitute the judgments completing the executive task in answering questions of what to believe have their characteristic merit if the beliefs they direct us to have are true.[6]

---

[5] For a more detailed treatment, see chapter 8, section 5.2, pp. 312–15, and my "Reason and Experience," *Noûs* 7, no. 1 (March 1973):56–67.

[6] For some modification of this, see this chapter section 2.3, The Force. For further discussion of directives, see chapter 8.

2.3. The Force

What I here call "force" covers several rather different aspects of directive reasons. But before I describe these in detail, we need to be clear about two wider distinctions. One (already mentioned) is that between reasons that are not and those that are capable of competing and conflicting with one another. I borrow the terms "monotonic" and "nonmonotonic" which are sometimes used for this distinction. The other concerns two subclasses of nonmonotonic reasons, pro tanto and final reasons. The "force of a reason" sometimes refers to a characteristic of pro tanto reasons, at other times to one of final reasons.

2.3.1. Monotonic and Nonmonotonic Reasons

As I said, monotonic reasons are immune to being affected by other reasons. The fact that a lump of sugar is a cube, is a deductive reason to believe that it has twelve edges, but this means that nothing can come to light about this cubic lump that could cast any doubt on its having twelve edges, let alone show that it has not. The reason is "logically" conclusive, not subject to being affected, whether weakened or strengthened, by other, rival or allied, reasons. Historically speaking, what first captured most of the attention of logicians and scientists was deduction and the search for *the* cause of things. It is only in relatively recent times that probabilistic reasoning and the search for a multiplicity of causal factors and conditions came to be investigated. For most people, I imagine, "logical" and "deductive" are still virtually synonymous.

As I said before, there are also conclusive reasons which are not "logically" so. Thus, their blood groups may be a reason to think John is not the father of Jack. But this reason can conflict with others, say, that John has been Mary's husband for an adequate length of time, that their marriage has been consummated, and so on. But since (if I am correct) the blood-group reason is conclusive, it defeats the others, irrespective of the point in time at which it becomes known. It is conclusive *ab initio;* we do not need to wait until all the relevant reasons have been brought to light before we can tell whether it will defeat the other applicable relevant reasons.

This is important since we may sometimes know right at the start, or at any rate before we have surveyed and weighed all the applicable rival reasons, that there is a reason which is conclusive and so will carry the day whatever other reasons may come to light. This will sometimes save us the trouble of surveying and weighing the other applicable reasons, since they can make no difference to the outcome.[7]

Finally, there will be reasons that clinch the issue not because they are conclusive *ab initio*, not because they defeat all possible conflicting reasons, but only because they defeat all actually existing rival reasons, though they would not defeat others that would be applicable if they existed but do not exist in this case. This is usually called "a reason all things considered." For various reasons, say, pressure of time, we may have to be satisfied with less, for example, all *discovered* reasons considered, although we know full well that if we had had more time to look, we might have found additional reasons that would have altered the balance of reasons we established in our hurried search. I shall borrow the legal term "dispositive" for such clinchers, whether genuinely "all things considered" or only "all discovered things considered."

2.3.2. Defeating Force

We can now examine the first sense of "force of a directive reason," to which I give the name "defeating force." As the name suggests, it applies to a pro tanto reason or to combinations of them, but not to reasons all things considered or even to dispositive reasons, since in such cases the "victory" of the reason in question is no longer open to challenge.

The conclusiveness of a nonmonotonic directive reason is the strongest defeating force it can have.[8] If all the reasons we have in a particular case are singly inconclusive and so defeasible, then we must examine the defeating force each of them has and try to compound these forces into an overall or resultant one to determine the dispositive reason or combination of reasons.

---

[7] See Judith Jarvis Thomson, *The Realm of Rights* (Cambridge, Mass.: Harvard University Press, 1990), 82–122.

[8] In his book, *Practical Reasons and Norms* (London: Hutchinson University Library, 1975), p. 27, from which I have profited greatly, Joseph Raz says, "*p* is a conclusive reason for *x* to *ø* if, and only if, *p* is a reason for *x* to *ø* (which has not been cancelled) and there is no *q* such that *q* overrides *p*." This seems too weak. Suppose I know that a given coin has a strong bias, and this is a reason for thinking it will come up heads more than five times during the next ten throws, *and that there is no other fact that overrules this reason*. Still, it is not conclusive. Of course, there is something else for which it will be a conclusive reason, namely, that the coin will *probably* come up more than five times. But is not the same fact also a reason, though far from conclusive, to think that it *will* come up more than five times? Furthermore, Raz also says (in a footnote on p. 26), "I am not assuming that of every two strictly conflicting reasons one overrides the other. It may be that a conflict of reasons cannot be resolved." This seems right to me, but, together with his definition of "conclusive reason," it would seem to imply that one can have a conclusive reason both for and against the same thing.

This idea of compounding such forces is, of course, only an analogy inspired by mechanics, and we should not expect to be able to apply it in detail. Actions are not geometrically simple paths of physical objects through space determined by the direction and magnitude of the physical or other forces impressed on our bodies or limbs. Nor do our motives and reasons represent measurable or measured forces by which our actions are determined nor could we compound our motives and reasons into a single resultant one by mathematical calculations. The alternatives we confront when we engage in deliberation and practical reasoning are few and highly specific. We compare and rank them in qualitative, rough, non-mathematical ways only vaguely understood (at least so far). That one reason "has greater defeating force" than another thus is the conclusion we draw from our qualitative compoundings rather than a prior discovery required before we can perform such a compounding. Nevertheless, the analogy seems useful and I shall attempt to give an account of the defeating force of reasons which will preserve the principle that it is in accordance with reason to perform in accordance with "the balance of reasons," that is in accordance with the reason, or combination of reasons, that has a defeating force greater than that of the competing reason or combination of reasons.[9]

In an actual deliberation, we normally end up with a reason (or a combination of reasons) that has defeated all the other reasons actually considered. We may know that the guidelines considered are all the relevant ones and so know what reasons are "applicable." Alternatively, we may not know, either because we are uncertain about the types of reasons that are applicable or because, though we know that, we have been unable to ascertain which of them actually apply to our case (for instance, in our earlier example, whether all the men of the same blood group as John who have cohabited with Mary at the relevant time have been identified), or because we have failed to see the relevance of certain facts, say, that John was abroad at the relevant time. Such "final," dispositive reasons thus may or may not be literally "all things considered." However, both in the domains of practice and of beliefs, in our dispositive judgments, we often have to make do with such inconclusive, still defeasible, dispositive reasons.

We can, however, attain greater clarity about whether a given reason defeats another if we distinguish a number of types of reasons which defeat one another, at least other things equal, on the basis of the type to

---

[9] For a different view, see Raz, *Practical Reasons and Norms*, 36ff.

which they belong. There is then the further question of whether the defeating force of an individual reason of a type that defeats another can be defeated by an especially strong reason of the inferior type.

Self-anchored reasons. Only practical reasons can be of this type. The first two cases I shall mention illustrate employing practical reasons when we judge a case "on its merits," as we say. In these cases, it is natural for the agent to take into account only what (for her) are the merits of the case, that is, how the various options before her affect her or those individuals, if any, about whom she is not indifferent, whom she loves or hates or toward whom she has some other positive or negative attitude. I call the kinds of reasons employed in such cases, "self-anchored reasons." (For a more detailed account see chapter 4, section 1.)

The most elementary reasons of this sort are those sometimes called "hedonic in a wide sense," that is, facts about the alternatives open to someone and their consequences on account of which they please her, or please those toward whom she has positive attitudes or displease those toward whom she has negative attitudes, and, mutatis mutandis, other facts about the alternatives on account of which they displease her and relevantly affect those others toward whom she has such relevant attitudes.

In the case of any such pair of single, or sets of, conflicting, pro tanto reasons, one of them will have a defeating force that is greater than or equal to that of the other. In the first such case, I shall say that one of them "outweighs," in the second that it "balances," the other. The first means that the practical judgment which constitutes the correct completion of the reflective task must be that she ought to do what the dispositive reason directs her to do. And if she arrives at this judgment, she will further conclude that it will be in accordance with reason to act as the judgment tells her she ought. Of course, as we have seen, in a justificatory context, after she has performed, the judgment whether she acted in accordance with reason may be based on slightly different grounds. I shall for the moment postpone the answer to what will be the correct completion of the reflective task when the reasons are balanced.

I turn next to another type of cases which we judge on their merits. Many people have argued that when we deliberate about what to do, we should try to attain certain ideal ends, such as our welfare, interest, good, self-realization, happiness, fulfillment, and so on. And most would agree that one or other or most of them are indeed things that should have a certain place in what can be called a good, a valuable, or a meaningful life, which is the sort of life we should attempt to lead. And so, many would agree that when on a particular occasion we deliberate about what to do, it will often be the case that the plan for such a life will require us to aim at such things as attaining certain skills or excellences, promoting our interest, our good, our self-realization and so on, and that attaining this will be incompatible with always following the strongest hedonic reasons, and that these "higher" reasons have greater defeating force than the "lower" hedonic ones.

Supposing this is correct, what is the relation between such higher and lower reasons? It is easiest to see in the case of so-called prudential or self-interested reasons. It is generally thought to be in one's interest to make the effort and undergo the tedium of the reading, rote learning, essay writing, and practicing involved in the acquisition of certain high-level skills, such as are involved in the study of medicine or in becoming a first-rate pianist, and to forgo the pleasures of play and companionship, especially rewarding at an age when such studies require one to renounce them. This will not of course be true for everybody. If, like myself, one has a tin ear, the study of music will not be in one's interest; if, like myself, one has no talent for tennis or for basketball, the sacrifices necessary to acquire the skill will be wasted. That is to say, one will not increase one's chances of reaping the especially rewarding payoffs of the activities requiring these skills nor the increased ordinary rewards (say, earnings) that normally go with having them. These particular things will then not be in one's interest, but that of course does not mean that there may not be other things that *are* in one's interest and for which one therefore has such higher reasons.

Thus, these higher reasons are "in the same ball park" as the lower hedonic ones, but they recommend improving one's abilities or acquiring additional ones in order to secure these and perhaps other more rewarding payoffs, and to improve one's defenses against the blows of fortune one may suffer. Thus, although these higher reasons draw on the same sorts of grounds as hedonic ones and involve judgments on the merit of the case, yet they deserve a certain "weighting" on account of the fact that they also take into account the whole of one's life and the prospects for reaping more and greater goods as well as guarding against more and greater evils.

Nevertheless, although higher reasons of self-interest defeat lower hedonic reasons, they do so only up to a certain threshold. Suppose prudence requires of Chuck, a commercial traveler, that he take out automobile insurance, covering him against collision damage, and so on. Suppose also that he would derive a lot more enjoyment from using that money on a vacation in the Bahamas. Yet, because the one is a prudential, and the other merely a hedonic reason, we think that the former outweighs the latter. But now suppose he has a unique opportunity for a significant increase in enjoyment: he has won a vacation for two in the Bahamas, which would cost him only the air fare, and his new love would be glad to fly with him. In such a case, it may well be thought in accordance with reason for him to regard the hedonic as outweighing the prudential reason, and so to take the risk of postponing renewal of his automobile insurance until he has paid off the cost of this vacation. Thus, in this case, too, we are still judging on the merits of the case, even though we attach to certain "higher" reasons a certain weighting that sets up a threshold below which lower reasons are prima facie defeated by higher ones. But that threshold itself is removed when we have adequate information that it would give greater defeating force to the higher reason than is warranted by the merits of the case.

Lexically prior reasons. The treatment of higher reasons on account of their weightings does not amount to a so-called "lexical ordering."[10] If R1 is lexically prior to R2, then the agent who has R1 and R2 may not follow R2 until she has attained the end R1 directs her to attain. As shown by the example of the commercial traveler who won a holiday for two, when the defeating force of a hedonic reason exceeds a certain threshold, the agent may in reason follow it rather than the higher reason. A lexically prior reason unconditionally defeats a lexically subordinate one; there is no threshold above which the subordinate one balances or defeats the prior one. Things other and more important than the merits of the case in hand have been taken into account in what is really such a lexically prior reason. Where a lexically prior reason applies, it is therefore not in accordance with reason to judge the case on its merits.

Society-anchored reasons. I turn now to a second class of cases, in which there is a conflict between "natural" reasons—the kind we have discussed so far—and another kind I call "artificial." This kind presupposes the existence of certain practices, such as promises or laws, which involve conventional rules and the recognition of authority. If I promise you to meet you at the club at five, I am taken to have such an artificial reason to be there at five. Such society-anchored reasons are like higher self-anchored reasons in that their defeating force is greater than that of hedonic reasons and in that it does not amount to that of a lexically prior reason. It is only a weighting up to a certain threshold. But there are at least three differences that should be mentioned. In the first place, such

---

[10] Rawls, *TJ*, 74.

reasons are not in the same ball park as hedonic and higher reasons—they are not based on the effects on herself of the alternatives open to an agent or on those toward whom she is not indifferent, as long as these effects are within the limits set by a certain threshold. Where the hedonic payoffs of these alternatives and their consequences exceed that threshold, the relevant persons are not merely the agent herself and those toward whom she is not indifferent, but also and especially those to whom the promise was made, and so the case is not correctly judged simply on its merits.[11] Finally, while higher self-anchored reasons defeat hedonic reasons, society-anchored reasons are thought to defeat both hedonic and higher self-anchored reasons. To indicate the greater defeating force of a society-anchored reason, I shall speak of it as "overriding" or "overruling" the other. (I prefer "overruling" because it indicates more clearly than does the more widely used "overriding," that the force is normative, not motivational.)

It may perhaps be thought that the main novelty is that the previous cases did not involve moral reasons, whereas the last one does. This sounds plausible, especially when one considers the appropriate sanction, which I shall take up in section 3.4. But the question whether these society-anchored reasons are moral ones is very complex and involves a number of contentious issues which we have to postpone until Book Two. (See chapter 7, section 4, especially 4.2.)

Exclusionary reasons. We need to consider briefly a special type of society-based reasons which defeat other conflicting reasons, not by outweighing or overruling them, but in an importantly different way, namely, by making them *inadmissible*. Whereas the other two kinds are sensitive to the merits of the case, exclusionary reasons are not: as in the case of lexical ordering there is no threshold above which the merits of the case defeat them. An exclusionary reason disqualifies a defeated reason from being taken into account in the determination of what is the dispositive reason of the case. What distinguishes the defeat of a reason by its exclusion from the other types of defeat is, that the excluding reason does not compete with the excluded reason; it does not oppose (or support) the target the excluded reason supports (or opposes). Indeed, an excluding reason may exclude several mutually competing ones, without of course itself competing with any or all of them. Such exclusionary reasons often occur in law where the party with "the better substantive

---

[11] Thomson, *The Realm of Rights,* 316–20. See also my review of Thomson in *Dialogue* 33 (1994):1–13.

case" may lose because of a procedural misstep, such as missing the deadline for an appeal or counsel's persisting in a line of questioning the judge has ruled out of order.

Nevertheless, there is a sense in which, though they do not compete with excluded reasons, excluding reasons conflict with them. For in excluding them, they eliminate the support or opposition the excluded reasons would otherwise provide for their common target; in doing this, the excluding reasons indirectly support, because they do not render mute, the remaining unexcluded reasons with which the excluded ones competed. We can therefore think of the excluding reasons as defeating or helping to defeat the excluded reasons. But, of course, this does not mean that the exclusion of a reason or group of reasons entails the defeat of their "cause" (in the sense that the judgment supported by these excluded reasons is defeated), for the exclusion of these reasons may not suffice to accomplish that. A judge's exclusion of a certain line of questioning may not suffice to make the opposing party victorious. Still, I think it not too misleading to speak of exclusion as a species of defeat, since, in the case in hand, it renders a reason mute, inadmissible, inactive.

But, it may be asked, are cases involving exclusionary reasons settled, like the earlier ones, by the balance of reasons? After all, the defeating force of exclusionary reasons is not added to that of the reasons in conflict with those excluded. This is true. Nevertheless, the final judgment does reflect the balance of reasons (if less directly than in the earlier cases) because the exclusionary reason determines which of the relevant reasons are to be balanced against one another. We can therefore retain this general principle.

2.3.3. Requiring and Permissive Reasons

The second sense of "the force of a directive reason" refers to its rational constraining force, the extent to which a reason narrows those options of a person that are in accordance with reason. Unlike the first, this sense does not refer to the defeating force of a pro tanto reason. It is not concerned with how well it would fare in competition with other pro tanto reasons, but how, if it were the dispositive reason, it would restrict the agent's choices that would be in accordance with reason.

By a "requiring reason" I mean one that entails that performing as directed by it is according to reason, and not so performing is contrary to it. By a "nonrequiring or permissive reason" I mean one entailing that performing as directed by it is according to reason, but leaving open whether not performing in this way is contrary to it. If one morning, at 5:30 A.M., I feel both sleepy and hungry, and if that constitutes a permissive reason to stay in bed and get some more sleep, that implies that it would be according to reason to stay in bed but says nothing about whether or not it would be in accordance with reason to get up and have breakfast. On this view, one could have both a permissive and a requiring reason to stay in bed. If neither is defeated, the requiring reason becomes dispositive.

It may perhaps be thought that there can be no merely permissive cognitive reasons. For this would imply the possibility that neither believing p nor not believing p (including believing not-p) is contrary to reason, whereas the only rational attitude would seem to be *not to believe either*, that is, to suspend judgment, to remain agnostic. If, at a crossroads, I find a crudely made sign, ROAD CLOSED—LANDSLIDE, which could be a hoax or a genuine sign made up by a motorist in a hurry, surely I should suspend judgment. Of course, I have to make a choice whether to take the supposedly blocked road or make the long detour, and the choice should be appropriate to my belief. Unfortunately, in such a case, I can do no better than toss a coin. This seems a strong point. Still, are there not cases in which one has equally good reasons for both rather than none for either? May there not be good reasons for thinking that Yeltsin will remain in power for at least another five years and equally good reason for thinking that he cannot last for more than two,[12] or for thinking that Kennedy was shot by only one person and that he was shot by two? But does this show that in such a situation anything other than agnosticism is contrary to reason? Perhaps there are certain situations, as when a spy master has to deal with his own team of spies, in which the only rational thing for him to do, really is to remain inwardly agnostic but outwardly to behave as if he completely trusted them and believed what they reported. In more usual circumstances, it would seem not to be contrary to reason to believe whatever these balanced reasons incline one to believe, as long as one remains responsive to new evidence. If Yeltsin's economic program fails, if war breaks out between several of the successor states, if economic help from the West is not forthcoming, and if a popular leader emerges, then perhaps one has sufficient reason to believe he will not last for more than two years rather than for another five. Thus, it would seem that the case against merely permissive cognitive reasons, reasons which permit

---

[12] This was written shortly after a visit to Moscow in 1987, when that question was frequently asked about Gorbachev. I hope I shall not have to replace this name again before this book finally appears in print.

either but require neither belief, is not conclusive. However, the issue is complex and I am not confident that I have this right.

2.3.4. Sanctions

We may want to include, under the force of a directive reason, a further aspect concerning "the relevant sanctions" we impose for malperformances of the reflective or the executive task or both, by those for whom there are such reasons. Someone is guilty of such a malperformance if, for instance, he overlooks or ignores such a reason or fails to give it its due weight, for he would not then perform in a way best calculated to achieve the relevant ideals (truth, the good, etc.). It would, therefore, be appropriate to judge such a flawed performance and its performer in the appropriate negative way. Epithets such as "foolish," "imprudent," "unreasonable," "irrational," and, as I shall argue later, "immoral," express such negative appraisals, based on the various kinds of malperformance we may commit. Of course, the kind of reasons that possess this kind of force are dispositive, not pro tanto reasons.

Exactly what epithet we should use to express our negative judgment would depend on the ideal involved and the gravity of the lapse. An important consideration in how to judge such a performance is whether the community may within reason expect of all or some of its members that they adopt the relevant ideal as their own, and what pressure, if any, reason would permit or require them to exert on members to do so. Judging someone imprudent implies that she has failed to give adequate consideration to a prudential reason. And although we expect (in the sense of "anticipate" or "assume") that a given person will pay heed to such reasons, we do not normally expect (in the sense of "demand") that she do so. On the contrary, we think that it normally is solely a person's own business whether she does or does not heed prudential reasons. Nevertheless, foolishness is regarded as a character trait that makes it reasonable to exclude those who have it from certain cooperative enterprises and to take self-protective measures against the harm their foolishness can cause one.[13]

Thus, by "the force of a directive reason" we could mean (among other things) the kind and severity of the individual and social pressures whose appropriateness is determined by the adequacy of the heed a person should pay or has paid to the dispositive directive reasons she has or had.

---

[13] Cf. Introduction, section 3, p. 20f.

In this last sense, then, a reason can be said to have greater force than another if a more strongly motivating sanction is appropriate to it than to the other. We shall have to return to this point later when in Book Two we look more closely at the nature of morality and the force of moral reasons. (See Book Two, chapters 6 and 7.)

2.3.5. Margin of Victory

There is yet another possible sense of "force," one applicable only to dispositive reasons, namely, the margin by which the dispositive reason has defeated its competitors if any. If a pro tanto reason is *ab initio* conclusive, then the margin is as wide as it can be. Performing contrary to it is as seriously contrary to reason as it can be. Of course if the dispositive reason is only permissive, one cannot perform contrary to it, hence the margin of victory would not matter.

Words such as "must" and "ought" can be used to indicate the margin of victory or its restrictive reach. By "you really *must* read Michael Frayne's new novel," I may well mean that this is a requiring dispositive reason, or it may mean "the reasons for reading it defeat any against it by the widest possible margin of victory." "You ought to get married again" may imply that although there are reasons against it, there is a *significant* balance in favor.

2.4.   The Ground

The ground of a directive reason is that on account of which we tell whether a given reason-statement has correctly linked the target of a reason to its constituent, and correctly specified the other dimensions. It is not difficult to see what is normally the ground of a cognitive reason. In our example of the cubic lump of sugar, it is of course the entailment that holds between being a cube and having twelve edges: the reason-statement, "the fact that a lump of sugar is a cube is a logically conclusive reason to believe that it has twelve edges," is true because—and this now states the ground—being a cube entails having twelve edges. Why is that the ground? Because the context in which we are employing this reason is that of thinking about whether or not to believe something, namely, that the lump of sugar has twelve edges. Our normal aim in such a context will be *the truth*, that is, to arrive at the true one of the two relevant contradictory beliefs. But since to believe something that can be true or false is to believe it true, we shall normally want to believe the true rather than the false one. For normally when we inquire into what to believe, say, whether to believe that a cube has twelve edges or not, we want to *know* how many edges it has, and that involves having a true belief about it.

But if we want to arrive at a true rather than a false belief, say, about whether or not a certain lump has twelve edges, then a conclusive reason to think that it has twelve edges is the best reason we can have to believe it, since it guarantees its truth, provided, of course, that its constituent (that the lump is a cube) is true.

It may be objected that we do not always want to know the truth, or want to believe something because and in as far as it is true. Someone may want, perhaps unconsciously, to deceive himself about something, say that the person he loves returns his affection, or he may want to believe that he will win the race not because it is true but because it will give him the confidence necessary for winning. And these beliefs may not be contrary to reason. This objection should be granted. We can distinguish between two kinds of cognitive reasons, epistemic and pragmatic, based on different grounds. The ground of the former is that their constituent guarantees or makes it probable that its target belief is true, that of the latter, that having its target belief has certain desired consequences, independently of whether it is true or false.

We can here ignore the problem of the relation between these two grounds and the rational limits on either. We need not here look into the difficult questions of when it is contrary to reason to follow epistemic and when to follow pragmatic cognitive reasons. We can be satisfied with the somewhat open-ended conclusion that, other things being equal, it is in accordance with reason to follow epistemic cognitive reasons, while leaving it open when it is in accordance with reason to follow pragmatic ones and in what circumstances which type of reason defeats the other when they conflict.

Turning to practical reasons, we face a difficulty since, obviously, their ground cannot be related to truth the way it is in the case of epistemic cognitive reasons, for the excellence of the target of such reasons cannot lie in its truth. Why not? Should we perhaps say, borrowing from Hume,[14] that, being "original existences (or facts or realities)" and not, like beliefs, "representations," actions cannot be true or false and, *therefore*, truth cannot ground practical reasons, as it can cognitive ones? But is this a valid inference? Suppose I say, "I shall be there at six"; can't this be a (practical) reason to be there at six? And is not its ground the fact that being there at six would *make true* what I said?

---

[14] Hume, *Treatise*, 458.

To this query it may be objected, plausibly, that being truth-generating can ground this practical reason only if and because I *wish to make true* some prophecy, prediction, expression of intention, promise, vow, dream, and the like, whether my own or someone else's. This objection may be granted, but then, it would seem, being truth-generating can ground a cognitive reason only if and because when thinking about what to believe, I wish to take cognizance of something, because then what I am after is true rather than false beliefs. If, however, I want to believe something in order to secure certain benefits, then pragmatic reasons may be more apposite than epistemic ones, and then being truth-generating will not be the ground of the apposite reasons for what to believe. Thus capacity for being true or false is neither a sufficient condition of being able to ground cognitive reasons nor a necessary condition of being able to ground practical reasons. It is only if the capacity for being true or false were a necessary and sufficient condition of the fact that being truth-generating can be a ground of cognitive reasons, that the fact that actions cannot be true or false would show that being truth-generating cannot be a ground of practical reasons.

However, the crucial question would seem to be a different one, namely when, if ever, it is in accordance with reason to substitute for the "normal" epistemic cognitive reasons (which are grounded in truth), pragmatic cognitive reasons which are grounded in some good or benefit; and what single ideal aim, if any, is the one by reference to which we can ground both pro tanto practical reason and its force, so that we can work out what is the dispositive reason, all things considered. However, I leave more detailed discussions of this complex topic for a later chapter.[15]

2.5.   *The Scope and the Range*

I discuss these two aspects of reasons together since both indicate limits beyond which a reason does not hold. The scope of epistemic cognitive reasons is universal: what is a cognitive reason "for" one person, is a cognitive reason "for" all. Even what, *relative to the same evidence*, is probable for one person is equally probable for all, irrespective of the availability of that evidence to them. Hence, it would, perhaps, be less misleading to say that epistemic cognitive reasons altogether lack the dimension of scope. Of course, what is warrantedly assertible for one person may not be so for another since, unlike truth, warranted

---

[15] See chapter 4, The Ground of Practical Reasons.

assertibility is relativized to the evidence *available* to the person thereby warranted to make the assertion.

The scope of practical (and pragmatic cognitive) reasons appears not to be similarly universal. That there is good swimming in Mallorca may be a good reason for you but not for me to vacation there, because you are a keen swimmer and I am not. Whereas epistemic cognitive reasons need not distinguish between truths "for" different types of persons, (at least some) practical reasons are essentially relativized to different types of persons and also to the different ways in which they are placed relative to their goals. Thus, this fact about Mallorca is a reason to vacation there, but only with a limited scope, including those who like swimming in the sea. Similarly, it holds only for a certain limited range. If at certain times of the year, the water is too cold or too polluted for swimming, then these times are beyond the range for which this reason holds.

We can maintain the universality of practical reasons by limiting their scope and range. Within these limits, the reasons hold universally. Somewhat like scientific laws, our practical guidelines can be developed by the initial assumption that their range is unlimited until we find restrictions on the range, such as the times during which the water is too cold or too polluted for swimming. However, unlike cognitive guidelines, practical ones also have limited scope, such as the differences in personal tastes. For many practical questions, such differences in taste determine the scope of reasons constituted by certain facts.

We can increase the scope of a reason by making it less specific. You go to Mallorca for the swimming and the sights and activities of the beach, I go to the Tyrol for the mountain scenery and the thrills of mountaineering. The constituent of what is a reason for you about where to vacation is the fact that there is good swimming in Mallorca (but not in the Tyrol), the target is to go to Mallorca; the constituent of what is a reason for me is the fact that there is good mountain scenery and mountaineering in the Tyrol (but not in Mallorca) and its target is to go to the Tyrol. Thus, you and I have different reasons (both in constituent and target) for picking our respective vacation spots. But, if we raise the level of abstraction, we also have the same reason, namely, that our respective vacation spots ideally cater to our favorite vacation activities. In this sense, you have the same reason to select Mallorca and reject the Tyrol, as I have to select the Tyrol and reject Mallorca. Thus, if we spell out our reasons more specifically, we have different reasons for different choices, if more generally, we have the same reason for them.

However, we cannot get rid of all restrictions on scope by raising the level of abstraction. People who do not have vacations or cannot go away for them are not within the scope of reasons about where to vacation. At the same time, raising the level of abstraction tends to reduce the usefulness of the guideline. We often want to know precisely what is a reason to do precisely what. A brochure that tells you that Mallorca caters to most vacation activities is less helpful than one that tells you exactly what activities. And the brochure that tells you that the Tyrol has splendid mountain scenery and climbing is less useful than one that tells you more exactly where in the Tyrol you will find what kind of mountain scenery, whether glaciers, forests, alpine meadows, spectacular rock faces to climb, and so on.

Let us remind ourselves of the two stages of our reflective task in practical deliberation. First, we must survey as far as possible all the relevant facts, that is, those that are constituents of practical reasons for or against the alternatives between which we want to decide, and so assemble the various applicable pros and cons concerning these alternatives. Second, we must try to compound these pros and cons into an overall, where possible all-things-considered, dispositive reason for one of these alternatives. To make it possible, preferably easy, for us to perform these tasks, the guidelines should satisfy certain conditions. In this section, I confine myself to a few remarks about the first task, and postpone discussion of the second to a later chapter.

It should be obvious that the guidelines must strike a compromise between two opposing principles, the *principle of parsimony* and the *principle of specificity.* Since people should be able to recognize the relevance of facts without looking up a list of guidelines, such as a legal code book, there should be relatively few so that they can remember all or most and so recognize which of the facts of their case can be subsumed under the constituent of one or other of the familiar guidelines. To satisfy this first principle, the guidelines would have to be comparatively nonspecific, abstract, or general, rather than specific, concrete, or particular. But as we have already noted, the more general they are, the less helpful they will often be. Fortunately, we can to a certain extent remedy the specificity problem by a division of labor. We can leave to experts the knowledge of specific guidelines of certain kinds, namely, those concerned with means to ends. When the kitchen clock stops or a tooth aches, we need not be able to determine what exactly we have reason to do, let alone to do it. It is enough to know that we have reason to get the clock fixed or the tooth treated by an expert, that the former is done by a watchmaker, the latter by a dentist, and that, if we do not know one, we can find one in the phone book. Of course, as we all know, it is often quite difficult or at any rate time consuming to determine who is an expert, let alone which of several experts is the best.

Section 3.   Abstract and Concrete Reason-Statements

It may be helpful to construct the canonical form of a directive reason-statement that lists all its dimensions. As I mentioned before, such statements involve two main things, the availability in a society of various guidelines for thinking about what to believe, do, and so on, which it has been able to work out, and the ability of its members to apply the relevant ones to a particular problem case for the purpose of solving it. I call the formulation of such a guideline an "abstract directive reason-statement," the claim that a given case can be subsumed under a certain guideline, a "concrete" one.

3.1.   *The Form of Directive Reason-Statements*

We can begin with a skeleton statement (a "sentence frame" or "propositional function"), in which the various dimensions of directive reason-statements are represented by variables, indicated by descriptive expressions followed in parenthesis by single letters and what they stand for. In the canonical form of the abstract reason-statement some key expressions are in brackets, whereas the corresponding "open" expressions accompanying them give the canonical form of a concrete directive reason-statement.

> For a certain range of conditions (r; the range), a certain [type of] fact (c; the constituent) is [would be], on a certain ground (g), a pro tanto directive reason of a certain kind (k; e.g., hedonic, prudential, etc.) and force (f) for people of a certain sort (s; the scope), to perform in a certain way (w).

An abstract directive reason is a guideline for us because it tells us what *type of fact* would be a directive reason for us, while giving enough detail to enable us to recognize whether it is relevant to the case in hand, i.e., whether performing as it directs us to, would be a solution to our problem, and to ascertain whether we can in the circumstances we are in, identify a fact which is an instantiation (or token) of the type of fact which the abstract reason tells us would constitute a directive reason.

Two further things should be mentioned. The first concerns the pair of terms that is appropriate for stating the constituent in such a pair of directive reasons. My choice of "fact of a certain type" instantiated or tokened in a token fact is awkward and perhaps misleading but no more so than other pairs I can think of, such as possible/actual fact, genus/species, species/specimen. Perhaps the reader will think of a less awkward pair.

The second is to reemphasize an important difference between cognitive and practical reasons, namely, that cognitive reasons do not vary in scope, as practical reasons do; or, perhaps more accurately, that the very idea of scope does not seem to fit cognitive reasons. We think of what there is to take cognizance of as a single world or aspects of it; by contrast, getting what one wants from the world may require transforming it or some aspects of it in ways that differ from one person to the next and indeed may be mutually incompatible.

Book One

The Order of Reason

PART TWO:
A THEORY OF
PRACTICAL REASON

CHAPTER THREE
Practical Reasons and Motives

Section 1.   Internalism versus Externalism

At this point, it will be most helpful, I think, to make clearer the relation between reasons and motivation before examining more fully what is the ground of practical reasons. So far, we have touched on the question of motivation only when considering the sanctions that are appropriately attached to various kinds of practical reasons for the purpose of supplementing the motivating force intrinsic to them. We noted the difference between the motivating force of a practical reason and its defeating force: the former is crucial in explanatory, the latter in justificatory and deliberative contexts. However, since practical reasons obviously also can play an explanatory role, they must be able, at least sometimes, perhaps always, to have a motivating force. The question now is whether that ability is essential to being a practical reason, in particular whether the motivating and the defeating force of a pro tanto practical reason must be the same (in a sense yet to be made clear), and whether the motivating force of a dispositive reason must be greater than that of any other conflicting practical reason or combination of such reasons, or greater than any other motive operative on the occasion.

I here assume it granted that directive reasons apply only where we have a measure of control, whether direct or indirect, over something, such as a belief, a feeling, or an action. It is over our actions we appear to have the greatest measure of control. We all think, I believe, that we often know what are at least some of the alternatives open to us, and that in such cases we can enter upon one or other of them as we see fit: that we can simply decide to do one of them, and then execute this decision "at will" as we say, that is, act as we decided.

Similarly, it seems we can think about what it would be appropriate to feel, though it seems we cannot exactly deliberate about *what* to feel, since it seems we cannot, for instance, feel anger or not feel anger at will, as we see fit. Nevertheless, over the long run, it would seem, we can at least try to change the kind of emotional reactions we normally have or make to certain sorts of situations and we can "work on" our emotional responses with a view to bringing them into conformity with our judgment; thus at least some of us, it seems, can do something along these lines about our irascibility or our jealousy or our envy or our fears.

Something similar appears to be true also for our beliefs. We may not always believe what corresponds most closely to what is recommended by what we believe we have the best reason to believe, but we can work on it. We can try to resist and to weaken those strong motives of ours (if any) that incline us to embrace or maintain certain beliefs in the face of overwhelming, perhaps conclusive, evidence to the contrary, even if (perhaps—if we can believe Tertullian—even because?) it is absurd.

The term, *Internalism*,[1] is now widely used for the view that if a fact is a reason for someone to do something, then it necessarily also is a motive for him to do it, in the sense that, if he knows or believes that this fact constitutes a reason for him to do something, then it also motivates, that is, inclines or disposes him to do it. Few philosophers, if any, would (I think) seriously question the claim that Internalism does not hold for cognitive reasons. It seems clear that our culture has worked out a serviceable regimented method for reflecting about what to believe, and that the conclusions of these reflections and reasonings, issuing in a directive (or normative) judgment of what (one ought) to believe, is capable of coming into conflict with one's motives. Thus, in our case of John, Jack, and Mary whose blood groups are such as to constitute, together, conclusive evidence, and so conclusive (cognitive) reason for everyone including John to believe, that Jack is not his child, I suggested[2] that this fact about their blood groups, established in court beyond any reasonable doubt, may yet not be capable of moving John to believe that Jack is not his child, and not because he knows of other facts which he regards as weightier cognitive reasons to believe that he is Jack's father, but because there may be virtually nothing capable of shaking his belief in his fatherhood. Thus, it seems clear that there are at least some directive reasons, namely, cognitive ones, for which Internalism is false. Some fact of which someone is now fully aware (and which he would perhaps in other cases acknowl-

[1] Thomas Nagel, *The Possibility of Altruism* (Princeton, N.J.: Princeton University Press, 1970), 7–12; Frankena, "Obligation and Motivation in Recent Moral Philosophy," 40–41; Bernard Williams, "Internal and External Reasons," reprinted in *Moral Luck*, ed. Bernard Williams (Cambridge: Cambridge University Press, 1981), essay 8, 101–13.

[2] See Introduction, p. 10f.

edge to be conclusive evidence for a certain other fact) can be a conclusive reason for him to believe that other thing to be a fact, even though he is not now moved or to any degree motivated to believe it. Of course, this does not show that one can believe something to be a fact and to believe that fact to be a conclusive reason for one to believe a certain other fact and yet not be motivated to believe that other fact.

What, then, about practical reasons? Suppose John's lover has AIDS; would we not think that this is a very weighty, perhaps dispositive reason for them to refrain from making love in their preferred but unsafe style, even if nothing could shake their determination to continue in their usual way? Would we not here, just as in the case of John's belief in his fatherhood, think that there are facts of which someone is fully aware and which are requiring practical reasons for him to do a certain thing even if he is not moved, or even to any extent motivated, to do it?

Is there a way of telling whether we are right or mistaken in thinking this? There appear to be two quite different types of reason to think that we must be mistaken. One is that there is a significant difference between beliefs and actions and that because of this difference a fact can be a practical reason for someone *only if* it is capable of suitably motivating her. The second grants that a fact could conceivably be a practical reason for someone even if it does not suitably motivate her but claims that in the domain of practical reasons there can be *no system of objective guidelines* comparable to that in the cognitive domain, hence that in the domain of practice we cannot advance beyond "motivating facts" to facts that tell us what we ought to be motivated to do, even when we are not.[3]

Section 2.   Different Types of Behavior and Their Explanations

Well, then, is there anything about human behavior, or perhaps human action (as opposed to human talk and thought) and the explanations it is capable of, that justifies the first of those two claims? Let me begin by sketching in a highly stylized fashion a few types of organisms in an order of ascending complexity so as to become clearer about some salient features an organism must possess in order to be capable of having practical reasons, and to see whether there is anything about the function of practical reasons that would require the truth of Internalism. The

---

[3] I discuss the first reason below, section 2.6, pp. 104–9, the second in chapters 4 and 5.

models are constructed as embodiments of our everyday conceptions of various types of human behavior and of the explanations considered appropriate for them. The survey of these types of organism makes it plausible, I think, that the main support for Internalism derives from a certain view of the role of practical reasons in the explanation of human behavior.

2.1. The Haunted Organic Machine

Let us mention, just to put it aside, the sort of behavior often called "reflex action," such as the behavior generated by the operation of the patellar or the pupilar reflex. Such behavior best fits the so-called stimulus-response model of explanation although, of course, in the present cases, we need not think of a human body as a black box, for we may know enough about the physiological mechanism that must be in good working order for the stimulus to elicit the normal response. We may assume that such internal mechanisms normally do not allow for internal forces modifying the simple causal relation between stimulus and response. It either "works" or it does not. There is normally no room for anything like "negative feedback" or "conditioned reflexes." If it works, the stimulus elicits the response; if it does not work, there may be no predictable behavioral response.

Such reflex action has a further characteristic that distinguishes it from some more complex types of behavior. Thus, in the pupilar reflex the creature need not even be aware of the stimulus and the response, nor need it—nor indeed can it—in any ordinary sense be *motivated* to respond in this way. We want to say it is the body, not the creature (not the individual or the person) herself, that produces the response; as far as the latter is concerned, she is not, or is only peripherally involved. Her response is like Dr. Strangelove's: his arm shoots up in the Hitler salute, her pupil contracts and her leg jumps up, irrespective of whether he or she intends it to do so. If all a person's behavior were like this, she would be (somewhat like Ryle's ghost in the machine)[4] what might be called "an organic machine occasionally haunted by an (observant) ghost," a being who may be aware of what the body she haunts is "doing" but who has no direct or indirect control over it. It would be a playball of the forces

---

[4] G. Ryle, *The Concept of Mind* (London: Hutchinson's University Library, 1949), 15f. Ryle's characterization of "the dogma of the ghost in the machine" is that minds are "ghosts harnessed to machines" (20).

impinging upon it. If someone or something "hits" one of its "buttons," the organism reliably responds in a certain fixed way, irrespective of whether the being haunting it is aware of the stimulus or the response. We would not wish to ascribe any of "her" body's doings to her.

2.2. The Prisoner in His Body

Let us then enrich the structure of such a haunted organic machine by endowing it with what we ordinarily call "urges," such as our urge to breathe after being forced to hold our breath for a while, say, by being submerged underwater, or to sneeze when sneezing powder is sprinkled on our nose, or to throw up during gastroenteritis.

Such a "prisoner" is more tightly related to "his" body than a "haunted organic machine" to hers. We find it less artificial to speak of "his" behavior since we assume that the sentience is in some way operatively related to his body's or the organism's behavior. However, for such a "prisoner" to yield to an urge, he need not be capable of having ends or of thinking that he occurrently has a certain end or (a fortiori) that certain ways of acting are suitable means of attaining certain ends, or that what he is doing is such a suitable means to his current end. Nor, of course, need the explanation of his behavior be or include that he thinks it is such a means. In yielding to (or satisfying) an urge, the creature need not be intentionally doing anything of a particular sort, he need merely "let go." Finally, if such a creature can resist an urge, he can do so only for a short time, after which a reflex takes over whether he likes it or not. In this respect he resembles us when we have held our breath for a certain time after which we become unable to do so, even if we are still held underwater and desperately want not to inhale. A creature, all of whose behavior is yielding to urges, is such a "prisoner in his body" because, although he may have "privileged access" to his body's behavior, he has at best only very limited control over it. Even if he could resist his urge for a time, in the end, a reflex would take over, just as in the case of ordinary reflex action.

In any case, it may well be that a creature capable only of reflex action and yielding to urges is an impossibility. For an urge, it seems, can be yielded to only when it arises and it cannot arise until the psychological pressure involved has reached a certain intensity. But this, it would appear, cannot happen unless the yielding to any pressure of the urge is somehow delayed. And that, in turn, seems to require some other counterforce with which we seem not to have endowed our "prisoner." By our hypothesis, it could only be either a "counter-urge" or some other kind of motivation, but an organism with urges and counter-urges might well be doomed to be eliminated by natural selection, and we have explicitly excluded other kinds of motivations. In other words, urges appear to presuppose something like desires whose satisfaction is, in certain circumstances, incompatible with yielding to the incipient psychological pressure of what, if yielding to it were delayed, would turn into a full-blooded urge.

However, although prisoners in their bodies may be impossible or unlikely creatures, there is good reason to bear the nature of urges in mind, since they provide us with the most conspicuous paradigm of motivation: a strongly felt, eventually irresistible psychological force, which is quite different from the workings of a reflex in reflex action. Still, prisoners in their bodies have no scope for practical reasons.

2.3.   *Simon, The Single-Motivation Agent*

Let us then endow our creature also with desires. Note that the "psychological force" operating on it when it has an occurrent desire may but need not be of the same sort as that in an urge. It is of the same sort when, as in hunger or a craving for heroin, the prolonged frustration of the desire generates feelings of steadily increasing discomfort or pain or some other unpleasant sensation, and relief or pleasure when it is gratified. It is not of the same sort when, for instance, it is the desire not to yield to the urge, say, to smoke on a long flight, or the urge when, late in the banquet, one is called upon to propose a toast, to relieve oneself; frustrating such a desire involves nothing like the hunger pangs or withdrawal symptoms when we do not yield to an urge, nor does satisfying the desire involve the relief and pleasure we get from yielding to one.

I should mention two other differences between urges and desires. As I implied earlier, desires always involve a more or less clearly envisaged end, a belief (or idea) about what sort of behavior would attain that end (otherwise it is at most a vague longing or yearning not for anything in particular), and the ability to generate that sort of behavior; hence the desiring organism must be able to behave in a way that is sensitive to changes in the environment and the resulting need to adapt its goal-seeking behavior to these changes. Desires do not, when their gratification is delayed or denied altogether, trigger a reflex that would satisfy them, even when the inclination they generate is of the same type as that in an urge.

The behavior of Koehler's ape is such as to suggest that he had a desire for the bananas suspended outside his cage and that he tried, and eventually managed, to find a way of satisfying it. Hypothesizing that he had such a desire explains his behavior, because his having it would motivate him to seek a way of satisfying it and, having found one, to engage in that sort of behavior, and because his actual behavior exhibited these two stages. In contrast, Jones's seeing a psychiatrist because of his desire to kill his (Jones's) mother is not this sort of explanation, because we may assume that Jones does not believe that seeing a psychiatrist is a step that will (help) bring about the death of his mother.

A second difference—one that has probably been overlooked in some discussions of the freewill controversy* is that, whereas in the case of an urge it eventually becomes *impossible*, because the matter is taken out of our hands when automatic breathing occurs, and so on, in the case of desires it is merely *difficult* to resist. We do not have to sit on our hands to prevent them grabbing the piece of cake we desire. The so-called freedom of the will implies (of course, among other things) the possibility of not acting as the dominant desire inclines one to act, a possibility that is absent at the point during one's resistance to an urge when a reflex takes over. That impossibility is different from even the highest degree of "difficulty," say, one experienced by an addict trying to resist her desire for crack when she tries to "say no." The former difference (that between the reflex stage of an urge and a desire) is one in kind: between there not being and there being an alternative open to one, the latter (that between different degrees of difficulty) is a difference in degree: between its being more or less difficult to enter on one or other of the courses open to one. Of course, an observer may rightly be as confident that an addict will accept crack when offered, as that, when her head is being held underwater, she will take a breath before ten minutes are up.

Our question then is, under what conditions this possibility of behavior contrary to the most strongly felt desire is realized. To get clearer about this, let us first consider what we may call a "single-motivation agent"— call him Simon—that is, a being with the following characteristics. His behavior is of three types: reflex actions, yielding to urges, and satisfying desires. Let us further stipulate that at any given time he can have only one aroused desire which, therefore, is dominant. That is to say, other potentially aroused desires will either be suppressed or else will supplant the currently aroused and so dominant desire. If a desire is aroused, Simon will forthwith set to work on satisfying it or, if he has no idea of how to do that, will immediately try to look for ways of doing so. If he finds a way, he will do what he thinks will satisfy his desire. If not, he will continue to look for such ways until the desire is supplanted by another, say, to rest. He ceases to have an aroused desire if and only if it is satisfied or supplanted by another. We stipulate that there is no time during his waking life when no desire is aroused.

Thus all Simon's motivated behavior (but of course not reflex actions or wholly unconscious doings, such as healthy digestion) is like that of a soldier sitting outside his trench ravenously wolfing his food when suddenly his hunger is forgotten (not just ignored) because supplanted by fear the moment the bombing begins and he also automatically switches from eating in order to satisfy his hunger to diving into his trench in order to satisfy his occurrent desire which is part of the fear aroused by the bombardment. He does not experience any conflict between these two conflicting desires because they are not (in a single-motivation agent, they cannot be) aroused (and so become motivationally operative) simultaneously.[5]

Nevertheless, we may wonder about situations when Simon has an aroused desire, but when no urge or reflex action has been triggered. Could he then act differently from the way his current desire inclines him to act? Obviously not, for our postulates have precluded that possibility. Since, ex hypothesi, no urge or reflex is operative on the occasion in question and since he cannot have another desire that is simultaneously aroused and in conflict with the first, there is in his case simply no room for any other motivation to bring about other behavior.

We may, then, want to call Simon "a slave of his passions," because he is not equipped to resist his dominant desire. But if so, we must not also conceive of him (as presumably we ordinarily do of "a slave of his passions"), as a being who can, and perhaps sometimes does, know when it would be best for him to resist his currently dominant desire, and who also has the resources to resist it but fails to draw on them when he should. As already noted, Simon, ex hypothesi, lacks these further abilities.

2.4.   Emma, The Multiple-Motivation Agent

The question therefore arises, what further powers or features we must ascribe to a single-motivation agent to get a creature capable of being a slave or even a master of her passions, in the ordinary sense of these

---

[5] Simon is therefore immune from the conflict between simultaneous desires generated by different parts of the soul that, on H. W. B. Joseph's reading, Plato believes can prevent a person from acting on a felt appetite; see Joseph, "Plato's Republic: The Nature of the Soul," *Essays in Ancient and Modern Philosophy* (Freeport, N.Y.: Books for Libraries, 1971), 52–53.

expressions. It seems that what is needed is that she not be designed in such a way that a desire becomes dominant the moment it is aroused, that it cannot be aroused unless it is stronger than any that is already aroused, and that, when it is aroused, she not instantaneously come to have what we may call "a propension to set to work on satisfying" it. In other words, it must be possible that, even if she already knows, or believes she knows, a way of attaining the end "indicated" by her aroused desire, she not immediately come to have that end and so enter on the course of action she regards as a suitable means of attaining it unless prevented from doing so by someone or something; or that, if she has no idea of how to attain it, she not immediately have a propension to do what she takes to be a way of finding out, such as experimenting or sitting down to reflect or waiting for inspiration, as Koehler's ape seems to have done.

In other words, the creature must be so constructed that gratification of an aroused desire may be delayed, even when she knows or has ideas on what would be suitable means for gratifying it. Let us then assume that she also has the ability to reorder in imagination the sequence of the gratification of her various desires in such a way that more of them get satisfied and to a higher degree than if the order was on the basis of their comparative intensity. Unsurprisingly, in some unfavorable circumstances, such attempted schedulings may mean not merely the delaying but the complete frustration of some of the aroused desires. In these cases, too, the desires that are completely frustrated need not be those of the relatively lowest intensity.

It seems possible, then, that if a certain further condition were satisfied, such a creature—such a "multiple-motivation agent," call her Emma—should come to act contrary to her most strongly felt aroused urge-like desire, and in accordance with some other weaker desires, though this may happen only up to a certain intensity of such a contrary desire. If her most strongly felt desire is above that intensity, the other motivations may not be sufficient to prevent it from immediately becoming dominant.

What further condition do I have in mind? It is that all desires below that threshold come to be processed as if they were "proposals" or "claims" or "demands" submitted to or pressed upon her by others, their satisfaction coming to be delayed until they have been sorted and ordered by some principle of priority not necessarily that of greater intensity. Whatever, up to the threshold I just mentioned, is the intensity of an aroused desire, it is possible (especially where it is unclear what is involved in satisfying and what in frustrating it) that behavior (supposedly) satisfying it will not occur immediately, and that the behavior that does occur may instead be a fuller investigation of these so far unclear matters.

Gratification of any of Emma's aroused desires may thus be delayed until she has sufficiently thought about and discovered what is involved in satisfying and in frustrating each of the claimants or until one of the urge-like desires exceeds the threshold of intensity. We thus postulate that Emma's motivated behavior need not necessarily be what she takes to be the best way to satisfy her most strongly felt aroused desire or combination of such desires. We suppose, rather, that her makeup is such that an aroused desire does not necessarily become dominant immediately, that more than one desire may become aroused and that (up to a certain threshold of intensity) the satisfaction of the most strongly felt desire may be delayed if she thinks a reordering of the sequence of actions will achieve the gratification of a greater number of desires or a higher level of satisfactoriness of such gratifications than if it were to occur in an order of decreasing intensity. Thus, Emma may be quite hungry as well as desirous of a dip in the lake. If, as the intensities of her desires dictate, she were to eat first and swim later, this would mean a less satisfactory gratification of these two desires, since she would either have to swim immediately after the meal with a full stomach to which she is averse or postpone her swim until after the sun has gone from the lake to which she also is averse. Because of these reflections she may be moved to postpone her meal until after her swim.

2.5. Motivating Beliefs

We may now wonder whether the motivation generating such an agent's behavior must be that of her aroused desires and of whatever motivation in some way flows from them, or whether things unrelated to her desires can also motivate her. Before answering this, let us first be clear about those cases in which Emma is motivated not by her aroused desires themselves but by other things that are suitably related to them. Remember that, as we noted, not all our desires are urge-like: frustrating them does not leave us in a state of steadily increasing discomfort or pain, but perhaps only with gradually diminishing feelings of frustration, disappointment, and the like, or not even that. Also bear in mind that not all desires are like hunger or thirst in that they are normally brought about by conditions of the body of which we normally are not aware. Some desires are brought about by our perceiving (or thinking we perceive) an event or state of affairs: a snake in the grass where we are picnicking, an approaching thunderstorm, a clogged drain. We can think of these as motivating events, states, or states of affairs, the perception (or misperception) of which by such a being motivates her to behave in a certain way. However, whereas hunger or thirst is always from its very nature a desire "for the same sort of thing"—food or drink—and so motivates all individuals to aim at the same sort of thing and so behave "in the same sort of way," that is, to behave in a way thought by them suitable for attaining that end, this is not so for motivating events, say, a mouse in the kitchen or a fly in the soup; these events may be motivating ones for one individual but not for another and what they motivate individuals to aim at or do may (and in the case of humans does) vary greatly from one individual to another. Hunger and thirst are motivations for certain (comparatively) specific things in all agents; motivating events and what they motivate to may vary from agent to agent.

Take, next, expected events, say, being hungry tomorrow. Suppose that in Emma (as in human beings) such expectations generate motivation, not of course to eat now, but rather to ensure that she will have something to eat tomorrow. Is this a desire or some other kind of motivation derived from a desire? Let us say it is a "standing" second-order desire, namely, one to ensure one's ability to satisfy a first-order urge-like desire whenever one expects it to be aroused, and that it may become aroused by a range of stimuli, say, by noting that one's refrigerator is empty. What is the relation between the two desires? Although when hungry Emma is not, like Simon, necessarily "in the grip" of her hunger—since she may be able to delay gratification—nevertheless, she is under the full psychological pressure of an urge-like desire of increasing intensity as time passes without her eating anything. Both types of agent are subject to this sort of pressure independently of whether they know what brought it on, but Emma (unlike Simon) may also be subject to the very different motivational pressure generated by her (possibly false) expectations about the future including the expectation that she will be hungry tomorrow, a motivation whose force depends on her attention to, and appreciation of the significance to her of, these expectations.

Note how different this second-order desire is from the urge-like desire involved in hunger. Obviously in having it, Emma is not already under the pressure of her future hunger, but only under the very different sort of occurrent pressure exerted by the expectation of that future pressure. And she may well be under the pressure exerted by that expectation even though she will never be under the expected pressure itself: she may die before she gets hungry or someone else may bring her food or she may get it herself before she gets hungry. Furthermore, the activation of her standing second-order desire, the disposition to ensure her ability to satisfy her first-order desires when she expects them to be aroused, does not generate anything like the psychological pressure of an urge-like desire; its nonsatisfaction (say, not filling the refrigerator with food for next week) does not produce any pains or discomforts of frustration nor does its gratification yield any noticeable pleasure or satisfaction, as happens in the case of hunger.

To summarize, in the case of a creature such as Emma we can distinguish four types of experienced motivational conflict: (1) between an urge and an urge-like desire or between two urge-like desires, (2) between an urge or urge-like desire and an expectation-based or (more generally) belief-based motivation, (3) between two belief-based motivations, or (4) some combination of these. Once a being is such that a delay of gratification can occur, urges and urge-like desires can come into conflict with belief-based motivations.

Suppose then that the soldier who ducks out of danger into the relative safety of the trench[6] is not Simon but Emma, then her response to the bombardment may not be immediate but could conceivably be a delayed gratification of her more strongly felt desire, to duck out of danger generated by fear, and so her relevant motivating beliefs may affect what she does. In her case there could then be two quite different types of conflict between different motivations: (a) the (blocked) conflicting motivations of two simultaneously aroused urge-like desires, say, hunger and the desire to seek shelter, and (b) the (blocked) conflicting motivations generated by the expected consequences of satisfying her hunger and frustrating the desire to seek shelter and those of satisfying the latter and frustrating the former. Hence, although in (a), her more intense motivation would not simply supplant (that is, evict from consciousness and practical efficacy) the less intense one, it would nevertheless eventually "win the day," that is, bring it about that she would come to be set on satisfying the (more intense) desire aroused by her fear rather than on satisfying her (less intense) desire for food. In case (b), by contrast, what wins the day may well be the motivation attaching to her expectations about the consequences of the alternative courses of action open to her on the occasion in question. Thus, in this case, there is the possibility of Emma's acting contrary to what *the most strongly felt desire* inclines her to do. She may then, if she is lucky, reap what she expected to get at the cost of having to endure the continued felt pressure of the frustrated desire, and in addition the (possibly unsuspected) costs (discounted by the benefits) of frustrating it. Thus, what actually motivates her are the *expected* costs and benefits of entering into the various alternatives open to her, not the *real* ones. Simon,

---

[6] See section 2.3, especially p. 95f.

we may say, necessarily "acts in the grip of desire," whereas Emma in certain situations acts as we may say, *"from* motivating beliefs," that is, from motivations attaching to the expected costs and benefits of the alternatives open to her.

Let us then accept the distinctions we drew between the case of Simon, the single-motivation agent, and Emma, the multiple-motivation agent. Simon is always necessarily in the grip of desire when he is not like a prisoner in his body in the grip of an urge, or is, as it were, ignored altogether, like a haunted organic machine when parts of his body behave in response to stimuli triggering reflexes. In the case of Emma, by contrast, the satisfaction of aroused desires may come to be delayed or frustrated altogether, so that she may have several simultaneously aroused desires whether of the urge-like or belief-based kind, and may behave in ways motivated by a belief-based desire rather than an urge-like one, even though the urge-like one has the greater intensity. Of course, even then we may want to say that the less strongly felt belief-based desire is the stronger one, in the different sense of "winning the day."

Still, Emma's standing second-order desire to ensure being able to satisfy her hunger would not be aroused unless the beliefs on which it was based were suitably related to a desire of hers—the expected future desire for food. If she had not expected that desire, she would not have the expectation-based desire either. The question now arises whether there may not be other beliefs that motivate Emma, beliefs that are not, even in this loose way, related to the motivating force of aroused desires. Let us examine this more closely.

Might Emma be motivated by proper attention to (true or false) beliefs, such as that she will need additional life insurance? If we acknowledge that she can be moved by a belief, even a false belief, that is harnessed to a desire, we ipso facto acknowledge that what she is motivated by is her attention to and appreciation of what she believes, that is, its activation, its coming to life, something playing the same role as arousal in the case of desire. So why should not there be cases in which it is activated beliefs and not aroused desires that motivate her? We need not think this means that there are creatures that can be moved by their beliefs even though they have no desires at all, though we shall shortly look at this possibility. For the moment, we are considering only the question of whether in some cases, it is beliefs rather than desires that should be *singled out as the motivating factors,* and desires rather than beliefs that should be *demoted to the background conditions* under which they do so. It would seem that all we mean by elevating some belief to being that which motivates us to do a certain thing is to single out, from a group of things that may be severally necessary as a group and jointly sufficient for us to be motivated or moved to do that thing, the one we regard as the salient factor, the one we think deserves that privileged role, whereas all the others are reduced to mere background conditions even though they, too, must be satisfied if the salient one is to be "operative."[7]

If this is right, then why could not a belief not thus suitably related to one of the agent's desires figure in such a salient role? Why, for instance, could not that prominent role be played by beliefs about the costs and benefits to the agent from entering on one or other of the various courses of action open to him? Is not Sidgwick right in stressing "the proper appreciation" of these supposed costs and benefits if the appropriate motivating power of the expected consequences is to be activated in deliberation, and is not this "appreciation" simply the agent's proper attention to these supposed costs and benefits to the agent of the alternative courses supposedly open to her in a given situation and their (supposed) consequences?

We may suppose, for instance, that Emma does not now have an aroused desire for a travel iron, and may not even come to have one when the iron is offered to her as a present, but she may nevertheless welcome it as something useful, though she never actually desired one and would not, if she lost it, then desire another one. And her regarding it as useful need not return desire by the back door, for what the iron is useful for—having uncrumpled clothes—may be something she would welcome if it came her way, but not something she actually desires to have and so is ready to expend resources to obtain when she does not have it. It may be like the after-dinner brandy that one enjoys when it is served but would not miss if it were not.

There appears to be a (rather movable) point in the transition from desire for getting and keeping something to merely welcoming it or finding it useful. It would seem that in our case of the travel iron we may well distinguish between those who desire one (normally a standing desire which comes to be activated in certain circumstances), those who would welcome having one or would find one useful and the like but who do not have even a standing desire for one, and those who would find it useless, not worth having, and so on, and who would get rid of it if someone gave it

---

[7] R. G. Collingwood, *An Essay on Metaphysics* (Oxford: Clarendon Press, 1940), especially 285–87; 296–311; Douglas Gasking, "Causation and Recipes," *Mind* 64 (1955): 479–87; Joel Feinberg, "Sua Culpa," *Doing and Deserving* (Princeton, N.J.: Princeton University Press, 1970), 204.

to them as a present. Of one in the second group, it may be true, not merely that she had never desired one, but also that she does not desire one now, though of course it may also not be true that she has for some time had a standing, and now an aroused, desire *not* to have such an iron, nor that she would find it something useless let alone a burden. Such an agent in the second group may be motivated to put it on a wish list for Christmas because it won't cost her anything and she has to put something on the list. But she will not buy one for its usefulness because, though she would prefer the freshly ironed look of her apparel to its usual crumpled appearance, she is not willing to do anything to get such an iron.

The connection between such motivating beliefs and one's desires may be looser still. Thus my belief that I may at some time in the future have a serious car accident or a costly illness (though I am hopeful, perhaps confident, that I never shall), may motivate me to take out expensive accident and health insurance policies. Even our belief, for example, that making a winning move in a game of chess is "the natural thing to do" when playing chess may be for us a motivating one, even if we do not have an occurrent desire to win the game or a currently aroused standing desire always to do what is the natural thing to do.[8] Thus, not only the belief that one actually has, or that one day one will have or is likely to have, a desire can be "for one a motivating belief" to do a certain thing.

One further step should now be taken before we return to the question we postponed at the beginning of section 2.4 of whether our multiple-motivation agent, Emma, may be a slave or even a master of her passions. The further step I have in mind is to postulate now that Emma has grown up in a group of multiple-motivation agents like herself, all of whom have learned to speak English in the process of growing up. I am not adding this point because I want to claim that our postponed question can be answered in the affirmative only for beings who have a shared language. I do not wish to maintain that apes or dogs, because they do not have a language, cannot believe things, cannot think, and cannot solve means-end problems more complex than those solved by Koehler's ape. My main reason for adding language is merely that an affirmative answer is more plausible if one supposes (as I have to some extent surreptitiously done already) that our agents have a language and are members of a society. Another reason is that, in my view, the more interesting and important uses of reason and reasoning do presuppose language. Indeed, in chapter 1, it will be remembered, I spoke of the behavior of Koehler's ape as if it

---

[8] Obviously, it would not make sense to explain a person's behavior by the fact that he has this desire and then prove that he has it by the fact that he behaves in this way.

involved forms of means-end reasoning and this did not seem strained or odd. Still, if this were the only type of reasoning there is, we would not need to distinguish between intelligence and reason, as I have done and as I think our practices make it desirable to do. At the same time, the cases that students of animal behavior report show clearly both the continuity between animal and human intelligence and the severe limits this necessarily individualistic, noncumulative approach to problem solving imposes.[9]

2.6.   *Custer, The Decision Maker*

With all this in mind, I now turn, finally, to the question, with what further powers or features (if any) we must equip a creature such as Emma, if it is to be capable of being a slave or a master of its passions. It would seem that that depends on whether it *can resist* the psychological forces—whatever they may be—that oppose the forces that "are on its side," or "are its" or "have been brought to bear by it." However, obviously, we have not so far introduced any distinction between these two sides of a creature, these two sets of forces, and whether, and if so how, it can mobilize, marshal, or muster them. It will be remembered that in Emma's case—unlike Simon's —it is "possible *that*" a force other than that of the most strongly felt aroused desire may "win the day," that is, generate the final propension to act; however, we have not equipped Emma in such a way as to imply that it is "possible *for her*" to resist that desire and to act in the way *she* really wants to act. So far, we have spoken only as observers noting the possibility of one or the other type of unimputed psychological force winning the day, but we have not yet involved "the agent herself" in the genesis of her behavior. The overall picture is still like that of balls rolling down inclined planes or being hit by others on a billiard table: the picture

---

[9] Jane Goodall in *The Chimpanzees of Gombe* (Harvard University Press, 1986), p. 31, reports the case of "a chimpanzee named Julia [who] was given two series of five locked transparent boxes, each of which opened with a differently shaped key. The last box in one series was empty; in the other series the last box contained a banana. The boxes from the two series were randomly placed among each other, except for two unlocked initial boxes. Given the choice between the two initial boxes, Julia was able to select the one that contained the key that opened the box that contained the key that opened the box . . . and so on, to the box that contained the banana. To do this Julia must have reasoned backward from her desired goal." Quoted by Peter Singer in "Bandit and Friends," *New York Review of Books,* April 9, 1992, 10–11. Cases of this sort seem to me to demonstrate very clearly that chimpanzees and other animals are capable of intelligent thinking and practical problem solving of a very high order, even without the benefit of language and the increase in power through regimentation and cumulation it makes possible.

of a creature that is the playball of (varied types of) forces, the outcome depending solely on their "direction" (conceived in terms of compatible or incompatible means to ends) and their relative strengths conceived in terms of their felt intensity or their ability to overcome others in determining the agent's behavior. Even Emma's aroused desires come to be delayed only if her desire to "think before leaping," that is, to assess the payoffs of the alternatives before her, is *stronger* than any of the desires pressing for immediate satisfaction. If a being is to be thought of as a genuine agent capable of genuine action, we must be able to distinguish between the forces that *impinge on it* and the forces *it brings to the battle*. It must not be merely a bystander or observer of the play of these forces determining its behavior. It must, in a sense, be a self-mover.

To achieve that, we must convert the multiple-motivation agent into a decision maker, call him Custer. But that requires adding a further power, one recognizably his, a power that enables him to "intervene in" the automatic balancing out of the various forces pressing on the machinery that determine his behavior according to their respective strengths. To count as his intervening in this way, the forces carrying the day must serve what we recognize as his own goals involving the outcomes he prefers over those produced by other forces at work at the time. He must have likes and dislikes of certain types of occurrences (including doings and nondoings) and states of affairs; he must know, at least about some, what they are; he must have preferences for some of these types over others, also in cases where they involve both elements he likes and others he dislikes; and he must be structured in the following way: at least in a certain class of cases, his having a certain belief (namely, that his doing a certain thing, A, will bring about a state of affairs he would prefer over another that would be brought about by his doing another thing, B) *brings it about* that he does A rather than B, even if he has an aroused desire to do B and none, or only a less strongly felt one, to do A. In such a case, the forces that are generated by his belief concerning the outcomes of satisfying one or other of his various aroused and conflicting desires are naturally thought of as the forces that *he* brings to this battle between his desires. Hence we can think of him as having a power to offer resistance to some of the forces impinging on him. The magnitude of this power then determines whether he must be a slave or can be a master of his passions.

I think imputing to someone the ability to deliberate about what to do and to make choices and decisions implies that he has such a power. When he engages in such deliberation, then the forces brought into play by this type of thinking are naturally ascribed to him because the deliberation involves "a standing back" from the play of forces, an envisaging of alternative possibilities, an evaluation of their relative desirability, and a resulting activation of those motivational forces that dispose him to act in ways which produce the preferred expected outcome. We may also suppose that Custer has acquired a standing desire to deliberate about what to do whenever he believes that the risks of making the wrong decision are significant, that deliberating will increase the chances of discovering the right decision and of being able, by suitably attending to the alternatives and their consequences, to carry it out. Such a standing desire will be activated when he comes to believe that these conditions are satisfied.

In view of the salience of Custer's prominent cognitive involvement in the generation of this sort of behavior, it is natural to impute to Custer himself—and not merely to his body—those psychological forces influencing his behavior which have come into play in this way. We naturally think of these forces as what he marshalls to initiate the sequence of events that constitute his actions and their consequences, as what makes him a sort of "prime" mover, and we may think of his arriving at and carrying out of his decisions as cases of what has sometimes been called "agent causation" or "immanent causation," though now naturalistically conceived.[10]

Such a decision maker can look at the world in a new way, different from that of Koehler's ape as we interpreted him and different also from Emma's. For the ape views the world from the perspective of one always doing—or if necessary first trying to discover—what he thinks would be a suitable means for attaining the end determined by his single necessarily dominant urge-like desire; while Emma views it from that of one trying to do what she will have a propensity to do after she has fully attended to and come to appreciate all the beliefs she can acquire about the alternatives open to her and their consequences. Custer, by contrast, views the world from the point of view of one who aims to discover, by adequate deliberation, *what* (as we may call it) *he ideally wants,* and then to do what is the best means to attaining it, including resistance to his aroused urges, urge-like desires, and motivating beliefs in conflict with that. Such a decision maker has (at least the beginnings of) a will, that is, the ability to try to resist at least some of his desires when they become aroused. Having

---

[10] See Roderick M. Chisholm, "Freedom and Action," *Freedom and Determinism,* ed. Keith Lehrer (New York: Random House, 1966), 11–44, especially 20ff.; and Nuel Belnap and Michael Perloff, "Seeing to It That: a Canonical Form for Agentives," *Theoria* 54 (1988): 175–99. Also: K. Baier, "Action and Agent," *Monist* 49, no. 2 (April 1965): 183–95.

it is a presupposition of the distinction between not even trying to resist and trying to resist but suffering defeat.

To avoid confusion, we must keep apart the aim of deliberation which in Custer's case we are calling "attaining what one ideally wants" and in Sidgwick's case[11] "what one really wants." We discover and do what we really want when (like Emma) we discover and do what we have a propensity to do after we have ascertained all the relevant facts and have attended to and have come adequately to appreciate them. We discover and do what we ideally want when in the course of our deliberation we arrive at a judgment of what we would prefer, all things considered. If that judgment is based on what, all things considered, we would like best, then the preferred course of action may not be the one we have, as a result of our deliberation, come to have a propensity to enter on.[12] Thus what we really want is a subclass of what we actually want,* but what we ideally want is not. Custer has not yet reached his aim in deliberating when he has surveyed and adequately attended to and appreciated the attractiveness or unattractiveness of the competing courses of action and thus found himself with a certain propensity to act. He must furthermore come up with a judgment of what he prefers all things considered (which alone satisfied what we have called the reflective task) and then, if this diverges from his resulting propensity, he must mobilize, in the way explained, the motivation at his disposal to conform to his judgment (which alone completes the executive task). Thus, we may on reflection conclude, for example, that we prefer the course that involves giving up smoking and so diminishes certain risks involved in continuing to smoke, over continuing to smoke and so incurring these risks, even though our most strongly felt inclination and so perhaps our propensity, may be to have another cigarette and so not to stop smoking.

Given these distinctions, we can also distinguish among the psychological forces that determine what I eventually do (in the absence of outside interference), between those that work for what I ideally want and those that oppose it, as well as some that I can bring to bear on the matter at will, by directing my attention to those of my beliefs that I believe or know incline me in the direction of giving up and away from those that incline me toward continuing. If I make the effort so to direct my attention, I try to resist the forces that drive me to continue; if not, I don't even try, and, of course, I may fail, even if I try.

---

[11] See Introduction, p. 12f.

[12] For a more detailed account of preference, see my paper "Rationality, Value, and Preference," *Social Philosophy and Policy* 5 (1988): 17–45.

If this is right, then Custer, the decision maker, differs importantly from Emma, the multiple-motivation agent, for in his case, there is an additional type of motivation, one that he can mobilize "at will," by directing his attention to certain of his motivating beliefs about that alternative among those open to him into which he ideally wants to enter, beliefs which motivate him to do what he ideally wants and to direct his attention away from those other motivating beliefs that motivate him not to do that.

Thus, this account of what one ideally wants enables us to distinguish two kinds of practical thinking: a cognitive one that enables us to perform the reflective task by finding out what we ideally want, and a tactical one that helps us perform, even in difficult cases, the executive task, that is, do what we "ideally" want when we do not "actually" want to do it.[13] If I am right, then Emma, the multiple-motivation agent, lacks the ability to do this, whereas Custer, the decision maker, has such ability because, unlike Emma, he is constructed in such a way that a certain subclass of his beliefs, namely, those about certain "evaluative properties" of the various courses of action open to him, may be motivating beliefs, and because he can determine in the second (non-Sidgwickian) way what he really (that is, ideally) wants, and he can also employ certain tactics of practical thinking that help him perform the executive task in those difficult cases when he does not actually want what he ideally wants and so has to maneuver himself into being disposed to do it.

But what, it may now be asked, is the relevance of all this to whether reasons must be motives. Well, to put it in a somewhat oversimplified way, it is this. Suppose, for the moment, that it is always in accordance with reason to do what one ideally wants and always contrary to it not to do so. Then, if Custer arrives at the conclusion that he ideally wants to give up smoking, it would be in accordance with reason for him to give it up even if he did not really want to, and so did not, give it up. But it is also possible for him to try to overcome, by the Sidgwickian technique I described, his motivation to go on smoking. Of course, though it is possible for him to try, he might well fail. Thus if the form of deliberation I described yields a judgment by Custer about what he has requiring reason to do, then he may have, and may believe or even know he has, requiring reason to do something but not have *sufficient* motivation to do it.

The crucial question for us is whether the Custer type of deliberation

---

[13] Bernard Bosanquet, *The Philosophical Theory of the State*, 4th ed. (London: Macmillan, 1923), chapter 5, especially 110–15.

makes sense, whether we can determine what we ideally want, assuming for the moment that that is what reason requires, by a method that involves assessing the merits and demerits of the alternative courses of action open to us in ways that are independent of the motivation actually generated by one's judgment of these merits and demerits. For if this sort of deliberation does make sense, if we can assess the computative merits of, say, taking out health insurance versus buying a new sports car independently of how strongly these merits motivate us towards them, then it may well happen that our judgment of what we ideally want diverges from what we are disposed to do. Now, in some of these cases we will, "from weakness of will," fail in our executive task, thus acting contrary to reason. What exactly is the explanation of this failure? Must it always be only the compound and never the particular (pro tanto) reasons that diverge from the corresponding particular motivations? Can it be also the particular weights of the particular reasons that diverge from the particular magnitudes of the corresponding particular motivations? Can a favorable assessment of merit never be paired with the absence of a favorable motivation or the presence of an unfavorable motivation? Can it not happen that when someone favorably assesses the merit of taking out health insurance, he is nevertheless not favorably motivated to take out any?

I believe the widespread acceptance among moral philosophers of Internalism is to a considerable extent due to the belief that we could not explain people's behavior when they act for a reason if it were not necessarily true that nothing can be a pro tanto reason for someone to do something unless it motivated him, at least somewhat, to do what it is such a reason for him to do. I find this implausible, on the face of it, and I suspect that its plausibility depends on a misunderstanding of the role of reason in the explanation of human behavior. I therefore turn to a discussion of this question.

Section 3.   The Peculiarities of Reason-Explanations

Bear in mind that, of course, not all explanations involve reasons for which something (someone) behaves in the way it does. Suppose a water pipe in our house has burst while we were away on vacation. When asking for an explanation, we may be given, as *the reason why* it burst, the drop in temperature below freezing, the consequent expansion of the water, or some other such salient factor. But in such cases, it would be quite inappropriate (indeed absurd) to look for a motive from which the pipe burst or a reason for which it burst.

By contrast, when Koehler's ape put two sticks together to reach the bananas outside his cage, the explanation of his behavior, the explanatory reason, the reason why he did so, may well be that he had a desire to eat them or that he believed that he could reach them by putting the sticks together, or both. We may allow that his desire (and/or his belief) explained, was the reason, why he behaved in this way, perhaps the motive for his behavior. But we might resist the suggestion that this desire and these beliefs were (practical) reasons *for him* to put the two sticks together and so were *his reason* for doing these things[14] and so were things done *for a* (i.e., *that*) *reason,* the reason for which he did them. Nor should we accept the suggestion that *the fact that* he could reach the bananas by putting the sticks together was *his* reason for behaving in this way. For we should resist the idea that anything done by the ape was done by him for reasons.

Compare this with Mary's running out of a house on fire. That may well have been something *done for a reason,* since things may *be* reasons for Mary to do something and she may be something like a decision maker and also a member of an order of reason. The case may well be one capable of being explained by a certain combination of explanatory and practical reasons. There are two ways of construing such a combination of explanatory and practical reasons, a lax and a strict one. In both cases, the explanatory function is dominant and the practical aspect of the reason enters into the explanation, but it enters in different ways in the two construals. Both are cases of acting for a reason, that is, acting from a motive which consists in two beliefs: that something is a fact (in our case, that the house was on fire), and that that fact is a practical reason for the agent to act in the way she did. Of course, her having these beliefs could be the explanation, the reason why, she acted as she did even if neither of them or only one of them was true. For it to be a case of acting for a reason, the agent must have these two beliefs and they must be the motivating, the

---

[14] Cf. Donald Davidson, "Actions, Reasons and Causes," *Journal of Philosophy* 60 (1963). Reprinted in *Essays on Actions and Events* (London: Oxford University Press, 1980), 3–19. Davidson defines an agent's "primary reason" for an action as the union of the agent's pro attitude toward acts of a certain kind with the belief that the action in question is an action of that kind.

operative factors,[15] the reason why she acted as she did, otherwise this could not be the explanation of her behavior.

However, in that case, the explanation might not be one in terms of *her reason, the reason* for which she ran, except on the lax construal. For on this construal what she takes to be facts may not be facts and so what she takes to be reasons may not be reasons. On the strict construal her beliefs may only be her motives (or in our terminology, her considerations) and not her reasons for her behavior. And if there *was* no other reason for her to run, then (strictly speaking) she did not act for a reason at all, though she may have thought she did.

These expressions, it seems to me, are not always used so strictly. "The reason for which she ran" is sometimes used elliptically for "the belief she rightly or wrongly took to be a reason for her to run and which moved her to run," and similarly for "her reason for running." In this looser use, we could say that she had a reason (although there was none), that she acted for one, and that that false belief was her reason for running. We then have to distinguish two different merits and demerits of such an explanation. If one or both of her beliefs are false, then her reason is a *bad* one and in some (e.g., moral) contexts it would not be *a justified exculpatory explanation.* But if her beliefs were the operative factor, then the offered explanation was *correct;* they *really were the explanation* of her running, even if they were not true.

I believe the looser use of these expressions (the use which allows us to say that *her reason* for running was that the house was on fire, even though, unknown to her, the house was not on fire and its being on fire was not a reason for her to run), has obscured the different ways in which motives and reasons function. Motives count when we want to explain someone's behavior, reasons count when we want to know whether it was in accordance with reason, whether it was "rationally justified." If we do not keep in mind that there are two quite different kinds of reason at work here, we may well ascribe the features of the one kind also to the other. I believe this has happened in the case of certain accounts of the relation between being a reason and being a motive.[16] In sum, if Mary (let us say) had not been moved to run, but had stayed in the house or walked slowly

---

[15] I do not here examine exactly what this means, e.g., whether it means that they can be said to be the cause(s) of her running. I think the problem here for the most part concerns the proper construal of "cause," which would take us too far afield.

[16] See, for example, Davidson, "Actions, Reasons and Causes" or Bernard Williams, "Internal and External Reasons," *Moral Luck* (Cambridge: Cambridge University Press, 1981), essay 8, 101–13.

out of it, then the fact that the house *was on fire* and that that *was a reason* for her to run out of the house, would not have been *her* reason for running out of the house (since that is not what she did) and so these two facts or her belief in these two facts could not have been the explanation of her behavior. Indeed, although there must, of course, have been an (explanatory) *reason why* she behaved the way she did, she may not have acted *for* any reason at all; nothing may have been *her* reason for doing what she did, not even something else she wrongly took to be a fact constituting a reason for her to run, for she may have acted on impulse or in the grip of desire rather than for a reason.

The fact that something is a reason for someone to do a certain thing on a certain occasion, therefore, does not imply that it moves her to do it. Of course, put thus generally, this goes without saying, since a fact may be a reason for me to do something, even though I do not know that it is a fact or that it constitutes such a reason for me. Similarly, it may be such a practical reason yet not a reason *all things considered*, or even if such an overall reason, yet not a *requiring* one—that is, not one such that it is according to reason for one to act in a certain way and contrary to reason not to do so. However, even if one knows that it is a fact and that it is an all-things-considered requiring reason for one to act in this way, one may yet not be moved to act in the way the reason directs one to act, since one may be *motivated* (i.e., somewhat inclined) to act in this way but not sufficiently to have a propension, to act in this way; one may instead be more strongly motivated by another less weighty reason because, for instance, one mistakenly took it to be weightier, or perhaps because one was more strongly motivated by a fact one judged to be a less weighty reason, perhaps because one was weak willed. Thus Mary may or may not recognize that in the circumstances her reason for not running, namely, that she wanted very much not to arrive at her job interview perspiring and disheveled, was inadequate.

Section 4. Reasons and Considerations

Several points must now be further clarified. I began by drawing attention to felt motivation, as in various urges (e.g., to throw up) and urge-like desires (e.g., hunger). It is characteristic of these that the conditions in which they operate do not include any of the agent's beliefs. Whatever these conditions are, the agent is motivated whether or not he has any beliefs about them and, if he has, whether or not they are true. I next spoke of motivating perceptions and expectations of events, states, and states of affairs. To this we might add the corresponding memories, say, of insults suffered and benefits received. Once we distinguish between on the one hand those urges and desires which are independent of perceptions, expectations, and memories and on the other those that depend on them, we can see that in the case of some of the latter, say, the expectation of losing a game of chess by not making a certain move, the desires involved are very different from the ones with which we began and their role in what motivates us to act diminishes and may altogether vanish.

I then added motivating beliefs and expectations, and we could add memories. Once we add beliefs we can also add facts, for we can think of them as whatever it is that makes one's beliefs true.[17] If someone shouts "fire," then someone else who hears and understands the shout will normally come to believe what he believes when he perceives a fire and that will usually motivate him, perhaps move him to run. In more sophisticated cases, when he is not under time pressure but deliberates in a cool hour about what to do, the beliefs will be about the merits and demerits of the alternative courses open to him, as he believes. Thus, corresponding to these motivating beliefs, there will be (supposed) facts which we can speak of as motivating facts, as what for him are considerations in favor of certain courses of action. What actually motivates him, of course, is his belief in these (supposed) facts, but when we speak of motivating facts or of what are for some considerations in favor of or against doing something, we actually mean true motivating beliefs, or facts such that if someone believed in them, his beliefs would motivate him one way or another. What is for someone a consideration in favor of, say, giving up smoking, differs from what is a reason for him to do so; the former has an Internalist definition, the latter does not. Thus, if the possible fact that smoking causes lung cancer is for me a consideration against smoking, then if I believe that this is a fact, I must be motivated not to smoke. By contrast, that something is, *for me*, such a consideration does not imply that it is a practical *reason for me*, since its being such a

---

[17] This may be denied on the grounds that facts are what is stated by factual statements that are true (i.e., by statements of fact) and that the question of whether factual statements are true, cannot be elucidated in terms of whether they state facts. Fortunately, we do not have to examine this difficult matter, for on either view the relation between on the one hand true beliefs or true factual statements and on the other hand the facts one believes when one has these beliefs or purports to believe when one makes these statements is this: that what one believes or states could not be true unless it was a fact. And that is all we need here. For relevant details, see "The Social Source of Reason," presidential address, APA Eastern Division, 1977, published in *Proceedings and Addresses of the American Philosophical Association* 51, no. 6 (August 1978): 707–33, and my paper on Stanley Benn, "Autarchy, Reason and Commitment," *Ethics* 100, no. 1 (1989): 93–107.

consideration does not imply that my being so motivated or moved is in accordance with reason, that I may or should in reason be so motivated. Conversely, that a fact is a reason for me to do something does not imply that it motivates, let alone moves me to do it. Of course, it would be odd if something was a reason for someone to do it and he believed or knew that it was, yet was *never* motivated by, nor acted for, this reason. It would be even stranger if it was a reason for a certain type of person and no one of that type was ever motivated by or acted for it. But the question remains just what role motivation plays in determining whether something is a reason for someone. Thus, it would not be surprising if people who think of practical reasons as considerations or as a certain subclass of them, also think that Internalism must be true for practical reasons. But if I am right in what I said before, then that line of thought is not compelling.

Perhaps it will now be granted that something could be a reason for someone to do a certain thing, yet not be for him the decisive consideration in favor of doing it, and so not move him to do it. But it may still be thought that nothing could be a reason for someone, say, to run unless it also was for him a consideration in favor of running, unless it at least motivated him, even if only weakly, to run. I know of no good reason to think so but, as I suggested earlier in this chapter,[18] there are two main reasons why it might be thought so. At this point I want to examine only the first of these, which is relevant here because it involves the belief that a person could not *genuinely believe* that something was a (pro tanto) reason *for him* to do a certain thing unless it at least somewhat motivated *him* to do it. (I postpone the other more important one to the next chapter, where it is more directly relevant.)

There are two related beliefs whose truth would indeed lend some credence to the view that one could not fail to be at least to some extent suitably motivated to do a thing by what one genuinely accepts as a practical reason for one to do it. The first belief is that all cases in which a person acts contrary to what she regards as a requiring reason, all things considered, are cases of weakness of will. The second is that all weak-willed persons act for reasons they recognize as inadequate. If both these beliefs were true, then, it may be argued, one would always regret not having acted in accordance with the balance of reasons. For, it may be argued, a weak-willed person sees the better course, but (with regret or remorse) follows the worse.

But this would seem to be wrong, for when one is, say, cussed,

---

[18] See p. 91.

obstinate, perverse or unrepentantly lazy and acts accordingly, then one may believe or know that one is acting contrary to the dispositive reason but one may not regret it. Thus, one need not have even the standing intention (or principle) of doing *whatever* one has requiring reason to do, *all things considered.* (Having that standing does not include sometimes intending to do something under some concrete description which one knows runs counter to the formulation of that standing intention: because one construes it as an exception built into the intention, or because one acknowledges one's behavior as due to a fault (weakness) of the will. In the case now under discussion, the behavior is construed neither as an exception built into a standing intention or principle nor as a deviation due to weakness of will.) For if one has that standing intention, then one could fail to behave in accordance with it only if one regards one's behavior as being a genuine exception to the principle expressed in the formulation of the intention (i.e., not covered by it) or as a regrettable weakness of one's will, but then one could never behave in an obstinate or perverse way or do something because one was obstinate or perverse. By contrast, when such an obstinate or perverse person is not *actually moved* to do what, as he believes, he has requiring reason, *all things considered, to do,* he does not do so regretfully, and so does not have even the slightest motivation to follow the requiring reason he thinks he has. He acknowledges that he is acting contrary to reason, perhaps even irrationally, yet has no regrets and may be set to act in the same way the next time he is in the same sort of situation.

Hence, such a person may also believe on some occasion that he has requiring reason, *other things equal,* to do a certain thing and *no overruling reason not to do it,* yet intend, without any regret, not to follow this unopposed requiring reason. But then he is not to any degree motivated to follow that reason. For if he were thus motivated and thought he had no other overruling reason not to do it, then he would have to be actually moved to do it. Of course, this inference is sound only if he is not prevented and does not act in the grip of desire. To clinch the point at issue here, we can simply postulate that we are speaking only of such occasions. For our question concerns only the conceptual possibility (not the probability or frequency) of someone's acknowledging that he has a practical reason to do something and is yet not motivated in the least to act in accordance with it.

If this is sound, then people may knowingly, intentionally, or deliberately act in ways that are irrational or contrary to reason, sometimes from weakness of will and sometimes (perhaps less frequently) from obstinacy or perversity. They may also act contrary to reason knowingly and without regret because, although they see the merit of acting in accordance with reason, they are too lazy to make the effort or to give up what they themselves regard as the lesser (but more ardently desired) good for the sake of the greater. (This last case need not be one of weakness of will since the agent may not regret acting contrary to reason, but it does imply that one can sincerely and correctly say that a certain course would be the better and therefore the course required or recommended by reason, even though one is not motivated to follow it and does not even wish one were so motivated.) As we shall see in chapter 5 and in part 2, this will be particularly important where moral reasons are concerned.

We can now state the motivation problem and my solution to it more clearly than before. The problem is, in the first place, how practical reason can motivate us at all and in the second place how, as seems to happen sometimes, reason can move us to do something it requires us to do when our most intense desire is to do something else.

My solution to the first part of the problem was to distinguish various kinds and sources of motivation including, most importantly, motivating beliefs and facts. This disposed of the question whether reason had "its own" sources of motivation or had to rely on the motivation inherent in desires. If there are motivating beliefs and facts, and if the motivation of considerations is that of beliefs or facts, we need not think that the motivating power of reason is either dependent entirely on that of our desires—that reason is and ought only to be the slave of the passions—or else is a faculty that has its own kind of motivation peculiar to it but capable of conflicting with and of overpowering the motivation of our desires.

The second part of my solution is my account of the "design" of the decision maker who is able to work out the consequences of various kinds of behavior in various kinds of circumstances, who has come to have a standing desire to do what he ideally wants and so to schedule the gratification of aroused desires as he thinks most suitable for the attainment of that end and who often becomes motivated to delay gratification and to deliberate in order to find out what he ideally wants, and finally, by attending tactically to those facts about the consequences of the alternatives he thinks open to him on a particular occasion, to mobilize the motivational forces of those of his beliefs that will motivate him to do what he ideally wants.

The important point about the solution of the motivation problem is to see that this problem must explain the possibility of conflicts between reason and desire (which certain versions of Hume's account of the relation between the two make impossible) and to be careful neither to underestimate nor to overestimate the ability of reason to master our desires. For the psychological facts (when expressed in this roughly commonsensical way) seem clear enough. We often could try to resist our desires though we do not, and we sometimes could succeed though we do not, because we do not try hard enough or do not try at all. At the same time, our will is also often not strong enough to succeed, and perhaps often would not have been strong enough even if we had, all our lives, made the greatest efforts of which we were capable to strengthen it. If my account of the will is on the right track, it is a power that depends a great deal on early and persistent training of the right kind, on the individual's conception of what he ideally wants, and on the intensity of his various desires, passions, and his chances of satisfying his needs.

I have so far assumed, but only provisionally, that it is always in accordance with reason to do what one ideally wants. But we must now take up the question of whether this is really so. This will involve us in a discussion of what I take to be the second and more powerful reason for the popularity of Internalism about practical reasons: that the differences between them and cognitive reasons show the impossibility of developing an interpersonally valid system of practical reasons even if it is granted that I have made a plausible case for saying that such a system need not be wholly dependent on people's personal patterns of motivation. I fully realize that what I shall have to say on this topic will strike some (perhaps all) readers as too imprecise, and I sympathize with them. I hope, nevertheless, that sketchy as my account is, it may not be entirely useless at least as a starting point.

CHAPTER FOUR
The Ground of Practical Reasons

Section 1. Subjective and Objective Practical Reasons

We have now reached a crucial point in our investigation. We must try to answer the question whether there is something that in the case of practical reasons can (or already does) play the part that truth plays in the case of cognitive reasons, something that ultimately grounds practical reasons, something to which we can appeal in disagreements about whether or not a fact is a practical reason with a certain target, force, range, and scope to do a certain thing. In chapter 3, I illustrated the nature and role of the ground of directive reasons primarily by examples from the class of cognitive ones because there are seemingly indisputable or at any rate undisputed such reasons, for example, those grounded in entailments. However, even in the domain of cognitive reasons, we noted, not all cases are thus undisputed. For one thing, not all such reasons are conclusive and where there is evidence pointing in different directions, there will be conflicting cognitive reasons of possibly disputable defeating force.

Even the ideal of truth which is the ultimate ground of such reasons is not as clear as perhaps one might expect nor as compelling as one might at first sight think. The case of pragmatic cognitive reasons is instructive in several ways. In the first place, it shows that there can be conflicts between epistemic and pragmatic cognitive reasons, that is, truth-based and advantage-based reasons to believe, in which the latter could conceivably defeat the former. In the second place, this gives us some hints about where to look for the ground of practical reasons since pragmatic cognitive reasons are essentially practical ones, for they treat believing something as if it were the success-crowned effort of pursuing some end, that is, the successful outcome of an effort to come to believe it. In the third place, it shows that, nevertheless, truth is not dethroned as the ground of cognitive reasons just because there are (or at any rate may be) special cases in which its claim on us is superseded by another ground. In the fourth place, it reminds us, however, that even a seemingly "ultimate" ground such as truth may have to give way, either because there is another even "more ultimate" ground or, alternatively, something that tells us when truth is outranked or rightly set aside and by what.

It seems clear, however, that it will not be as easy to find for the practical domain an ideal that is even as appealing and unassailable as truth is for cognitive reasons. In view of the many pervasive uncertainties and persistent disagreements in the field of the practical, it will probably not come as a surprise that, even though I devote a whole chapter to this question, my answers are even sketchier than before and that I am even less confident about them than about those offered in earlier chapters.

The difficulties are compounded by the fact that the literature on this topic is vast and labyrinthine, and that many of its authors' claims proceed from quite different initial assumptions, so that their relative merits are very difficult to assess. An adequate survey and fair discussion of it would require a whole book and cannot here be attempted.[1] I therefore thought it best to begin by discussing two authors, Henry Sidgwick and G. E. Moore, both very influential in their lifetime and even now, whose general approach of tying practical reasons to the good seems to me on the right track, though I regard their central theses as seriously flawed. Nevertheless, matching their very different approaches to the good against one another, and especially exploring some of their undeveloped suggestions, will help us with the central problem of this chapter, that of identifying the ideal which constitutes the ultimate ground of practical, as truth does of cognitive reasons.

In his great work, *The Methods of Ethics*,[2] Sidgwick conceives of ethics as the whole of practical philosophy, and its methods as the ways of determining what is rational (or reasonable—he appears to use these terms interchangeably), and so what we ought to do. He finds that there are two mutually independent such methods: Egoistic Hedonism, to maximize one's own good,[3] and Universalistic Hedonism, to maximize

---

[1] Since writing this, some time ago, I encountered an excellent article, "Toward *Fin de siècle* Ethics: Some Trends," by Stephen Darwall, Allan Gibbard, and Peter Railton, in the January 1992 special centennial issue of *The Philosophical Review* 101, no. 1: 115–89, which illuminatingly surveys some of that literature as well as other closely related writings, from which I have learned much but, alas, too late to incorporate the lesson in this chapter.

[2] See Jerome B. Schneewind, *Sidgwick's Ethics and Victorian Moral Philosophy* (Oxford: Clarendon Press, 1977).

[3] Sidgwick, *ME*, book 2, especially 119–21.

universal (or general) good.[4] He explicates *a person's good* "as what he would desire if all the consequences of all the different lines of conduct open to him were accurately foreseen and adequately realized in imagination"[5] and *the good*, that is, the universal (or general) good as a whole composed of parts where each part is the good of a single person, with no person's good excluded from that whole. But he also claims that "the good of one individual is of no more importance from the point of view (if I may say so) of the universe than the good of any other," hence "as a rational being I am bound to aim at good generally—so far as it is in my power—not merely at a particular part of it."[6] However, he does not think that the reasoning for "the reasonableness of aiming at happiness generally" amounts to "a logical transition from the Egoistic to the Universalistic principle."[7] Furthermore, "even if a man admits the self-evidence of the principle of Rational Benevolence [i.e., Universalistic Hedonism[8]], he may still hold that his own happiness is an end which it is irrational for him to sacrifice to any other."[9] From this Sidgwick derives the conclusion—which he thinks is held by common sense—that "a harmony between the maxim of Prudence [i.e., that of Egoistic Hedonism] and the maxim of Rational Benevolence [i.e., that of Universalistic Hedonism] must be somehow demonstrated, if morality is to be made completely rational."[10]

Sidgwick appears to think of these two maxims or principles as independent and so capable of coming into conflict with each other, but not necessarily and not irreconcilably so. However, he also thinks, very plausibly in my view, that we know from experience that in this world these principles sometimes do come into conflict so that we must sometimes choose between following the one or the other. He envisaged, although (unlike Kant) he did not go so far as to *postulate*, the existence of a benevolent god who maintains coextensiveness between the two principles, so that the same results are achieved by following either, and the conflict between them is thus eliminated.*

How serious is Sidgwick's problem? In my view, as I have suggested in

---

[4] Sidgwick, *ME*, book 4, chapters 1 and 2; see also 381–82.

[5] Sidgwick, *ME*, 111–12.

[6] Sidgwick, *ME*, 382.

[7] Sidgwick, *ME*, 498.

[8] See Sidgwick, *ME*, 496.

[9] Sidgwick, *ME*, 498.

[10] Sidgwick, *ME*, 498.

the Introduction, it is quite serious, especially if one starts, as many do, from Sidgwick's unfortunate formulation of it. Thus, his bifurcation of practical reason need not give rise to a contradiction, even on those occasions when, as surely sometimes happens, the two principles do conflict. A contradiction would arise only if both the reasons they supported were what I called requiring rather than merely permissive, and even then only if they were indefeasible. If even only one of them is merely permissive, if it is simply perfectly rational or reasonable, say, to act for one's own good, but not necessarily always irrational or unreasonable not to act for one's own good, then one could act for the general good and contrary to one's own without its necessarily being the case that when the two principles offer reasons for incompatible actions, one both ought to act for the universal good and not for one's own, *and* that one ought to act for one's own and not for the universal good.

However, as Sidgwick seems to have sensed, there is still a problem even if this is granted. For if my argument in the preceding paragraph is sound, then Sidgwick's position would allow that it may always be in accordance with reason to promote the universal good and always in accordance with reason to promote one's own good and that, when one cannot do both, it is in accordance with reason to do *either.* Nevertheless, Sidgwick also appears to have thought, and it would seem to agree with common sense, that moral reasons, which he took to be those based on the universal good, defeat, if not all other kinds, surely at least prudential ones.

But then, even this further problem could be solved if we allowed the distinction between, on the one hand, indefeasible reasons and, on the other hand, defeasible reasons of different defeating force, and could show that moral reasons always have greater defeating force than conflicting prudential ones. Thus, it seems that in order to solve Sidgwick's problem (when correctly stated), it may not, after all, be necessary to discover some "mechanism" which ensures that prudential and moral reasons remain coextensive. For what would do at least equally well would be an account of moral reasons which shows that they have greater defeating force than prudential ones when the two conflict. We shall deal with this problem in two stages, the first in chapter 5, the second in Book Two.

Sidgwick seems to have grasped this much, even if perhaps only obscurely. For in various places in which he produces arguments designed to persuade the Egoist to see the rationality of Universal Hedonism, their thrust is always to show not merely that the Universal Hedonist is *also* or *equally* rational, but that the Egoist ought to give up his position and become a Universal Hedonist. The thrust of his argument "from the Point of View of the Universe," for example, appears to be that everyone should look at things from that point of view, and that anyone who does must adopt the principle of Universal Hedonism as defeating that of Egoistic Hedonism when the two conflict. Thus Sidgwick seems to have sensed the need for a demonstration that moral reasons have a greater defeating force than prudential ones, hence his argument from the point of view of the universe. In any case, whether or not he sensed it, he is surely wrong in his claim (quoted above) that a completely rational morality requires a demonstration of a "harmony" (i.e., coextensionality) between the maxims of prudence (i.e., in his view the maximization of one's own good) and of benevolence (i.e., in his view, the maximization of the universal good and so the dictate of morality). There is an alternative to proofs of such a harmony, in my view more promising and more in tune with common sense, namely, a proof that when the two conflict, the requirements of morality defeat those of prudence, though the identification of morality with the principle of benevolence may then have to be given up. Sidgwick hints that this alternative can be established by looking at the matter from a certain elevated point of view from which, when the two are in conflict, the preeminence of the requirements of morality over those of prudence can be seen; I believe this hint is well worth pursuing.

However, Sidgwick's own choice of such a point of view does not appear to do the job. In the first place, it is open to a number of different interpretations and Sidgwick does not make clear which he has in mind. Presumably, to "have" a point of view at all, the universe must be conceived of as a person or in important respects like one. But what attitudes does she have toward humans? Is she well disposed or indifferent or hostile to humanity? Is she impartial, neutral, indifferent as between individual humans? What attitude must we attribute to her if each of us is to have a reason to conform to, or even to take into account, practical judgments made from her point of view? Suppose she is benevolent toward humanity but indifferent about individuals. Then presumably she will (like a utilitarian) care only about the total good but not about its distribution. But why should individuals respect or follow judgments made from that point of view, especially if they could in reason believe (as Sidgwick suggests) that it would be irrational for them to sacrifice their own happiness? Or suppose the universe is wholly indifferent to individual human concerns but has an agenda of her own, say, the advancement of her chosen people. Such a point of view, too, would fail to satisfy the demands we make on that ideal. Or suppose the universe aimed to perfect herself. Should we set aside our own good to make the world a better one? And what would make one a better world than another? (I shall shortly return to this point.)

However, before considering other more promising points of view, it will be helpful to look briefly at an approach that starts from the opposite end, so to speak: that of G. E. Moore. Whereas Sidgwick starts from the supposedly indubitable and irrefutable claim to rationality of what he calls the maxim of prudence (maximizing one's own good) and builds on it a conflicting, either equally or more rational, maxim, that of maximizing the universal good, Moore begins with objective, absolute goodness and tries to find within its confines an appropriate place for the good of individuals. Thus, for Sidgwick, "ground floor" reasons are subjective, agent based, that is, based on each agent's good, itself construed as whatever it is the agent "really wants," (as we put it), whereas objective reasons, for example, those based on the maxim of benevolence, have to be established by argument, such as that from the point of view of the universe. For Moore, by contrast, "ground floor" reasons are objective, whereas subjective, agent-based reasons have to be established by arguments taking off from objective ones.

For Moore, the ideal that grounds practical reasons is *the good.* He conceives of it as whatever and only what is good intrinsically (for its own sake, on its own account, and the like) or extrinsically (as a means to something intrinsically good). Our aim in determining what it would be in accordance with reason to do on a particular occasion, is to either maximize "goodness," that is, *the degree or magnitude of intrinsic goodness* inherent in all the things brought about by the actions open to us on that occasion, or "the *amount of good*," that is, the quantity of things that are, to some degree or other, intrinsically and/or extrinsically good. Thus, the ultimate reason we have for doing a particular thing is that by doing it we maximize goodness or the good *in the world,* or, putting it differently, we make *the world* as good as we can.[11]

On this view, what someone on a particular occasion has reason to do is to do whatever is the objectively best thing he can do. To the extent that his doing this is, on that occasion, the best thing to bring about something that others, too, have reason to welcome and help him in doing it, as far as possible. Supposing that the world is a better place if I am not run over by a bus, then there is a reason for me to get, and for you standing next to me

---

[11] Cf., G. E. Moore, *Principia Ethica* [hereafter *PE*], (Cambridge University Press, 1903), section 112.

to pull me, out of the bus's path, and for anyone else to do what would have a tendency to help prevent my being run over. On this view, these are well-grounded reasons irrespective of whether or not the persons in question have any desire for or interest in my surviving unscathed. They are "objective" or "person neutral" in the sense that they are grounded in the goodness of the world which is affected more favorably by one's acting according to these reasons than it would be by acting in any other way open to one.

Moore rejects views that would ground all or indeed any practical reasons in "the agent's own good," as for instance Ethical and Rational Egoists do.[12] He rejects Ethical Egoism on the ground that it "holds . . . that each man's happiness is the sole good—that a number of different things are *each* of them the only good thing there is—an absolute contradiction."[13] Alas, what makes this form of Ethical Egoism self-contradictory is only the ascription to it of the view—which any adherent of Ethical Egoism worth her salt would reject—that practical reasons must be grounded in something that is objectively and absolutely good, rather than in the agent's own good. Moore rejects the notion of someone's good as a confused amalgam of two quite different things: what is desired by someone or is in his interest, and its being an objectively and absolutely good thing that he should have what he desires or what is in his interest.

Against this, adherents of Ethical Egoism typically argue that the fact that something is in a person's interest (or, what is closely related to it, for his good) can ground practical reasons for that person, but, of course, such reasons are subjective, person relative; they are reasons only *for* the person whose interest or good is promoted by following them. On this view, that it would be in my interest or for my good not to be run over by a bus is a reason for me to step aside so as to avoid being run over, but normally it is not a reason for anyone else to step aside, for one thing simply because— not being in the path of the oncoming bus himself—*his* stepping aside would not promote anyone's best interest, more importantly, because the fact that *his* doing something else, say pulling me aside, would help *me* avoid getting run over, is not on this view a reason for him to do it unless his good or interest is in some way tied to my unscathed survival. Even if

---

[12] By Ethical Egoism I mean, as I believe most philosophers do, the theory that *the morally right thing* to do is always to do what will maximize one's own good or best interest. By Rational Egoism I mean the theory that *the rational thing* to do is always to do what will maximize one's own good or best interest. For details see, for example, my "Egoism," in Peter Singer, ed., *A Companion to Ethics* (Blackwell Reference, 1992), 197–204, especially 201–3.

[13] Moore, *PE*, 99.

the world would be a better place if I do not get run over, that, Ethical and Rational Egoists would hold, is not a reason for anyone else to do what he can to prevent my getting run over unless it also happens to be in his interest to make the world a better place. Moore avoids the problem of the relation between these two competing conceptions of practical reasons mainly by the claim that there are no independent subjective ones. But this seems too short a way with these dissenters.

Moore's objectivist account of practical reasons[14] was revived some years ago by Thomas Nagel in a brilliant and influential book, *The Possibility of Altruism*,[15] in which he argued that apparently subjective reasons, such as those based on the agent's own interest or good, are really reasons only if they can be backed by genuinely objective ones. In other words, he thought, like Moore, that for a subjective consideration to be a practical reason, it must be an objectively good thing to be motivated by that consideration. In his more recent work,[16] Nagel drops the terminology of objective and subjective reasons and adopts instead a dichotomy, borrowed from Parfit,[17] between agent-neutral and agent-relative reasons, neither of which is dependent on, derived from, or reducible to the other.

Despite these changes, Nagel has retained one conviction about the type of reason he now calls "agent-neutral," which he originally ascribed to what he then called objective reasons:

> An objective principle provides reasons for everyone to desire a common goal in a different way from a subjective reason which happens to yield a common goal for everyone. The latter depends on some appropriate relation between each of the individuals and the end in question, whereas the former does not. Thus, what has objective value [i.e., what, in Moore's language, is intrinsically good, or has intrinsic value, or ought to exist for its own sake], is not thereby of value *to* anyone, not even to everyone. [The emphasis in this quotation is mine and the passage in brackets is my interpretation of Nagel in Moore's terminology.][18]

Thus, if I have an objective or person-neutral reason to get out of the bus's way, then *everyone* has pro tanto reason not indeed to step aside but to do what *he* can to prevent *my* being run over. And *I* have such a reason if and because my unscathed survival has objective value irrespective of whether

---

[14] But without Moore's nonnaturalism which I have felt justified in ignoring here.

[15] Thomas Nagel, *The Possibility of Altruism*, especially 90–98.

[16] Nagel, *The View from Nowhere*, 152n.

[17] Parfit, *Reasons and Persons*, 143.

[18] Nagel, *The Possibility of Altruism*, 120, n.i.

it is of value to (or promotes the good of) anyone or everyone. If I have only a subjective or agent-relative reason to evade the collision, no one else has even pro tanto reason to do what he can to prevent my being run over unless it is of value to him (or promotes his good), quite irrespective of whether doing it is objectively or absolutely good or has intrinsic value or whether this even makes sense. Thus, Nagel now thinks that there are independent agent-relative reasons, but retains the view that there are independent agent-neutral ones which cannot be reduced to general subjective ones.

It may be helpful to the reader if I compare the distinction between subjective/objective and agent-relative/agent-neutral practical reasons with the terminology introduced in chapter 3. A reason may be subjective or objective on the basis of two different criteria. One is what I have called the ground, the other the scope, of a reason. Thus a reason may be called subjective either because its ground is based on something specific to the agent, for example, that doing something will give *him* pleasure or make *him* famous or save *his* life, or else because its scope is subjective in the sense that it is a reason *for the agent* but not necessarily for anyone else. It is natural to infer from the subjective/objective distinction that if the ground is subjective, then the scope must also be subjective and that, if the ground is objective, so must be the scope. The person-relative/person-neutral distinction is similar, but the emphasis is on the scope and there is no suggestion that there is a necessary connection between the agent relativity of the ground and the scope of a reason. On the contrary, some of those who use this distinction (e.g., Nagel) suggest that the fact that I am in danger or that something would cause me pain or give me pleasure which is, in a fairly obvious sense, person-relative (as today's being January 1 is not) has person-neutral, that is, *universal* scope: it is a reason for anyone and everyone.

The claim that certain practical reasons are objective or person-neutral may suggest to us (as it did perhaps to Moore) that they have the same structure as cognitive reasons. It may suggest, in other words, that their ground generates a reason with a single target and universal scope; that such reasons are reasons for everyone to do the same thing; that, just as the fact that this lump is a cube is a reason *for everyone* to believe the same thing, namely, that it has twelve edges, so the fact that *I* (Baier) am in danger of being run over by a bus is a reason for everyone to do the same thing, namely, to do what will prevent *my* (Baier's) getting run over.

However, this is not what, at any rate some believers in agent-neutral reasons (e.g., Nagel) have in mind and, in any case, not something that can be plausibly maintained. There is a difficulty concerning the target, which can be met. For although there is a sense in which, even if the fact that I am in danger of being run over by a bus gives rise to a person-neutral reason, that is, one not only for me but also for others, it is a reason for us to do different things, for me to step aside, for you to pull me out of the bus's path, and so on, there is also a way of saying what we have reason to do which is the same for all of us, namely, to prevent Baier getting run over. Thus, to achieve a single target for a person-neutral practical reason, we need to formulate it not in terms of what there is reason *to do* for those who have it but in terms of what there is reason for them *to aim at*, but of course in the various different ways appropriate to the different ways in which they are positioned relative to that end.

This point brings out a significant difference between cognitive and person-neutral practical reasons. The scope of the latter is not genuinely universal, as is that of cognitive reasons. In the case of the latter we do not really need the dimension of scope at all, since it is always the same: it is a reason for everybody. By contrast the scope of a person-neutral practical reason is only "all those who are in a position to do something or other to attain or help the agent attain his end." Thus the scope of such reasons is not universal but is limited to a certain class of people, namely, those who stand in a certain sort of relation to the attainment of an end for the attainment of which the agent also has an agent-relative practical reason.

Person-neutral practical reasons thus have the same structure as what are generally taken to be moral reasons. The case under discussion, my being in danger of being run over by a bus, gives rise to a prudential reason on my part and to Good Samaritan reasons whose scope is related in the way described to my agent-relative reasons. I believe Nagel is right in thinking that there are such agent-neutral reasons but I think that they arise in a very different way from the type of practical reasons so far considered. To anticipate a little, I believe they are what I have called "society-anchored" reasons, not "self-anchored" ones,[19] as are most of the practical reasons so far discussed. It seems to me that the central question now under discussion (what is the ground of practical reasons) is best approached by adopting a highly artificial simplifying supposition intended to govern the reflections in this chapter, but which will be dropped in the next. This initial and merely provisional supposition will enable me to ignore, for the time being, a large class of practical reasons—society-based ones—whose inclusion at the start of our search for the ground would greatly and unnecessarily complicate my exposition of it. This

---

[19] See above, 72ff.

simplifying supposition enables me to proceed with the fiction that there could be an order of reason which recognizes only "self-anchored" and not "society-anchored" ones.

What exactly do I mean by "self-anchored practical reasons"? They are self-anchored in four ways. First, their ground is some agent-favoring property of the action for which they are reasons, as, for instance, prudential reasons or those favoring the agent's loved ones are. Second, they are independent of other people's actions, as my preventing myself getting run over by the oncoming bus may not be. In other words, they are reasons for doing something an agent can do without the help of others and the doing of which confers a benefit on him. Third, they are independent of others' following the same reasons in the same circumstances, as the reason I have for refraining from leaving trash on the beach may not be, since I may have reason to restrain my inclination to leave my trash there only if others do likewise. Fourth, the motivating force of the constituent of such reasons normally is not and should not be reinforced by certain sorts of social sanctions.

An order of reason which provides practical guidelines only for such self-anchored reasons would have a much more limited task than the societies with which we are most familiar. It would construct merely the sort of guidelines that each person could work out for herself provided only she had (or had access to) the vastly superior intelligence, information, and other resources which society, drawing on its culture built up by large numbers of individuals over many generations, can bring to the task. In other words, such a society either would not contain any institutions that impose corrective sanctions, as do law and custom and some established religions, or else would not give the directives of these institutions the backing of practical reason by appropriate guidelines. In such a society it may be unlawful to defraud someone but it would not be thought contrary to reason to disobey the law. The fact that something is unlawful or unconventional or frowned on by society would not, as such, count as a reason against doing it. The only thing that in such a society would count as a practical reason for someone are those facts which, looking upon a choice situation from a certain point of view, he would, knowing everything society can know, want to overrule his actual disposition on that occasion.*

The discussion in the next few sections will, I hope, make it clearer what self-anchored reasons are and what is the appropriate point of view which can ground all of them and can determine the defeating force of each. The need and grounding for society-anchored reasons in general will be examined in chapter 5, and their relation to moral reasons will be discussed in Book Two.

Section 2.   Practical Reasons and the Good

The views I considered in the previous section agree on one thing, that the ground of practical reasons is somehow related to the good, but they have very different conceptions of the good. It seems to me that the main difficulty with the theory of objective reasons is the point made by Nagel[20] and apparently embraced by most or all believers in objective or agent-neutral practical reasons, namely, that they are grounded in something that is objectively or absolutely good, that is, is good in a sense which does not imply that it is therefore of value to everyone or even to anyone, or for everyone's or even anyone's good.[21] The problem with such a view is that no such theory has been able to provide—and I believe no one could provide—a plausible account of how we tell that anything is objectively or absolutely good. It seems to me more promising to construe the good in the way we ordinarily do, for that at least does not leave us without any idea of how we would tell what it is.

There are two basic uses of "good" relevant to our purposes here: "a good thing from a point of view" and "a good thing of a kind."[22] I may say, "a good thing I went back—a burglar was just trying to break into our house." We understand this to mean a good thing from my point of view, not necessarily from any other including, of course, the burglar's. When we say of something that it is a good knife or a good book we appraise it as knives and books go. We can judge a great variety of types of things in this way: things with a use or purpose or function, such as clothes, knives, or air conditioners, but also persons, lives, institutions, societies, and even (possible) worlds.

It seems probable we all believe that it would be a good thing (at least other things equal) if I were not run over by the bus coming at me or, more

---

[20] See above, p. 126.

[21] I am not here endorsing the suggestion I detect in my quotation from Nagel and in other writings, that being for someone's good and being of value to someone comes to exactly the same thing. For a more detailed discussion of the concept of value, see my "Value and Fact," *Ethical and Social Justice*, vol. 4 of *Contemporary Philosophic Thought*, ed. Howard Kiefer and Milton K. Munitz (Albany, N.Y.: State University of New York Press, 1968, 1970), 93–121.

[22] I borrow this distinction from J. O. Urmson, *The Emotive Theory of Ethics* (London: Hutchinson, 1968) 98–116.

generally, if there were fewer accidental deaths or if AIDS could be cured or if there were fewer mosquitos. We may even agree that if these things were to come true, ours would be a better world than it otherwise would be. Can this be explicated in terms of "good from a certain point of view"? We may agree that my not being run over may be a good thing from some point of view, mine or that of my friends but not from that of my enemies or my heirs; but probably even the latter would not hold that it would be a better world if I or more people got run over, suffered pain, and so on. Let us then agree that the change on account of which a world would be a better one is not that the change is a good thing from a certain person's or group's point of view. Does this show that a change can make our world a better one only if the change is a good thing not just from a point of view but objectively or absolutely a good thing? Might it not be that a change makes the world an objectively better one if it is judged better by criteria that are objectively appropriate for judging the merit of alternative worlds? In one sense of "objectively or absolutely better," a knife is better in that sense than another if it is sharper, for it is a better one, not because it is so for "subjective" reasons such as that I like it better than the other or that it better serves the purposes for which *I* want to use it. It is a better knife if and only if the criterion of merit is that it better serves the associated standard purpose—cutting well. This will, by and large, be true if it is sharper though, of course, not universally so: paper knives cut "better" if they are not very sharp; the knife in question may already be too sharp, so it won't be a better paper knife if it is still sharper. What is more, the extent of the objectivity of such quality judgments is achieved by the existing standardization of the user; these judgments abstract from particular individuals' deviations from that standard and can be fully understood and made practical use of only by those who know about this standardization and know their own deviation (if any) from that norm and know how to adjust for it.*

The connection between having a practical reason to do something and something being a better thing of a certain kind is much less clear when the kind of thing in question is the world. For whereas in the case of appraising knives there is an associated standard purpose—cutting well—which determines the criteria (usually, sharpness) by which standard appraisals of knives are made, this is not so in the case of appraising worlds. In the case of knives, the criteria are based on a standard and "privileged" point of view, that of a standard knife user. Thus, in the case of the "objective" merit of knives we can give an explication of that objective merit in terms of these criteria. In the case of the world, by contrast, it is not clear what would be this privileged point of view. Is it that of the appraiser's own good, or the excellence of his life, or that of his loved ones, or that of all sentient creatures, or that of humanity, or that of certain aesthetic criteria by which we (or the Sierra Club, etc.) judge the beauty of the earth, and so on? The question then is whether there really is such a privileged point of view from which the world must be judged if any change of the world brought about by someone's action is to be judged an improvement and to constitute a reason for him to do it, and if so what that point of view is.

It seems to me that if a society had the limited aim described above of providing for its members guidelines determining what I called "self-anchored" reasons, that is, reasons based on the individuals' preferences and motivational patterns and the most complete relevant information available, but the society developed no guidelines for the purpose of remotivating them for some purpose or other, then the questions the society would have to ask and answer are those formulated in the preceding paragraph. And of course the most important would be the question about what exactly would be that privileged point of view—call it the point of view of self-anchored reason. I shall attempt to answer this question in the remainder of this chapter.

Perhaps it will now be agreed that closer attention to the two important matters to which Sidgwick and Moore draw attention can put us on the right track, even if their theories taken as a whole are deeply flawed. The two matters I mean include Moore's insight (in his argument against Ethical Egoism) that in many cases it may not be an objectively good thing if someone does what promotes his own (or for that matter someone else's) best interest and that, *therefore,* the fact that his doing it would promote his best interest, would not constitute an adequate reason for him to do it. Of course, the exact nature and significance of this point may remain hidden from one as long as one remains wedded to Moore's reading of the claim that something is (or is not) a good thing. For, if I am right, Moore failed to note that one's fully understanding and supporting the claim that something was, is, or would be an objectively good thing requires knowledge of the point of view from which it is one. Sidgwick, by contrast, recognized the importance of reference to the appropriate point of view when one wanted to determine what one had reason to do. He thought that when one looked at the possible clash between doing what promotes one's own and what promotes the universal good, which appeared to be equally sound ultimate grounds for action, then one can adjudicate this clash only from that point of view. Again, the exact nature and significance of that insight may remain hidden from one as long as one thinks both that promoting one's own and promoting the universal good are equally in accordance with reason and that when the two conflict only promoting the universal good is. And as long as one thinks that, the relevant point of view may seem to one to be that of the universe in one or other of the various senses which that expression suggests to one.

Section 3.   Points of View

What exactly is a point of view in the sense here required? Note, to begin with, that we have a bewildering variety of expressions for singling out specific points of view: the farmer's, soldier's, educator's, politician's, scientist's, clergy's, housewife's, lawyer's, unskilled laborer's, and so on; or the agricultural, military, pedagogical, political, legal, religious, economic, moral, and so on. The first type of expression refers to a point of view by indicating merely *who* is likely to have it rather than by defining, specifying, or in other ways making clearer exactly *what* that point of view is. The second type, by contrast, does say something, though not a great deal, about that.

Specifying a point of view, saying what it is, as opposed to referring to it by a more or less informative label, such as "the educator's" or "the pedagogical" point of view, consists in spelling out what one needs to know in order to employ the method for answering practical questions associated with that point of view. What we need is a criterion of relevance and a criterion of soundness. These criteria should, of course, be so chosen that following the practical guidelines based on them will bring about the end also associated with that point of view. The criterion of relevance tells us what properties of the various actions open to an agent are to be taken into account and which ignored. The criterion of soundness tells us how these relevant properties of the actions open to the agent are to be ranked. A point of view defined by these two criteria determines a method for answering practical questions, for these criteria enable us, with the help of suitable know-how, to construct guidelines for answering them.

Suppose I am trying to define the point of view of self-interest, or as it is often (somewhat misleadingly) called, the prudential point of view.[23]

---

[23] For an insightful account of prudence, see, for instance, David Falk, "Morality, Self, and Others," in *Morality and the Language of Conduct*, ed. H. Castaneda and G. Nakhnikian (Detroit, Mich.: Wayne State University Press, 1963), 25–68.

Then the criterion of relevance is how doing something affects me or my life. Thus, I must ignore, because irrelevant, those aspects of an action which do not affect anyone or only other people. If I think that throwing away the orange peel will affect no one or only other people, then my criterion tells me that from this point of view nothing is relevant to whether or not *to* throw away the peel, hence this criterion generates no directive to curb either my desire to throw away the peel (if that is what I desire) or to keep it (if that is what I want). Suppose, however, there were a sign, saying NO LITTERING—$200 FINE, then there would be something relevant from this point of view, because throwing away the peel might cost me $200, clearly an unfavorable effect on my life.

Exactly how would this be relevant? Would it direct me to throw away the peel or not to do so? To answer that, I need a criterion of soundness. Obviously, if I consider the matter from the prudential point of view, my criterion of soundness will be that, if the action or its consequences affect me or my life *favorably*, then that counts in favor of engaging in it; if *unfavorably*, then against it. It will also tell me that *the* thing to do is that one among the actions open to me which affects me or my life *most favorably* or *least unfavorably*. So in these circumstances the thing to do from the prudential point of view is not to throw away the peel. If there is no such prohibition and my car is already full of various kinds of garbage, the thing to do would be to throw it out, because (as we can also put it) it is a good thing from the prudential point of view. From the aesthetic or the environmental point of view, a different directive would be generated.

Although such a definition of a point of view determines a method for answering practical questions, it plainly does not imply that it is a method of practical reasoning; that what, from a given point of view, *counts in favor* of doing something is a *reason for* doing it; or that what, from that point of view, is *the thing to do*, is ipso facto *the rational thing to do*, the (only) thing which is in accordance with reason. For so far nothing has been said to show that adopting and acting from this point of view is always or indeed ever in accordance with reason. We cannot, simply by arbitrarily selecting criteria of relevance and soundness, define practical rationality into existence. We must show that the adoption of this point of view, based on these particular criteria of relevance and soundness, is a good thing from what we may call the "point of view of reason." Let us review the four candidates that have already surfaced in our discussion: the excellence of the world, the agent's good, the excellence of the agent, and the excellence of the life of the agent.

Section 4. One's Own Good

One of the most popular candidates for the point of view of reason (even more so than for that of morality) has, I think, been that of a person's own good. To see whether this candidate has the necessary qualifications, we need to get clearer about what exactly one's own good is and how it differs from other related matters to which it is often assimilated. Putting it very roughly, we can perhaps say that a person's good is everything that favorably affects her or her life, including doing her good, doing good to her, making her feel better, bettering her state or improving her position, being good for her or being for her (greatest) good or in her (best) interest. A state of affairs, event, or action (e.g., a love affair, coffee break, or sip of brandy) *does someone good* if it improves her *state,* whether her health or her state of mind, in a way that will at the same time make her *feel* better, when she is in a bad or poor state and feels bad or poorly though it need not actually *make* her better, that is, cure her illness or malaise. If I give someone who is perfectly well and contented a sum of money, I have perhaps *done good* to her but it cannot be said to do her good, although it may well benefit her, that is, make her in some sense better off. Nor, probably, will giving her money be *good for her,* in any one of the following three ways: make her better *at* something, as learning a foreign language would be good (though not beneficial) for her, or make *her* better (which will also be beneficial for her), as giving her antibiotics and so curing her infection will make her better, nor finally, will it ipso facto or even probably make her *a better person,* as a father's meting out deserved punishment to his daughter is supposed to be good (and beneficial) for her, because it is supposed to improve her character.[24] However, giving her money will in all likelihood be *in her interest,* because it will probably favorably affect *her position* in life. That is to say, it may position her more favorably in her (likely) efforts to bring her life closer to what she wants it to be or to prevent it from slipping further away from it.

Is the prudential point of view, after all, the point of view of self-anchored reason? Does one have self-anchored reason to do whatever is a good thing from that point of view, and self-anchored reason against doing whatever is not a good thing or is a bad thing from it? Note first that what is for one's good favorably affects one and typically, but not necessarily, also favorably affects one's life, that is, makes it a better life.

---

[24] I have discussed these matters more fully in "Preference and the Good of Man," in *The Philosophy of G. H. von Wright,* Library of Living Philosophers, vol. 19, eds. Paul A. Schilpp and Lewis E. Hahn (La Salle, Ill.: Open Court, 1989), 233–70.

Thus, a person may improve his skills and his character and so become better in some respects, better at things and even a better person, yet not be better off or fare better or enjoy himself more and so on, that is, lead a better life. Conversely, we should also note—what so-called Rational Egoists tend to overlook—that something which detrimentally affects a person's interest or his good, and thereby that person, may nevertheless favorably affect his life.

Suppose Fred and Frieda are married graduates on the job market. Fred has received several offers; his top preference is Harvard, his bottom ranking goes to the University of Houston. Frieda, too, has received several offers; her most preferred is the University of Texas, Austin, and the least preferred is a small college in Boston. Since they love each other and want to have children, one of the desiderata high on the list of each is being together. Each knows that, if both take the job each ranks highest, they could not realize what each wants, namely, to be together and have a family.

For simplicity, we suppose that these are the only desiderata that weigh with them. The job preference is mainly self-regarding and self-referring; being together, though other-referring, is also mainly self-regarding; and their love for each other involves (let us suppose) mainly other-referring and other-regarding desires, including the second-order wish for things to happen that will satisfy this or that of the other's desires or will be for the other's good, and including the desire, where appropriate, to do what will satisfy this second-order wish. Because of their love for each other, we can thus ascribe to each of them a concern for the good of the other, but we may suppose that both are concerned for their own good as well.

Their decision about what jobs to take will, therefore, require finding out both what is for their own and what for the other's good. Suppose for the moment that on this question they are Sidgwickians. They therefore try as best they can to be "adequately informed" in Sidgwick's sense. Fred finds (let us suppose) that, when not taking into account what Frieda wants, he would prefer himself to take the Harvard job and her to take the Boston job, so that he can satisfy his own top job preference and they can be together. Similarly, Frieda would want herself to take the Austin job and Fred the Houston job. Let us also suppose that both attach more importance to being together than to advancing their career. Then, taking into account only their self-regarding desires, the "Massachusetts solution" requires Frieda to sacrifice her good for the sake of his, and the "Texas solution" requires Fred to sacrifice his for the sake of hers.

Now let us suppose that both also know what the other would choose if he/she disregarded his/her other-regarding desires and that both now take into account also their other-regarding desires. Does that change what is for their good? When Fred desires Frieda's good—which, on the basis of only her self-regarding desires, was the Texas solution—is he now still desiring that, or is her good now something else when he takes into account also her other-regarding desire for his good? Let us distinguish two cases.

Case A. Suppose that Frieda's desire for Fred's good is stronger than for her own and stronger than Fred's for her good, and suppose that after some discussion they come to realize this and decide to go for the Massachusetts solution. On Sidgwick's view, this means that that solution is for the good of both, that there is no conflict between her good and his, that neither side has made a sacrifice, since both sides did what, when both were adequately informed, they were inclined to do. But, surely, this is counterintuitive. We think that their good is in conflict and that one or the other has to make a sacrifice; in this case, Frieda ranks Fred's good above her own and makes the sacrifice.

However, with a few modifications, the case of Fred and Frieda turns into one in which we can construe their love for each other as eliminating the overall conflict of good. Suppose Fred cares a lot more about being together with Frieda than about his career and more than she does about being together with him, and that Frieda cares more about her career than he about his and that she cares less about his career than about hers. In that case, the Texas solution is not an overall sacrifice for Fred. For although he is sacrificing something in choosing the low-ranked Houston position, he is doing so to satisfy his greater interest, being close to his love. Since she is not prepared to give up her chance of starting at Austin, he has to choose between his career and being together with her, and ex hypothesi this is of greater importance to him than his career.

Note, however, that here, too, it is only his self-regarding (though other-referring) desire of being together with her, not his other-regarding desire for her good, that is involved in the determination of his good. Like someone who gives up smoking, he may overall gain more than he loses. In the movie *Klute,* if I remember it correctly, the heroine's love produces a change in her conception of the good life (from call girl to faithful wife) and thereby a change of what is for her good. In the second version of case A of Fred and Frieda, his love for her produces a new self-regarding (though other-referring) desire which he ranks as more important than his career and so, without a change in his conception of the good life, eliminates the overall, though not the partial, conflict of good. (Of course, if his love fades and his career ends in failure, he may come to think that he made a mistake in the evaluation of his interests.)

Case B. Now suppose that Fred's and Frieda's desires for the other's good are equally strong and stronger than their desire for their own good. So Fred insists on the Texas solution, and Frieda on the Massachusetts solution. How is this conflict to be described? On Sidgwick's view, both are holding out for their own good. But this, surely, is counterintuitive. Surely, because of their love for each other, each is holding out for the good of the other.

Both cases A and B appear to imply that one's good is something constructed out of one's self-regarding, but excludes one's other-regarding, desires. But this appearance is deceptive. As we know only too well, sometimes doing what is for other people's good may be for one's own good, if one considers more than the present moment. The others may be inclined to reciprocate later and, if one's readiness to promote the good of others becomes known, even people who have not directly benefitted from one's beneficent actions, may help one when in need and so on.

Thus, it would be a mistake to conceive of one's good along Sidgwickian lines, even if one were to restrict to self-regarding ones the inclinations that go into the construction of one's good. What is the mistake? It is the attempt to identify one's good, (or acting for one's good), with (acting on) those of one's overall inclinations that result from adequate information. It overlooks the fact that it must be possible to work out what is for one's good independently of what one would be inclined to do if one were adequately informed. One can, of course, act for one's good, even if one has not first worked this out on the occasion, for one may have done so before on similar occasions or have learned it from one's culture, and so can now intuitively see, without first working out, what is for one's good. One can even act for one's good without in any way knowing what is for one's good, but then this is an accident and only other people can know at that point whether or not one has acted for one's good.

The so-called Enlightened Egoist—who does what is for other people's good only if and when doing so is, at least in the long run, for his own good—is not necessarily a person who has no other-regarding desires. He is a person who, whatever his desires may be, runs herd over them in such a way that he satisfies them when and only when doing so is for his own good; and he does what is for other people's good if doing so is for his good, even when he has no inclination, perhaps a strong disinclination, to do these things for other people.

Of course, when he knows that doing something, say, writing a letter of recommendation for someone, is for that person's good and that his now doing what is for that person's good will be for his own good, at least in the long run even if it is not so right now, then he is not a perfect Enlightened Egoist unless he writes that letter. But one can be an imperfect Enlightened Egoist: one may adopt the principle of Enlightened Egoism and *thereby* become an Enlightened Egoist, but then, perhaps from weakness of will, fail to live up to that principle on some occasions. The point relevant here is that a person could not adopt and act on that principle unless he could work out, prior to knowing what his overall disposition to act will be, what is for his own and what for other people's good. For he is trying to "determine," (in the sense of "create," not "discover") that overall disposition to act, irrespective of what, as he may suspect or even know in advance, his overall inclination will be. The weak-willed Enlightened Egoist can know what to do—for instance, to give up smoking—even though, from weakness of will, he will not do it and perhaps knows he will not.[25]

As we have seen, Sidgwick's definition of one's good is a definition of what one really wants. Perhaps, most people most of the time really want their own good above all else, but surely few, if any, always do. Nor is it plausible to think that they would, if only they were adequately informed. As Bishop Butler[26] convincingly argued, love and hatred of others, greed, lust, pride, envy, and other passions may often be too strong to be held in check by one's desire for one's own good.*

Although a lot more could be said to clarify these notions, I think I have said enough to show that we must distinguish favorable impacts *on us* from those *on our life* and that we should recognize the possibility of something favorably affecting one but unfavorably affecting the other. The importance of this, of course, lies in the fact that there is a difference between the point of view of one's own good, and that of the good life as one conceives it, and that pro tanto reasons might be grounded in either point of view. It should also be clear that if one of these two must be the point of view of self-anchored practical reason, then it cannot be that of our own good. For if it were, then we would have to say that it would necessarily be contrary to reason to do what is contrary to our own good or interest even when it promotes or protects to a significant extent the good or interest of one we love and the loss to ourselves is comparatively insignificant. But surely it cannot be contrary to reason to do what makes our life better just so that we can promote our good. Surely, the promotion

---

[25] For a more detailed discussion of the difference between acting from inclination and acting for reasons, see chapter 3.

[26] Joseph Butler, *The Works of Joseph Butler,* vol. 2, 171. Sermon XI at the Rolls Chapel, section 18.

of our good is according to reason only when and to the extent that it makes our life a better one, as it so often does.

Section 5.   One's Own Point of View

Recall that we are in search of the point of view of self-anchored reason, one such that, if from it one's doing A would be a good thing, then that fact is in these circumstances a self-anchored pro tanto reason for one to do A. What are the desiderata such a point of view must satisfy? I want to stress two: strong universal appeal and strong authority. It must have strong appeal since the motivational force of self-anchored reasons normally is not and need not be artificially strengthened by strong social sanctions. At the same time, as we noted, that appeal need not be and is not strong enough to ensure that all our actions are in accordance with reason including self-anchored ones. The much-discussed phenomena of weakness of will and the less often discussed phenomena of cussedness and perversity imply that the motivating force of self-anchored practical reasons is sometimes inferior to their defeating force, or to that of nonrational motivation such as that of urges and irrational desires. Nevertheless, to ensure that even in the absence of such reinforcing sanctions and the failure of such reasons' intrinsic appeal to us in certain circumstances, the point of view of self-anchored reason should be such as to wield considerable authority from its nature so that people are motivated to bring their will into play to discharge the executive task.

We have already cast doubt on the suggestion that the point of view of self-anchored reason is that of the universe or the world or even (more modestly), our planet, partly because it is unclear and in dispute what would be an improvement in or of the universe, the world, and even the planet, and partly because even where it is clear, this ideal lacks the strength and universality as well as the authority that the point of view we call that of self-anchored reason should have. Nor does it have the sort of appeal that one's own happiness has, or one's own good or the avoidance of pain; nor does it have the authority and incontestability that truth has in the domain of cognitive reasons.

Similarly, I have argued, the point of view of one's own good cannot be that of self-anchored reason because that would rule out, as acting contrary to reason, anyone's promotion, motivated by love or friendship and the like, but to his own detriment, of the good of others. I rejected this because for many people (if not all) a life that contains such other-regarding concerns comes closer to a good life as they conceive it than one without such concerns. But, it seems, the point of view of self-anchored reason must not exclude such other-regarding consideration when they direct us in ways that make our lives better.

Much the same considerations, it would seem, hold for the ideal of one's own excellence or perfection. For that, too, could come into conflict with the ideal of a good life for oneself, as one conceives of it. There may be many directions for self-perfection, an even moderate pursuit of which would conflict with a good life for oneself as one conceives of it. If I think of a good life for myself as that of an explorer like Scott or Hilary or as that of an organizer of help for the sick and starving, I may have to postpone, curtail, or abandon my efforts at self-perfection in many or most of the directions that I might consider indispensable to one pursuing the ideal of self-perfection. Again, if one judged after careful reflection that one's life would be less good, worthwhile, or fulfilling if one had to curtail or abandon one's efforts to prepare the exploration of the Amazon or bring relief to the starving in Africa in order to improve one's singing or one's knowledge of history, or other excellences and virtues, or to work on one's impatience, irascibility, and arrogance, or other character flaws or vices, then it would seem that one would have a self-anchored reason to do the former, which has greater defeating force than the reason directing one to do the latter. If this is sound, then it would seem that the point of view of self-anchored reason is the last one, namely, the agent's own point of view (as I shall call it), that is, the point of view of the good life for the agent as he himself conceives of it.

What, then is this point of view? The criterion of relevance is any action that favorably or unfavorably affects the excellence of the agent's life. The criterion of soundness is that the action must more favorably affect it, or less unfavorably, than other actions open to the agent. But what are the criteria of favorable and unfavorable impacts on a life? The appropriateness of the criteria depends on the kind of appraisal of a life we are engaged in. We can appraise a life, whether our own or someone else's, up to a given point in that life as far as it has already been lived. In that case we may use the criteria based on our own conception of the good life for that person, or that person's own conception for it, or we may use our conception of a good, or the best possible life, for any human being, irrespective of whether such a life is accessible to the person in question as when (in the spirit of Aristotle) I give fairly low marks to my daughter's life as so far lived because she has allowed little or no space in it for "theoria."

More important for our immediate purposes here is the appraisal of a life insofar as it has yet to be lived. For human lives can be *led,* not simply *lived* as, I imagine, those of animals are. As we deliberate, we often think of what to do as a task, the task of leading our lives so as to make our life conform as best we can to our conception, not indeed of the best human life possible, but of the best possible, or less ambitiously, a good or acceptable life among those accessible to us through our choices, within the limits set by "the lottery of nature" (as Rawls has felicitously called it[27]), that is, our innate capacities, our talents and tastes (in the broadest sense), as well as by our social starting point, and by the opportunities, helps, and obstacles we can in reason suppose we shall encounter.

As we all know, the biological human life begins at conception and ends in death.* We can, however, distinguish between the biological and the experiential life which appears to begin later than conception and may end earlier than death, depending on exactly when the particular biological individual begins and ceases to experience things she lives through. The content of the experiential life—what we include when telling someone about what it contained or was part of it—is quite broad since one can experience things secondhand, as it were, when one does not witness them but learns about them through information or misinformation. One may have the experience of hearing of one's son being run over by a bus and of learning that the report was an error due to a mix-up of names, or perhaps never learning about the error because one dies upon receiving the "bad news" but before learning about the mix-up. One even may have the experience of something without ever knowing that one had it. John tells his daughter that her mother died in childbirth, whereas in fact her mother ran off with an actor while John was fighting in the Vietnam War, abandoning the girl when she was only two years old. The girl presumably had the experience of being abandoned by her mother even though she may never learn that she had it. Nevertheless, if my folk psychoanalysis is right, then this may be one of the more important experiences of her life. Thus, someone's experiential life contains or is composed of all those things or supposed things, whether events, states of affairs, or actions, including the things brought about by her own actions, of which she can be said to have the experience, in the widest sense of that expression.

There is, of course, a fairly long period of development, first in the womb, then throughout infancy and early childhood, "before reaching the age of reason," during which there is no question of the human being "leading her life." I imagine no one denies or doubts this in regard to the prenatal and immediate postnatal period, but I do not here go into the

---

[27] Rawls, *TJ*, 74.

question, at exactly what point of one's development that ability emerges or in what terms that point can be specified. It seems clear, though, that that point is reached before the individual acquires a (less or more detailed) conception of the good life for herself. During that intervening period she will (have to) learn to lead her life in accordance with the directives of the authority figures in her life—her parents, relatives, teachers, and others. With growing experience, knowledge, and maturity, she will "normally" form her own conception of the good life for herself and will begin to lead her life according to her own lights. Of course, her conception of the good life for herself may include the recognition of certain authorities—say, those of the law—as legitimate, though that recognition need not be clearly formulated or indeed formulated at all. However, as will become clearer in chapter 5, that recognition is not necessarily a good thing from her own point of view, since she may discover that it would be a better thing from that point of view if she did not recognize some or any of these laws as legitimate.

Obviously, there are many ways in which a person can come to have such a conception. He may admire someone and be inspired to emulate him. He may want to combine in his life the aims that he has found admirable or worthwhile or exciting or valuable in the lives of various people he has encountered or read about. Or he may want to explore a variety of lifestyles he has observed and found interesting but is not sure about, and so on. His culture may help him in this choice by its traditions, its religion(s), its literature, and its media by acquainting him with the possible or probable rewards and risks involved in various walks, modes, and styles of life.

Note, further, that different people's conceptions of the good life may comprise very different ultimate aims. We can, somewhat artificially, bring them under a single hat by the expression "what one wants from life" or, more actively, "what one wants to make of one's life," though some people's conception of the good life may be some variant or other of "The Land of Cockaigne" in which labor-saving devices are taken to the limit of ingenuity, where food and drink drop into one's mouth from the sky and wishes need only to be expressed to be instantly fulfilled. Such people want something from life but they do not want to make anything of it; the good things are all effortlessly provided for them, as for infants and for the senile. But most people recognize that to get what they want from life, success depends on acting appropriately to get it; and for many the activity of getting it is at least half the point. One may, like Bentham, want a life filled with the greatest possible balance of pleasure over pain or, like Mill, one may want a life devoted to the "higher pursuits" which if successful yield the higher pleasures and through them the best life as he conceives of it but which, by his lights, makes a better life even if unsuccessful, than that of "pigs" or "dunces" whose pursuits, even when successful, yield "only" the "lower" and less rewarding pleasures. Or one may want, as some contemporary game theorists appear to think we all do, or at least the rational ones among us do, a life devoted to securing the greatest possible satisfaction of one's own consistent set of "revealed" preferences. Or we may want a life in which we are able to attain the satisfaction of all our needs, or a life of achievement for its own sake, or such a life as a means to recognition, fame, and influence, or the life of the pursuit of power over others, or of wealth, whether for its own sake or for the ability that goes with it to satisfy whatever wishes to which the moment may give rise, or the dilettante's life of the fullest possible cultivation of all one's talents and tastes though not for the sake of achievment or recognition, but for the sophisticated pleasures derived from their skillful exercise and indulgence, or the life of the cultivation of deep and rewarding personal relations with others, or some ordered combination of some or all of these and yet others I have not mentioned. Bear in mind also that a conception of the good life for oneself, as I understand it here, is not the same as a plan of life. The former tells one what one wants from life or what one wants to make of it, the latter is a plan of more exactly how to proceed so as to come as close as possible to realizing the former.

Section 6.   Flawed Conceptions of the Good Life

I have so far ignored a complication which must now be exposed to view. One's conception of the good life for oneself can be sound or flawed. It seems to me that the point of view of self-anchored practical reason is that of the agent's conception of the good life provided it is sound in a certain respect. To the extent that such a conception is flawed in that respect, what is a good thing from that point of view will not determine what that person has self-anchored reason to do, though he may be justified in thinking that he has, provided only that he is justified (though mistaken) in thinking that his conception of the good life is not thus flawed. I shall speak of someone's "own point of view" if and only if she has adopted a conception of the good life for her which is free of the relevant flaws.*

To get clear about what I mean by one's own point of view, we must distinguish between what we may call external and internal flaws in a conception of the good life for oneself. External flaws are those that run counter to practical reasons other than self-anchored ones. If someone's conception of the good life for himself is that of a gangster or a dictator or a mass murderer and if there are indefeasibly weighty non-self-anchored requiring reasons, say, society-anchored ones against anyone leading this sort of life, then these conceptions are externally flawed. That does not mean that they are also internally flawed. Hitler or Stalin, looking back on their lives during their last few hours may think that their lives were highly significant and fulfilling and that, for all they or anyone else could tell, no other kind of life would have been equally significant or fulfilling.

Let us first distinguish between the things which such an ideal life free from internal flaws is to contain for their own sakes and those which it is to contain because they are necessary for the former. Suppose our answer to this is that our life should be crammed full with the greatest amount of pleasure. Then, first, we must discover what kinds of thing give us pleasure, what more, what less, and how we must space them to experience the greatest pleasure overall—we cannot continuously eat gourmet meals or play the violin. And, second, we must satisfy the conditions necessary for being able to engage in these pleasure-giving activities and for undergoing these pleasure-giving experiences. We should have the required physical and mental strength, health, money, opportunity, the willing cooperation of others, and so on. The more specific such a conception becomes, the closer it will be to a life plan, that is, a sort of blueprint that can tell us what to do when, so that our life will be as close as possible to the enactment of our conception of a good life for us.

Of course, very few, if indeed any, people have a full-fledged life plan. As everyone knows, the difficulties of working one out in detail are enormous. A person's actual life is determined by many factors other than what she does herself and over which she has little or no control at all. The most obvious are three: the innate limits of her talents and tastes, the things that, foreseeably or unforeseeably, befall her in the course of her life, and what others (among whom, for the moment, I include "society") do to and for her. What she can do herself may include the things the doing of which is part of her conception of a good life for herself, such as giving fun parties or composing an opera, also those things that help to bring about the things she wants to happen to her, the things she wants to undergo, and to prevent the things she does not want to befall her, as well as creating the opportunities and providing the wherewithal for the doing of the kinds of things just mentioned. In short, we can think of her life as composed of the things she does for their own sakes, the things she does to make doing the first kinds of thing possible, the things that regrettably befall her and those that she gladly undergoes, and finally the things she does in order to prevent the former or bring about the latter.

Thus, there are two main problems: "the basic challenge," and its implementation. The first is to decide (or somehow find out) what we want to make of our lives, the second to mold our lives to come as closely as possible to our conception of a good life for us. What is presupposed by and creates the basic challenge is that (as we all confidently assume) we can do some things at will, can know in advance some consequences of the alternative actions open to us and so can bring about some wanted and prevent some unwanted things; that we are not, like plants, the helpless playthings of the forces of nature entirely at the mercy of the elements, so that the quality of our lives does not depend entirely—though it does, of course, to a very considerable extent—on our good or bad luck.

We need not here dwell on the well-known problems of implementation. Plainly, we have only very limited knowledge of impending threats and approaching opportunities and of what would avert the former or exploit the latter, as well as only very limited power to take advantage of such knowledge as we have. However, the natural and applied sciences have vastly increased that knowledge and power, though we have not (yet?) mastered to a satisfactory degree the art of coordinating our activities with those of others, even where we have common aims, let alone developed the willingness to abandon or compromise conflicting ends instead of using our knowledge and power to frustrate or harm one another.

The problems with the basic challenge itself are less obvious. As mentioned already, what gives rise to it is something whose content we inevitably to some extent determine by our own actions. Since it (inevitably?) appears to us that we often can at will determine it one way or another, we can and naturally do ask in what way we should determine it, what we should regard as favorable, what as unfavorable modifications of our life, and finally what is and what should be our conception of a good life for us. Plainly, this conception should be influenced by what we may regard as, in the widest sense, our tastes, that is, the things that constitute criteria of what is a favorable, what an unfavorable impact on our life. Clearly, some, if not all, of our tastes change in the course of our life. Between puberty and ripe old age we find ourselves having varying sexual needs and tastes of which, prior to puberty, we know little or nothing and to which, after we have lost them and the relevant powers, we look back perhaps with nostalgia or amazement or relief. It is similar with other tastes, such as liquor and tobacco, or football and poetry. Having heard about or eaten the fruit of some or all of these and other trees, we soon learn about the inherent and the resulting rewards and penalties of indulging these tastes and form judgments about the exact importance and place they should have in our life as we want it to be—similarly, for the great variety of other positive and negative payoffs that accrue to us throughout the wide range of activities and undergoings open to us.

At any point in our life we can question the adequacy of the more or less detailed conception of a good life for us recommended by our parents or other authority figures or the one that has so far appealed to us. Every such conception comprises three interconnected aspects: an evaluative, a descriptive, and a normative one. The evaluative tells us that and why a life going a certain way would fulfill us; the descriptive specifies in descriptive language the things which are, for their own sake, contained in a life going that way; and the normative aspect, spelled out in our life plan to the extent we have one, tells us what we need to do on particular occasions if our life is to go as the descriptive aspect specifies. Plainly, the evaluative aspect is basic to a conception of a good life for us. It is the steady, but not inflexible, vision of how, given our knowledge about ourselves and the world, we want our life to unfold as we move from one of its stages to the next.

For many, it seems, the conception of a good life is that of a happy or fulfilled life. Happiness, I suggest,[28] is the positive feeling we experience on account of our horizontally and vertically nonfragmentary perception or judgment of our actual life as going the way the descriptive aspect of our conception of a good life for us specifies. Happiness may not amount to fulfillment for it may be unfounded; our life may not really go as we perceive or judge it to be going. The economist with the common name who has been notified, by mistake, that he was awarded the Nobel Prize for his work in economics may be happy, even radiantly so if only for a very short time, but not fulfilled though for that short time he may think he is. The discovery that his happiness was unfounded exposes his belief that he was fulfilled as false, but it only terminates his happiness, it does not show he never was happy. In such a case, our life is flawed by, perhaps built on, an awful mistake, for contrary to our belief it fails more or less significantly to live up to our conception of a happy life for us. Of course,

---

[28] For a more detailed account of happiness and fulfillment, see my "Maximization and the Good Life," in *Akten des 5. Internationalen Wittgenstein Symposiums 25. Bis 31.* August 1980. (Vienna: Hölder-Pichler-Tempsky, 1981), 33–42.

this reflects unfavorably on our actual life, possibly on us, but not necessarily on our conception of a good life.

However, there can be internal flaws in one's conception itself. An obvious such flaw is its ill-suitedness to one's talents or tastes. Many children have conceptions which to their parents seem obviously inappropriate in this way: they want to become race car drivers, pop singers, neurosurgeons, or, more recently, terrorists. As they grow older, some of them come to realize that they are not cut out for these modes of life. For some, the insight comes late or never. Their mistake shows itself in their continued inability to cope with the demands made on them by their chosen role or the frustrations, disappointments, or regrets that result from success in coping with them.

To avoid or correct this sort of mistake requires a grasp of one's actual talents and tastes or, more accurately, one's lack of the talents and tastes needed for one's chosen role. The necessary changes may require courage and resolve; the longer one has persevered in the wrong pursuits and so made greater investments in time and other resources, the harder it usually is to change one's conception of a good life for one and the necessary life plan to translate the new conception into action. If one has such an ill-suited conception of a good life for one, one may not have to correct one's beliefs about how (descriptively) one's life is actually going, but one has to change one's way of life to conform it to a life plan based on the corrected conception of a good life for one.

Another very different flaw consists in having unsatisfactory tastes, that is, tastes whose satisfaction does not generate fulfillment. One enjoys the social whirl, the gorgeous people, the superb food, the exquisite wines, the outrageous flirtations and the successful seductions, but, one may ask, what does it all add up to, what is there to show for it in the long run and for one's life as a whole? Perhaps, one comes to think that there should be, there must be, more to it than that. One wants a life whose pursuits fulfill one, a life such that when it is all over and done, one can say, on one's death bed (or wherever) that it was a worthwhile life, not a wasted one, a life of which one can be proud, a life one is glad to have lived, a life that, if one had it all over to start again from scratch, one would be glad to work again with the same conception of the good life.

Some people think that, to be such a worthwhile life, it must be a meaningful, a significant one. Actual lives can be ranked in terms of their degree of meaningfulness, some more meaningful than others, and some being so little meaningful that we may feel compelled to judge them meaningless. A life of outstanding achievement, for instance, is more meaningful in this sense than one of mediocre achievement, and such a life more meaningful than one of failure. In this sense, "meaningful" means much the same as valuable or important or significant.

When we assess actual lives, we often do so in respect of contribution, either by achievement, such as scientific discoveries or works of art, or by the good the person has done to others. We then judge such lives as more or less meaningful because more or less valuable, for by the value of a life we usually understand its valuableness, its excellence assessed on the basis of the benefits a person has directly or indirectly conferred on others. (The conception embraced by some economists of the value of someone's life as the amount of dollars for which she would be willing to run a given risk of losing it, concerns not the content of the life but the person's attachment to staying alive which may be relatively independent of its content.)

At other times, we compare lives on the basis of the extent of its impact or influence on the lives of others; we assess such lives as more or less important. The lives of Churchill, Roosevelt, Hitler, and Stalin were probably more important than are yours and mine. Of course, important lives are not necessarily valuable, but they are in this sense meaningful.

Plainly, some lives, probably many, are not valuable or important (because less valuable or important than a certain degree which is the minimum necessary to earn these titles) and so not meaningful in this sense. But this does not imply that they cannot be fulfilling or worthwhile, for whether or not they are depends on whether those living them find them so; it is not a matter of showing to the person that he has achieved much or contributed much or made many people happy, for the question now is whether this is what fulfills him and of this, it would seem, he is the best if not the only qualified judge.

The same is true if fulfillingness is tied not to having meaning via having value or importance, but directly to a certain mode of living, say, the life of pleasure or the contemplative life. Here, too, the question is simply whether such a life is in fact found fulfilling in the sense explained. This is a different question from whether such a life is the most valuable, for that, as ordinarily understood, is a question about what it contributes to the lives of others and neither the life of pleasure nor that of contemplation is likely to earn high marks on that score. But it should by now be plain that not everybody will find the type of life that is most valuable also to be the most fulfilling.

There is another widely employed sense of a life being meaningful or having meaning, which is often thought to be a condition of its being fulfilling. "What is the meaning of life?" in this sense is somewhat like asking "what was the meaning of that meaningful look you gave me?" It seems that, like that look, our life must have a meaning, but it is not immediately clear what it can be. This sense tends to come to the fore when we are struck by the inordinate amount of unavoidable and undeserved suffering which so many people have to endure in their earthly lives, and by the forced abandonment of all projects, the irreparable sundering of all associations, and the bitter rupture of all attachments in death. How, we find ourselves asking, can human lives, on the surface so plainly futile, be fulfilling unless they have a deeper, hidden meaning that belies their surface futility? If our lives did not have that hidden meaning, would it not be better for all of us not to have been born or even to commit suicide rather than go on living to the bitter end? And is it not outrageously unjust that some people, through no fault of their own, fare so much worse in this life than do others? How different it would be, we might want to say, if only our lives had (such a hidden) meaning!

This sort of meaningfulness consists, not simply in a life being more or less significant, valuable or important, but in being one that, simply as a human life, has a universal underlying meaning that explains why we lead this life which on its surface is so obviously futile; a meaning we cannot discover by empirical observation; and a meaning that transforms the character of human life as such. If every human life had such a hidden meaning and if it could somehow be unearthed, then the differences between important and unimportant, valuable and valueless, fulfilling and unfulfilling lives would fade into insignificance. Even the least valuable and least important lives would have such a hidden meaning and so be meaningful in this sense and their meaning would explain the suffering and compensate for it and for their lack of meaningfulness in the earlier senses. When we attend only to what we can observe, we may find truth in Schopenhauer's melancholy reflection that the road from the beginning to the end, "goes, in regard to our well-being and enjoyment of life, steadily downhill: happily dreaming childhood, exultant youth, toil-filled years of manhood, infirm and often wretched old age, the torment of the last illness and finally the throes of death—does it not look as if existence were an error the consequences of which gradually grow more and more manifest?"[29]

It all looks different when we discover the hidden meaning. Suppose (to remind ourselves of the central ideas of, and the consolations provided by, what is probably the most widely accepted version of such a hidden

---

[29] Arthur Schopenhauer, "On the Vanity of Existence," anthologized in *The Meaning of Life*, ed. Steven Sanders and David R. Cheney (Englewood Cliffs, N.J.: Prentice Hall, 1980), 36.

meaning) that human lives extend beyond the observable time from conception or birth to biological or brain death with all the hardships, adversities, and drudgeries to which that stage is prone. Suppose it to be merely a comparatively short and transitory phase in our total life and that it may be followed by another everlasting stretch of bliss free from all suffering and hardship and deeply fulfilling, but that we cannot enter this further blessed stage unless we pass certain tests of endurance, acceptance, and probity in the earlier stage. This would make some sense of our suffering and death, for we would understand that our forced march through this vale of tears is simply an experiment to test our mettle and worthiness, and that passing the test is the condition of our being allowed to enjoy the beatitude of the more important part of our life. When we have discovered this hidden meaning then we know, somewhat like Haroun al Rashid, that the beggar's life we lead is only one, the unimportant one, of our two lives; that we can be blithe about the hardships, insults, and losses we have to endure in this temporary life, for what counts is the eternal life of our real selves in the palace beyond.

There is a certain tension between two sorts of complaints I have listed against the character of human life as it appears on the surface. One is, as Schopenhauer has it, that all lives go from comparatively rewarding to very bad and that our knowledge of this inevitable downhill progression makes none of them worth living. The best fate, therefore, is not to be born, the second best to commit suicide in good time. Since the wish not to be or to have been born cannot be fulfilled, Schopenhauer's second best is therefore really the best. The widespread decline in people's belief in an afterlife has convinced many that this is right and, since we all must die, our conception of a good life for us and our life plan should include a timely death with dignity, if not in the prime of life, before decline sets in, at least before it becomes too awful.

Concerning this first complaint, I think it must be admitted that, in the absence of a satisfactory hidden meaning, human life has indeed this dark side. But several things should be borne in mind. First, no hidden meaning can alter this dark side of our lives. We still have to cope with it as best we can. Second, we may learn to accept our mortality and in the appropriate conditions embrace death as a friend, as Hume and others have done. Third, one can lead a valuable, significant, worthwhile, and fulfilling life despite life's dark side and even without its having a hidden meaning. In this respect, those who think it has a hidden meaning are no better off than those who don't. For what makes human life more fulfilling if it has a hidden meaning is simply that this hidden meaning promises a life so fulfilling that leading it compensates us for the suffering we have to endure in this one. But this second life does not have yet another hidden meaning on which its fulfillingness in turn depends. We know quite well in what way the afterlife would have to be fulfilling. We need not hope to provide specifics, such as that it will be filled with buffalo hunting or with a succession of houris sitting on one's knees or with contemplating the eternal verities or our navels; we can, indeed must, be vague about what this life will be like. But we can be confident that, if it is to do its job of outweighing the miseries of our earthly existence, it must contain the things which, in our condition as presumably disembodied spirits, we will regard as good things from what will then be our point of view, and it must be free of the things which we would then regard as bad things from it. But if this blessed afterlife can be supremely fulfilling without a hidden meaning in this ordinary sense, so our earthly life can be at least acceptably fulfilling without such a hidden meaning.

The second complaint is that it is unfair that through no fault of ours, our lives differ enormously from one another in fulfillingness. We have not yet discussed any moral notions such as fairness, but, relying on our pretheoretical understanding of them, we can say that this would be true if someone had arranged our lives in this way. To the extent that humans have done so, this is indeed outrageous and justice may well require that we all make what efforts we can to change it. To the extent that humans are not the cause of it and if human lives do not have the particular hidden meaning envisaged or one of the many other similar ones, then this complaint does not arise; the inequality is not iniquitous but merely unfortunate. Thus, those of us who are more fortunate and do not believe that the less fortunate will eventually be more than adequately compensated for their misfortune should find it harder to be content to leave remedying their plight to cosmic agencies. In any case, many versions of the consequences of failing the test are a hell of a lot worse (so to speak) than even the worst suffering on earth, and some versions (such as Calvin's) of whether it is up to us whether we shall pass the test in no way improve the parameters within which we are condemned to lead our lives.

I conclude that neither of the two complaints against human life without a hidden meaning seem convincing, and even if they were, the addition of a hidden meaning, at any rate of the sort with which we are most familiar, would not dispose of the cause for complaint about our earthly life, particularly in view of the seeming heartlessness of the imposition of the test, the difficulty of passing it, and the penalties for failure. If this is right, then our construction of a conception of the good life for ourselves is an attempt to imagine what sort of life would fulfill us, what ultimate aims that life would involve, and how we can go about attaining them. It seems then that we cannot assume that everyone would find fulfillment in the pursuit or even attainment of the same ultimate ends and that the chances of attaining or even coming close to attaining one or the other will vary greatly from person to person. Although the relevant sciences of human nature have made remarkable progress, it has to be admitted that the assistance we get from our culture in constructing such a conception, let alone a life plan, is far from adequate. By and large, we have to rely on our own hunches and on some more or less well-established conventional beliefs about what would constitute internal, what external, flaws in such conceptions. Of course, our society is more concerned about their external flaws because lives based on such conceptions may adversely affect not only the life of the one whose conception has them but many others as well; indeed they may not affect him at all, or not adversely but favorably. But for our problem at this point—the identification of the point of view of self-anchored reason—we need to be concerned only with internal flaws. Of course, a full account—beyond the scope of this book—would require not just a few examples of such flaws as I have offered here, but a systematic treatment of them.

If I am right in thinking that a conception of the good life for oneself free of internal flaws is the point of view of self-anchored practical reasons and that such reasons must be a part, perhaps the basis, of any system of practical reasons that also comprises other kinds, such as society-based ones, then my conception would seem to capture what is sound in Sidgwick's conviction that what he called Egoistic Hedonism, the pursuit of one's own good, is, indubitably an element of practical reason, even if there are other types of practical reason that can defeat these. I have tried to make clear what is unsound in Sidgwick's formulation of this—as it seems to me—important insight.

I have not, of course, proved that what I call one's own point of view, in the sense explained, really is the point of view of self-anchored reasons. But I think I have given some reasons to believe that it rather than that one or others of the three alternative candidates I have mentioned is that point of view. Perhaps the weightiest reason to believe this is that it satisfies better than any of the others the two demands that the point of view of self-anchored practical reason must meet. The first, it will be recalled, is that it must have a very strong appeal, in the sense that it must be a point of view concerning which we all can see the point of adopting it when deliberating about how to lead our lives and what to do on particular occasions. The second is that it is a point of view that yields practical directives which, on particular occasions, we may not be adequately motivated to follow, even if we adequately attend to all the relevant (i.e., remotivating) information. Contrary to what Sidgwick suggests, there remains a gap between what we have dispositive reason to do and what we are moved to do even with adequate information because, as we have seen, not all motivation (not, e.g., urges and urge-like desires) are affected at all or adequately by factual information. Admittedly, this second demand may be called in question because it relies on our commonsense intuitions about what is in accordance with practical reason. However, it seems to me (1) that such intuitions cannot be altogether dispensed with as support of a claim about what is the point of view of reason; (2) that most would find the intuition plausible, that if one's fulfillment requires that one resist certain urges and urge-like desires, then one has reason to do so even when adequate information would not motivate one accordingly, as when, for instance, one lacks adequate strength of will; and (3) that it is hard to see what could be wrong with this intuition.

This concludes my case for saying that the point of view of self-anchored reason is one's own point of view in the sense explained.

CHAPTER FIVE

Society-Anchored Reasons

Section 1. Abandoning the Simplifying Supposition

In chapter 4, it will be remembered, I identified the point of view of self-anchored practical reason with the agent's own; I mean the point of view of one whose ultimate aim is to lead a life that comes as close as possible to a conception of a good life for her that is free of internal flaws. However, the thought that led to this conclusion was made on the basis of a simplifying supposition, namely, that the only kind of practical reasons for which societies develop guidelines, the knowledge of which they make available to their members, are what I call self-anchored reasons. Since we want to identify the point of view of practical reason and not merely that of self-anchored practical reason, we must now review this highly artificial limitation. We must ask whether there are not other kinds of practical reasons as well and, if so, how they differ from and are related to self-anchored ones.

The simplifying supposition implies, you will remember, that, as far as the practical part of the enterprise of reason is concerned, society has only two functions: to turn those of its members who are "capacity rational" into "fully rational" beings, and to make available to all who want it, the best information (both general guidelines and particular facts) relevant to and needed for the solution of their concrete practical problems. This supposition yielded a greatly oversimplified picture of practical reasoning: all rational behavioral choices are made on the basis of facts showing that a given alternative open to one is a good thing from one's own point of view.

By contrast, many of the practices and institutions of the societies we know best serve functions that impinge a good deal more on their members' talents, tastes, desires, preferences, and so on, than the two envisaged in the simplifying supposition. In these societies, all members, to a greater or lesser but always to a considerable extent, and prior to adolescence often entirely, are the "products" of their socialization, whether produced inside or outside the family. We can distinguish two very different kinds of impact our society has on us. First, we are shaped during our most pliable years by institutions, such as the family, schools, churches, and more or less organized peer groups, whose impact we have little chance of escaping. And some of that impact is continually reinforced and extended later on, in various contexts into which life in such societies inescapably leads us, through exposure to newspapers, television, movies, books, and so on. Second, and even more important for our purposes here, the freedom of our choices is restricted by the more or less coercive pressures exerted on us by social institutions, such as the law, custom, public opinion, and social morality.

By the first kind of impact, society more or less directly creates or modifies at least some of the very weights we must employ in weighing the alternatives before us. It determines a great deal of what we come to believe through the information and misinformation which it pumps into, launches toward, or withholds from us. In this way and in others, it also molds the desires, tastes, and preferences on the basis of which we build our conception of the good life for ourselves, and it overtly or covertly indoctrinates us on many matters, such as the will of God, the destiny of our state, the evil plotted by certain empires, the inferiority of certain races to our own, and so on, which affect our conception of the good life. Thus, not only our ability to choose but even what we "choose freely," that is, without extraneous weighting by threats and the like, is to a considerable extent *the result of* the prior social forging of the very equipment necessary for free, rational choice. Furthermore, by the second kind of impact, namely, the sanctions it attaches to the guidelines embodied in law, custom, and public morality, society narrows the scope of what we are conventionally *free* (i.e., conventionally not required not) to choose and so normally *able* to choose *freely*.

It would seem quite impossible to eliminate all social influences on the paraphernalia of free choice. Nor would it seem to be desirable to do so, if we could. For since it would be impossible or impossibly onerous for individuals to generate by themselves information about what sort of life a particular one would find fulfilling and how to make it so, it also seems desirable for society to integrate, at an early stage in his development, the motivational and aspirational aspects of his psyche so that when he comes to form his conception of the good life for himself, and so to know what he has self-anchored reason to do, he will, in Plato's words,[1] be able to greet

---

[1] Plato, *Republic*, tr. Francis MacDonald Cornford (Oxford: Oxford University Press, 1941), 88 [402a].

reason as a friend; so that his motivational machinery will be a help, not a hindrance to the development, the suitable modification, and the execution of an appropriate life plan, and that where such a conflict nevertheless occurs, that he will have sufficient strength of will to follow reason.

Educators, whether parents or teachers or others, thus face a very important and difficult task. They are expected, by normal adults who have already been socialized in this way, to turn all capacity-rational (that is, all normal) children into social-rule-abiding members but also into fully rational ones. This would seem to require the bringing about of a certain degree of integration of the motivational and attitudinal elements in the child's psyche, without however doing violence to the child's innate psychological structure. The educator must try to shape the child's personality without forcing it into alien molds. She must at the same time enable the child, if reason requires it, to break out of the mold into which he has perhaps unwittingly been forced by his education.

What is of immediate concern to us here, however, is the impact of social pressures on adults. We must ask whether societies could exist without more or less severely sanctioned rules, such as are embodied in the law, in custom, and in social morality, and if so, whether it would be desirable to do away with at least the most intrusively coercive ones, as anarchists believe. Would everyone or indeed anyone be rationally justified in trying to keep them in existence or in resuscitating them once we have gotten rid of them? Would such a rational justification be available for every member of society irrespective of social position, or only for those in favored positions (for the slave as well as the master, or only for the master); can everyone have adequate permissive or even requiring reason to support the existence of a social system with suitably sanctioned rules? Can everyone also have such reason *always* to act as these rules require? If everyone can or does have such reason, can or must these reasons be self-anchored ones or must they be reasons of a *new kind*, and if so, what kind, and how is this kind related to self-anchored ones? I shall address these and a few related questions in the remainder of this chapter.

Section 2.   The Rational Limitations of Good Will

Can sanctioned rules be rationally justified? On the face of it, they seem undesirable, for their point is to weight our choices extraneously; they turn some things which it would otherwise be in accordance with (self-anchored) reason for us to choose and which we then could and would choose freely, into things it is now either contrary to reason to choose or else into things we are no longer free to choose or able to choose freely or both. If we still choose to do them, we must now expect to pay a price for doing so, which in a society without such rules would not have been exacted from us by it, perhaps by anybody. (Though this last point is questionable. The vendetta or individual retribution might well take the place of custom or law.)

It may be thought that this need not be so, that such rules push us to choose only those things that are in any case according to self-anchored reason to do. But this is implausible. For sanctioned rules are rigid and uniform in a way in which self-anchored reasons are not. Although, of course, such rules do not hold literally for everyone, they do hold for everyone of a class of people, such as men or children or homeowners, and are, therefore, in some respects like Moore's objective reasons or Nagel's agent-neutral ones. Thus, they abstract from things such as the various class members' conceptions of the good life, their tastes, their ages, and so on, from which their self-anchored dispositive reasons cannot abstract. Indeed, it would be virtually impossible to administer sanctions attached to what people have adequate self-anchored dispositive requiring reason to do. It seems highly plausible, in other words, that a person's self-anchored reasons will tend to come into occasional conflict with the sanctioned rules of his society and that these rules are therefore on the face of it undesirable because they may occasionally or often require behavior that is contrary to self-anchored reason.

It may, of course, be possible to give a rational justification of them, even one in terms of self-anchored reasons. Indeed, that is the position I hope to establish eventually. However, for the moment, I shall suppose the opposite. I shall suppose that, other things equal, it would be better from the points of view of all or most of those living in a given society if that society did not have any sanctioned rules, especially any coercive ones. It is an important implication of this, that fully rational members of a society without such sanctioned rules must, when interacting with others, choose what to do on the basis of "strategic reasoning" along game-theoretic lines but based on their own self-anchored reasons.[2] In such strategic reasoning

---

[2] For an account of strategic reasoning, see Jon Elster, *Ullysses and the Sirens: Studies in Rationality and Irrationality* (Cambridge, England: Cambridge University Press, 1979). There is some similarity between one's acting for self-anchored reasons and maximizing one's utility (as understood by Elster and many others), but I believe there are serious difficulties with their conception of preferences on which their concept of utility is based. See my "Rationality, Value and Preference."

they must, of course, take into account what other people could or probably will do. If they have reason to think, furthermore, that others are always not only fully but also evaluatively rational, they will also have to take into account what these others have self-anchored reasons to do and what they have reason to expect their fellow "interagents" to do.

Accordingly, the following questions arise. In the absence of sanctioned rules, what weight would it be rational to attach to the concerns of others? What conception of a good life for themselves would it be rational to expect those to have about whom one knows little or nothing? In trying to answer these two questions, we discover what I call the Rational Limitations of Good Will and with it the inescapability of what I call the Problem of General Egoism. Let me now elaborate this.

I do not here mean "egoism" as typically used in everyday conversation where it has a pejorative sense, meaning much the same as selfishness. In that ordinary sense, I suggested, it refers to an attitude leading to the promotion of one's own best interest or good, *beyond the morally permissible*. It is widely held to be one of the most common moral faults. Indeed, the behavior is thought by many to be so common that they find considerable plausibility, at least initially, in an explanatory psychological theory, often called Psychological Egoism, which holds that all human behavior at a certain level of sophistication (say, all chosen, deliberate or intentional, but not involuntary or reflex behavior) is what the agent takes to be promotive of his own best interest or greatest good.

As every philosopher knows, many textbooks on ethics expound a theory entitled "Ethical Egoism" which holds that the morally right thing to do is *always* to promote one's best interest or greatest good (this often baffles students because they feel the name to be an oxymoron). This theory thus denies by implication what I believe is one of our most widely held moral convictions, namely, that in certain circumstances it is morally wrong to promote one's own best interest or greatest good. This is no doubt one of the reasons why Ethical Egoism is not very widely espoused even by philosophers, although many think they can detect highly sophisticated versions of it in Spinoza and Hobbes.

What I here mean by "Egoism" is neither Psychological nor Ethical, but what I have earlier called "Rational Egoism." At this point, we need to distinguish three different versions of it. One is what I shall call (1) "Egoism," which can be ascribed to someone if and only if he always acts *in accordance with* the Principle of Egoism, that is, the principle of always

doing whatever there is adequate (cognitive) reason for one to think will
be in one's own best interest, irrespective of whether or not he actually
subscribes to and *acts on* that principle. The second might be called (2)
"Principled Egoism," which can be ascribed to a person if and only if he
actually subscribes to, and acts on, the Principle of Egoism. A person is a
Principled Egoist quite irrespective of the reason(s) for which he has come
to hold this principle, even if he has no reason at all to hold it, although of
course we may suppose that there always is a reason (explanation) *why* he
holds it, even if neither he nor anyone else knows what it is. The third is
what might be called (3) "Principled Rational Egoism" (PRE). This can be
attributed to someone if and only if he subscribes both to (a) the Principle
of Rationality (PR), *always to do* what he has adequate (cognitive) reason to
think has the weight of (practical) reason behind it, and to (b) the Theory
of Rational Egoism (TRE), that the fact that S's doing A would be in his
best interest is *the only*, or is *an indefeasible*, reason for him to do A.

The Problem of General Egoism seems inescapable not because we are
all egoists in the ordinary sense (though no doubt some of us are), nor
because we are *all* Egoists, Principled Egoists, or Principled Rational
Egoists, or because Psychological Egoism is true, for there is no good
reason to believe that any of this is so, and good reason to believe that
none of it is.[3]

The Problem of General Egoism seems inescapable if it is plausible to
hold, as I do, that many, perhaps most of us, are what might be called
"Limited Egoists,"[4] that is, people with the following differential attitudes
to others. They love or are friendly with or have sympathies for or are
concerned about the well-being of *some* others, for example, lovers,
parents, children, friends, family, fellow citizens, and therefore would set
aside their own good *to some extent* if they would thereby prevent harm
from coming to those people or even merely to make them better off than
they now are, as we assumed Fred and Frieda to do.[5] They may even love
some others more than they love themselves and would therefore be
prepared to sacrifice their own greater good for the lesser good of these
loved ones. They might even give their life for them. At the same time, as
far as quite large numbers of people are concerned (say, people of other
races or living in other distant lands), such Limited Egoists, though
perhaps not entirely indifferent, still care a lot less about those strangers

---

[3] For a more detailed discussion, see my "Egoism." See also chapter 4, the endnote to p.
139, p. 397ff.

[4] Here my views are close to those of David Hume. *Treatise*, 486–87.

[5] Cf. above, chapter 4, pp. 135–40.

than about themselves and about their loved ones, so that their concern for these others will not show itself much or at all in their interactions with them. This probably large number of people is (in the absence of suitably sanctioned rules with suitable content) disposed to behave in relation to the bulk of humankind in much the same way as if they were Egoists, Principled Egoists, or Principled Rational Egoists.

Mutatis mutandis, much the same would seem to be true for people's negative attitudes toward others. In some conceptions of the good life, hatred of and struggle against some people will be an important valued element. For such people, fulfillment requires battles and crusades against some "infidels," or "barbarians," or "subhumans," perhaps their extermination. However, even most such crusaders' conception of the good life for themselves identifies only a relatively small number of villains. Concerning the rest, their attitude is usually concern and affection for some and indifference for the bulk of people. I should perhaps add that it seems there are not many if indeed any genuine misanthropes. For most people the fact that some *stranger* (hence not known to be a villain) is in peril is an (admittedly rather weak) pro tanto reason to throw the (cost-free) rope rather than to administer the (cost-free) kick. When neither costs much, I believe, and I think most of us believe, that most of us tend to come to the aid of strangers in peril rather than to finish them off.[6]

It also seems plausible to think that where this is what such Limited Egoists are inclined to do on impulse without prior reflection, most would also do it on reflection. They might well be prepared to adopt a principle to that effect and they would probably think that to act in this way would be rational. They would then be "Limited Principled Egoists," and "Limited Principled Rational Egoists." The last would hold that, perhaps because of one's limited resources, reason requires one to allocate them in ways which reflect the differences in one's actual concern for different people.

But then it seems that, in the absence of sanctioned rules, this sort of Limited Egoism is bound to become general in our relation to strangers. For our reflections suggest that a lot of people, whether or not themselves Egoists or Limited Egoists, will have (cognitive) reason to expect that they often will be, and on any particular occasion may well be, interacting with a stranger who is such a (Limited) Egoist. If rational, they will be interacting with one another in accordance with strategic reasoning, as

---

[6] But see Colin Turnbull's depressing account of the Ik, in his *The Mountain People* (New York: Simon & Schuster, 1972), which gives plausibility to the view that whether, in the absence of a reason to the contrary, we are benevolent or malevolent, depends on the climate of life in which we grew up and now find ourselves.

taught by game theory. But if a person's attitude toward another is the one he would adopt toward a stranger if he thought the stranger might well be an Egoist or a Limited Egoist, then on very many occasions his response will be indistinguishable from that of (Unlimited) Egoists or one of the other varieties of Egoism. This is what I mean by the Problem of General Egoism.

The crucial question, then, is whether for these cases, people fare better with or without sanctioned rules designed suitably to modify strategic egoistic interaction. If my reflections in the last few paragraphs are sound, then many people interacting with one another are likely on many occasions to act as Limited Egoists would. It will therefore be important to examine the behavior of people in a world in which they find it plausible to regard one another (other things equal) as one or other of the three kinds of Egoists I distinguished, and in which they interact with one another in accordance with strategic reasoning, whether this means in accordance with the principle of maximizing their preference satisfaction or on the basis of self-interested or self-anchored reason.[7]

Section 3.   Prisoner's Dilemma

In recent years, many philosophers[8] have been influenced by this sort of reflection which goes back at least as far as Hobbes. I want to stress, what should already be clear by implication, that the Problem of General Egoism does not depend on everyone's actually being an Egoist of one or the other kind described. Rather, it arises out of the plausibility of the belief that persons one does not know may well be or may well (at best) behave like Principled Limited Egoists. Nor is the problem avoided if

---

[7] As should by now be clear, the main difference between the principle of maximizing one's preference satisfaction and the principle of acting on the balance of self-anchored reasons is that the former imposes only very few if any constraints on what are admissible preferences whereas the latter restricts relevant preferences in various major ways. We already noted that they are those based on what is a good thing from one's own point of view. And we shall shortly note another restriction. For a discussion of the relevant limitations on preferences, see my "Rationality, Value and Preference"; Amartya Sen, "Behaviour and the Concept of Preferences," *Economica* 11 (1973):241–59; and Gauthier, *Morals by Agreement*, 26–38.

[8] Including myself (see my paper "Rationality and Morality," with a reply by Sen, *Erkenntnis* 11 (1977): 197–223; also notably Gauthier, e.g., *Morals by Agreement*, especially 79–82; Sen, e.g., "Choice, Orderings, and Morality," along with J. W. N. Watkins's reply "Self-Interest and Morality" and Sen's rejoinder, *Practical Reason*, ed. Stephan Körner (New Haven, CT: Yale University Press, 1974), 54–82; and Derek Parfit, "Prudence, Morality, and the Prisoner's Dilemma," *Proceedings of the British Academy* 65 (London: Oxford University Press, 1979), 539–64.

everyone always acts on self-anchored reasons, since it is plausible to think that, in the absence of suitable socialization and suitably sanctioned social rules, many or most people will adopt conceptions of the good life for themselves in which their prudential reasons are outweighed only by the strong positive or negative attitudes which they develop, in the course of their lives, toward relatively few people with whom they stand in a special relation of love, friendship, and affection, or hate, enmity, and dislike; and, of course, the latter is no help anyway.

The Problem of General Egoism (as I call it) has been explored most fully in game theory, which officially operates with the theory of the rationality of agent-utility maximization, but then usually proceeds as if everyone's preferences were "nontuistic" (that is, self-regarding) and as if, in the absence of contrary evidence, people with whom we interact had acted on the principle of always doing what accords with reason. Together, these two assumptions come to the same thing as that which I have called "Principled Rational Egoism." However, if my reflections on the previous section are sound, then the Problem of General Egoism arises not only out of these strong, and, I think, psychologically unrealistic, assumptions of game theory. As Hobbes saw, in the absence of suitably sanctioned social rules with suitable remotivating content (as in his state of nature), the problem may arise, even if people interacting with one another are not themselves Principled Limited (let alone Unlimited) Rational Egoists. It does arise if, in such a "state of nature,"[9] it is plausible for people to suppose, when interacting with strangers, that these may well be (Unlimited) Egoists and also be rational and that they will in turn suppose that those strangers with whom they interact may well be (Unlimited) Egoists and rational. Under these conditions, it seems, they would interact with one another in the same way as they would if they were Principled Rational Egoists. We can therefore rely for our investigation on game theoretic discussions of the topic most relevant here, namely, whether in view of certain types of interaction—of which so-called Prisoner's Dilemma is the best known—Rational Egoism is a tenable theory of rationality.

The story of Prisoner's Dilemma (PD) (attributed to A. W. Tucker) is by now so well known that I can be very brief. It concerns two prisoners, say, Ann (A) and Bill (B), accused of jointly committing crimes, who have been told that, if both confess, both will be sentenced to two years in prison; if

---

[9] Of course, if my account of reason is sound, people cannot be rational (in my sense) in a Hobbesian State of Nature (if indeed such a state is conceivable), but they can be rational in the sort of society we considered in chapter 4, that is, one which provides guidelines only of practical reasons that are self-anchored (if that sort of society is conceivable).

neither confesses, both to one year; and if one confesses while the other does not, the former will get off free, while the latter will get three years.[10]

What makes this a PD situation are three things: (1) that the outcome for each depends on what both do, but what one does is independent of what the other does: each must choose in ignorance of which of the alternatives the other will choose, though each knows what are the choices before both of them; (2) that it has the following "payoff" pattern when ranked in terms of each prisoner's first-order preference ordering; in this case, each has a preference for shorter over longer prison terms for himself;

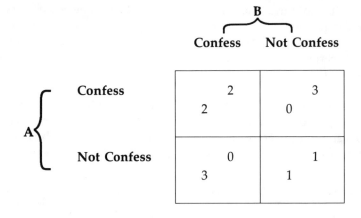

B

	Confess	Not Confess
A Confess	3rd Preference for B 3rd Preference for A	4th Preference for B 1st Preference for A
Not Confess	1st Preference for B 4th Preference for A	2nd Preference for B 2nd Preference for A

---

[10] Fo˜ those if any not yet familiar with PD, here is the pay-off matrix in terms of years in prison:

B

	Confess	Not Confess
Confess	2 2	3 0
Not Confess	0 3	1 1

and (3) that each knows that the other is (what I have called) "evaluatively rational," and knows also what the other's preference ordering is. This shows that by not confessing, A either gets her fourth preference (if B confesses) or her second preference (if B does not confess); whereas by confessing, she either gets her third preference (if he also confesses) or her first preference (if he does not confess). Thus whatever B does, A does better by confessing than by not confessing (third rather than fourth or first rather than second preference). And since the payoff pattern is symmetrical for A and B, each does better by confessing than by not confessing, whatever the other does. Hence confessing is A's *best reply* to whatever B does. Hence if people have adopted and act on the Principle of Rationality, if the only reasons in which they believe are self-anchored ones, if they subscribe to the theory of Rational Egoism (rather than, as I do, in the theory that bases self-anchored reasons on the agent's own point of view which does not imply Egoism), and if that theory requires them always to make their best reply (where there is one), then each will confess. At the same time, *both* will *fare better*, in terms of their preference satisfaction, if both do not confess. Thus, we have the seemingly paradoxical result that *each does better* for himself or herself by confessing than by not confessing, but *both fare better* if they do not confess than if they do;[11] and not only that, but *each* fares better if *both* do not confess than if both confess. But bear in mind that, as things are set up, A's and B's choices are made independently of each other: neither knows what the other is or will be doing. Indeed, in the absence of suitably sanctioned rules, neither would seem able to acquire reliable evidence of what the other will be doing, since, as I argued, it is plausible to think it not unlikely that the stranger with whom one interacts is an Unlimited Egoist and is only pretending to be a Limited, or no sort of Egoist at all.

Does this show that the Theory of Rational Egoism is unsound, that no society should teach it, and that people who want to be rational should not accept it? To clarify this, let us borrow a few further distinctions from game theory. The first is between "zero-sum" and "cooperative" interactions. In the first type, what one party gains, the other loses. If you win our game of chess, I lose it. In a cooperative game, all parties may do better if they act "in a cooperative way" than if they do not. PD is a cooperative type of game (interaction). Both fare better if both follow "the coordinative

---

[11] In this formulation, I have followed Derek Parfit, "Prudence, Rationality and Prisoner's Dilemma," 550.

guideline," that is, if neither confesses, than *either or both* would if each made his "best reply" to the other. Let us use "cooperating" as short for "following a joint coordinative guideline in a cooperative type of interaction."

A second distinction is between "independent" and "interdependent" interaction. Suppose that I like my job but am dissatisfied with my present salary, but would be satisfied with a modest raise. I also know that my own company would at least match any offer I may receive from some other prestigious firm, but will not give me a raise unless I receive such an offer. Lastly, I know that my firm believes I shall not get such an offer unless I seriously look for one, an activity they know I hate. I also know that my company is convinced that if I make a serious effort to get such a job, I will succeed and that for this reason, the moment I start seriously looking, they will offer me a modest raise. If I receive such a modest offer from my firm before I receive a good offer from another, I stop looking because I hate spending my time on doing it and the moderate raise will satisfy me. But, if I have received an outside offer before my firm offers the moderate raise, then I shall expect a matching offer from them or else leave. If all this is known both to me and the firm, then my interaction with my firm is interdependent since what I do depends on my knowledge of how they would react to my behavior, and vice versa. I begin to look for a job because I know that though they would match an offer, they will not give me even a moderate raise if I don't make efforts to find another job because they know I would not get such an offer without such an effort. The firm risks losing me because they think I may well never start looking for another job or that they can keep me if they give me a moderate raise the moment I start looking. By contrast, in PD, the interaction is independent. Each interacting agent knows only what his and the other's options are and what his relevant preferences are, *but not which of them the other will choose,* so they cannot make their own action dependent on what they know the other will do. In such a situation, it is natural for them to make their best reply, *whatever the other may do,* that is, to do whatever is the best thing for them to do from what, as they believe, is the point of view of practical reason.

A third distinction is between "coordinated" and "uncoordinated" interaction. Eight men rowing a boat will do better if they coordinate their rowing than if they do not.[12] They may do better still if they have a cox

---

[12] But see the qualifications J. L. Mackie makes to this Humean claim in his book, *Hume's Moral Theory* (London: Routledge and Kegan Paul, 1980), 88–90.

coordinating their strokes. Coordinated differs from interdependent interaction. The latter is interaction on the basis of each agent's knowledge of how the other will react to his actions. In the former, each agent follows the coordinating guideline in the hope, belief, or knowledge that the others are also following it. Where all would gain equally, as in the rowing example, it is in accordance with reason to assume that, if all are rational, all will cooperate and that all are sufficiently rational to know that the coordinated behavior is in accordance with reason, the uncoordinated contrary to it.

PD is different in that the fact that both would gain equally if both behaved cooperatively does not enable either to infer that it would be in accordance with reason for either to act cooperatively, since neither can infer that his "partner" is rational, that his partner knows he is rational, and that his partner knows that he knows his partner is. Unless both know at least this much, neither can infer that the other will act cooperatively. For if either of them, say A, is unsure of some of these matters, she may think one or both of two things: she may think that the other (B) will hope that he (B) can, one-sidedly, act uncooperatively (i.e., confess) and so obtain his most preferred outcome; and/or she may think that (B), though he would be disposed to act cooperatively if he knew she, too, was so disposed, would not risk doing so unless *he knew* that she was so disposed and that *she knew* that he too was so disposed. The possible unwillingness of either to renounce her or his most preferred outcome by acting cooperatively (that is, their possible Unlimited Egoism), and/or the possible unwillingness of either to risk the other's possible unwillingness to renounce his best outcome[13] make it contrary to reason for them to act cooperatively.

It is not even crystal clear that this additional knowledge about one another's rationality would help to resolve the problem. For how could anyone acquire such knowledge? Suppose both my partner and I have that knowledge. Am I *locked into* doing what is rational? Could I not, assuming that the other is rational and so "locked into" the cooperative strategy, act uncooperatively myself? But if, when he knows that I am rational, I am not locked into the cooperative strategy, why should he be so locked? But since, it would seem, nothing could literally lock us into that strategy, the hope that we could acquire this sort of knowledge would seem to be naive. For if the "knowledge" that the other is rational implies that he is locked into cooperative behavior, then the fact that no one ever is locked into this

---

[13] That is, their "conditional limited good will," as I shall call it; for details, see this chapter, section 5, especially pp. 187–90.

or any sort of such behavior would seem to make that knowledge hard or impossible to acquire.*

In any case, even if we could in principle acquire that sort of knowledge, it is unlikely to be available to most or indeed any of us in the circumstances typical of interaction with strangers.[14] It seems to me that, therefore, in many or most such cases, going for the best worst outcome (two years in prison) thereby avoiding the worst worst (three years in prison) and still having a chance of the best best outcome (getting off free), though precluding the worst best outcome (one year in prison) would seem the only course in accordance with reason.[15]

It seems plain, then, that what TRE (the Theory of Rational Egoism) tells individual agents to do depends on the circumstances in which they find themselves. If they face one another as strangers, neither having any special reason (such as love, friendship, hatred, or revenge) to take into account (one way or the other) the interests of the other, neither to be concerned to harm or to benefit the other, but merely to promote their own good, and if neither has any *assurance* that the other will or will not follow the coordinative guideline, even though both know what it requires, then depending to some extent on how bad the worst and how good the best outcome, and on how risk prone or averse it is in accordance with reason to be,** the TRE sometimes tells them to play it safe, to go for "the best worst" outcome, in this case for the third preference. In the absence of any assurance of cooperation, that theory may often require them to make their best reply despite its relatively poor payoff to both of them.

And this advice by that theory seems right. In such circumstances, the best thing one can do is to make the best reply, as one sees it. No guideline of practical reason can in this sort of situation *ensure* a better outcome for an individual. At the same time, it is plain (as Hobbes clearly saw) that from the point of view of an optimizer, this is unsatisfactory, since both *could* fare better if both followed the coordinative guideline. What follows

---

[14] For a different view, see Gauthier's claim that we are, all or most of us, sufficiently "translucent" for others to know whether we are "straightforward" or "constrained maximizers," that is, whether in PD we will always make our best reply, or whether we will cooperate provided others also do so. *Morals by Agreement,* 174.

[15] I am not denying that in stable conditions, where so-called "iterated PDs" occur, mutual confidence can be built up by certain strategies, such as "tit for tat," but not all circumstances are like that and in the absence of a social order with its trust-building institutions, such situations are likely to be rare and short-lived. Of course, once there are these institutions, the matter is very different. Indeed, it seems to me that the assumption that these transactions would occur in a genuine "state of nature" is incoherent.

from this, however, is not that, according to TRE, it would in this situation be in accordance with reason for each to follow that coordinative guideline, but rather for each *to try to change the situation* so that each can in reason do so.

The first thing to be done according to TRE therefore is to solve the so-called assurance problem,[16] that is, the problem of obtaining assurance that others will follow the coordinative guideline. For in the absence of that assurance, following it risks being saddled with one's worst outcome. How can the assurance problem be solved? We have already cast doubt on a solution based on acquiring certain complex knowledge.

Could we perhaps solve this problem simply by getting the agents in such situations to agree to follow the coordinative guidelines? This idea, at the heart of the social contract tradition, raises at least three very difficult problems. The first is a purely practical one, though it is sufficient, I think, to dispose of the idea that the assurance we seek has actually been brought about by such an original social contract.[17] One thing that prevents this ball from ever starting to roll is simply that it would be impossible in the circumstances envisaged to get all the people together and to agree on a given set of guidelines sufficiently detailed to provide guidance for the major practical problems arising even in a small group of interacting people.

The second difficulty, usually called the coordination problem[18] is of considerable theoretical importance. It concerns the question of what would be a rational set of coordinative guidelines and how those to be guided by them would come to know the particular one from among the various possible ones which *actually is to coordinate* their behavior. It is easy to forget the magnitude of this problem when one thinks only of PD. For its structure is so simple that there can be only one coordinative guideline: not to confess; and it is completely symmetrical, hence the question of its justice or fairness does not arise: both prisoners gain and lose the same amount by the only two options open to them. But in the enormous numbers of PD situations which arise in real life, there will be many alternative sets of coordinative guidelines which, while benefitting some or all, would not benefit them equally

---

[16] Cf. Rawls, *TJ*, 269.

[17] See David Braybrooke, "The Insoluble Problem of the Social Contract," *Dialogue* 15 (March 1976): 3–37.

[18] Cf. Rawls, *TJ*, 269.

or equitably. (I shall return to this point at greater length in Book Two, chapter 7.)

The third problem is this. It may well appear to be required by the Theory of Rational Egoism that people in PD situations draw up coordinating guidelines and make agreements to follow them rather than make their best reply to whatever others can do. But since it is in accordance with that theory to do this only if one's cooperation is both a necessary and sufficient condition of other people's cooperation, it cannot be in accordance with it to keep the agreement one has made. For even though one's making the agreement may be a sufficient condition of *other* people's cooperation, one's own actual cooperation is not a necessary condition of it. One can sometimes profitably break such agreements. But if one's own cooperation is not a necessary condition, then it may not be in accordance with this theory to adhere to the agreement, since one may be able to do better for oneself by breaking it as long as the others keep it. And conversely, since one's own cooperation may not be a necessary condition of others cooperating, no particular other person's cooperation is either. But that shows that the agreement itself is not a sufficient condition of other people's cooperation. Therefore it is not in accordance with TRE for oneself or anyone else to cooperate, since the existence of an agreement alone does not solve the assurance problem. As Hobbes pointed out, contracts alone are empty words[19] (for a subscriber of TRE, as he appears to have been).

The coordination problem does raise doubts about the soundness of TRE, however, for it would seem that its adherents are committed, by their conception of what is in accordance with reason, to a choice that produces a suboptimal state of affairs, since different choices could produce a better one for at least some of them without it being less good for anyone, and perhaps better for all, perhaps even better for all alike. I shall return to this point shortly.

The upshot of these reflections is to confirm that TRE is plausible only if it is interpreted as requiring the pursuit of one's own good in whatever *happens to be the best possible way* in the particular circumstances in which one finds oneself. If it were interpreted as specifying or implying a certain specific method or policy or strategy, namely, the strategy of making the best possible uncoordinated reply in interaction, then it could not be acceptable. For if it turns out, as it seems to, that one's good depends at

---

[19] Hobbes, *Leviathan*, 201.

least as much on what others are doing as on what one is doing oneself, such an uncoordinated, individualistic approach to the promotion of one's own good is clearly not always the best possible.* It would surely be preferable, from a rational point of view, to work for a state of affairs in which one's own promotion of one's own good is reliably coordinated with other people's promotion of their own good, so as to avoid the suboptimal outcomes necessarily produced by uncooperative strategies in PD and similar situations.**

Let us then look at the oldest solution to the assurance problem: a suitable change in the PD situation making the uncoordinated best reply either impossible or undesirable. Hobbes thought of the condition in which PD arises as a State of Nature, that is, one in which, although (implausibly) all can work out for themselves roughly what the "best" coordinating guidelines would have to be, there is no way of agreeing on the necessary details and there is no assurance of reciprocity. Such a state, Hobbes argued, is governed by what he called the Right of Nature, for in that state it is rational, that is, prudent, for anyone and everyone to do whatever in his judgment is necessary for the promotion of his good (which Hobbes appears to have located above all in the preservation of his life and secondarily in "commodious living"). But although in his view a rational person would be willing, *on a basis of reciprocity*, to lay down whatever part of his Right of Nature necessary to avoid the mutual harm caused by each person's untrammeled exercise of the Right of Nature in his pursuit of his own good, no one can have assurance of reciprocity as long as he lives in a State of Nature. But since only reciprocity makes it beneficial for anyone to lay down any part of his Right of Nature, so in the absence of assurance of reciprocity, it is not prudent and so, in Hobbes' view, not rational for anyone to do so.[20]

Hobbes thought that the existence of an effective social order with adequate sanctions guaranteed the prevalence of the conditions which assured its members of reciprocity. For promulgation of the guidelines ensures that those willing to cooperate *know how* to do so, thus solving the coordination problem. And their enforcement ensures the prudence of cooperation, thus making it prudent for anyone and everyone to follow, and imprudent to break, whatever (with minimal exceptions, such as the requirement to commit suicide) are the coordinative guidelines promulgated and enforced by one's society. This solves the assurance problem.

---

[20] Hobbes's exception: *Leviathan,* 203–5.

Hobbes thought it right to identify rationality with prudence, for although he admitted that it might in some cases turn out to have been in one's best interest to break it, he argued that it could never be prudent to break it, taking into account the probability and the seriousness of being caught.[21] However, this argument depends on two claims, only one of which is sound, namely, that under the conditions Hobbes envisages, anyone who violates the law can gain from his violation only by "the errors of other men." The second, namely, that one "could not foresee nor reckon upon such errors" and that therefore one always necessarily acts contrary to reason in breaking the law, is open to two serious objections.

The first objection, for argument's sake, grants Hobbes the possibility of a flawlessly efficient state, one capable of catching and convicting all (or very nearly all) lawbreakers and of inflicting such heavy punishment on them that in such a state it is indeed always necessarily contrary to (Hobbesian) reason for anyone to break the law. The problem with this is that, if such a state is indeed possible, the cost of maintaining it would be staggering. It is more than doubtful whether, under such a monstrous police state, the loss in freedom and the risk of false conviction by a court could possibly be outweighed by the gain in having rationality and prudence coincide, as Hobbes's theory of practical reason would seem to require.

The second objection looks more closely into the possibility of such an absolute state composed of Hobbesian individuals. All the members of a community (if that is not here an oxymoron), or most of whom are, and suspect one another of being, Principled Rational Egoists, have reason to want to be in a position to break the law and get away with impunity, but at the same time want also to ensure that others will never be in that position. Every one in such a community thus has reason to ensure, through supporting stringent policies of "law and order," that crime never pays *other* people, while at the same time ensuring that it pays *him*. He therefore has reason to attempt, perhaps by bribes, threats, and other methods, to induce officials to bend the law in his favor or simply to close their eyes when he breaks it. Conversely, its officials whose task it is to ensure that the laws are enforced, have reason to bend the law in favor of those who are able and willing to make it worth their while. Given the unequal ability of people to promote their own interest in these various ways, a society of consistent adherents of this the-

---

[21] Hobbes, *Leviathan*, 203–5.

ory will tend to depart from stringent uniform enforcement of the laws. What is worse, every such person will want, by lobbying and similar methods, to ensure that the laws are written so as to favor him more than others. As officials find it in their best interest and so rational to exempt some from punishment and to pass inequitable laws favoring some more than others, it will become more and more in the interest of more and more of the socially disfavored to try and break the law, even as the risk to themselves of being caught increases, because for them the advantage of obeying the laws tends to diminish, whereas that of breaking them to grow. Such egoistic societies will, therefore, tend to be unstable, with periodic upheavals and revolutions and many of the drawbacks of Hobbes's State of Nature, which they were supposed to remedy.

It is sometimes argued that Hobbes's mistake lies in his account of human psychology: we are not as egoistic as he makes us out to be. This may well be true, but it does not solve the problem Hobbes faces. If TRE (the Theory of Rational Egoism), to which Principled Rational Egoists subscribe, is sound, then in certain situations such as Prisoner's Dilemma, setting aside one's own interest to promote that of others is irrational unless one has very good reason to think that others will do likewise. All that is needed, then, for optimal outcomes of our interactions might seem to be two things. One is a slight change in our theory of rationality: the point of view of practical reason is not that of the agent's own greatest good or best interest or maximization of revealed preference-satisfaction, but what I have called his own point of view, that is, that of his own sound conception of a good life for himself. The other is a more altruistic attitude of people toward one another, a greater concern for the good or interests of a greater number of one's fellow members.*

Section 4.   Altruism

But might not increased altruism alone resolve the problem of PD? In what sense are we to understand "altruism" here? Not in the ordinary sense (the opposite of egoism) in which it means the disposition to promote and protect other people's greatest good or best interest *beyond the morally required*. For what we want to know now is whether a general increase in people's concern for others would make it the case that one's own point of view as defined earlier would constitute the point of view of reason, and, if so, exactly how great the increase would have to be. Thus, presumably, the increase required (if any) is not one beyond whatever other-regarding concern beyond the morally required already exists, but the increase in the extent of other-regarding concern (if any) that is rationally required—irrespective of the extent that is morally required. The question, in other words, is about the extent to which individuals must have other-regarding concerns if it is to be true that for them to do what is a good thing from their own point of view is in accordance with reason. If we could find a way of specifying this extent of other-regarding concern and if we could find a way of generating it in an entire population, generation after generation, then perhaps the only practical reasons really would be self-anchored ones.

Note that this approach no longer conceives of a person's rationality as a function of his *actual* desires or preferences. This is, of course, a serious drawback since at this point we do not know how these ideal desires or preferences can be generated. Perhaps it is unrealistic to assume that there are unobjectionable ways, or indeed any ways at all, for changing people's other-regarding desires and preferences concerning all the people with whom they are likely to interact in PD situations, including those whom they do not now and never will know personally. Perhaps the monetary and the psychological costs of such an educational and reeducational scheme would be prohibitively high. At the same time, the solutions relying solely on suitably sanctioned social rules—call it "the political solution"—even if they are more sophisticated and less brutal than Hobbes's, involve considerable costs of a similar kind and do not work all that well, especially in social orders whose members suspect one another of being Principled Rational Egoists or even Principled Limited Rational Egoists. Thus, if a change in their psychology could generate cooperative behavior without that costly and dangerous enforcement machinery, simply on the basis of self-anchored rationality, that would surely be a significant gain.*

Note also that we must now drop the equivalence of the various interpretations of strategic reasoning we assumed earlier.[22] Thus, the theory of rationality we are now examining is, strictly speaking, no longer that of Rational Egoism (TRE) but that of the maximization of *admissible* preferences, which I shall abbreviate as TRP.

---

[22] See above, this chapter, section 2.

Section 4.1.   Sen's Version of Increased Altruism

At this point it will be helpful to examine a fascinating and highly imaginative article by A. K. Sen on this "psychological solution" from which I have learned and borrowed much.[23] In it, Sen suggests two degrees or patterns of increased altruism which, he thinks, might dispose of PD. He introduces them by way of two "games," similar to the "game" of PD, which he christens "AG," for Assurance Game, and "OR," for "Other-Regarding" Game. These two games differ from PD only in terms of the preference orderings of the two prisoners playing these games. Sen specifies the games by the following matrices:

	PD		AG		OR	
	A	B	A	B	A	B
1st Preference	a_1b_0	a_0b_1	a_0b_0	a_0b_0	a_0b_0	a_0b_0
2nd Preference	a_0b_0	a_0b_0	a_1b_0	a_0b_1	a_0b_1	a_1b_0
3rd Preference	a_1b_1	a_1b_1	a_1b_1	a_1b_1	a_1b_0	a_0b_1
4th Preference	a_0b_1	a_1b_0	a_0b_1	a_1b_0	a_1b_1	a_1b_1

In these matrices, "a_1 and a_0 stand respectively for prisoner A confessing and not doing, and similarly b_1 and b_0 for prisoner B confessing and not doing it."[24] Sen, in other words, indicates the preferences of prisoner A in column A and that of prisoner B in column B. In PD the top preference of A is for her (A) to confess and for B not to confess, while the top preference of B is the reverse: himself (B) confessing and A not confessing. Their second preference is the same: both not confessing; and so on down to their bottom preference. AG differs from PD only in that the positions of these two top preferences are reversed, while OR differs more radically, as we shall see later.*

However, before examining these preference patterns and the games they characterize, we must note that this (quite helpful) way of representing the prisoners' behavior and preferences does not exhibit certain

---

[23] Sen, "Choice, Orderings, and Morality." The remarks in this section follow ideas expressed in my paper "Rationality and Morality."

[24] Sen, "Choice, Orderings, and Morality," 56.

important aspects of the nature of the preferences and of their internal relations. Traditionally, it is assumed that the prisoners prefer one of the two strategies open to them, confession or nonconfession, not on account of anything intrinsic to confession or nonconfession itself, but solely on account of the outcomes they produce, in this case different prison sentences. If we are to indicate what they prefer in a way that exhibits the individual rationality of their choices, we should specify also the outcomes, not only the behaviors themselves. Next, we should note that a prisoner's overall preference for an outcome may be based solely on his own prison sentence implying indifference to the fate of the other prisoner, or it may be based on both outcomes implying a positive or negative attitude to the fate of the other. Also, we must not specify the outcomes in terms of specific prison sentences, because what defines the game is not the specific prison sentences attached to the various behaviors but rather the prisoners' preferential ordering of the outcomes, which is compatible with considerable variations in the prison terms attached.[25] Sen's matrix also does not represent the fact that the two prisoners' preferences are exactly the same so that the prisoners are interchangeable in the matrices. This can be indicated by replacing "A" and "B" by "S" (for Self) and "O" (for Other). We can then indicate *either* prisoner's preferences in terms of what he (S) prefers *for himself* and what he (S) thinks O prefers *for himself.* Lastly, Sen's matrix does not show that, although some of the preferences of the prisoners are different in each of the three games, some of their preferences are the same in all of them. After all, although Sen's two new games, AG and OR, are variations on PD, all three are versions of another type of game: one in which each of two persons has only two strategies, confess/not confess, in which the same strategies have the same outcomes, and in which both prisoners have *the same* "intrinsic first-order preferences," namely, for lower rather than higher prison sentences.

I call someone's preference of X over Y "intrinsic," rather than "derived" or "overall," if he is more inclined toward something, or less inclined away from it, insofar as he takes it to be X rather than Y. Both prisoners intrinsically prefer two years in prison to twenty. However, if one of them believes that the gang to which he belonged will try to kill him the moment he comes out, and if he intrinsically prefers being in prison and staying alive to being free and getting killed, then he may well *derivatively* prefer twenty years to only two, although of course he still

---

[25] Cf. Sen's rejoinder to J. W. N. Watkins's "Self-Interest and Morality," 80.

intrinsically prefers two years to twenty. Not all derived preferences are overall preferences. Thus, the prisoner who derivatively prefers twenty years to only two may yet overall prefer two to twenty years if he suffers from an incurable disease and desperately wants to be reunited with his family before he dies even at the risk of being killed by his gang. As we shall see shortly, the distinction between intrinsic and derived preferences is relevant to rationality in action.

I call preferences "first-order" if the formulation of their content (that for which they are preferences) does not involve reference to preferences, "higher-order" if it does. They are $(n+1)$th-order preferences if the preferences referred to in the formulation of their content are nth-order.

To exhibit these features unexhibited in Sen's matrices more clearly, I have redesigned them. I construe all six of these games as *versions* of (rather than variations on) what I now call PD′, because in all of them the prisoners have the same choices, confront the same outcomes, and have the same relevant intrinsic first-order preferences. I have therefore changed the name of Sen's first game from "PD" to "SF" (for Self-Favoring), a version of PD′; the justification of this change will become clearer shortly. I then rewrite the matrices as follows. Instead of indicating the four possible outcomes in terms of the strategies leading to them, as Sen does, I indicate these outcomes in terms of two rankings: (1) S′s (i.e., Self's) own ranking of the joint outcome on the basis of his own first-order intrinsic preferences for shorter over longer prison sentences; and (2) S′s estimate of O′s (Other's) corresponding rankings. I thus replace Sen's representations of the four possible outcomes, that is, a_1b_0, a_0b_0, a_1b_1, and a_0b_1, by [1,4], [2,2], [3,3], and [4,1]. In my matrices the prisoners' top first-order intrinsic preference is indicated by "1," the second by "2," and so on down in numerical order to the bottom preference.

Since, ex hypothesi, both the intrinsic and overall preference patterns of the two prisoners in one and the same version of PD′ are symmetrical, we need to give only one ranking of the outcomes so indicated, namely, S′s *overall preference-ranking*, for this applies equally to prisoner A and to prisoner B. This overall ranking is made explicit in the left-hand column. Sen's three games, with PD suitably renamed "SF," would then be represented as follows: the left-hand column indicates, for each of the three games, Self's second-order preference-ranking for each of the four possible outcomes in each game, the rank order based solely on which of Self's and Other's intrinsic first-order preferences (the latter as judged by S) the outcomes satisfy.

		SF	AG	OR
		S O	S O	S O
	1st Preference	[1,4]	[2,2]	[2,2]
S's	2nd Preference	[2,2]	[1,4]	[4,1]
	3rd Preference	[3,3]	[3,3]	[1,4]
	4th Preference	[4,1]	[4,1]	[3,3]

Thus, the first (top) preference shown above in SF, [1,4], indicates that among the four outcomes possible, each prisoner gives top second-order preference to the outcome which satisfies his or her own top first-order intrinsic preference and what they judge (in this case rightly, ex hypothesi) to be the other's bottom first-order intrinsic preference. The matrices indicate how the preferences distinguish the games from one another, namely, by their intrinsic *overall* preferences (shown in the left-hand column) based on *whose* first-order intrinsic preferences are satisfied and to what extent (shown in the column with two figures). Only in SF is there a completely obvious pattern: it is that the satisfaction of S's own first-order intrinsic preferences is S's dominant concern; the pattern is completely self-favoring.

Thus, S's overall preferences are based on his first-order intrinsic preferences (the length of prison terms) and the weight S gives to O's getting his preferences. In SF, S gives no (choice-influencing) weight to the latter: his overall preference pattern is the same as that of his first-order intrinsic preferences. I shall speak of the relative weight one gives to the satisfaction of one's own preferences and that of those of one's partner (or opponent) in interaction, as one's "self-involving distributive" (or SD) preferences. Not all second-order preferences are "distributive" (D) preferences. I should, for instance, prefer to have certain first-order preferences which I do not in fact have, e.g., to use Sen's example,[26] I have a preference that I prefer a vegetarian to a meat diet. This is a second-order but not a D preference. But if, when there is a serious meat shortage, I prefer that my own first-order preference for meat be satisfied rather than that of my neighbor's, then I have a D preference, to wit, an SD one. Of course, not all D preferences are SD ones. If of two of my students, Ann and Bill, I like Ann better, I shall to that extent prefer that her preferences, whatever (within limits) they happen to be, be satisfied rather than his.

---

[26] Watkins, "Self-Interest and Morality," 56.

Thus, if both have applied for jobs (1) and (2), and both prefer (1) to (2), I should prefer her getting (1) to his getting it. The difference is important, as we shall see, for where the D preferences are not SD preferences, the satisfaction of the agent's intrinsic first-order preferences is not necessarily affected by the satisfaction of his D preferences, but in the case of SD preferences it necessarily is. This is at the heart of the difficulties in PD. I shall return to this point.

We can now resume our discussion of the question of whether the difficulties for TRE (the Theory of Rational Egoism) are removed by an increase in our altruism, say, by moving from SF to AG or OR preferences. Let us begin with AG. As far as the relevant preferences are concerned, there is only one difference between the two: their first two rankings are reversed; [2,2] moves from second position in SF to first position in AG, and [1,4] from first position in SF to second position in AG.

If that is the whole difference between SF and AG, then in the real world it still is rational by TRE for S to confess; perhaps confessing would be the only rational course for him. For although, ex hypothesi, both S and O have AG preferences, from this it does not follow that *either knows* that this is so. For in the real world (though not in the world assumed by PD), it will quite often happen that one person does not know what sort of SD preferences the other has. But then it will be in accordance with reason for S to cooperate if and only if it is in accordance with reason for him to assume that the other will cooperate, too. If he has to choose in ignorance of these preferences, then it might seem to be merely a question of whether he prefers to play it safe or to go for the big chance. For the crucial alternatives are between Self's having and knowing that he has AG preferences while assuming either that O has and knows that he has and thinks that S also has AG preferences or assuming that O thinks that while he (O) has AG preferences, S has SF preferences. In the former case, if both are rational, both will cooperate, for then both will in fact get their top overall preference, [2,2]. In the latter case, however, O, if rational, will not cooperate, since O will expect S not to cooperate and since by not cooperating either, O will avoid getting his bottom SD preference, [4,1], and can get away, at worst, with his third-highest SD preference, [3,3], and (if O misjudged S and S cooperates) then O will even attain his second-highest SD preference, [1,4]. Thus, by cooperating, S risks reaping the worst for the chance of getting the best. The question is, "Which of these two assumptions about O is it most reasonable for S to make?" If it is equally reasonable for S to assume either strategy on the part of O, then cooperating and not cooperating would seem to be equally reasonable, a matter merely of personal temperament and outlook.

It seems to me, however, that these two assumptions may not be equally reasonable. For it is not reasonable (or so it seems to me) for S to assume that *p*, i.e., that O thinks that S has AG preferences, unless it is reasonable for S to assume that *q*, that is, (1) that O in fact has AG preferences *and*, (2) O does not think that S has SF preferences, *and* (3) O does not think that S thinks that O has SF preferences. But if that conditional is true, should not S conclude that the chances that O will think that S has AG preferences are less good than that O will not think this? For if I am right, O will believe that S has AG preferences only if O believes that *all* three propositions are true, whereas O will not think so if he believes *any one* of these propositions to be false. If this is sound, then it would seem not to be reasonable for S to cooperate even if both S and O *in fact* have AG preferences, but S lacks adequate reasons to think this about O. The mere change in the interagents' preferences from SF to AG thus appears not to remove the problem raised by action in accordance with TRE (the Theory of Rational Egoism), in PD′ situations.

AG does, however, have the following advantage over SF: the *assurance* that others have AG preferences removes the requirement of TRE, that each do whatever promotes his intrinsic first-order preferences. Hence, if interagents themselves have AG preferences and know that the others with whom they interact also do, then they could cooperate without running foul of TRE, as they would if they had SF preferences. It is plain, however, that even in this case the mere conclusion of a contract without enforcement would not provide the necessary assurance. For people with SF preferences would have reason to pretend that they are people with AG preferences, and adherents of TRE with AG preferences would need better assurance on this point than other people's word. In their absence it would not be reasonable for them to cooperate.

If what I have argued above is sound, then the main difference between SF and AG is the following: whereas in SF it is reasonable (by TRE) for each prisoner not to cooperate whether or not he has adequate assurance that the other will cooperate, in AG it is reasonable not to cooperate if one lacks the assurance that the other will cooperate, but not if one has that assurance. Thus, although AG players will not be tempted to break their contracts when they have adequate assurance that their contract partners will keep them, they will, if reasonable, break their contracts when they lack that assurance.

My two conclusions from this rather involved discussion are the following: first, the problem for TRE in PD′ situations is aggravated by certain types of SD (second-order self-involving distributive) preferences, particularly SF (self-favoring) preferences. For a follower of TRE with SF preferences cannot in reason cooperate even when, indeed particularly when, he has the assurance that others will do so. Such a person cannot thus honestly enter, or be accepted, without error, into a cooperative scheme whose success depends on *all* participants cooperating. For a person with such SD preferences is required by TRE to ignore that scheme's coordinative guidelines in PD' situations when he can do so with impunity, whether or not he has adequate assurance that others will follow them. It is therefore, as Hobbes saw, not in accordance with reason, according to TRE, for other people to allow such a person to enter or remain in such a cooperative enterprise. What Hobbes did not see (or wish to acknowledge), however, is that the existence of a coercive social order does not dispose of the theoretical problem raised by PD' for Principled Rational Egoists or even Principled Limited Rational Egoists with SF preferences.[27] Contrary to Hobbes's claim, it is not always necessarily contrary to reason (by TRE) for such a person to break the coordinative guidelines, even when they are enforced. It is always contrary to reason only if the system creates such certainty of discovery and such severity of punishment that he can always expect to do better for himself by following than by breaking the guidelines. However, as I suggested earlier, it would seem not to be in accordance with reason to create or maintain such a social order. So such a Hobbesian move would seem not to be a satisfactory way to deal with the SF version of PD'.

Second, a shift from TRE to TRP (Theory of Rationality as the maximization of admissible preferences)[28] coupled with a change in SD preferences would not seem to help either. For their modification, such as a shift from SF to AG preferences, would not suffice to remove the problem, although it would ease it. For we would still need adequately to enforce the guidelines in order to provide AGs with adequate assurance that, even if others had SF preferences, it would be in accordance with reason for adherents of TRP with AG preferences to follow them. However, given adequate sanctions and the assurance resulting from them, AGs (unlike SFs) would act contrary to reason if they did not follow their society's coordinative guidelines.

Is there, then, any further general shift in the direction of "altruism" of SD preferences that, while posing no problem for TRP, would make it reasonable for such "altruists" to cooperate with whatever others are

---

[27] But, as I said, Hobbes's second Law of Nature seems to imply that Hobbes regarded SF preferences as contrary to reason, so that the problem of PD' with SF preferences would arise only for people who had SD preferences that are contrary to reason. But it is not clear to me whether, and if so why, Hobbes should have supposed that people in a State of Nature could not have such SD preferences or that it was contrary to reason for them to suppose that other people had them.

[28] See p. 173ff.

doing so that there is no need for the coordinative guidelines to be suitably sanctioned? Sen's OR-preference pattern would seem to represent such a shift, for these SD preferences really do remedy the major "weakness" of AG preferences: dependence on mutual knowledge of like behavioral dispositions by others. It really would always be according to reason (by TRP) for an OR prisoner to cooperate, whatever his partner does. For, given his SD preferences, S gets his top overall preference, [2,2], if O does not confess and his second overall preference, [4,1], if O does confess, whereas if S confesses, he can only get his third or fourth overall preference, depending on whether O confesses or does not. Since by TRP it would be contrary to reason not to aim for the satisfaction of one's highest overall admissible preferences, confessing would be contrary to reason, because it would satisfy only his third or fourth, while not confessing would satisfy his first or second.[29]

Sen's paper does, however, support the general line of thought already adumbrated at the beginning of section 4, which holds that a person's rationality or irrationality, etc., cannot be a function of his actual preferences or desires. We have already seen in our discussion of AG that, if we want to resolve the PD′ paradox without abandoning TRP or invoking the political solution, then interagents must not have certain (e.g., SF-) preference patterns. I want now to ask if certain preference patterns themselves are contrary to reason, so that rationality cannot be defined as a function of actual preferences irrespective of their pattern. It seems to me that an OR pattern of overall preferences is contrary to reason because of the way an OR's first-order intrinsic preferences are related to his overall preferences by way of his SD preferences.

To get clearer about these questions, consider three further versions of PD′, which I shall call, respectively, OF (for Other-Favoring), OH (for Other-Hating), and SH (for Self-Hating). They are all importantly different reversals of SF. Here are their matrices shown together with SF for easier comparison:

		SF	OF	OH	SH
		S O	S O	S O	S O
S's {	1st Preference	[1,4]	[4,1]	[1,4]	[4,1]
	2nd Preference	[2,2]	[2,2]	[3,3]	[3,3]
	3rd Preference	[3,3]	[3,3]	[2,2]	[2,2]
	4th Preference	[4,1]	[1,4]	[4,1]	[1,4]

---

[29] Someone may object to this or any other such "psychological" solution on the grounds that in real life there are many multiperson situations, analogues to PD or PD′ and that they are not susceptible to this solution. This seems plausible but I cannot pursue the matter here.

Whereas in SF, S's overall preferences *mirror* his own first-order intrinsic preferences; in OF they mirror O's; in SH they mirror a *reversal* of his own; and in OH, a reversal of O's first-order intrinsic preferences.

Consider SH first. S's overall preferences are (at least in part) due to S's SD preferences. If these underlying SD preferences are themselves intrinsic ones, then they are groundlessly self-hating: S's actions are chosen *as* self-hating, *because* they are self-frustrating. I think our commonsense conviction that such preferences are irrational is correct. This is not so because self-hate is necessarily irrational: a person may have good reason to hate himself, perhaps for what he has done or for what sort of person he is, but then such SD preferences are derived, not intrinsic. The reasons for his self-hate may defeat the *intrinsic reasonableness* of his self-love. Nor is self-hate irrational just because in such a case one's second-order preferences conflict with and outweigh one's first-order intrinsic preferences. The vegetarian's wish he had intrinsic first-order preferences for vegetarian over meat dishes need not be contrary to reason. He may have excellent self-anchored reasons for his vegetarian convictions. Acting on them may be good for his health, or his conception of the good life may include an ideal self-conception which, for good reasons, excludes eating meat. But, again, this self-conception is not normally an intrinsic second-order preference, but a reason-based one: for example, that feeding the world on meat is inefficient, prohibitively costly, and unfair to the starving Third World; or that the slaughter of cattle and pigs and sheep is cruel and barbarous; or that killing sentient creatures is brutalizing and morally wrong, and that eating meat is conniving at and helping to finance such practices, and so on.

A meat lover's second-order preference for a first-order intrinsic preference for vegetarian over meat dishes is like an SH pattern of second-order preferences in that in both cases the second order is in rational tension with the related first-order preference and may outbalance it. But the former is unlike the latter in that it is based on reasons whereas the latter is intrinsic. In the vegetarian case the second-order preference, because of the reasons on which it is based, may defeat the natural rationality of the first-order preference though without necessarily having the stronger motivating force, as when the person continues to eat meat dishes despite his acknowledgment of the superiority of the reasons for vegetarianism. In our case of the self-hater, the second-order preference, which conflicts with the first-order preference is ex hypothesi intrinsic or based on inadequate reasons; it is a preference for frustrating all one's first-order preferences simply because they are that, or because one has certain weak or bad reasons against satisfying any of one's first-order preferences. I conclude that, in the absence of adequate specific reasons against a specific first-order preference, or of adequate general reasons for hating oneself and so against satisfying *any* of one's intrinsic first-order preferences, one has no reason for having a second-order preference that is in rational tension with one's first-order preferences. Such an SH pattern of SD preferences must therefore be regarded as contrary to reason.

This has three important corollaries: (1) SD preferences may be intrinsic or derived; to be in accordance with reason, intrinsic SD preferences must not conflict with first-order ones; derived ones, even if in conflict with first-order ones, are in accordance with reason only if they are based on adequate reasons showing the superiority (by TRP) over the first-order preferences with which they conflict; (2) a particular choice may be contrary to reason even if it maximizes the agent's actual overall preferences, because some of these, e.g., his SD preferences, may themselves be contrary to reason, as under 1; (3) the rationality of a person's set of preferences is not guaranteed by their internal consistency. The beef lover's preferences may be contrary to reason if he has a second-order preference for being a beef lover rather than a vegetarian when that second-order preference is based on unsound reasons, such as that a healthy diet for him must include beef or that his country's economy would suffer if people stopped eating beef.

Intrinsic OF preferences, too, it seems to me, are contrary to reason though this is not quite so obvious. While in SF, S gives a uniquely favored position to *his own*, in OF he gives the same favored position to O's, that is, someone *else's* first-order preferences. In chapter 4, it will be remembered, I argued that this need not be contrary to reason, as when one loves someone more than one loves oneself and when the flourishing of this love is an important part of one's conception of the good life. However, in the absence of adequate reasons for such a reversal in particular cases, it would appear to be contrary to reason. Furthermore, if one has an OF preference for a particular person without having a reason for this, but simply because he is another, one would seem to be committed to adopt this SD pattern with respect to anyone, even those concerning whom one lacked a special reason either to have an OF or some other less extreme other-regarding SD preference, such as, say, OR. But any such intrinsic other-favoring preference would seem contrary to reason if not absurd.

The SF pattern thus has a very special position among SD preferences.

It would appear to be the one pattern which does not, as such, stand in need of rational defense. (Of course, if one's intrinsic first-order preferences are inadmissible, they not only stand in need of rational defense, they cannot be rationally defended.) This is so, of course, precisely because it reflects the agent's first-order intrinsic preferences. This throws a new light on the importance of Sen's arguments to the effect that people with SF preferences (for instance, those interacting in PD) would do better, even in terms of their first-order intrinsic preferences, if they acted *as if* they had AG or OR preferences. If Sen's arguments were sound, he would indeed have provided the necessary rational defense for having AG or OR preferences or for acting as if one had them. However, as we saw, Sen failed in the case of AG preferences. Let us see whether he succeeded with OR preferences.

OR preferences do indeed ensure the satisfaction to a higher degree of the prisoners' overall preferences, and do so independently of what each prisoner believes are the overall and the SD preferences of the other. But, if my argument in the last few paragraphs is sound, this apparent strength is really a weakness from the point of view of practical reason, even if it is not by TRE or TRP. For although an OR prisoner would in terms of his overall preferences do well by cooperating whatever O does, he would in some cases not do well in terms of his intrinsic first-order preferences, as when he interacts with an SF Other, for he might well do so one-sidedly, thus satisfying only his fourth, his lowest intrinsic first-order preference, whereas O, who presumably would confess, would then satisfy his top intrinsic first-order preference. But if an OR's overall preferences[30]—which are in conflict with his own intrinsic first-order preferences—lack the support of adequate self-anchored reasons, then they are contrary to reason and the OR prisoner lacks adequate reason to cater to them. But this seems a strong reason against cultivating an OR pattern of overall preferences and also, in their absence, of *acting as if one had them.* Of course, if interagents knew of one another that they were ORs, then cooperating would give them their top overall preference. But if both had such knowledge of others' preferences, something less perverse and dangerous—such as AG—would suffice to give both interagents the satisfaction of their

---

[30] I here ignore the complicated question of how we would express an OR's SD preferences. It is not immediately clear how his overall intrinsic preferences could emerge from his first-order intrinsic preferences on the basis of some suitable SD preference. But what else other than SD preferences could produce the difference between his first-order and his overall preference patterns?

first overall preferences, and what is more, preferences that are not in rational tension with one another.

I conclude that the introduction of OR preferences cannot, any more than that of AG preferences, dispel the appearance of paradox which TRE and TRP generate in PD situations. For relying on OR preferences could resolve the PD problem only if a person's practical rationality could be conceived in terms of the maximal satisfaction of one's actual overall preferences, quite independently of their internal structure, quite independently, for instance, of how one's second-order (including SD) preferences are related to one's intrinsic first-order preferences and to one another, and so independently of whether these second-order preferences are themselves in accordance with reason. But that, it seems to me, would be to erect rationality on an unsound foundation.

Section 5.   Conditional Good Will

What then, would be the ideally rational SD preference pattern? We first consider what we may regard as the "standard" case. Its conditions are as follows: there is interaction; people's actions are independent of one another; many people are indifferent about one another's well-being and/or are ignorant of one another's SD preferences; there are no socially recognized and adequately sanctioned uniform coordinating guidelines; and/or, even where people can easily determine such guidelines for themselves (as in PD), they lack the assurance that others will follow them. In such a situation, any SD-preference pattern other than SF would be contrary to reason since in this standard situation—where "other things are equal" e.g., the other is not one of the comparatively few whom one loves—it would be contrary to (self-anchored) reason to put anyone else's concerns as high as, let alone higher than, one's own.

However, since, when generalized, interaction on an SF-preference pattern leads to suboptimal results in PD situations, there is then reason for everyone to try to change this standard situation so as to make it according to reason to act in ways that would generate both individually and collectively optimal results, as would be achieved in PD by all cooperating. If, as I have argued, changes in one's second-order preferences will not suffice to achieve this, then three other changes would seem to be needed or at any rate helpful: the promulgation by a rational order of uniform coordinative guidelines generally recognized as defeating what are reasons in the standard situation, the creation of the assurance that people, whether ideally rational or not, will follow these guidelines by attaching suitable sanctions to them, and a suitable modification of SF preferences to make the effectiveness of the sanctions less crucial. For if we all retain our SF preferences and know that we all do, then we ourselves are not trustworthy, and we know others not to be either. But then it would be contrary to reason for others who are trustworthy to include *us* in a cooperative scheme capable of ensuring optimal results, since these results depend on all their members being sufficiently trustworthy, even without perfectly effective sanctions. Similarly, if some people with whom we interact are not trustworthy, then it would be contrary to reason to include *them* in our cooperative scheme. If a group consisting entirely of untrustworthy people nevertheless set up such a cooperative scheme, then the best they can hope for is the sort of Hobbesian order (or disorder) I described earlier. If a mixed group, some trustworthy, some untrustworthy, forms such a cooperative scheme, then the trustworthy ones will tend to be exploited by the untrustworthy ones.

Grant, then, that reason requires not only a change of external conditions but also a modification, on a basis of reciprocity, of interagents' SF preferences. But exactly what is the ideally rational change? Hobbes appears to have hit upon the minimal change necessary: the mutual laying down, on a basis of reciprocity, of those parts of what he called the Right of Nature that stand in the way of the optimal working of a cooperative scheme. But, of course, Hobbes's second Law of Nature tells us what reason requires us to do in "ideal" circumstances and what it requires in others. In conditions of imperfect assurance of reciprocity and of imperfect rationality of our own and other people's preference structure, it tells us to do things that have suboptimal outcomes. Applying the preceding reflections to Hobbes's point, we can say that in these "ideal" circumstances reason requires that wherever the coordinating guidelines, whose universal adoption would ensure optimality, require us to set aside or modify our own actual SD preferences, we do so even if we cannot also suitably change our conflicting first-order ones. We must, if necessary, change or curb our SF preferences so that we are prepared always to follow the coordinative guidelines—of course, provided others do likewise—even when our current SF preferences would require us to ignore them and especially when we know or have reason to believe that others are following them.

I call this modification of SF preferences an attitude of "Limited

Conditional Good Will." It is limited in that it is not a disposition to promote or protect other people's good on all occasions, but only when it is required by certain coordinative rules that apply to one. And it is conditional in that one's willingness to do so is dependent on a certain contingency, namely, that all others to whom the rules apply do likewise, or, if not all do so, that those who don't do not profit from their nonconformity and preferably are treated in a way intended to remotivate them (e.g., punished). This attitude need not, of course, be based on a concern for others, though the practical effects will be the same as if it were. It need only be an attitude based on the recognition that oneself and others alike are dependent on one another for our attainment of the good life, and that each of us should therefore be prepared, on the basis of reciprocity, to contribute his or her share to the good life of others by making the necessary modification in the untrammeled pursuit of his or her own good life. The main modification of SF preferences required by reason is thus only the willingness to recognize the fact that in PD and similar situations all will fare better by everyone following certain coordinative guidelines, than by each making his (uncoordinated) best reply.

Thus Limited Conditional Good Will is not a straightforward other-regarding or benevolent, let alone an altruistic, SD pattern, like OF or OR, or even like AG. Nor is it a utilitarian willingness to generate the greatest total of preference-satisfaction with no concern about whose preferences thereby get satisfied or are left unsatisfied. It is, rather, a willingness not to seek to achieve the good life by making what one thinks the best reply, in those types of situation in which everyone's doing so has suboptimal effects, but instead to follow uniform publicly recognized guidelines, designed to achieve optimal outcomes (or at any rate better ones than would result from independent reasoning by all) and where there is adequate assurance that all concerned, or a sufficient number of them, will follow these guidelines. Persons of limited conditional goodwill may thus be motivated primarily by concern for their own good life, and their conforming with the guidelines is a contribution to the concerns of others, which (since they may not care about these others) is made mainly or only because the realization of their own ends is seen to depend on the contributions made by others, and because they are prepared to recognize the reasonableness of reciprocity in this matter.

At the same time, behavior so motivated is not a case of treating others merely as means to our ends, for one asks for and accepts their contribution to the promotion of one's own good on a basis of reciprocity. Such interagents are not using or exploiting one another, but participating in a mutually beneficial scheme, even when they don't do so from love, affection, kindness, benevolence, or pity. It is a paler substitute for these in those cases when all they feel for one another is the respect they have come to recognize as reasonable if and to the extent that they all play their part in such a mutually beneficial cooperative scheme. They have come to recognize this respect as reasonable because they recognize one another as fully rational beings who conform their behavior to self-anchored reasons except in those cases in which everyone's doing so has suboptimal consequences, when they think it contrary to reason not to conform to known coordinative guidelines which eliminate the suboptimality of consequences, provided only they have adequate assurance that others do likewise.

If we suppose, as seems plausible, that the guidelines that overrule self-anchored reasons would sometimes be followed only very grudgingly and sometimes not followed at all, then an additional change may be necessary. For, given their function, these coordinative guidelines really will at times, perhaps often, conflict with people's self-anchored reasons. That additional change could be brought about by a suitable method of socialization and/or the imposition of appropriate sanctions. But if we are not to have an incoherent system of practical reasons, the coordinative guidelines must be recognized not merely as self-anchored reasons that defeat others in virtue of the sanctions attached to them, as Hobbes may sometimes seem to imply, but as practical reasons that from their nature, independently of the sanctions, defeat self-anchored ones when they conflict. Since, as we supposed, these guidelines are developed, promulgated, and sanctioned by a society, we can think of the reasons based on them as society anchored.

Conflicts between society- and self-anchored reasons differ in certain respects from conflicts between two or more self-anchored reasons. One is that people may occasionally hope, sometimes with good reason, that they can ignore the society-anchored reasons without suffering the consequences of not following them that one inevitably suffers if one follows the less weighty *rather than* the weightier self-anchored reason, and even when one follows the weightier, *thereby* ignoring the less weighty one. The usual reason for this hope is, of course, that the sanctions may not be effective.[31]

The second difference is that such society-anchored reasons are

---

[31] A less usual reason is that someone may be perfectly willing to endure the sanction, as when someone hates another so much that he will choose certain death rather than refrain from murdering his enemy.

dependent in a sense in which self-anchored reasons are independent. One has an independent reason to do a certain thing if one has it independently of whether other people have and follow the same reason on the same or on other occasions. The reason I have cut down on carbohydrates is an independent one because I have it and benefit from acting on it even if no one else has it or acts on it. By contrast, a society-anchored reason is more or less dependent on others also having it, *and* following it when they have it.

The third difference resulting from the other two is that the question of whether or not we conform is always also other people's business and so our compliance is inevitably of some (greater or lesser) importance to others, and theirs to us, so that compliance is of importance to all parties in a cooperative scheme whereas this is not so in a system of merely self-anchored practical reasons.

Note that such reasons though society-anchored may (and perhaps must) also be indirectly self-anchored, and this in two respects. The first is that their primary appeal may be of the same kind: that following them promises a better chance of leading a good life for those governed by them. The second is that *what* they recommend us to do is determined by the contribution which the doing of it by all who have the reason, makes to each agent's chances of leading a good life as he conceives of it. However, they are not "directly" self-anchored, because the direct contribution of action in accordance with them is to *other* people's lives, whether or not the agent cares about them. Nevertheless, if sound, they are indirectly self-anchored because each person with limited conditional goodwill follows them mainly or only because he assumes that (by and large) each person governed by them is willing to follow them and so to contribute to others, on condition that others do likewise. All are willing to contribute on a basis of reciprocity or mutuality, and those (necessarily few, if the system is to work) who do not, will (by and large) be dealt with in a way designed not to make their failure to comply profitable for them or harmful to their victims.

The question then arises whether society-anchored reasons can be thus indirectly self-anchored and if so, exactly how. How could they be, one may ask, when they are in conflict with self-anchored ones? Well, is it not enough that everyone will fare better if such society-anchored reasons are recognized in and by the society that creates (that is, formulates, promulgates, and sanctions) them? Can we not say that what makes such reasons superior to self-anchored ones is that everyone fares better if everyone acts in accordance with them rather than in accordance with the self-anchored reasons with which they conflict?

I think this Hobbes-like argument is on the right track, but it has at least one very serious flaw. Surely, a slave in a slave society or an untouchable in a rigid caste society would not rightly regard all the coercive rules of her society, at least not all those concerning slavery or the subordination of untouchables, as adequate reasons to do what they require of her. Would it not be a mistake to regard such a society's customary or legal requirements as reasons defeating their self-anchored ones, even if life really were better even for slaves or untouchables, relative to some plausible benchmark, than if they were not so regarded? Why would it be a mistake to hold that the requirements of any such coercive social order are *rightly* regarded and so *really constitute* adequate reasons for members of such an order to act accordingly?

The mistake, I think, is this. If these requirements are really to defeat self-anchored reasons when they conflict, then *everyone* must have *adequate* self-anchored reasons to want them generally so regarded. Now if my earlier argument was sound, then it may well be the case that, whatever (within certain limits) the nature of the social order, everyone is better off under it than in a Hobbesian state of nature or at any rate in a society that recognized only self-anchored practical reasons, and still better off if the social requirements are regarded as defeating reasons than if they are regarded as necessary but irksome obstacles to promoting one's own good or the good life as one conceives it. Nevertheless, this shows only that everyone has *some*, but not that he has *adequate*, reason to want these requirements regarded as reasons that defeat conflicting self-anchored ones.

What, then, would make them adequate? It seems that the society and its sanctioned rules would have to meet certain standards of excellence. The following is a very high standard which, if reached, would yield adequate reasons so to regard them: that the society be so organized that everyone has *the best possible self-anchored* reason *anyone* could in reason *demand* for wanting the social requirements regarded as paramount reasons, namely, the best possible reasons everyone could have. A person's self-anchored reason for wanting the social requirements so regarded would be the better, the more favorable the social rules are to him and those he cares about. Of course, a person could always ask for better self-anchored reasons than he already has, for there seems to be virtually no limit to the advantages and privileges a society may grant him. It does seem, however, that there is a rational limit to the improvement of a self-anchored reason anyone can in such a context demand: he cannot *in reason* demand a better reason than *everyone* can have. It would seem, therefore, that the best self-anchored reason *anyone* can in reason *demand* for wanting the social requirements generally regarded as paramount reasons (that is, the best self-anchored reason *everyone* can *have*) is that the social order be not simply for the good of everyone (almost any social order might achieve that) but for the good of everyone *alike*—that, in other words, it be *equitable*. The main reason for this is that socially recognized and suitably sanctioned coordinative guidelines for PD and similar situations are intended to guide people to promote the best possible life for themselves but burdened by a contribution by all participants in such a cooperative scheme to one another's good life. The reason why they must make that contribution to other people's lives is that everyone would fare worse if they did not make it. For this reason, everyone must admit that the guidelines based on such social rules must override self-anchored reasons whenever they conflict but (unless there is another way of showing that they constitute overruling practical reasons) they must indirectly be grounded in adequate self-anchored reasons. Everyone who is to have adequate reason to regard these social rules as society-based reasons must have adequate self-anchored reasons to want these rules recognized as paramount over self-anchored ones with which they conflict. But no one has reason to accept any such reason as adequate unless it is as good as anyone can have without thereby making someone else's reason less good than his. For why should any fully rational person welcome a transition from a system of merely self-anchored reasons to one in which self-anchored ones are defeated by society-anchored ones or resist a transition in the opposite direction, unless the contribution to other people's lives they require of him is no greater than that which they require of others, and that general conformity to them equally improves other people's lives? It seems that if a social order comes up to this standard, then everyone has adequate self-anchored reason to want its requirements generally recognized as reasons defeating self-anchored ones. And in that case they are rightly so regarded, and therefore really are such paramount reasons.

However, it seems plain that this is an unjustifiably high standard of adequacy for recognizing social requirements as such paramount reasons. For one thing, it is not clear that a society's requirements could be so formulated that the "sacrifices" (frustrations of self-anchored reasons) each is asked to shoulder are the same and that the improvements thereby made to each life also are the same. Even if such an arrangement is possible, no one may know what it would be like, or how one could get to it from the current social structure, or whether one had reached it as far as this is possible. Again, it will often be very difficult to tell how close to one's conception of the good life one would get by strategic reasoning based on self-anchored reasons in a social order that recognized only self-anchored reasons but also had sanctioned social rules not recognized as society-anchored reasons, and then it would be difficult to tell just how much better or worse one's life is made when these social requirements come to be recognized as society-based reasons, or how great a further improvement or deterioration would be brought about if the rules were changed so as to be equitable.

All the same, the advantages of having the requirements so recognized would seem to be great and should, it seems to me, be allowed to outweigh some of the disadvantages to those whom the social order appears to treat less favorably. So perhaps we should be satisfied with the following lower standard. Since equity is hard to attain and since it is also hard to know when it is and when it is not attained, there should be institutions (such as a supreme court) set up to keep check on the equity of the guidelines and empowered to set in motion recognized processes of correction. Clearly, this would seem to be a minimum condition of regarding inequitable guidelines as practical reasons defeating self-anchored ones. But if the machinery for detecting and correcting them is well designed and reasonably effective, and if the society encourages critical discussion of both the social requirements and the institution of correction, then this may well be the best we can do to get as close as possible to a truly equitable society, especially in view of the vagueness and unavoidable contentiousness of the idea of equity. But in that case, even the requirements of such an inequitable society which, however, is trying as hard as possible to become equitable may constitute paramount society-based reasons. If so, then there would also be justification for the imposition of appropriately sanctioning the social rules that impose these requirements. If this is right, then it solves the problem I raised in section 2 of this chapter.

This concludes my account of the order of reason. It also concludes, for the time being, my discussion of society-anchored reasons and their relation to self-anchored ones. I shall, however, return to this question in Book Two where I attempt to show that the moral enterprise is the same as the enterprise that gives rise to society-anchored reasons.

Book Two

The Moral Order

PART ONE:
A THEORY
OF MORALITY

CHAPTER SIX

The Social and the Moral Order

Section 1. The Concept of Morality

If our examination of reason, in book 1, has been on the right track, we have established two important points. First, there is no necessary connection between rationality and self-interest: even practical rationality does not *consist in* doing what one has adequate reason to think will be in one's best interest. Our distinctions in book 1 between self-interested and self-anchored reasons, and between these and society-anchored reasons, loosens the often supposed equivalence between a practical reason for someone to do a certain thing and an adequate (cognitive) reason to believe that her doing that thing will be in her best interest, as that latter term has most frequently been interpreted, that is, in terms of maximizing her happiness or the satisfaction of the preferences she happens to have.

Second, our account of irrationality as a particularly flagrant way of performing contrary to reason, that is, contrary to the balance of reasons one has on a particular occasion, makes it plausible to say that it is not always irrational not to do what morality requires of or recommends to us. But, of course, this is so, it will be remembered, only because we may have both requiring moral reason to do something and weighty, possibly even requiring, nonmoral (e.g., prudential) reason not to do it. Hence not doing on a particular occasion what morality requires of us need not be irrational because, even if the moral reasons for doing it defeat the nonmoral ones against doing it, and not doing it is therefore contrary to reason, still, because of the weighty nonmoral reasons against doing it that are present on this occasion, this contrariety to reason is not sufficiently flagrant to amount to irrationality, in the sense in which we have here, quite naturally, interpreted it.

However, even if all this is accepted, as I now assume, the question remains whether moral reasons always defeat at least all self-interested and perhaps all self-anchored practical reasons. They would, of course, if they were of the sort which I have called society anchored. To answer the central question raised in the Introduction—what is the relation between reason and morality?—we must be clear about the nature and force of moral considerations. But that question, whether moral considerations are practical reasons and, if they are, whether their force is that of society-anchored ones, cannot be answered without a thorough examination of the nature of morality and of the place of moral considerations in the scheme of practical reasons developed in Book One. In this chapter, I therefore turn to these broad questions.

My first task is to spell out my conception of the concept of morality, along the lines I followed in Book One for the concept of reason. In this case, too, there appears to be a part of the concept that would seem to be well entrenched and adequately established in our linguistic practice, and which someone's conception of it therefore gets either right or wrong, but also another part concerning which one's conception spells out a more or less detailed interpretation or specification. The first part concerns what it is for some person or society to guide their thinking, feeling, and acting in a specifically moral way, while the second part concerns the criteria by which we distinguish sound from unsound ways of being guided in this way. The first is concerned with distinctions such as those between the moral and the nonmoral, the second with such as those between the moral and the immoral.

As before, we must bear in mind that the family of relatively specific concepts that make up the general concept of morality is a large one, with some of our terms, such as the adjective "moral" itself, referring to concepts in both parts. Thus, in the first ("descriptive") part, there are, besides the moral/*non*moral distinction, also concepts such as that of (individual and social) moralities, the moral institution, the moral order, the moral enterprise, and the moral point of view. While in the second ("normative") part there are, besides the moral/*im*moral distinction, also those of right/wrong, duty/freedom, obligations/rights, justice/injustice, commendability/reprehensibility, virtue/vice, responsibility/irresponsibility, innocence/guilt, and many more. In my elucidation of the concept of morality, I hope to shed light on some of these, and on the relations between them.

Section 2.   A Moral Order

I begin with what, for reasons that will become clear as we proceed, I consider the central concept of the first ("descriptive") part of the concept of morality, namely, that of a moral order. In Book One, I discussed the parallel (though at first sight perhaps less obviously called for) concept of "an order of reason" (or "a rational order"), and we can analogously speak of legal and political orders. Philosophers have conceived of these orders in a variety of ways. Plato's Theory of Forms conceived of "the order of reason" as a single system of actually existing perfect prototypes of things whose relations to one another and to the good were from their nature necessarily in accordance with reason and so, he thought, could serve us as a model of how to think and act in accordance with it. In the same vein, the Divine Command, and Natural Law, theories of morality conceive of "the" moral order as a single actually existing perfect prototype of a legal system with a perfect legislator, perfect laws, and a perfect system of enforcement, which they offer as a model for our own moral thinking and acting.

In my view, the idea of a moral order is not only useful but indispensable for our understanding of morality. However, it seems to me, as it does to many contemporary philosophers, that such a Platonistic construal is ultimately unhelpful. Its main asset must have seemed to be its providing a criterion by which to judge the soundness or acceptability of our thinking and acting. However, it only seems to do so, for it succeeds in creating an indubitable and infallible authority of this prototype only by (stipulatively) defining it so, and by making it altogether distinct and separate from our ordinary fallible thinking and acting, but thereby also making it useless for improving our actual practice. As soon as that gulf is bridged—as in the claim that *we* (humans) have "the light of reason" or that the precepts of reason and morality are written "on the hearts of man"—these prototypes are brought down to earth and made useful for application to our own guidelines, but by that same move their infallibility is destroyed and they are opened up to criticism, doubt, and disagreement, for whose elimination they were introduced in the first place.

I therefore think we would do better to construe the moral, the way we already construe the legal order, namely, as a social order that satisfies certain conditions. This allows for the possibility that many societies very different from one another can satisfy them and so qualify as legal and moral orders. This approach has the drawback of seeming to open the door wide to relativism, since it begins from the actually recognized and accepted moral guidelines within a society. But this relativism is less invidious than it may look at first sight, since neither the criteria by which we tell whether a social order is a legal, moral, or political one nor those by which we evaluate such orders need themselves be society relative. But I am jumping ahead of myself.

With these preliminaries out of the way, we can begin to examine the first of two questions crucial for our inquiry: under what conditions does a social order constitute a moral one, and how do we assess the merits and demerits of different moral orders?

What, then, is a social order? I conceive of it as a certain character or quality possessed by every society. By "a society," I do not of course here mean a voluntary association such as Alcoholics Anonymous or the American Automobile Association. The societies about which we are now talking are associations of which people typically become members by being born into them and which they join or leave voluntarily only in (fortunately, still) exceptional circumstances. Societies in this sense now are usually political orders. In view of the gapless occupation of the earth by territorial states, it is now virtually impossible for anyone to live outside every existing state, perhaps in what Hobbes and others have called a state of nature. For even legally stateless persons must now live in or under a state. The reluctance of most states to welcome new members or residents, and the difficulties many states put in the way of anyone's leaving them, highlight the importance of what Albert O. Hirschman[1] felicitously calls "exit" and "voice." Since exit is usually difficult and costly, the demand for voice, for having a say in the structure of one's state, becomes an important interest and is naturally conceived of as a natural right.

We can think of such (more or less involuntary) societies as Strawsonian Individuals,[2] that is, entities resembling things and persons that exist for a time and can be reidentified during that time. The distinctive nature of a particular person may be called her personality, that of a particular society its culture. (Here, of course, I have in mind, not the nature of personhood or of societyhood, that is, what it is that makes something a person or a society, but something that distinguishes one person or society from another.) Either may undergo changes during a given period, although both remain in some sense one and the same throughout the change. Conversely, just as two or more ("numerically") different persons may have ("qualitatively") the same or at any rate closely similar personalities, so two or more ("numerically") different societies may have ("qualitatively") the same or closely similar cultures.

---

[1] Albert O. Hirschman, *Exit, Voice, and Loyalty: Responses to Decline in Firms, Organizations, and States* (Cambridge, Mass.: Harvard University Press, 1970). For a detailed critique, see Brian Barry, "Exit, Voice, and Loyalty," review article in *British Journal of Political Science* 4 (1974), reprinted in Brian Barry, *Democracy and Power*, Essays in Political Theory 1 (Oxford: Clarendon Press, 1991), chapter 7, 187–221.

[2] P. F. Strawson, *Individuals* (London: Methuen, 1959).

We can (roughly) distinguish between different parts of a society's culture: its art, its religion, its knowledge and understanding of the world in which the society is placed, and so on. For our purposes here, the most important part is its *mores*, the generally recognized and more or less suitably sanctioned directives regulating the members' behavior and attitudes which the society teaches its new members in the course of their growing up and being socialized. This part of the culture includes the society's customs, traditions, manners, law, religion, and morality. I take it that a group of people is a society if and only if they constitute a Strawsonian Indvidual possessing a culture, and that a society is a social order only if it can be said to have mores. I am inclined to think that nothing could be a society, however primitive, unless it had mores, but I shall leave open just what kind of impossibility this might be.[3] If my thought is sound, then every society has or is a social order.

I shall not examine the difficult question of how societies and social orders (as opposed to countries, polities, peoples, nations, communities, clans, and so on) are individuated, even roughly. It seems least difficult to explain, though even that only roughly, how we individuate societies that are political orders or states. The main question is, what changes such a society may undergo and yet remain (numerically) the same. Obviously, a society's identity is not normally changed by visits and immigrations, by births of babies born to members or residents, or by their deaths and emigrations, nor necessarily by the acquisition or loss of territory or by changes in the constitution, even revolutionary ones. However, one may think of, say, France after the French Revolution, as being a (numerically) different state from that before it, even though one also thinks of it as being the same society, nation, and perhaps culture (but are we even tempted to count cultures, as we count states and perhaps nations?) Nor need states, like persons, persist continuously throughout their existence. Poland, after its several divisions, may be considered the same state as before them, and Austria the same state after its "liberation" from Nazi Germany as before its annexation. Group identity, even in its more fully developed cases, would seem to be considerably less sharply delineated than personal identity.

Given the conquest of the earth by territorial states, I shall think of the identity of societies as that of states or political orders. I suggest that moral

---

[3] The impossibility may be the same, or nearly the same, as the impossibility, according to Hart, of a municipal system of "beings constituted such as men are" where there are no sanctions in place to provide at least minimal "forms of protection for persons, property, and promises." *The Concept of Law* (Oxford: Oxford University Press, 1961) 189–95.

orders, too, can be individuated along the same lines as states, that we think of each single state as also being a single moral order, even though, as is now so often the case, the moralities of its individual members and of its religious and ethnic subgroups differ so radically from one another that we may be inclined to say that a given state has (and that not just its members and subgroups have) several different moralities.

I shall not attempt to individuate moralities of social subgroups because, as we shall see, they are composed of moral convictions or principles and corresponding practices which may overlap with one another in a great variety of ways. Those who agree that abortion is not always wrong may disagree with one another on more things than they disagree with most of those who think it always wrong. But we must for the moment postpone, until we are clearer about moralities, any discussion of whether there is something in every order individuated in the way suggested that can be called *its* morality, and if so, what is the relation between that morality (if there is one) and the moralities of the individuals and subgroups in that society.

Section 3.   Mores and the Moral Order

Suppose, then, that every society is a social order and so has its own more or less peculiar system of mores. Are we adding anything, and if so what, when we think of it as also a moral order? Or, to put it differently, could any social order (any society with mores) fail to be a moral order?

It will be helpful to begin by examining the analogous relation in the political domain. A social order is a political one if and only if it has the specifically political institution, that is, if and only if it is a state. Bear in mind, though, that we sometimes think of the state (as Marx did) as a certain sort of *part* of *any* political order: its specifically political institution, made up of its government and governmental apparatus, its various ministries with their personnel, the armed forces, the judiciary, the police force, and so on. But we can also think of a state as a particular society with political institutions, that is, as *the whole* of a *particular* political order. Similarly, we can think of "the moral institution" as a certain sort of part of a social order, a part that would presumably be missing from any premoral social order (if there can be such a thing), just as *the* state is missing from a prepolitical and from Marx's truly communist (classless) social order in which the state has withered away. But we can also think of "a moral order" as constituted by any social order that has the specifically moral institution, just as we think of "a political order" as any social order that has the specifically political institution we call "the state." Note, however, that we have no special name, comparable to "the state," for the specifically moral institution.

Thus, comparison with a political order suggests that we look for the moral analogue of the state, that is, for the specifically moral institution. If the analogy holds, then no society can be a moral order unless it has this sort of institution. But what can that institution be? Is it simply the society's mores or could a society have mores without being a moral order? In other words, does a moral order have an additional institution, one that goes beyond the society's mores? (I ignore the question of whether a society could be a moral order without mores since I have assumed that no group of people—or society in the sense here in question—could be a social order unless it had mores.)

What institution does a society have when it has mores? We can perhaps say of the mores of a social order, at all levels of complexity, that its members' behavior and attitudes are (more or less effectively) regulated by rules which, as they know of one another, they have learned in the course of their socialization and which, as they know and know of one another that they know, are backed by certain negative or positive social sanctions, the former consisting in other members' unfavorable responses to culpable nonconformity, the latter in their favorable responses to meritorious conformity, with these rules.

We can best characterize the institution involved in a society's mores by describing the roles which constitute it and the tasks specific to them. There is a primary role, call it that of "the social agent," and several second-order roles designed to improve and transmit from one generation to the next the ability and the willingness to accomplish the task of the social agent. That task is, of course, to behave, and to cultivate attitudes, in accordance with the directives embedded in the mores. The tasks of the secondary roles are the teaching of these directives to the young, the monitoring and judging of social agents in the performance of their specific role task (conforming to the mores), the carrying out of the negative social sanctions for others' culpable failure to conform and of the positive social sanctions for meritorious conformity, and the improvement of the guidelines of the mores themselves. There may be higher-order roles, such as the monitoring of the performance of those doing the teaching or carrying out the sanctions.

To answer the question whether a social order could fail to be a moral order, it will be helpful to look more closely at the evolution of a social order because, it seems, once a society reaches a certain higher stage, it necessarily is a moral order. Our two main questions, therefore, would seem to be whether a social order could conceivably fail to be a moral order and, if so, what would have to be taken from or added to a social order in such a transition from its simpler to its more complex stage. An answer to that last question should make it clear what is that feature whose addition or loss makes the differences between a social order that is and one that is not a moral order.

Consider, then, a society that is what I call an order of "Pure Custom," that is, one the whole of whose mores takes the form of custom. In such a social order, members learn the regulations of behavior and attitudes they are to live by, partly through other people's example and through the social responses they encounter when they culpably or ignorantly violate these regulations or when they meritoriously or pleasingly conform to them, and partly by being taught explicitly formulated rules. In such an order there often (but not necessarily always) will also be suitable ways of characterizing these practices. People will learn that in violating the mores, a person has failed to do *the done thing,* that what he did was *against custom,* that it was *not customary,* and that violators of custom should expect to encounter certain unfavorable reactions from their fellows. In such a society everyone is required and expected to conform unquestioningly to these generally recognized guidelines which are changed and sanctioned in the haphazard, relatively unorganized and unsystematized, but often extremely severe ways characteristic of such simple unsophisticated orders of Pure Custom.

H. L. A. Hart[4] illuminatingly describes the transition from such an order to a legal one. In his view (and mine), what such a simple order lacks, is any role specialization of the three distinguishable functions performed under the society's mores: the function of the ex officio enforcer (police, prisons, punishment), that of the ex officio judge (arbitrators, courts, juries), and that of the ex officio law changer (the legislator). In a Pure Customary Order, anyone may and perhaps should perform at least the first two functions, each when the circumstances are appropriate. As a result, all three functions are likely to be performed inadequately. In the absence of "specialist officials," application and enforcement of the mores are likely to be sporadic, haphazard, and unjust; lynch mobs, vigilante justice, and "democratic people's courts" are survivals of, or reversions to, this nonspecialist administration of the mores. Lastly, attempts to change

---

[4] Hart, *Concept of Law,* 89–96.

the mores, apart from their almost certain ineffectuality, are likely to be risky because they are probably seen as attempts to overthrow the social order, and therefore rare.

An order of Pure Custom develops into a legal order when these functions are entrusted to officials, that is, persons who alone are authorized to perform them, and who do so "ex officio," "in their official capacity," as we say, while the ordinary members' role in performing these functions is correspondingly reduced. What is left for them is, ideally (in a democratic legal order), only the discussion of the merits and demerits of the laws and participation in the accepted procedures for the appointment and dismissal of some or all officials.

Despite these changes, there is an important continuity: the directives embedded in the mores, both of an order of Pure Custom and of a legal order,[5] are essentially "positive," that is, generally recognized, in the sense of being generally known and accepted, and so amount to an at least minimally effective or operative method of social coordination and regulation. A member of either type of social order acquires knowledge — in the case of Pure Custom by the process of socialization, in the case of law by that same process or by consulting the appropriate experts (lawyers) — of what sorts of behavior and attitudes are required of, and what forbidden or permitted to, the society's members.

In an order of Pure Custom the way to find out what Custom requires, forbids, or permits is to find out *whatever the members, in more or less nearly uniform agreement, think* that Custom requires, forbids, or permits. A legal order, by contrast, provides a more reliable way to determine what law requires, forbids, or permits; it is a matter of the authoritative say-so of the relevant officials, namely, legislators and courts. Putting it very loosely, legislators provide the general rules by which individuals wishing to be law abiding can guide their own behavior, while courts give authoritative rulings when there are uncertainties or disagreements about what the law intends or provides in particular cases. Because of these authoritative rulings, there is scope for a further function of legal specialists: to advise laypersons on how courts would probably rule in their case if they took legal action, and to represent their interests in court.

There is a reasonably clear difference between the question of what the Customs or laws of a particular society are at a particular time, and of what they morally ought to be, even if what they are at that time is what the

---

[5] For complications arising in a legal order, see Hart, *Concept of Law*, chapter 6, section 3, "The Pathology of a Legal System," 114–20.

relevant authority—the members collectively or the appropriate official—
"found" or "decreed" them to be on the grounds that that is what in their
judgment they morally ought to be. For even then nothing is, simply
because it morally ought to be, that society's Custom or law, and nothing
fails to be its Custom or law simply because it morally ought not to be. But,
of course, in a particular case, a given statute (or even—mirabile dictu
—all the statues) of a given legal order may in fact be what they ought
to be.

Once a social order becomes a legal one and so, of course, is no longer
one of Pure Custom, part of its mores has become its law, but only a part;
law has not swallowed up all of the mores. The remaining extralegal part
of the mores is what we now call "custom" which, however, differs from
Pure Custom in tending to regulate only matters that are relatively
unimportant in both of two respects: it does not matter much just what is
according and what contrary to custom, and it does not matter much when
some or even many people do not do what is customary. Thus, it usually
does not matter very much whom it is or is not customary to tip and how
much, whether a man walks on the street side or on the left of a woman,
whether or not men take off their hats in elevators, and so on. And it does
not matter very much when people do not observe these customs. For after
the development of law, the important matters tend to be incorporated in
the law and so to be dealt with by the machinery of law, while the
unimportant ones continue to be dealt with by the informal and now
relatively lax sanctions of custom. *De minimis non curat lex.*

Does a society necessarily become a moral order when it becomes a
legal one? Is it the institution of law that generates it? Can there be no
prelegal moral orders? Can there be a legal order that is not a moral one?
As I mentioned before, it does not seem implausible to think that there is a
conceptual connection between law and morality and so not implausible
that a legal order is necessarily also a moral one. The question is complex
and cannot here be treated adequately, but I think we may assume a
minimal conceptual connection between being a legal and being a moral
order which can accommodate the Legal Positivist insistence on a sharp
distinction between what *the law* is and what it morally ought to be, and
the main concern of Natural Law theory that *law* (properly speaking)
imposes a (prima facie) moral obligation of obedience.[6]

---

[6] On the obligation to obey the law in Natural Law theory, see Saint Thomas Aquinas,
Summa Theologica, excerpted in *The Political Ideas of St. Thomas Aquinas*, ed. Dino Bigongiari
(New York: Hafner, 1953), 58, 71–77 [Question 95, Second Article; Question 96, Fourth
Article]; Lon L. Fuller, *The Morality of Law* (New Haven, Conn.: Yale University Press, 1969),

We think of a society's law (municipal, of course, not scientific) as that part of its mores which uses the characteristic machinery described by Hart. But we also think of it as something that it is a good thing for a society to have and that deserves our respect and support. In this use law is from its nature respectworthy. It is primarily when we think of it in this sense that we think of it and the state (which is tied to the law by the role of the legislator) as importantly different from a "robber band writ large," even though the latter may use similar regulative machinery for governing its members. When we think of it that way, we sympathize with Plato's claim that the ruler in the precise sense looks after the interest of the subject.[7] For we are rightly ambivalent about the state: we see the need for a generally accepted and acceptable system of adequately sanctioned directives that regulate interaction among people who want to interact with one another and hope to benefit from such interaction, but we also see the possibility of even greater inconveniences, sacrifices, and dangers involved in the existence of such a system of mores. For its powerful institutional machinery, especially when it reaches the level of a state, may and is quite likely to impose unnecessary and inequitable regulations which can make life unbearable, at least for some. Furthermore, since even necessary and equitable ones may and are likely not to be universally obeyed, scofflaws may be turned into rejoicing free riders and the law abiding into seething suckers, dissatisfied with virtue as their only reward. We see the great potential benefits of the state and its institution of law, and its even greater benefits if law is obeyed voluntarily because of its reputation as a good thing to have and to obey.

But we also want it, unlike a robber band writ large and its rule, to *deserve* that reputation. However, if the state and its law are fully to deserve that reputation and the resulting respect and support, then, unlike the rule of a robber band, its law must be formulated equitably and must mete out justice to the law abiding and to the lawbreaker. For this reason, it is not enough for law to spell out clear rules for interaction supported by adequate machinery of enforcement: it must also include machinery for producing conformity of its directives with the society's morality. Hart's account of the transition from Pure Custom to law provides the machinery for adequate expert determination of the general principles and rules embedded in the law (so that the law-respecting members can guide themselves with their help) as well as the specific legal requirements in

---

33–94; John Finnis, *Natural Law and Natural Rights* (Oxford: Oxford University Press, 1980), 281–350.

    [7] Plato, *Republic*, 23 [342e].

particular cases (including hard ones), and adequate machinery of enforcement to ensure an adequate level of conformity. However—for a variety of reasons we need not go into here—Hart does not find any need for additional institutional machinery to ensure continued conformity of the law at all levels of specificity with the society's morality, even when the law and the society's morality undergo significant changes.

What sort of institutional machinery, if any, would tend to ensure that? Unfortunately, this is a question for a detailed answer to which I lack the necessary legal expertise and which in any case, goes far beyond the primarily ethical interest of this book. My guess would be that things such as morally inspired constitution or elections by a morally motivated electorate might be worthy candidates.[8]

If there is this sort of conceptual connection between law and morality, then every legal order would appear to be a moral order since, for any part of its mores to constitute law in the honorific sense (rather than merely the quasi-legal machinery of a robber band writ large), it must to some extent be controlled by the society's morality; conversely, the society could presumably not have a morality unless it was a moral order.

If this is right, then for a society to be a legal order and for part of its mores to be law, the mores must have, in addition to the institutional machinery described by Hart, also some "morally corrective" machinery of the sort I suggested. If this is right, then *law,* from its very nature, must have this conceptual tie to morality, and so must be what *it* morally ought to be, a system of legal machinery controlled by some adequately effective "morally corrective machinery." At the same time, *the* law, that is, the legal provisions of some particular legal system (contextually identified), may well not be what *it* (they) morally ought to be, because its social machinery of moral self-correction has not yet done its job and perhaps will never do it.

That we recognize something like this conceptual connection between a legal and a moral order is supported by the fact that we think of the law as always purporting and always able to purport, to be meting out justice though not necessarily always actually doing so. Suppose the jury finds the accused guilty of murder in the first degree, although he passionately protests his innocence, and the judge, prior to sentencing, whispers to the now convicted prisoner, "Of course, I know you are innocent; I killed him myself," and then goes on to pronounce his sentence of thirty years in prison without parole. The judge, the prisoner, and anyone who heard

---

[8] Fuller, *Morality of Law,* 38–39; Philip Soper, *A Theory of Law* (Cambridge, Mass.: Harvard University Press, 1984).

the judge's remark would know that this was a travesty of justice and so of law. The judge therefore cannot say aloud what he has whispered to the prisoner without exposing it as a travesty, a deliberate abortion rather than merely a miscarriage of law. Spoken aloud, this performance cannot even purport to be a meting out of justice and therefore cannot purport to be, and therefore cannot be, the law of that society.

There are two questions here. The first is whether this verdict can be the law of that society, even though clearly it ought not to be. There would seem to be two answers to this first question, between which we need not now decide: either, yes, it is, or at least it is justifiably, though erroneously, thought to be the law, provided the society is a legal order and the recognized procedures have been followed. This proviso raises the second question: can this society be a legal order in that sense if it makes such travesties of justice possible? Again, the answer seems to be yes, it can be if (as we may assume) it were generally held in that society that this sort of performance amounts to a travesty of justice, that if the facts were known, the judge would be severely dealt with and the prisoner released, and that this is why the judge had to whisper rather than say out loud what he said to the prisoner.

Or consider Thrasymachus's notorious theory that law is the advantage of the stronger. This cannot be *what law is* because administering principles and rules that are openly proclaimed to be designed to serve the advantage of the ruling class could not purport to be acts of meting out justice. Indeed, no ruling class worth its salt would be foolish enough to proclaim such a design. At the same time, Thrasymachus could be right in thinking that this is often what some laws of a given society or of most societies in fact are. Of course, the legal practice of a society must not go too far in this direction, if the application of this guiding principle of legislation is not to become the normal legal practice rather than the carefully concealed exception. If it does, then that practice may no longer be able even to purport to be the practice of meting out justice and so no longer even appear to deserve the honorific title, *law*, and so nothing in that society may be *the law*.

Grant me, then, that it may well be the case that every legal order is also necessarily a moral one. Is there a comparable case for saying that every order of Pure Custom must be a moral one? It seems not. It is not merely that there is no contradiction in the supposition that at least some directives of the mores of a certain order of Pure Custom are contrary to *our* morality, but also that it is not the case that its mores are or even purport to be in accordance with *its* morality. There seem to be two possibilities: either that that social order is a moral order and has a morality but that its mores are and purport to be conceptually unrelated to it, or that the society in question is not a moral order and has no morality.

However, the former assumption seems incoherent. For a social order that is a moral order and has a morality, but whose mores do not even purport to be in conformity with its morality, can find no fault with its mores when some of its directives conflict with its morality. Such a society would seem to be unable to regard its condition as needing rectification when one part of its social order requires what another forbids. But this seems incoherent, especially if that other part is its morality which, if it is to deserve that name, must be recognized as paramount over the rest of the mores. This fact alone, that in this society, a conflict between its mores and its morality is not taken as something that calls for rectification either of its mores or its morality, seems sufficient to show that the society does not have a morality and therefore is not a moral order. It therefore seems to me more plausible to embrace the second possibility and to assume that an order of Pure Custom could conceivably fail to be a moral order.

Suppose, then, that a particular order of Pure Custom is not a moral order, what is missing or superfluous? What would turn a premoral order of Pure Custom into a moral one? If I am right, then it is not simply the development of the institutional machinery characteristic of law, for that alone (I argued) would not turn an order of Pure Custom that was not a moral order into a legal-cum-moral one. If the transition from Pure Custom to law described by Hart has the consequence that a legal order necessarily is a moral order, then it must have been a moral order even at the prelegal stage. It seems, then, that a particular order of Pure Custom that, according to our supposition, is not a moral order, could become one without at the same time becoming a legal order. And, of course, conversely, such an order of Pure Custom that is not a moral order could develop the Hartian machinery of defining and enforcing a part of its mores without thereby become a legal order because, if my account of law is sound, law carries a certain moral connotation not carried by a social order simply in virtue of possessing that institutional machinery.

What, then, is the required change? There appear to be two connected steps. One is a change in the attitude of the society's members to its mores and in the factors determining that change. The members no longer accept the prevailing mores uncritically and unquestioningly as sacrosanct, as is characteristic of the premoral stage of Pure Custom. They now can and sometimes do stand back from the accustomed way in which they live and explore the possibility and desirability of improvement. Once people travel abroad and observe other ways of life, the possibility of living by other very different mores is driven home. The Greeks are said to have been shocked out of their unquestioning acceptance of their own mores when they observed the Persian practice of burning their dead and noticed the equally shocked reaction of Persians when observing Greeks burying theirs. Of course, this is only a first step, often accompanied by doubt, skepticism, cynicism, and nihilism, stemming from the suspicion that there is in the end nothing to choose between ways of life, that one is as good or as bad as another, that the differences reveal not even a deep (e.g., racially determined) difference in taste, but the mere accident of birth that determines what way of life one comes to find right, as it determines one's mother tongue.

The second step is the development of critical judgments of the mores, especially one's own. The development of these judgments usually goes hand in hand with a vocabulary that marks greater differentiation and precision of what is judged than the simple "in accordance with/contrary to custom." For one thing, it allows judgments of some of the directives of the mores themselves in place of the earlier unquestioning acceptance, but it may also distinguish between various matters to be regulated, such as actions, dispositions to act, motives, character traits, and agents, all to be judged on their accordance/contrariety to these directives as well as on the extenuating/aggravating or the merit-increasing/decreasing nature of the circumstances in which these conformities or nonconformities occurred.

If a society is a moral order, its language may (like ours) imply which part of its mores constitute its custom, which its law, and which its morality, and which practical issues are regarded as matters of custom, which of law and which of morality. The judgment that it is *customary* for men to walk on the street side of women stamps this as a matter of custom; that it is *illegal* to drive on the left side of the road as a legal matter (though a directive about this sort of behavior could have moral implication, as when it is customary for wives always to walk several steps behind their husbands); and that it is (*morally*) *wrong* to lie, a moral matter.*

Custom, law, and morality share a central dichotomy: "according/ contrary to" custom/law/morality. We can distinguish between what, in a given order of custom, law, or morality, is rightly or wrongly thought to be according, what contrary to the relevant part of its mores. When we ask whether something is really in accordance with or contrary to a given society's custom or law, this is just another formulation of the same question: what is *rightly* thought to be according, what contrary to a society's custom, law, or morality. But in the domain of morality, we can ask a question which has no analogue in the domains of custom and law:

"Is what is (rightly) correctly thought to be according/contrary to a given society's morality, rightly (correctly) thought to be according/contrary to morality?" We can grant that a single member or all members of a certain moral order rightly think that, say, infanticide is contrary to the morality of that moral order, and still ask whether it is against morality. Or, putting it somewhat differently, we can grant that all members of that moral order *think* that infanticide is (morally) wrong, and still ask whether they rightly think so, whether it really is.

Thus, one thing that distinguishes a morality from other parts of the mores is that we can construe the prevalence of a certain morality in a given society as the prevalence of a sound or unsound belief that what (in that society) is according/contrary to that morality is (in that society) according/contrary to morality (or "Morality," as it were, with a capital "M").[9]

A moral order (whether at the stage of Pure Custom or law) thus is a social order which raises certain critical questions about its mores and which tends to modify them in light of the answers it gives to them. These questions therefore function as the society's own tests of soundness, that is, tests of the belief that certain directives contained in its mores (and possibly in those of other societies as well), and purporting to be moral directives and so to pass a certain appropriate test, really do pass it; furthermore, the soundness of the morality may depend not only on this appropriate test being passed by the directives actually incorporated in the mores but also on its being passed by those that are not thus incorporated though they ought to be.

A society's morality (or moralities; I return to this point in the next section), therefore, is or involves that part of its mores which purports to pass the appropriate test of acceptability, just as what someone asserts, or what is contained in a government report, purports to pass the appropriate test of verification or confirmation.

Thus, when we claim that whereas in the U.S. it is, in Australia it is not, *customary* to tip waiters, we are of course saying *something* that purports to pass an appropriate test of soundness, namely, that the corresponding parts of the mores of these two social orders, namely, their custom, differ in this way on the question of tipping. By contrast, when we say that both according to the U.S. and the Australian moralities it is morally wrong to lie, we imply that two other corresponding parts of these two systems of mores do not differ in this way on the question of lying, but we also imply

---

[9] For further details, see this chapter, section 4.

that there is an additional appropriate test of soundness which they may or may not pass. If the mores of some third society contained the directive, "it is morally permissible to lie," then that third morality would differ from the U.S. and Australian moralities on the matter of lying, but it too would imply that it should and does pass that additional appropriate test of soundness. However, as hardly needs saying again, the fact that this is implied does not mean that it actually is so; but, if we know what that additional appropriate test is and if we can carry it out, then we can ask (and perhaps discover) not only whether the claim that this really is what *that* morality directs, but also whether that prohibition or that permission concerning lying is sound. And, of course, if it is, then (as I mentioned before and will more fully defend later) we can say that this moral directive is true (or false) since, unlike many other directives, it says or implies something that can be true or false, namely, that it passes a certain test.

In sum, the custom and the law of a society differ from its morality in that, whereas we can ask, about all three of them, whether claims to the effect that a certain directive is part of them can be true or false, only the moral directives, not those of custom and law, can also themselves be true or false. I have already mentioned, in Book One, why this is so with regard to all normatives, and the same applies here. Since, as we noted, those judgments that purport to be moral *imply* that the directives embedded in them (thus, "stealing is morally wrong" embeds the directive, "no stealing," "not to steal," "one is not to steal," or something along these lines) meet the appropriate criterion of soundness, and therefore can be true or false. They are sound if and only if they meet it. But since asserting these directives implies that they do, they are true if they do, false if they do not. Thus, claims that contain only directives can only be sound or unsound but not true or false. The pure directive, "no stealing," can be evaluated by this appropriate test as sound or unsound but not as true or false. By contrast, normative claims, such as "one ought not to steal" or "stealing is morally wrong," which also imply that the pure directive embedded in it meets an appropriate criterion of soundness, can also be true if, but only if, it passes that test. It is perhaps worth stressing that claims to the effect that something is a directive of some society's custom or law do not imply that they meet an appropriate criterion of soundness, but that this does not mean that they are not open to criticism on the basis of appropriate criteria of merit and demerit.

Our most important next question, therefore, concerns the criterion and test of soundness implied by directives that purport to be moral. However, to be able to tackle that, we must first be clearer about several other matters, including, the relation between moral orders and moralities and that between moralities and Morality, as it were, with an upper-case letter.

Section 4.   Individual and Social Moralities*

Do individual moralities presuppose moral orders in a sense that makes a moral order prior to the several moralities—or the single morality, if any—it happens to have? Or are moral orders simply social orders in which all or most members happen to have the same individual morality? Or are there moral orders in which, though different members have different and at least in part conflicting moralities, there is some other unifying factor such as a generally accepted nonmoral (perhaps legal) procedure for authoritatively determining the proper directives for the mores that would otherwise be determined by the agreed moral judgments of the members? Or is even that much of a unifying common method for adjudicating individual moral disagreements unnecessary for a moral order to have a single morality? We can pick up clues from our term "rationality," for "morality" resembles it in many ways.**

To begin with, let me reemphasize that a morality is normally "owned," that is, ascribable to a (Strawsonian) individual, whether a person, a society, or some other collective such as a religion, a corporation, or an association (say, Christianity, General Motors, or Greenpeace). I think we would not ascribe a morality to a group which is not such a collective, say, a crowd watching a juggler or the people waiting for a train.

Begin then with the morality of particular persons. To say of someone that she has a morality would seem to imply that she is or can be moral (analogous to being rational), at least in the capacity sense if she can also acquire the ability to be moral, that is, be moral in the ability sense. And one has that ability if one has acquired—to an adequate degree—the ability to tell what is morally wanted of one in the various situations one finds oneself in, and also the ability to satisfy what is thus wanted of one. Can one have a morality without being moral in these two senses, without having this capacity and ability? It seems to me that one cannot. For if one is not moral in these two senses, one cannot be moral in the two others, the evaluative and dispositional sense, either. For one takes oneself to be moral in the evaluative sense if one acts in accordance with rather than contrary to the precepts of one's morality. But one cannot take oneself to be acting in this way if one does not at least have what one takes to be the ability to tell what is morally wanted of one and to satisfy that want. And one could not have acquired that ability unless one had the corresponding capacity on account of which one can acquire this ability. Of course, taking oneself to have that ability is not the same as having it. One may have many misconceptions about what is morally wanted of one, and it is often extremely difficult to demonstrate to another who disagrees with one, that it is his and not one's own that is a misconception. So one may, without knowing it, be under so many misconceptions that one not merely has that ability to a low degree, but does not have it at all.

But this does not affect the two points, (1) that one could not be able to be moral in the evaluative or dispositional sense without having these two abilities and the capacities presupposed by them, and (2) that one could not have the ability to any degree unless one had begun by acquiring a rough idea first, and a method of correcting the mistakes one has picked up in the course of the learning process, together with a method for eventually correcting errors in the method by which one's society had taught one that ability.

There is a further reason to think that one cannot be moral in the evaluative sense without being moral in the capacity and ability senses. For if one simply happened to hit on what was the moral thing to do, then one did it by fluke, accidentally, without knowing that one was doing so. But when one acts in this way, one gets no credit for it. But, surely, being moral is something for which one can claim credit.

Consider, then, the converse question. Can one be moral in the capacity and ability senses without being moral/immoral in the evaluative and without having a disposition—at least in a significant range of circumstances—to be moral rather than immoral? It seems to me that if one is moral in the ability sense, then, other things equal, behavior that runs counter to what is morally wanted of one counts as immoral, behavior that satisfies it as moral. For since, ex hypothesi, one had that ability, one must have known that one ought to use it to determine what was morally wanted of one and to satisfy the want. And if one did not use it to find out what was wanted of one, then one was immoral; and if one did find out but did not satisfy the want, one also was immoral. Of course, these things are true only other things equal. If, through no fault of one's own, one made a mistake in what one worked out to be wanted of one, then in not doing it one was not immoral; similarly, if there was an exculpatory explanation of why one did not do what one rightly thought was morally wanted of one, one was not immoral.

Comparable considerations support the view that if one is moral in the capacity and ability senses, one must also be moral in the dispositional sense. If that were not so, then the amoralist, too, could have a morality.

For the amoralist may be moral in the capacity and ability, but not the dispositional sense. If we ascribe a morality to her, then having a morality may have no practical significance, no influence on one's behavior. Ascribing morality to her would then be like ascribing ancient Roman law to any currently existing society in which that law was widely known, for the amoralist's morality seems as dead as Roman law is now and would remain so even if everybody knew what it was; of course, her morality may have been alive earlier before she became an amoralist, just as Roman law was once alive in ancient Rome. It may perhaps be objected that she has that morality in the sense in which a certain gambit invented by Smith and named after him is Smith's, even though he never uses it because he does not think it "good enough" to risk in an actual game of chess. Perhaps one can know and understand "the moral game" but think of it as a gambit not "good enough" to use in "the game of life." "No" may then be one's answer to "should I be moral?" and "no good reason" to "why be moral?" However, the morality the amoralist regards as not good enough to follow need not be her own invention and, unlike Smith, she rejects not only her own but all moral "gambits." She thinks that, from their moral nature, none of them is good enough for her, perhaps for anyone, to use. She thinks of it as essentially a sucker's game.

If the answer to what a person's having a morality comes to is along these lines, what is it for a society to have one? What exactly is the relation between the morality of a society and that of its members? Which is primary? Must a social order have a uniform morality, one accepted by all its members, if it has one at all? And does it have one if and only if all its members have the same individual morality, or is it sufficient that the bulk or a majority or a plurality of its members have it? Can a society be a moral order even if it does not have a morality at all or not a uniform morality? Can a person have an (individual) morality, even if his society does not have (a uniform) one?

A comparison with legal orders should be instructive. The law, it seems, is much more closely tied to the legal order whose law it is than a society's morality is to the moral order whose morality it is. There simply is no legal analogue of a person's morality; there is nothing that is a person's law, the law of that person. Again, when someone travels or even emigrates to another society, she takes her morality with her, but not her former society's law. Conversely, it does not seem to make sense to say of a society that it is a legal order unless it has *at least and at most* one legal system. This, of course, is not to deny the possibility of federal legal systems, but such systems must draw consistent dividing lines between the federal and the local legal spheres. The concept of morality does not seem to require, indeed even to permit, a parallel subdivision of its realm. Abortion may be illegal in New Jersey and legal in New York, and it may be *believed* morally wrong in one state and not in another, but it would seem impossible that it should (other things equal) *be* morally wrong (that is, on account of what it is, not because it is illegal in a state) in one but not in the other.* By contrast, it does not seem inconceivable that a single moral order should house conflicting individual moralities. Indeed, in so-called pluralistic societies we expect it, though we also see it as a weakness and a difficulty. It bothers us about our own moral order that there are many important moral issues on which we are deeply and passionately divided, but we do not deny therefore that these purportedly moral disagreements could be, and in all likelihood usually are, genuinely moral, nor do we think that our social order cannot, on account of such disagreements, constitute a moral order.**

Does this make sense? I think so. The concept of a legal order imposes fairly strict requirements of consistency on the directives, principles, and rules that compose its law. The reason for this, I think, is that law requires social enforcement and that justice requires high standards of consistency for social enforcement.[10] This ideal of consistency is built into the (honorific) concept of law itself. If an inconsistency between two laws is discovered, it seems to follow that both cannot remain law; and even in retrospect, in many if not all cases, it would seem that both cannot *have been* law.*** But since society suitably enforces its morality to the extent that it is incorporated in the society's law or custom or both, justice does not require equally stringent consistency of the directives, principles, and rules of the society's morality as such. Of course, consistency is a desideratum also in a social and in an individual morality, but it conflicts with another even more important desideratum for a moral order, namely, every member's (legal and moral) freedom to express disagreement with opposing moral views, though perhaps only if he supports it by reasons. This is so because improvements in the society's morality can occur only by changes in the members' morality and these are best brought about by the members' own efforts at convincing one another by their discussions with others (and, of course, themselves by their own critical reflections).

At the same time, as in court cases, where the desirability of allowing further factual investigations by the parties, by cross-examinations of witnesses, and by presentations of legal arguments, must be weighed against the desirability of reaching final enforceable settlements without

---

[10] But see Carlos E. Alchurrón and Eugenio Bulygin, *Normative Systems* (Vienna: Springer-Verlag, 1971), 144–64, especially 158–63.

undue delay, so in the case of important moral issues, it is desirable for them also to be regulated by law so that they, too, will come to be authoritatively settled in good time. However, it would seem that even in the case of very important moral issues, the reasoned moral disagreement should be allowed to continue beyond the enforceable legal settlement of particular cases, at least as long as there is reasonable hope of an eventual reasoned agreement.*

Thus, this difference between a moral and a legal order appears to be due to the different ways in which the two enterprises, those of morality and of law, divide up the common tasks between society and its members. The law is the creation of the authoritative decisions of society, that is, its officials, its legislators, and judges, who are essential role players in societies that are legal orders. In relation to the making and applying of the law, the members of a legal order are merely subjects. But, of course, through the political order, with which a legal order is typically, perhaps necessarily, paired, these subjects play some role at least in the selection of the legislators and judges who make the authoritative decisions.**

By contrast, a society's morality is the joint product of the moralities of its individual members. As far as its content is concerned, individual members are its joint makers, not merely its subjects. At the same time, each of these personal moralities is the result of the members' socialization. Even if the members of a new generation are socialized by parents, priests, teachers, peers, media, and so on, all of whom, as now rarely happens in pluralistic societies, have the same individual moralities, these new members will, as they grow up and develop their critical faculties to a greater or lesser extent, develop increasingly divergent individual moralities.***

This divergence is likely to be increased by a number of factors with which we are only too familiar: immigration on a large scale by people of very diverse moral traditions; more widespread and thorough critical examination by adolescents and minorities of the prevalent type or types of morality; an expanding number, scope, and influence of ethical theories by theorists trained in quite different disciplines, (such as philosophy, theology, literary criticism, sociology, anthropolgy, history, economics, game theory, sociobiology, jurisprudence); and, last but not least, the activities of passionate and persuasive pundits ardently selling, in the guise of justice, morality, decency, and salvation, the advantage of powerful interest groups. Pummeling by these forces is likely to push up the rate of change in interpersonal and intergenerational individual moral convictions.

At the same time, however, a greater knowledge of facts and a better understanding of their bearing on the soundness of these convictions may eventually have the opposite effect. One may hope, for instance, that the facts about the so-called population explosion and its impact on our lives and thereby on the soundness of our current population policy and of what we take to be our relevant moral views about such practices as birth control, abortion, poverty, racism, conservation of resources, protection of the environment, and so on, will eventually seep into public consciousness, and that this increase in knowledge and understanding will bring about an improvement and a convergence in our views concerning the policies that would promote human flourishing.

Thus, if my account is correct, then the question of what comes first or what is primary, the society's or the members' morality, makes as little sense as the analogous chicken-and-egg question. What is fundamental and relatively stable is the moral framework, the society's moral institution consisting of its various roles and constituting its moral order. It is this which makes possible the cyclic process of passing on, from one generation to the next, the knowledge and skills needed for the various practices that constitute the moral enterprise, and it is this which ensures that each member of a new generation will have an (individual) morality. For a society to have a morality, for something to be a social morality, it is sufficient for that society to be a moral order, for that is sufficient for the production of new generations with individual moralities.

We can speak of "the contours" or "the shape" of the social morality which, at any particular time, is determined by the individual moralities the members have at that time.* Thus we may wish to say—and can do so without being misleading—that every social order that is a moral order has a single morality composed of the members' individual moralities which, because they may diverge from or even be incompatible with one another, determine its possibly changing contours that define its character. It is because of the different ways in which the tasks of society and those of its members are parceled out in the legal and the moral enterprises, respectively, that we should not expect social moralities to have the internal consistency of legal systems. Indeed, we should not expect that level of consistency even within all or most individual moralities in the same moral order. For a person's morality is likely to undergo significant changes in the course of his life. In all probability, he will at first acquire a morality closely resembling those of his parents and containing all the internal inconsistencies of each and (some of) the conflicts between them. As he acquires critical skills, he will discover and remove some of these inconsistencies, but he will also modify some of the moral views inherited from his parents on grounds other than their inconsistencies. In the process, he will probably import new internal inconsistencies which again it will take him time to discover and to iron out, and so on throughout his life as long as his morality is not frozen into immobility. It would be surprising if, by that time, he had succeeded in eliminating all inconsistencies.

What is prior, then, is neither the individual nor the social morality, but the moral order. For the members of a social order could not have acquired an individual morality unless they had grown up in a moral order, that is, one in which they have learned to play the various constitutive roles of its moral institution, have been taught a set of purported middle-level moral precepts and principles (such as the Ten Commandments) and their application to a large variety of more specific types of case, have lived through, confronted, and coped with many moral problems, and have absorbed or been told some generally recognized criterion or criteria by which to judge the soundness of the more or less generally recognized purportedly moral precepts, such as conformity to the will of God as expressed in the Ten Commandments.

It is in reference to these matters that I speak of the social roots of morality. Of course, nothing could be further from my intentions than a wish to deny or belittle the importance of the role of the moral critic and reformer.

Section 5.   Moralities and Morality

In the preceding section, I distinguished between individual and social moralities, but I have also sometimes spoken of Morality, as it were, with an upper-case letter. Moralities are like belief systems, in that they are typically those of a (Strawsonian) individual and purport to be sound (in the appropriate sense to be discussed in chapter 7), though, of course, they may not actually be so.

Moralities also resemble belief systems in two other respects. One is that they are subject to a consistency requirement, though, as I noted, it may be less strict for a social morality than for an individual one and less strict for either of them than for belief systems. But there are important parallels. Thus a person can without contradiction or absurdity say that he believes or feels certain that some of his beliefs contradict others, but he cannot say this in the same breath of two particular beliefs of his, such as that the earth is round and that the earth is flat. Similarly, he can say that he believes or feels certain that some of his moral convictions contradict others, but he cannot in the same breath say this of two particular moral convictions of his, such as that lying is always wrong and that lying is not always wrong. The second resemblance is that first-person moral claims, like first-person assertions of observational fact, can give rise to Moore's paradox. One cannot without absurdity claim (although it may be true) that one went to a movie on Wednesday but that one does not believe one did. Similarly one cannot without absurdity claim (although it may be true) that it is always morally wrong to lie but that one does not believe it is.

Similarly, although of course one can say that someone else believes a certain thing, for instance, that the earth is flat but that this is mistaken and that he ought not to believe it, one cannot assert that the earth is flat and in the same breath maintain that what one is asserting is mistaken and that one ought not to believe it. Equally, one can assert about someone else that he believes it is always wrong to lie but that this is a mistake and that he ought not to believe it, but one cannot in the same breath make these assertions about oneself. Such claims would disqualify one from deserving to have one's factual or moral judgments taken seriously, for they give rise to the suspicion that one does not understand what one is talking about or that one is not serious when making such claims.

These linguistic facts support the view that (at least normative) moral judgments purport to satisfy, or imply they satisfy, a certain criterion or test of soundness. This in turn implies that moral judgments can be true or false. At first sight, this seems impossible because the mores, to which both social and personal moralities are conceptually related, are designed to regulate interactions between the society's members, and such regulations when explicitly formulated must be, or embed, directives, that is, forms of words depicting types of human behavior, such as John's opening the window which those who understand them can *follow* or *ignore*: e.g., "John, open the window," "John, you are to open the window," "John will open the window," and so on. The last expression shows that what makes these sentences directives is not their grammatical form—whether they are imperatives, gerundives, or indicatives—but whether they depict someone's behavior and how that depiction will in certain contexts be taken. Taking it as a directive is different from taking it as a description or prediction of it, and in the same context it cannot by the same person be taken as both, though it can rightly be taken differently in different contexts. Thus in one context, "The procession will enter the Town Hall at

10 A.M." can be taken as a prediction (e.g., by spectators reading a program) and by others as a directive (e.g., by the leader of the procession reading the same program).[11]

As I have suggested in various places before, our term "Morality" (as in "she often acts contrary to Morality") is sometimes used in the sense of a possible ideal morality—not necessarily one actually embraced by some society or person—which is sound in toto. However, such a use raises various doubts, for instance, that such a wholly sound person- and society-neutral morality may be impossible, because moralities may have to develop out of particular actual moralities of particular societies, through the impact of actual moral critics and reformers. I believe moral orders and their moralities develop from different social starting points and with different conceptions of soundness as guides for improvement. Thus, even if we can reasonably hope that a single criterion of soundness will one day become accepted in all moral orders, it may yet be utopian even to hope for, let alone expect, a development in the direction of a single sound social morality, perhaps with everyone in all societies subscribing to it. I am suggesting, in other words, that there may be a number, perhaps a large number, of different but equally sound social moralities, though they may necessarily have common cores.[12]

There is another doubt I should perhaps mention, although we are not likely to reach a point in the near future by which we may need to resolve it. The doubt concerns the relation between the sound code of a social and that of an individual morality in a single moral order. I have argued that in a given moral order the codes of individual moralities may differ from one another and from the dominant code (if any) of its social morality. A reason for thinking such a diversity acceptable or even desirable is that probably at least parts of most people's individual moralities are unsound, even if, perhaps especially if, all subscribe to the same moral code, and that such diversity will generate critical comparisons and through them improvement in the direction of greater soundness. But can this be true also of the relation between the *sound* code of a dominant social morality and those of its members' *sound* individual moralities?

There seems to be a strong reason against this. Suppose we come to understand more clearly what the appropriate criterion of soundness is and we learn to subject various moralities to a test of soundness, and so discover that a certain code is sound for our moral order. Will we not then

---

[11] I shall discuss this point in greater detail below in chapter 8, section 2, 293–98.

[12] Again see Hart, *Concept of Law*, 189–95.

reach the point at which the argument for insisting that individual moralities conform with the one morality we have found to be sound become as compelling as those for a single legal system? This is a difficult question because the fact that we have found one morality sound does not imply that there could not be different ones that are equally sound. Then it might well be unfair for a society to select one in preference to another, yet harmful for it to have more than one morality, even if all are sound. Perhaps it is fortunate that the point at which this question becomes important is not at hand, although the frequently noted contraction of the human world and the increasing interdependence of its parts may take us there sooner than the current state of our moral convictions and of our ethical theory might lead us to expect.

CHAPTER SEVEN

The Moral Enterprise

All normative moral judgments, I argued in the preceding chapter, imply that the directives embedded in them meet a criterion—and would pass a test—of soundness, and that in different moralities, the accepted criterion and test may be different. I postponed to this chapter, the discussion of what this test and this criterion is, or should be, in our morality, and whether they should be the same for all moralities. As will become clearer in the course of our discussion, this will involve a closer examination than attempted so far, of the moral enterprise and its most important characteristics.

Section 1.   The Divine Command Theory

It will be helpful to remind ourselves of the great strengths of a conception of morality which, in this country, is probably embraced by more people than is any other conception. I mean, of course, the conception exemplified by what is often called the Judeo-Christian morality. For our purposes here, we can neglect its many denominational divisions and theological subtleties and single out for review one simple persistent and highly influential model, the so-called Divine Command Theory. Its basic moral precepts are represented as spelled out in sacred and therefore authoritative texts, and as sound because they are or relay God's commandments. Thus, the criterion of the soundness of these purported moral precepts is that they are or conform to the expressed will of God.

Probably the most influential Christian version of this theory[1] represents a human morality as sound, if and only if it conforms to *the* moral order which it identifies with *the* legal order of the universe. It conceives of that order as a single flawless supernatural legal system with a single supremely powerful, perfectly wise, just, and omniscient divine being as

---

[1] One version of this part of the theory can be found in St. Thomas's *Summa Theologica* 1/II, Q90–108.

legislator, judge, and enforcer. This legal order enacts part of the plan according to which this perfect being has created and rules the whole universe. It is the part intended for human beings, who can understand commandments and are endowed with a free will enabling them to obey or disobey as they choose. He has also adequately promulgated these commandments to us, informed us of our subjection to them, and told us about the rewards and punishments he will mete out to us for obedience and disobedience, respectively. As conceived by this theory, the reason why the soundness of human morality is made to rest on its conformity with the divine plan for humans, thus lies in the perfection of that plan by which this perfect being perfectly governs the universe of which our earth and we humans are the center.

Consider, then, some of the strengths of this theory. One is that the moral order is conceived as a legal order freed of the most glaring flaws of earthly legal ones: the ignorance, deceivability, weakness, and injustice of its legislators, judges, and enforcers. A second is that it represents its precepts as binding on us irrespective of whether or not doing what they require of us is what we want to do either for its own sake or for its consequences, at least *in this world*. On this point, it is superior to theories such as Ethical Egoism and many versions of Utilitarianism.

A third strength is the admission of, indeed insistence on, the possibility, or even likelihood, of conflicts between the requirements of our own good in this world and those of morality, and its idea of the reconciliation of these conflicting requirements in an afterlife with more than adequate compensations for the disadvantages suffered by the moral and law abiding. It thus offers an uncomplicated account of the relation between duty and interest according to which moral choice is construed as always harmonious with prudent choice. A fourth is the force and plausibility of the reasons and motives it provides for compliance. One is fear of the punishments meted out by this supreme being for disobedience. Another is gratitude; gratitude to him for creating our original ancestors and placing them in the magnificent world of the Garden of Eden; and even greater gratitude for sending his own son to deliver us from those evils into which their offspring had been plunged, after our Ur ancestors had wasted their good fortune by disobedience. A third is the nobility of the behavior in which he orders us to engage. And a fourth are the more than generous rewards he holds out for such obedience. On the face of it, then, this conception of morality would seem to offer everyone sufficient reason and motivation to be moral.

Nevertheless, despite its important insights into some aspects of the moral enterprise, this theory has several weaknesses. I do not here need to dwell on the well-known difficulties relating to our knowledge of the existence of God and of the content of his will, beyond stressing the obvious point that they block the crucial move from accepting the implied criterion to performing the test of soundness: if God does not exist or if we do not know his will, we cannot use that criterion as a test of, as a method for, finding out whether a purported moral precept is sound or unsound.

What I do want to dwell on, however, is an ideal aim (or should I say, hope?) for humanity that is central to all versions of this conception of morality and that I believe distorts the nature and function of the moral enterprise when so conceived: I mean salvation. That aim owes some of its appeal to an infectious pessimism about human life on earth conjoined with an excessive optimism about the accessibility to us, simply through compliance with the supposed divine commandments, of a life that is everlasting, toil free, painless, and beatific, perhaps better even than life supposedly was in the Garden of Eden; a life whose blissfulness is not the fruit of effort and ingenuity, but is laid on, merely on condition of obedience to his will, by our heavenly father, as it was laid on, when we were good, obedient children, by our earthly father.

But quite apart from exhibiting this striking disparity in the assessment of our prospects, where life before and life after death are concerned, the ideal of salvation seriously distorts morality by an interesting and not widely examined egocentricity: one's salvation is wholly independent of anyone else's; it depends solely on one's own desert earned by obedience. Others get into the moral picture only indirectly, only insofar as the author of the moral precepts has forbidden or required us to treat them in certain ways. Moral wrongness is construed on the model of sinfulness, that is, disobedience or rebellion against the supreme ruler of the world, as lawlessness is rebellion against the highest authority of the state, and the wickedness of a child is rebellion against the highest authority in the family. Thus killing is a sin if and because God has forbidden it, not because it has caused someone's death. After David arranged for Uriah to be killed so that he could bed Uriah's widow, Bathsheba, David could say to God, quite correctly, "To thee only have I sinned." But, we may ask, could he have said, correctly, "Thee only have I wronged"? Can one wrong God? In any case, has he not wronged Uriah even if he has not wronged God or sinned against Uriah? And is it only by sinning against God that he has wronged Uriah?[2]*

This egocentric aspect of the ideal of salvation blinds us to the

---

[2] I here borrow ideas from Joel Feinberg's paper, "The Nature and Value of Rights," *Journal of Value Inquiry* 4 (Winter 1970), 243–57.

importance of the causal role of others in our chances of attaining a good life for ourselves. If a good life for us cannot be achieved by us simply by coming to deserve it through obedience, and if others play an important causal role in our achieving it, then, if (as the Divine Command Theory holds) morality plays a crucial role in our attaining a good life for ourselves, others must play a more prominent role in morality than the Divine Command Theory and the ideal of salvation provide for them.

It may perhaps be thought that a second and more sophisticated version of the Divine Command Theory is immune to these objections, because it embraces the view that God commands certain types of behavior because they are morally good (or right) and forbids others because they are morally bad (or wrong). Against this, it has to be said, in the first place, that this version, too, is open to all the epistemological difficulties to which I alluded earlier in this section. More interestingly, it is open also to an additional one which the first and cruder version escapes. For this second version faces a well-known problem, raised by Socrates in Plato's *Euthyphro*.[3] If, as claimed by the first version, certain kinds of behavior are held to be good (or right) because God's command-ments require them (and bad [or wrong] because it forbids them), then, as we have seen, that theory is open to the objection that it conflates moral badness (or wrongness) with sinfulness, and moral goodness (or right-ness) with its opposite. But if, like the second version, it embraces the converse view, then the theory is open to another objection, namely, that it deprives God (or the gods) of the indispensable role the first version gave them in the differentiation between sound and unsound versions of morality. On this more sophisticated version, God has a reason why he should and does command certain types of behavior and forbids others, and it is the very same reason for which, quite independently of divine commandments, we should do the former and not the latter. On this version, God is not now needed to *bring the basic moral differences into existence* by his fiat. His role cannot even be to tell us what things are morally good and what things morally bad, not so much because it is not the case that we often get this wrong and he does not, but rather because he appears to have no way of communicating his superior knowledge to us that is not also open to bad supernatural powers. We thus will find it easier to distinguish for ourselves between what is morally good and what is morally bad, than to distinguish between *the good and the bad voices* purporting to convey that superior knowledge. We are more likely to be

---

[3] Plato, "Euthyphro," *The Trial and Death of Socrates,* tr. G. M. A. Grube (Indianapolis, Ind.: Hackett, 1975), 12–14 [10a–11b].

able to distinguish between these voices on the basis of *what* they are telling us than by their peculiar *timbre* or *volume*. Looking, as Legal Positivists do, for the pedigree of a supposed edict to determine its legal validity makes sense, for there are relatively easy ways of doing so, but it does not make sense to hope for a comparable method to determine whether or not it was the supreme supernatural legislator or some supernatural opponent or rebellious underling who issued a certain commandment we seem to be hearing.

Section 2.   Is Our Inquiry Possible?

To avoid the important weaknesses of the Divine Command Theory, it will be necessary to become clearer about the moral enterprise itself. So far, I have tried to establish only claims that do not directly involve reliance on any moral value or normative judgments, such as the following: that a social order is engaged in the moral enterprise if and only if it is a moral order; that it is a moral one if and only if it has the moral institution (the analogue of the institution of law in a legal order); that it has that institution (perhaps if and certainly) only if it engages in the characteristic types of practice with the characteristic first- and second-order roles that are also present in a legal order, though with the difference that their moral analogues are not restricted to certain officeholders, as they are in the law, and that some of the principles and precepts relied on by these role players are taken to imply that they would meet a certain criterion and pass a corresponding test of soundness.

So far, however, I have not yet touched on several difficult questions, some of which directly or indirectly involve evaluative and normative issues. Thus, one of these (e.g., "Why should one *morally* condemn someone for his heterodox sexual view?") questions whether a given practical judgment is such as to imply that it is (rightly) taken to be a moral (rather than a nonmoral) one. A second (e.g., "How do we tell whether abortion is always wrong?") inquires into what the appropriate or right criterion and test of soundness are. A third (e.g., "What is the good of justice?") delves into matters that hinge on the nature, structure, end, and function of the moral enterprise.

It is natural to think that, in the last resort, the answers to both the first and the second, as well as to many other questions about which this is not so immediately obvious, hinge on these aspects of that enterprise. For it is plausible to think that its structure implies that its end is the bringing about of a state of affairs in which behavioral guidelines (in a very wide sense which includes dispositions to behave, attitudes, and the like) are generally available and which are such that general conformity with them achieves a certain desirable result, the achieving of which is their proper function and the end of the enterprise.

However, this immediately raises a well-known difficulty: how can we hope to state that function without begging the evaluative/normative issues these guidelines are supposed to settle? For there appears to be as much disagreement about that function as there is about more specific moral issues and, at this level of abstraction, we seem at a loss about where to find any, let alone adequate, support that favors some particular settlement over its rivals. How are we to choose between humanity as an end in itself (Kant), the greatest happiness of the greatest number (Bentham), the greatest self-realization (T.H. Green), the harmonization of conflicting interests and concerns (Toulmin), the promotion of liberty and justice and the reduction of inhumanity and oppression (Philippa Foot), the amelioration of the human predicament (Warnock), and so on and on?[4]

Indeed, some have questioned whether we even can distinguish between the moral and the nonmoral without begging important substantive (evaluative/normative) moral questions. For in trying to identify the moral and distinguish it from the nonmoral, must we not assume a specifically moral method for answering practical questions, or a specifically moral end of the moral enterprise, a specific criterion of moral relevance and soundness, or a specifically moral point of view? But do not these involve precisely the very general attitudes and commitments on which we disagree in ways that cannot be settled simply by further questions of empirical fact? And whatever our answer, it surely will have a decisive bearing on our determination of what is morally required and thereby on how we distinguish the moral from the immoral. Indeed, if that were not so, distinguishing the moral from the nonmoral would not be very important or morally interesting.

From these and similar reflections most contemporary moral philosophers appear to have concluded that all definitions or accounts of "the moral" (as opposed to "the nonmoral") which allow us to derive substantive moral judgments are objectionable or at least suspect and, it

---

[4] Immanuel Kant, *Groundwork of the Metaphysics of Morals*, tr. H. J. Paton (London: Hutchinson University Library, 1948), 95, 428; Jeremy Bentham, *A Fragment on Government* (Cambridge: Cambridge University Press, 1988), 3; T. H. Green, *Prolegomena to Ethics*, 5th ed., ed. A. C. Bradley (London: Oxford University Press, 1906), 206–28; Stephen Toulmin, *The Place of Reason in Ethics* (London: Cambridge University Press, 1950), 145; Philippa Foot, "Morality as a System of Hypothetical Imperatives," 167; G. J. Warnock, *The Object of Morality* (London: Methuen, 1971), 26.

would seem, incurably so. They appear to think, in other words, that in order to be aboveboard, definitions or accounts of "the moral" must be morally neutral, that is, noncommittal. Any acceptable distinction between the moral and the nonmoral must be compatible with any distinction between the moral and the immoral. They seem to think, as Frankena has put it, that such definitions must not imply "either a substantive normative or evaluative principle or a principle of inference . . . i.e., . . . a principle that tells us a certain fact or kind of fact is a reason for a certain (or a certain kind of) evaluative or normative judgment."[5]

R. M. Hare is probably the best-known spokesman for this position[6] but not all are as purist as he. Some, e.g., John Harsanyi,[7] allow such "normatively laden" definitions of "morality," as long as it is understood that from the fact that something is "morally required" of someone according to such a definition and that he therefore "morally ought" to do it, it does not follow that he has justifying, let alone requiring, *reason* to do it. However, Harsanyi, to my knowledge, does not raise or answer questions such as what to do when one morally ought to install antipollution equipment but also has adequate reason not to do so.

Others[8] agree with Harsanyi up to the last point, but then appear to imply that when one *morally ought* to do something, then one *really ought* to do it, even when one has *no reason* or no *adequate reason* to do it, or even has adequate reason not to do it. They seem to suggest or imply this[9] because, unlike Harsanyi, they play down the importance of practical rationality and play up the importance of morality.*

We have already examined Sidgwick's position according to which one really ought to do only what one has adequate reason to do, and one always has adequate reason to do what morality requires of one but, in the absence of a divine retributive system favoring morality, also what one's own good requires. On this position, too, there is no single ultimate objective justifier.

---

[5] William K. Frankena, "Three Questions About Morality," *The Monist* 63, no. 1 (January 1980): 127.

[6] Cf. e.g., Hare's review of Stephen Toulmin's *The Place of Reason in Ethics* in *Philosophical Quarterly* 1, no.4 (July 1951): 372 ff.

[7] John Harsanyi, "Ethics as a System of Hypothetical Imperatives," *Mind* 67 (1958). Reprinted in *Essays on Ethics, Social Behavior, and Scientific Explanation* (Dordrecht, Holland: D. Reidel, 1976), 24–36; also *Rational Behavior and Bargaining Equilibrium in Games and Social Situations* (Cambridge: Cambridge University Press, 1977), chapter 1, especially 13f.

[8] E.g., Philippa Foot, "Morality as a System of Hypothetical Imperatives," 167.

[9] Foot seems to me to do this; however, she does not say so in so many words, so I may have misunderstood her.

In light of this discussion, one might well conclude that any normatively noncommittal definition or account of morality must be useless for
settling moral disagreements, and any normatively committal one must
ipso facto be begging the question.

However, this dilemma is not as formidable as it may appear at first
sight. Note, first, that the problem Frankena spells out appears not to be
peculiar to morality but to arise for any definition that implies a principle
according to which a certain fact (or kind of fact) is a reason for a certain
(or a certain kind of) evaluative or normative judgment. But if that is so,
then the inadmissibility of *any* such definition would appear also to
exclude any sound definition of "modus ponens." For such a definition of
"modus ponens" must license us to infer that some inference (call it "I") is
a valid one, from the fact (call it *p*) that "I" conforms to modus ponens.
And is not the conclusion—that "I" is a valid inference—which we draw
in this inference (call it *q*) an evaluative judgment? I infer *q* from *p* in
accordance with modus ponens, so the inference to *q* is a *valid* one, so I
ought not to reject it; if I know that *p* is true, I should not deny or doubt *q*,
and so on.

Thus, Frankena's claim that definitions of "the moral" (as opposed to
"the nonmoral") must be morally neutral (noncommittal) or else they
simply beg the question, itself faces a dilemma: either all normatively or
evaluatively committal (nonneutral) definitions, including those of logical
principles such as modus ponens, are objectionable—which seems absurd
—or else the objectionability of such committal definitions of "the moral"
cannot lie in its being *normatively committal*, which robs the claim of
objectionability of its supposed ground. As I see it, the objections to
embracing *neither horn* of this dilemma are more serious than Frankena's
objection to embracing *the second horn*, namely, accepting some committal
definition of "the moral" (as opposed to the nonmoral).

At this point, I leave this horse, even though to some it may still seem
worth flogging. For if my account of directive reasons in general, and
practical ones in particular, is sound, then it would appear that we can
safely embrace the second horn of Frankena's dilemma. And if my account
of prudential reasons is sound, then there is no reason to think that
Frankena's objection rules out definitions of all principles of practical
inference that rationally justify us in drawing evaluative or normative
practical conclusions from certain facts, conclusions about what it would
be better for us to do or what we ought to do, drawn from facts, such as
that doing one of these things would be in our best interest, whereas the
other would not. Of course, such conclusions would hold only if other

things are equal; nevertheless, they surely would amount to substantive evaluative or normative conclusions. And with further relevant information (i.e., that nothing is the case that could rebut such a conclusion), we might well convert them into all-things-considered ones.

Of course, this is only the thin end of the wedge against the Frankena objection. For even if what I have just said is right—as I have argued in Book One that it is—it shows only that this objection does not have the broad scope it purports to have. It may still be true, for reasons *peculiar to the moral enterprise* that, although this objection is without force against the enterprise of reason itself, or against that of cognitive reason, or against some branches of practical reasoning, it still is valid against the enterprise of morality. However, it is my aim in this book to show that moral considerations are one kind of practical reason and that the peculiar regimentation of practical thinking that counts as moral constitutes a branch of practical reason. It will by now be clear that, according to my thesis, moral reasons are one kind of practical reasons, those I called "society anchored."

At this point of our inquiry, then, I take myself entitled to assume that the dilemmatic problem sketched by Frankena for practical inferences other than moral ones is best met by embracing the second horn of his dilemma: that we can, without necessarily begging any questions, rely on definitions of the end of the rational enterprise in our definition of principles which justify us in deriving from empirical facts conclusions that are evaluative or normative judgments. At this point, our main question, therefore, is whether we can, from the conception of morality developed so far, extract a conception of the nature, structure, end, and function of the moral enterprise which, similarly, will justify us in deriving from empirical facts conclusions that are moral (evaluative or normative) judgments. I turn, then, to this crucial task.

Section 3.   The Design of the Enterprise of Society-Anchored Reason

The task just described would be easiest if we could simply identify the moral enterprise with some part of the rational enterprise, for then we could think of moral considerations as reasons and so as providing valid licenses from empirical facts to evaluative and normative conclusions. We could achieve this result painlessly by recommending that we construe the moral enterprise so as to satisfy all the conditions satisfied by the enterprise of society-anchored reason to which it clearly has some resemblance. But that would leave us with some uneasiness. For such a move might raise the suspicion that we have ignored important, perhaps the most important, features of the moral enterprise. We must therefore attempt to find out whether what appear to be, at least at first sight, two different enterprises, the enterprise of society-anchored reason and the moral enterprise, really are two or are only one, their identity hidden by their different names, descriptions, and different conceptual histories: the first an enterprise that in our thinking is associated with that of prudence and self-anchored reason, the second an enterprise that has for a very long time been identified with the religious enterprise and is only gradually and against determined resistance freeing itself from this confusing entanglement.

To make this task easier, I distinguish between four main aspects of an enterprise: its nature (or type), its structure, its end, and its function. I then examine these four aspects in each of the two enterprises to be compared. If it turns out that there are significant differences between them in one or all of these respects, then they are sufficiently different to count as two different enterprises, as they may seem to be. If, however, they are indistinguishable in all four, then, as far as our interests here are concerned, they really are one and the same (type of) enterprise.

The task thus neatly divides into two parts. The first requires the spelling out in greater detail of the nature, structure, end, and function of the enterprise of society-anchored reasons. The second requires assembling and assessing the evidence that, as we conceive the moral enterprise, its important aspects (nature, structure, end, and function) are indistinguishable from those of the enterprise of society-anchored reason. I deal with the first task in this section and with the second in section 4.

3.1.   *Enterprises: Their Natures and Ends*

By an enterprise, I understand a comparatively difficult and long-range activity, such as taking and passing the exams for a university degree, bringing in the harvest, or winning an election. By contrast, preparing and getting one's breakfast is too easy and short range to qualify. But the distinction is not sharp; getting a drivers' license may be too easy for some, but difficult and protracted enough for others to qualify.

There are, of course, many ways in which we can and do classify enterprises. For our purposes here, it will be most helpful to distinguish three natures or types: individual, collective, and an important subclass of the latter, social. Trying to bring in one's harvest or shopping for a suitable used car typically are individual enterprises, even though more than one person may be involved in achieving its end, that is, in bringing about the event (the harvest's being brought in or the finding of a suitable used car) or the state of affairs (the harvest being in or the used car having been found) at which it aims. What makes it an individual enterprise is that the questions of whose it is and what its end is, are both answered by reference to the same single individual (the person who is bringing in his harvest or is shopping for a suitable used car).

We need not try to draw sharp borderlines. "Joint enterprises," as when six are together trying to lift their car out of a ditch, involve a number of people with the same end. More than one but fewer than six may be required to attain the end of this enterprise. If all one's neighbors help one in bringing in one's harvest or if one gets one's friends' help in scrutinizing ads and cars, then there normally seems to be little point in deciding whether these are individual or collective enterprises. A particular business, say, a corner grocery shop run by a single person, may begin as, unquestionably, an individual enterprise but grow into a collective one as the number of its employees and outlets increases. We can think of it as an enterprise of an individual type or nature as long as its end is determined by reference to a single individual with that end and it ceases to be the same (token of its type) when that individual dies or loses control of its end.

Thus, the fact that the neighbors' help is needed to bring in one's harvest or that the owner of the grocery shop hires an assistant would appear not to affect its status as an individual enterprise. But when the enterprise becomes very large and the determination and implementation of its end depend on a large number wanting it and carrying it out, then the question of whether it still is an individual enterprise becomes increasingly less determinate. This is so largely because it also becomes less clear whether the end of the enterprise and its implementation is still actually determined by its (now more or less nominal) head, or whether there are among its various role players some whose opinion and will will have to be accommodated by that head and to what extent his originally dominant position has been modified in the direction of a "primus inter pares."

An enterprise moves out of this grey area on the border between an individual and a collective nature, and becomes an unquestionably collective one, not so much by a further increase in size as by the existence of a recognized collective decision procedure. In some cases, there no longer is a question of whose enterprise it is (as with General Motors or the Church of England), and its end and its policies of implementation are now determined by a formal procedure involving explicitly formulated steps by explicitly identified role players, consisting, for instance, of the questions to be decided, a well-defined voting procedure, and a list of the role players entitled to vote.*

Collective enterprises may be more or less voluntary. One can always leave one's job if one does not like it but one cannot get just any job one likes. And even if one can get it, one usually has to be satisfied with the wage one is offered. One cannot always join a trade union even if there is one, and one cannot always leave one or refuse to join it if one wants to keep one's job.

For our purposes here, the most interesting and perhaps the least voluntary type is the social enterprise. That is not, of course, (as should by now be clear) a one-shot individual enterprise, such as working for a degree, in which complete success is achieved when one gets the degree, and which also comes to an end at that point. The state of affairs of having the degree, which is a (conceptual) consequence of getting it, does not require the continuation of the enterprise, nothing more needs to be done to maintain it.** Although the number of migrants appears to have increased in this century, the typical way of joining a society, and the social enterprise it is engaged in, is still by being "born into it," that is, born to parents who are already members of it. Even those who manage to become members of a society they actually want to join are often refugees from the society into which they were born, or those who would have preferred to join another which, however, refused them entry. Many of them were allowed into any country only because they had rare skills, large amounts of money, or powerful sponsors; were not of an "inferior" race, sex, or age; did not have unpopular political or religious convictions; and were unlikely to become a burden to their new home on account of a physical or mental disability or an infectious disease. Thus, even apparently voluntary joinings of a society often are not, on closer inspection, entirely so.

Every society, through its members and others living in its territory, necessarily engages in (its token of) the social enterprise. Every individual enterprise conducted in that society by one of its members is regulated by its mores, which also, either through its custom or its law, determines the decision procedure by which the end of the (token) social enterprise and its implementation are determined. Because the mores must, from their very nature, determine a particular way of coordinating the individual enterprises of its members and of distributing the joint product of its cooperative enterprises, and because "exit" from a social order is often very limited and in any case usually a very undesirable step, members for good reasons tend to have a strong interest in having a voice in that collective determination of these important matters.*

However, even the existence of some procedure ensuring that the end of a given social enterprise is (at least by and large) in accordance with the will of its members would seem not to provide an adequate assurance of such ends being rationally acceptable. For one thing, the mores make their impact on members' lives long before these members can make their voice heard. For another, an individual's voice is often lost in the babble of voices that tends to flood societies in which all members have a voice. As has long been quite clear, Mill's apprehensions about the tyranny of the majority are not baseless or exaggerated. Principles limiting what ends governments may legitimately adopt and pursue, or lists of natural or human rights, are drawn up to protect members against the worst forms of oppression and exploitation generated by a variety of widely held prejudices against different but rationally unobjectionable behavior patterns and lifestyles often associated with the race, gender, religion, age, language, and so on, of the people exhibiting these hated deviations.

However, even this seems inadequate. After all, such rights are interests conventionally protected and guaranteed by the imposition of correlative duties on others whose interests may be adversely affected by that imposition. Such adversely affected interest groups may clamor for the recognition of their interests as rights. Interests of employers and employees, husbands and wives, of one industry and another, may conflict and if their interests are converted into rights, the rights also conflict. But the move from interests to rights was, in the first place, not simply to provide conventional recognition and protection of all interests but also an adjudication between conflicting interests, a determination of whose interests are to be protected and to what extent.

Thus what is needed is a system of reasons that adjudicate when different people's self-interested, and more generally self-anchored, reasons come into conflict. The enterprise of society-anchored (practical) reason (which I shall call "the enterprise$_R$") provides just such reasons.

3.2. The Nature of the Enterprise$_R$

What, then, can we say about that nature (or type)? If my account in Book One is correct, then the enterprise$_R$, as a crucial part of the enterprise of practical reason, has to be a part of the social enterprise. For the degree or extent of success of that enterprise depends on the transmission of the knowledge of these guidelines from one generation to the next, on their continual improvement, and on the appropriate sanctions, and this in turn depends on the proportion of the members of society who do their part in playing the various roles which constitute a society's engaging in the enterprise$_R$.

Note, however, that although its success depends on appropriate sanctions being provided by the mores, the guidelines of society-anchored reason are not necessarily the same as those contained in and sanctioned by the mores. Rather, the guidelines of society-anchored (practical) reason (and the reasons based on them) tell us what the guidelines of the mores and the sanctions in support of them should be, what they would be if they were in accordance with reason. Thus although both the enterprise of the mores and that of the society-anchored (practical) reasons are parts of the social enterprise, they are different though importantly related parts. The former is an important part of the subject matter of the latter, and the latter is the rationally ideal version of the former.

3.3.   The Structure of the Enterprise$_R$

Postponing for the moment a discussion of its end and its function, let us remind ourselves of its structure—"the structure$_R$" for short. By "the structure of an enterprise," I mean the way in which its members are expected to attain its end. Applied to the enterprise$_R$, this means that its members are expected to play, at the appropriate time and place, the various roles it involves: learner, teacher, agent, critic, reformer. For all or most of these roles, the society provides guidelines, more or less specific, more or less generally recognized and accepted. All members are expected always to apply those applicable to their situation and then to follow them because its complete success is thought to depend on everyone's doing so.

Bear in mind, though, that these guidelines are, at best, the best that the society can generate at that time, and sometimes they fall short of that, even considerably so. A member, therefore, is not in reason expected to follow them when the following conditions are satisfied: when he is especially well qualified and positioned to judge *whether,* and when he judges *that,* a particular guideline applicable to his situation and generally accepted is unsound and when he has good reason to think he knows what it should have directed instead, and what it would be best in the circumstances for him to do (whether to follow it nevertheless or else what to do instead). Under these conditions, members are also expected to play the role of reformer, that is, to communicate to their fellow members that and in what way the guideline is unsound and in what way it should be reformulated.

When, as a critic, he forms the opinion that someone has failed to follow a sound guideline, he is expected to convey that critical judgment to the culprit, and if (as will usually be the case) the matter is regulated also by the mores, to mobilize the appropriate sanctions, whether those of the law or those of custom. And he should, where necessary, also advocate the appropriate changes in custom or law. Thus, in the role of teacher, learner, and agent, a member helps to perpetuate currently accepted practical judgments and practices, whereas in the role of critic and reformer, he tries to influence the direction in which he thinks opinion and practice should move.*

If I am right in this, then there is both a close connection and an important difference between the judgment- (or practical reason-) oriented approach of the enterprise$_R$ and the response- (or will-) oriented approach of the mores. For the mores *purport* to be reason based, and the society-anchored reasons accepted in an enterprise$_R$ *purport* to be those on which the mores ought to be based. Thus, the two enterprises are mutually complementary; the mores strengthen (via their sanctions) the members' motivation to do what they purport is in accordance with society-anchored reasons, while the society-anchored reasons of an enterprise$_R$ purport to provide rational content for the mores. Neither would make sense without the other.

Two further related features of the structure$_R$ deserve our attention. The first is their universality and the varying degrees of what is often called their generality (but which I have subdivided into their scope and range[10]). They are "universal," but only in the sense that all the members to whom they are applicable are bound by them. Not all are equally general, not all maximally so; that is, not all are applicable to the same proportion of the members of an enterprise and in the same proportion of circumstances for which their formulation makes them applicable, let alone applicable to all members and in all circumstances. "People with headaches and sensitive stomachs ought not to take aspirin but Bufferin" is universal because it purports to be true of all to whom it applies, but not very general, since the proportion of those to whom it applies is not very high.

Thus, one of the most important features of any particular token of the enterprise$_R$ is the way it classifies its members. Few, if any, of its guidelines are likely to apply to all of them, but any one of them applies to and binds all the members of the class defined in it. Just as, in the law, there may be different regulations for tenants, unemployed, retirees, sailors, resident

---

[10] See above, chapter 2, section 2.5, pp. 81–84.

aliens, and so on, so, in an enterprise$_R$ there may be different guidelines for parents and children, teachers and students, friends and strangers, the old and the young, and so on. As we shall see more clearly, we tell whether the classifications of an enterprise$_R$ are well or ill chosen, by reference to its end. It is because the end of the ideal legal enterprise does not justify different provisions for the employment of men and women that we think such laws are (in most cases) discriminatory, that in such cases gender classifications lack rational justification.

A second feature we should mention concerns the appropriate way of improving the guidelines. For a variety of reasons (such as fear of seriously suboptimal outcomes of interactions based on self-anchored reasons), a society may come to have society-anchored guidelines even if its members are still unclear about their proper scope and range and so they may at first be treated as having a wider scope and range than some may suspect are warranted. Thus, they may start with a very broad principle to the effect that it is contrary to society-anchored reason for anyone ever to kill a living being. Taking into account only the typical cases on which they must initially focus, its recognition in that society would appear to have better consequences than its nonrecognition. Then, as their knowledge of conformity with and violation of this principle by various classes of agents and patients in various circumstances increases, they may be able to improve such overgeneral, hard and fast rules by adding certain exceptions to them, for example, killing animals, killing another human being in self-defense, or killing oneself in certain circumstances.

Such advances in knowledge and sophistication thus justify changes in two contexts. One is at the point where an agent needs to employ such a guideline prior to action. At that point, agents must determine whether they fall within its scope and range and so are bound by it or whether they fall under one of the established exceptions, and so are not bound by it.

The other is at a point at which we advert to such a guideline in judging the performance of an agent. We judge him by the general rule unless there is reason to think that he falls under one of these exceptions. The distinction between guidelines that "hold other things equal" and those that "hold all things considered" may also contain rules about who (e.g., whether the "accuser" or the "accused") has the burden of providing the relevant evidence to show what version of the guideline applies to the case in hand.

We can call this practice "methodological conservatism." It provides, at any particular time, a complex, but relatively neatly organized and so relatively manageable, body of established knowledge, into which new knowledge can be incorporated without unnecessarily uprooting established beliefs and modes of behavior, while yet allowing members to take advantage of new discoveries. If I am not mistaken, a similar method is employed also in the natural sciences—though only up to a point at which exceptions become unmanageably complicated, and we would do better to replace the "mother guideline" with its proliferating "epicycles" by a simpler one if it can be found.

3.4.   The End of the Enterprise$_R$

By "attaining the end of an enterprise" I mean its bringing about an event, or its bringing about and maintaining, for the appropriate length of time, a certain state of affairs, in which that enterprise's achievement of complete success consists. In the case of a typical individual enterprise, such as working for a university degree or getting in one's harvest, its end is the aim of the individual whose enterprise it is. As we have seen, in the case of collective, and especially social, enterprises, their end need not coincide with the aim of all or indeed the aim of any of its members' individual enterprises. What the end of such an enterprise is may be a difficult matter to determine.[11]

In the case of the enterprise$_R$, the question is particularly difficult. I therefore begin with relatively simple and uncontroversial peculiarities of that end. In this discussion, a further distinction between two types of enterprise$_R$ has to be drawn. The first type and its tokens may have different structures$_R$, leading to different degrees of success, that is, different degrees of excellence of the state of affairs the bringing about and maintaining of which constitutes various degrees or extents of its success. In the case of this first type and its tokens I shall speak of "success$_R$" and of "the end$_R$," when the relevant state of affairs may be brought about and maintained at any level of excellence, the end$_R$ attained with any degree of merit (barely, acceptably, adequately, satisfactorily, well, perfectly), and success$_R$ achieved to any extent (minimal, acceptable, adequate, satisfactory, considerable, great, full).

The second type and its tokens are ideals. Although they also may have different structures$_R$, they must be such as to attain the relevant end perfectly, that is, achieve complete success, that is, bring about and maintain the relevant state of affairs at the highest level of excellence. I shall speak of this type as "the Enterprise$_R$," of any of its tokens as "an

---

[11] For an interesting classification of enterprises and their ends, see Jacob Marschak, "Towards an Economic Theory of Organization and Information," *Decision Processes*, ed. R. M. Thrall, C. H. Coombs, and R. L. Davis (New York: John Wiley and Sons, 1954), 189.

Enterprise$_R$," of its end as "the End$_R$," and its success as "Complete Success$_R$." Achieving Complete Success$_R$, attaining the End$_R$, requires not merely the coming about of the appropriate state of affairs but also its indefinitely continuing prevalence. One of the crucial questions we have to answer is whether achieving Complete Success$_R$ depends on a certain special "process" through which the relevant state of affairs has come about and continues to prevail or whether it is sufficient that it has come about and continues to prevail in some way or other. Could it be simply a matter of luck? Could it be the outcome of the choices, by one or other member or a group of members, of means suitable for its attainment or must it be the appropriate behavior of all its members?

Let us remind ourselves of what is the End$_R$. It will be recalled that the enterprise$_R$ is a crucial part of the enterprise of practical reason which itself is a major part of the enterprise of reason. The end of the enterprise of practical reason is the good, in the sense of the bringing about and maintaining of a state of affairs which the members of a society can collectively bring about and maintain and which is, from the point of view of each of its members, the best that is possible for all (though not the best possible for any one) of them. This clearly is also the ultimate end of the enterprise$_R$, for the attainment of which the attainment of the end$_R$, its own (or proximate) end, is essential.

Its own end, it will be remembered,[12] is the correct formulation of society-anchored reasons and their incorporation in the mores, so that they will be generally recognized and followed. Where the context makes it clear, I shall here use "the end$_R$" to refer to either or both of these two, its own or its ultimate end.

If, as I have argued in Book One, the rational enterprise as a whole is an attempt to arrive, in certain sorts of activities (which I called "the activities of reason"), at "performances" as good as the suitably pooled resources of the human mind and body can generate, then the process by which Complete Success$_R$ is achieved cannot be a matter of luck. Indeed, luck can at most play a peripheral role.* Of course, the quality of people's lives will always be affected by good or bad luck, but the rational enterprise, and especially the Enterprise$_R$, are concerned only with what does not depend on luck. Indeed, part of the enterprise of practical reason, including the Enterprise$_R$, is concerned to reduce the impact of bad luck on individuals' lives as far as possible.

Again, the structure of the rational enterprise as a whole, and of the

---

[12] I have discussed this matter more fully, but from a different angle, in book 1, chapter 5, especially in sections 3 and 4.

Enterprise$_R$ in particular, makes it clear that they are concerned to provide the best guidelines that organized human ingenuity can develop for those who can take advantage of these aids in leading a life that comes as close as appropriate choices can take it to a realization of their (unflawed) conception of the good life for themselves.

However, the Enterprise$_R$ differs from other parts of the rational enterprise in that its guidelines are so designed that conformity with them, though yielding benefits, does not necessarily or even typically yield them for the complying member, but for someone else. Hence everyone's deriving benefits from the availability of these guidelines depends on everyone's complying with them. If everyone is to benefit, then everyone must "do his bit." Thus any enterprise$_R$, in which not every member does his bit, is not an Enterprise$_R$, not an instance of the Enterprise$_R$, but an enterprise$_R$, one that does not achieve Complete Success$_R$.

Why have and follow such curiously designed and "chancy" guidelines? Because they are needed for optimal outcomes in certain situations (such as prisoner's dilemma) in which more uncontentiously rational behavior, such as strategic interaction based on what I called "self-anchored" reasons, would have suboptimal outcomes.

The need for such guidelines seems to have been (at least obscurely) grasped by most societies (by all in my use of "society"), perhaps because their very survival has been sensed to depend on their having "mores," that is, recognized guidelines forbidding some and requiring other types of conduct which, by its nature, would be in accordance with self-anchored reasons. This may well also be the (at least obscurely) understood rationale for the frequent ascription of a special status inspiring fear, awe, reverence, or at least respect, to considerations with the content of such society-anchored reasons, and their usually being backed by sanctions, sometimes quite severe, so that members are more strongly motivated to follow them rather than their self-anchored reasons which, in the absence of such additional motivators, might well gain the upper hand.

The Enterprise$_R$ thus generates reasons which members are not simply welcome to comply with if they wish to heed these signposts to the good life (as is the case with self-anchored reasons), but which are treated as *requirements*, that is, as guidelines members *must* follow whether or not they desire to do *what* they prescribe, or revere whatever is required by reasons offered under such an awe-inspiring name, or even desire to do whatever is required by what really is a society-anchored reason.*

Clearly, then, the Enterprise$_R$ is a collective one, not merely in the sense that its guidelines are generated, transmitted from one generation to the next, and improved, by a collective effort, and one that is enormously superior to anything a single individual could generate, but also in the sense that its end is attained collectively, by the organized cooperation of its members, and not by individual action, let alone by luck. An Enterprise$_R$ comes the closer, other things equal, to Complete Success$_R$ the closer it comes to universal conformity with its guidelines.

Can we spell out the conditions of Complete Success$_R$? It would appear to be accomplished by an enterprise$_R$, if all its members always acted as they would if they always correctly performed their cognitive and executive tasks; if, in other words, they always arrived at their all-things-considered practical judgments by correctly applying all the relevant and sound principles of cognitive and practical reasoning to the practical problems they are confronting and if they always followed these practical judgments.

We can sharpen this point a little by spelling out the three conditions that are jointly sufficient for Complete Success$_R$ (call all three together "the Sufficient Success Condition"). (1) All the members of the Enterprise$_R$ know all the purported rational guidelines relevant to the practical problems they encounter, and they have the ability and the will to solve them by constructing all-things-considered practical judgments that correctly apply all the relevant rational guidelines to these problems (call this "the reflective-task condition"). (2) All the members always follow their all-things-considered practical judgments (call this "the executive-task condition"). And (3) all the purported rational guidelines are sound (call this "the Sound Principles Condition").* I call any rational enterprise that satisfies the Sufficient Success Condition "a perfect rational enterprise," and any social order whose members engage in such a perfect rational enterprise "a perfect rational order."

Condition (3) (the Sound Principles Condition) makes it clear that Complete Success depends on more than a sound structure of the Enterprise$_R$ and the perfect practical rationality of its members. It also depends on their perfect rationality in other relevant domains of reason outside the practical, for example, the cognitive. Furthermore, their perfect rationality would not, together with the other conditions, amount to the Sufficient Success Condition, unless it included perfect rationality in what I have called "the dispositional sense" as well, that is, a sense which implies that all the members of the Enterprise$_R$ also have the perfect motivation generated by appropriate mores. For, if some lack it, then considerations recognized in an enterprise$_R$, and so purporting to be sound society-anchored reasons, would not necessarily be, and in all probability often would not actually be, such (sound) reasons. For in that case, those members who lack this motivation, in all probability would, at least at times, not follow the purported society-anchored reasons. And then some of these purported society-anchored reasons in all probability would, at least for some members and for some occasions of their applicability, fail to constitute sound reasons of this (paramount) type. For if their content has been worked out as it should have been, namely, on the supposition that they will generate optimal outcomes if they are universally followed, then the state of affairs actually generated and maintained by such spotty conformity with such sound guidelines may well not be the outcome which would justify the belief that they are reasons which defeat self-anchored reasons that conflict with them. Thus, if these correctly designed guidelines are not universally followed, the belief that they are sound paramount reasons, all things considered, is probably not justified. When this is known, it will tend to disincline even some of those who would otherwise be disposed to comply with these purportedly sound society-anchored reasons, from doing so. Hence the importance for Complete Success of general compliance with these guidelines.

I now assume it granted that the Enterprise$_R$ has a certain end, that it is the end I said it has, and that the sufficient condition of its attainment is what I said it was. But it may be doubted (or indeed denied) that that sufficient condition is also a necessary one. In particular, it may be suggested that this end *can be attained* even if some members do not do their bit. Thus, it may be thought that even if not every member did his bit, there might be other external factors that could attain the End$_R$; perhaps some powerful and well-meaning spirit may bring it about and maintain that state of affairs for people who follow his commandments; or some unusual combination of natural forces may do it for all of us.

I think we can ignore this type of alternative as too farfetched and born of wishful thinking. Suppose, however, we think of attaining the End$_R$ as the being brought about and maintained of a certain specific state of affairs, specifiable in empirical (descriptive, observational) terms, just as a car engine's idling, after having been started and before being put in gear, is a certain state of affairs specifiable in such empirical (engineering) terms, which is brought about and maintained by the turning on of the ignition, provided that the various parts of the engine *function properly*. But surely, this same state of affairs can be brought about in different ways by engine designs involving different parts that work in different ways.

The suggestion is that it is possible to design the enterprise$_R$ in such a way that its working would bring about and maintain the same desirable state of affairs without requiring that all members do their bit, and that such an alternative design would be preferable for a variety of reasons. Perhaps the most important one is that such an alternative design of the enterprise$_R$ would not be afflicted by a weakness that threatens to send the Enterprise$_R$ to the junk heap. For its design is such that the Sufficient Success Condition would never be satisfied by any token enterprise$_R$ whose guidelines generate optimal results only if everyone follows them. No one can seriously believe in a "perfect rational order," in which everyone always does his bit, where that requires everyone often to act against what is best from his point of view. But if it is quite unrealistic to hope that we shall ever get an enterprise in which everyone does his bit so defined, would we not, as I suggested a few paragraphs ago, lack adequate reason always to follow even (other things equal) sound society-anchored reasons when they conflict with our self-anchored ones? For is not one of the conditions of our having adequate reason always to follow them—that everyone else always follows them—always false? Would it not, then, be sometimes, probably often, contrary to reason for us to follow even these rightly purported paramount reasons? Should we not try to construct an alternative design of the Enterprise$_R$ which does not rely on the unrealistic assumptions required by the Enterprise$_R$?

This seems to me a very serious objection and I propose to discuss it in two stages. The first examines whether we could so design the enterprise$_R$ that its function could be performed without the members doing their bit. The second examines whether participation in the enterprise of practical reason can have any point if the enterprise$_R$ accomplishes success only to an extent that falls short of Complete Success$_R$. I shall deal with these two questions in the next two sections.

3.5. *The Function of the Enterprise$_R$*

As I understand the term "function," things other than enterprises can have one, and not all enterprises do. Carburetors, safety valves, kidneys, none of which are enterprises, have a function, and getting a driver's license, designing a rock garden, or climbing Mt. Everest are enterprises, but they do not have one. Like "end," "aim," "goal," and "purpose," "function" is a teleological term; each refers in a special way to one or several aspects of an assembly of things of which the following three are central: a state of affairs, conceived as a good, which tends to be brought about and maintained by the normal or characteristic behavior of a certain thing. I shall use the term "telos" as the generic term for "end," "aim," and so forth, which are its species. Things are said to *have* these teloi and there is always something, some event or state of affairs, whose being brought about or maintained by their behavior constitutes their telos being attained, accomplished, reached, realized, performed, and the like.

I turn now to the species I mean by "a function." We can discover whether kidneys and vermiform appendixes have a function, and if so, whether or not particular ones perform it, or perform it well, or function well, but we cannot assign a function to them or impose one on them nor can they assume one. By contrast, a teacher can assume a function, for example, to teach the dyslexics or ancient history, and the headmaster can assign or impose that function on her, and she may perform it well or poorly or may altogether fail in it, or may not even try, but we cannot discover whether teachers, from their nature have these functions, or whether a particular teacher has it, but only after she had already assumed it or had it imposed on her, and in that case and only then can we discover whether or not she is performing it and how well she is doing so.

I shall not here examine in general how having a function differs from having one of the other teloi, but draw only those features that are relevant to a better understanding of the function$_R$ (i.e., the function of the enterprise$_R$).

For something to be capable of having a function, it must be part of a thing with a complex structure involving other parts, each with its own characteristic mode of behavior tending or intended to attain a certain end of its own, where all of these modes of behavior and the ends they attain are coordinated with one another so as to bring about, and maintain for an appropriate time, a certain state of affairs the bringing about of which is the overall end of that complex thing. That complex thing attains its end (with a certain degree of merit, that is, brings about and maintains the state of affairs brought about and maintained in attaining its end, at a certain level of excellence) if each of its parts with a function performs that function (with a certain degree of merit).

Not all enterprises that have an end and attain it have a function and perform it or function at all or with a certain degree of merit. Many individual enterprises lack the complexity of structure and the need for a coordination of parts toward a single end which an enterprise must have if there is to be anything that can count as performing its function and functioning. There is nothing in my bringing in the harvest, studying for a degree, or making preparations for a large end-of-term party that could be *that which* has and does or does not perform its function. Nor are these enterprises part of a larger one with an end of its own for whose attainment it is sufficient (and perhaps necessary) that each of the parts attains its own end, so that the larger enterprise attains its end because its component parts perform their function.

The enterprise$_R$, by contrast, can (and does) have a function, for it has an end of its own and is part of a complex larger enterprise with an overall end for whose attainment it is sufficient (and perhaps necessary) that each of its parts attain its own end. Thus, an enterprise$_R$ performs its function if it attains the end$_R$, because it is a part of an enterprise of reason, the attainment of whose overall end (i.e., the good, in the sense explained) depends on that particular enterprise$_R$ and the other parts of that particular enterprise of reason attaining their own ends. Thus, the enterprise of reason attains its end (more or less well or even perfectly, that is, with Complete Success) if all its parts, including its enterprise$_R$, perform their function (more or less well, or even perfectly).

It seems clear that we cannot conceive of a structure of the Enterprise$_R$, such that the Sufficient Success Condition does not include appropriateness of the members' behavior. For, as we have seen, Complete Success depends on members knowing what are the paramount general guidelines, how to apply them to their practical problems, and having acquired the motivation to act as their application of them to the problem in hand directs them. But then Complete Success is inextricably tied to the appropriateness of the members' behavior.

It may perhaps be thought that, since what matters is the ultimate end of the enterprise$_R$, there may be other ways of attaining complete success in attaining *it*, not just with a radically different structure of the enterprise$_R$, but without it altogether. But what could these other ways be? Should we rely on luck, or on supernatural powers or forces as the Divine Command Theory does, or simply on the mores of our society without conceiving of them as subject to correction through the enterprise$_R$? Even Hobbes thought it desirable for the sovereign to conform his laws and his actions to the guidelines of practical reason spelled out in the Laws of Nature (though, no doubt, he relied too much on the sovereign's fear of God, good sense, and decency to ensure that his laws did so conform.[13]

If this is right, then abandoning the enterprise$_R$ altogether cannot lead to a better way of achieving complete success in the enterprise of practical reason. I conclude that we cannot dispense with that enterprise as a condition of complete success in the Enterprise of Practical Reason. But is Complete Success$_R$ necessary for it? Well, it would certainly appear so, for it is an ideal of perfection which could not be accomplished without Complete Success$_R$, since it is success such that the state of affairs brought about and maintained is of the highest possible excellence, and so could

---

[13] E.g., see Hobbes, *Leviathan*, 265, 354; see also Jean Hampton, *Hobbes and the Social Contract Tradition* (Cambridge: Cambridge University Press, 1986), 242–46.

not be improved upon in any way. But then every member's doing his bit is a necessary condition of Complete Success$_R$, because a state of affairs brought about and maintained by every member's doing his bit would necessarily be better from the point of view of reason than the same state of affairs brought about when some members are not doing theirs.

Exactly why is this so? "Every member is doing his bit" implies that every member always follows reason, that is, always follows society-anchored reasons even when they conflict with their self-anchored ones. Call the ensuing state of affairs, S_1. Suppose, then, that contrary to our assumption in constructing society-anchored reasons, someone, say A, were not to do his bit but were to follow his self-anchored reason instead, then someone else, say B, would be less "well off" in terms of his self-anchored reasons than if A had followed society-anchored reason. But then the ensuing state of affairs, say S_2, has two quite different evaluative characteristics: it resembles S_1 in that it is dispreferable from one person's point of view, who has been adversely affected by the other's self-anchored choice: S_1 from A's and S_2 from B's. But S_2 also differs from S_1, and in a more important way, for it is also objectively less excellent than S_1, from the point of view of reason because, unlike S_1, it does not give all of the members (i.e., not B) adequate reason, all things considered, to accept it. S_1 does because, though dispreferable from A's point of view because from it it would be contrary to reason for him to accept it, it is nonetheless objectively more excellent than S_2 because it is acceptable to both A and B from the point of view of reason, the point of view that takes into account not only self-anchored but all practical reasons, including the paramount society-anchored ones.[14]

It may be helpful to summarize briefly what has been argued so far in this section. We examined the nature, structure, end, and function of the Enterprise$_R$, the perfect type of the enterprise of society-anchored reason, itself an important part of the enterprise of practical reason whose complete success depends on Complete Success$_R$ (i.e., the complete success of the Enterprise$_R$). We spelled out three conditions which, I argued, are jointly sufficient conditions of Complete Success$_R$. One of these is that all members always follow practical reason which implies that they follow society-anchored rather than self-anchored reason when the two conflict. Finally, I argued that this is also a necessary condition of Complete Success$_R$, because there is no state of affairs brought about and maintained by some members doing and others not doing their bit that is

---

[14] As will be recalled, I have explained more fully why this is so in book 1, chapter 5, especially sections 3 and 4, and I shall briefly return to this point in section 3.5 of this chapter.

as good, that is, as rationally acceptable, from everyone's point of view, as one that has been brought about and maintained by every member doing his. I conclude that, if we allow that complete success in the enterprise of practical reason depends on the enterprise$_R$ performing its function and if we allow that the nature, structure, and end of that enterprise is as I have claimed, then we must allow that the complete success of the enterprise of practical reason depends on the enterprise$_R$ performing its function perfectly, at least in respect of requiring every member to do his bit and every member in fact doing it, for, without that, the state of affairs thus brought about and maintained would be one which some member would have less good reason to accept than one brought about and maintained by every member doing his bit, even if the two states of affairs are equally excellent in other ways; say, the "overall happiness" of its members is the same.

And what holds for this part, namely, (1) and (2), every member doing his bit of the conditions, which jointly constitute the Sufficient Success Condition, also holds for the other part, namely, (3), the soundness of all the guidelines of reasons that are relevant to members performing their reflective task, and, of course, especially the soundness of all the guidelines of society-anchored reason. For if any, perhaps many, of these relevant guidelines are unsound in some particular enterprise$_R$, then Complete Success$_R$ cannot be achieved in it, hence that enterprise$_R$ cannot be expected to perform its function perfectly and that enterprise of practical reason will not achieve Complete Success, that is, attain its end with the highest level of merit.

3.6. Society-Anchored Reasons in the Real World

The preceding argument and its conclusion should not, however, be construed as denying the force of the suggestion I mentioned in the preceding section, that the actual enterprises$_R$ we normally encounter are never Completely Successful$_R$. I would have to agree that they are not instances of the Enterprise$_R$, or only in the sense in which the circles we draw on the blackboard are instances of the geometrical circle, or actual democracies instances of true democracy, or our free markets instances of the perfectly free market. That, I agree, is the hard reality, hence critics and reformers of an enterprise$_R$ should not expect ever to transform it into an instance of the ideal type here envisaged.

Why then bother with this utopian ideal? Only because it—and perhaps nothing else—can indicate the direction in which we should try to move our (imperfect instance of the) enterprise$_R$. What is more, it is, like a world free of all diseases or all crime or all barriers to free trade, a type of ideal we do not expect will ever be realized. But, surely, that does not ipso facto disqualify them as something to which we can come closer or from which we can move away.

Admittedly, there are dangers with such unattainable ideals: knowing where we want to go does not tell us how to get there or even how to get closer. But this danger threatens not only ideals that are unattainable even in principle, such as the perfectly free market; a world free of illness and hunger may not be unattainable in principle (as the perfectly free market is) and yet be *practically* unattainable, because we may never *find out how* to attain it, or, even if it is already widely known *what would have to be done by whom* in order to attain it, we cannot agree on *how to ensure that it is done by them.* Still, do we not rightly think it important to be clear about what it is to come closer to realizing this ideal, to develop methods for coming closer to it (whether or not we can ever fully realize it) and to employ these methods as best we can, because we can improve our lives not only by attaining the ideal but also by coming closer to it?

At the same time, we must guard against two related difficulties. One is that, by using one of these methods to come closer to one of these ideals, we may be driven away further from another. The second is that not everyone will be willing to curb his desires and pet projects "just because" their pursuit clashes with certain society-anchored reasons, even if he acknowledges that they are such reasons; and, of course, there will in all probability be some, perhaps many, who will not recognize that there can be any such reasons for them or for anyone, or that those that are widely recognized as such, really are. But I shall not now rehearse once more the case against those who reject the method for determining society-anchored reasons and the rationale for accepting the restraints they impose.

Even if all this is granted, another doubt may be raised: is not my conception of the Enterprise$_R$—call it the Ideal Cooperation Theory (ICT)—vitiated by exactly the same flaw as the Divine Command Theory (DCT)? That theory, it will be remembered, requires us, yet cannot furnish us with adequate reason, to believe that acting in accordance with what we take to be divine commandments will enable us to live a supremely blissful life in another better world. Similarly, it may be said, ICT requires us, but cannot furnish us with adequate reason, to believe that the world we live in is such that always following society, rather than self-anchored reasons, will put us in as good a position as we all can be, to lead a life that comes *as close as possible* to our (internally unflawed) conception of the good life for ourselves.[15] Do we not in fact have adequate reason to believe the contrary? Is not our world such that we shall sometimes, probably quite often, come closer to an optimal life, as we conceive it, if we follow self-anchored rather than society-anchored reasons? Indeed, will we not sometimes suffer irreparable harm, unbearable hardship, or even death, unless we follow self- rather than society-anchored reason? For will it not sometimes or even often be the case, for instance, that others, by not following society-anchored reasons, keep us away from the good life as we envisage it? And could we not, in such cases, come closer to it by, instead, following self-anchored reason ourselves, too? And would not reason recommend this course, rather than that which is dictated to us by society-anchored reason?

I have already conceded that no actual enterprise$_R$ can be Completely Successful and so none can give each of those guided by one the compelling self-anchored reason that a Completely Successful$_R$ one could give, for always following society-anchored reason. To acknowledge this unfortunate fact is not, however, to acknowledge a flaw in ICT, but simply to reject an unrealistic demand. Some moral theories are deeply flawed because their authors thought it necessary to cater to one such unrealistic demand: that a satisfactory moral theory must have the resources to prove that satisfying the requirements of justice will always also satisfy those of one's greatest happiness. Prichard famously argued[16] that this was true of Plato's moral theory. Many think it is true of Hobbes's. I argued above[17] that Sidgwick's theory is flawed, not because he could not show that his "two methods of ethics," egoistic and universal hedonism (to which my enterprises of self-anchored and society-anchored reason are analogues, though admittedly only rather rough ones), never require incompatible behavior of anyone, but because he took this "ideal" relation between the two methods to be something in the nature of a postulate of practical reason. And DCT is driven by the same demand, which it satisfies (despite its gleefully exaggerated pessimism about life in this world) by the postulation of an ideal afterlife which ensures that complying with the

---

[15] For the distinction between internally and externally flawed conceptions of the good life, see book 1, chapter 4, section 6, and chapter 5, especially section 5.

[16] H. A. Prichard, "Does Moral Philosophy Rest on a Mistake?" *Mind* 21 (1912). Reprinted in H. A. Prichard, *Moral Obligation,* ed. W. D. Ross (Oxford: Clarendon Press, 1949), 1–17; also reprinted in *Readings in Ethical Theory,* 2nd ed., ed. Wilfrid Sellars and John Hospers (Englewood Cliffs, N.J.: Prentice Hall, 1970), 87.

[17] See Above, Introduction, Section 2.

requirements of morality (the Divine Commandments) in this world will never conflict with satisfying the requirements of one's overall happiness.*

Thus, the practical impossibility of Complete Success makes it impossible to prove that it is in accordance with reason for *everyone always* to follow the society-anchored guidelines of their enterprise$_R$, but it does not make it impossible for anyone ever to have adequate reason to do so. For we may be able to show that there are enterprises$_R$ which are sufficiently close to Complete Success$_R$ for it to be in accordance with reason for every member either always to follow the society-anchored guidelines of his enterprise$_R$ or to do so at least in respect of some of its guidelines. Clearly, the practical impossibility of Complete Success$_R$ greatly complicates our task. We must develop something like a measure and the direction of the distance from Complete Success$_R$. And we must, in proportion to the magnitudes of this distance, suitably modify the general guideline requiring members of an enterprise$_R$ always to follow its society-anchored rather than self-anchored guidelines when the two conflict.

Two Types of Flaw. The three conditions which, together, constitute the Sufficient Success Condition indicate the dimensions along which an enterprise$_R$ can fall more or less short of Complete Success$_R$.

(A) I begin with the one which, for obvious reasons, is most frequently discussed by philosophers: the unsoundness of the socially entrenched guidelines which purport to ground society-anchored reasons. It is not necessary to repeat my account, in book 1, of the criterion of soundness, but it may be helpful if I remind readers of the difference between its two parts. The first states a condition the subject matter of a guideline must satisfy to be properly a guideline in an enterprise$_R$ at all: it must be such that, if members in relation to this subject matter were simply to engage in strategic interaction on the basis of self-anchored reasons, then this would yield suboptimal outcomes, that is to say, a state of affairs worse for every member than it would be if one or other from a range of guidelines came to be generally entrenched in the society and recognized as society anchored and so paramount. However, this still may leave room for a number of alternative such rules; thus, each of quite a few such guidelines for sexual and reproductive behavior may be an improvement on strategic interaction on the basis of self-anchored reasons.

To narrow the range, the second part demands optimality from the point of view of everyone affected by universal compliance; the outcome must be not merely some improvement over strategic interaction, but better than any produced by universal compliance with any other guideline, not merely better for some and worse for others, not merely better for some and no worse for others, but equally good from every member's point of view, not merely "satisficing" (in the sense invented by Herbert Simon), not merely "Pareto-optimal," not merely perfectly efficient.[18] It must be the best for everyone alike, both optimal and equitable.

I here suggest, tentatively, as a working hypothesis, that other things equal, an enterprise$_R$—call it E_1—is at a greater distance from Complete Success$_R$ than another, E_2, if in E_1 there is an entrenched guideline purporting to ground a society-anchored reason to act in a certain way such that universal compliance with it does not improve every member's life over what it would be without any guideline, whereas in E_2 universal compliance with its guideline on the same subject matter does generate such an improvement.

And E_2 is at a greater distance from Complete Success$_R$ than another enterprise$_R$—call it E_3—which has another guideline on the same subject matter such that universal compliance with it produces a state of affairs in which everyone's life in respect of the subject matter regulated becomes as good as it can without someone else's therefore becoming less good.

Finally E_3 is at a greater distance from Complete Success$_R$ than another enterprise$_R$—call it E_4—which has another guideline on the same subject matter such that universal compliance with it generates and maintains a state of affairs in which everyone has as good a chance as everyone can have to lead a life which in respect of the subject matter regulated by this guideline comes as close as everyone's life can come to the good (internally unflawed) life as he conceives of it.*

Suppose, then, that we can sometimes determine the distance from Complete Success$_R$ of an enterprise$_R$ by examining its guidelines individually for soundness. We can then distinguish three respects in which it may fall short of such success. One is the *degree* of the unsoundness of particular guidelines—the guideline in E_1 being the most unsound of the four considered, the second the *proportion* of guidelines that are unsound, and the third the *importance* of the unsound guidelines. If, finally, we develop a way of compounding these three "dimensions" of soundness into a single magnitude, then we can compare such enterprises$_R$ on the basis of their greater or lesser unsoundness and can determine whether, assuming there to be no other flaws, their unsoundness is low enough to bring the enterprise$_R$ sufficiently close to Complete Success$_R$ for its

---

[18] See Herbert A. Simon, e.g., *Reason in Human Affairs* (Stanford, Calif.: Stanford University Press, 1983), 85.

guidelines to constitute reasons that are, other things equal, paramount; or to put it differently, that members have, other things equal, adequate permitting or requiring reason to follow these guidelines rather than self-anchored ones.

Fortunately, the difficult determination of that sufficient proximity is not always required for answering our practical questions; in some cases, the answer hinges solely on the soundness of a single or a few such guidelines. Suppose that, as a conscientious parent, I am discussing with my son whether he ought to use a condom in his love-making. Suppose also that our enterprise$_R$ embodies a guideline that absolutely forbids the use of condoms but that I have concluded, after careful reflection, that it is unsound and that while there is no other relevant guideline which would prohibit, there are several I regard as sound and important that recommend, or require, their use. It seems then that I can answer my practical question without having to assess my enterprise$_R$'s distance from Complete Success and whether it is sufficiently close to it for its guidelines to generate paramount reasons.

Still, my conviction of the unsoundness of a given guideline may not always be an adequate reason not to follow it. Not following a widely accepted one may be undesirable even if it is unsound, for noncompliance may well tend to undermine other people's disposition to conform with other such widely accepted guidelines even though they are sound or at any rate sound enough. But a smoothly working enterprise$_R$ in which most of the members reliably always follow them is a great good. It generates and maintains a "social climate" in which its members can lead a life that gives scope for planning and for carrying out one's plans, safely and without obstruction, by strategic interaction on the basis of self-anchored reasons but within the confines drawn by the generally accepted society-anchored guidelines. And such a social climate not only is a great good, it is also one that is easily undermined and destroyed, but hard to rebuild.

The case in favor of following even an unsound guideline is, of course, the more persuasive the less seriously flawed the particular guideline is, the more it resembles the one in E_3 or E_2, rather than E_1. For if it is only as unsound as that in E_3, the adverse effects on people's lives of complying with it may well be less severe than those of not complying. The fact that we can or might be able to think of other guidelines on the same issue which would yield slightly greater improvements for everyone, or would distribute the improvements with somewhat greater equity might not be sufficient gains for which to risk undermining the existing level of success.

There is a further reason for this caution, even when the guidelines "*are* unsound" as I put it. For often one does not *know* that they are unsound, but at best has the best reasons available to one that they are. Given the widespread disagreements and uncertainties about the criterion and test of soundness and about whether one has applied it correctly, we should be especially cautious in our judgment of unsoundness when they are generally or widely accepted as sound. Often, a better policy would be to conform or, as in civil disobedience, openly to break the rule, but in either case to draw attention to the issue and discuss it with those who support the rule, to see whether agreement can be reached.

Of course, in certain types of case, this policy would be quite inappropriate. It would, surely, have been absurd to expect American Blacks (or their sympathizers) in pre-abolition America to obey the Fugitive Slave Act, or the Jews (or their sympathizers) in Nazi Germany the Nuremberg Laws, while arguing with slave owners or Nazis about their soundness. When an enterprise$_R$ is as far from Complete Success$_R$ as these two enterprises$_R$ were, when the basis of cooperation between certain classes of its members is not merely inequitable (as may be the distribution of wealth in some societies), but monstrously iniquitous, then the risk of undermining or destroying that flawed part of the social order cannot be an adequate reason for conforming with those of its guidelines that are as far away from soundness as they can get. However, even in these cases, the appalling unsoundness of one or a whole set of such guidelines does not necessarily suffice to invalidate all or even any of the others.

(B) I turn now to the second type of such flaw already mentioned earlier: that a certain proportion of the members of an enterprise$_R$ are *failing to conform to one or more of the only widely recognized guidelines* applicable to their practical problems, or fail to *take these guidelines into account* in arriving at their all-things-considered practical judgments about their practical problems thereby causing those who do conform to lead less good lives than they would if all conformed. Our question is whether someone's knowledge or justifiable belief that she is a member of an enterprise$_R$ such as we have just envisaged, is an adequate reason for her not to do her bit, that is, not to follow or take into account some or all of the recognized guidelines she knows or justifiably believes to be sound. (I here ignore the complication already discussed that she may not have adequate reason not to do so even when she knows or justifiably believes that they are unsound.)

Note, to begin with, that, in some of these cases, such nonconformity, and so on, by this proportion of members will amount to their not doing their bit, but in others it will not.* For, as we said, conforming to such guidelines or taking them into account in this way in an enterprise$_R$ that lies at some distance from Complete Success$_R$, may sometimes be contrary to reason, whereas doing one's bit can never be; when conforming to such guidelines (and so on) is contrary to reason, then not doing these things is not failing to do one's bit.

Suppose, then, that this proportion of members is not just failing to conform, etc., but is failing to do their bit, for reasons other than that a certain proportion of members are not doing theirs. Our question now is whether someone's knowledge or justified belief about this flaw in the enterprise$_R$ of which she is a member is an adequate reason for her not to do her bit.

Note, to begin with, that not doing one's bit includes two importantly different types of case: that in which one fails (perhaps from weakness of will or obstinacy) to act according to one's correct all-things-considered practical judgment although one knows that this risks adversely affecting others or actually does so; and that in which one follows one's all-things-considered practical judgments when, for no adequate exculpatory reasons, one has got these judgments wrong and when one knows that doing so risks adversely affecting others or actually does so. The flaw in an enterprise$_R$ we are now considering is not that a greater or smaller proportion of its guidelines is known or justifiably believed by a proportion of its members to be more or less seriously unsound—for in such a case their nonconformity, and so on, normally would not amount to a failure to do their bit. The primary flaw in the case we are considering is the more or less serious malperformance of their cognitive or executive tasks by a larger or smaller proportion of the members, for these are the primary cases of members failing to do their bit.

To simplify things, I shall here ignore another difficult problem, namely, how the magnitude of such an enterprise$_R$'s flaw is affected by how large a proportion of the failures to conform to guidelines is due, not to inadequately reasoned steps but to the erroneous epistemic convictions generally accepted in a community. I concentrate, instead, on examining the doing and failing to do one's bit in two importantly different types of case, which have been widely discussed.

The easier one is that in which doing one's bit involves following a sound guideline requiring one to behave in a way which does not risk inflicting, or does not in fact inflict, harm of a certain specific sort on some other person, or in a way such that one thereby confers a benefit of a certain specific sort on him. Typical instances are guidelines requiring members not to kill other human beings or to rescue them when they are in mortal or other serious danger, such as losing a limb. These cases involve a single agent and a single patient and they favor the patient at the possible expense of the agent, for the latter is forbidden or required to do a certain specific thing, in order thereby to improve the life of the patient, a thing he might not already have been disposed to do, from inclination or self-anchored reason.[19]

The two main subclasses of this class of guideline (prohibitions of harm and behests of benefit) differ in one important respect, namely, in the number of people who must not act as directed, if the patient's life is to be suitably affected. In the case of society-wide prohibitions of harming others, all members who can choose between acting or not acting as the guideline directs must always conform, if the life of a given person is not to be adversely affected; a single person not conforming on a single occasion suffices to affect that person's life adversely. And the same is true, a fortiori, if no person's life is to be adversely affected. In respect of this prohibitory guideline *everyone* must do his bit *by everyone*.

Benefit-requiring guidelines require less. For a certain benefit to be conferred on a particular person, say, Ann, it is enough for one member to act toward her as the guideline requires. Suppose a guideline requires that all persons in danger be rescued, then if Ann, now in danger of drowning, is to be rescued, it is not necessary that every member rescue her. If one person has rescued her, then others who have not done so have not failed to do their bit by her in respect to this guideline, even though they have not done anything toward her rescue. But if one person harms Ann, then he has not done his bit in respect of the relevant guideline, irrespective of how many others have not harmed her. The fact that Jack and many others have conformed to the guideline does not mean that Bert may now fail to do so without thereby failing to do his bit by her in respect of this guideline. Thus, knowingly not acting as a guideline directs may be failing to do one's bit in respect to it but, as benefit-requiring guidelines show, this is not necessarily so.* In respect of such guidelines, it is sufficient for everyone to receive the required benefits if, for each recipient and occasion, one person acts as the guideline requires.

The question, then, is whether someone's knowledge (or well-supported belief) that a "telling" number (I do not here examine how we determine such a number) of other members is not doing their bit in respect to a certain guideline of this sort, constitutes an adequate reason for her not to do hers in this respect. We have already remarked that other

---

[19] More on this in chapter 9.

known or believed kinds of flaw—such as the known or justifiably believed unsoundness of a given guideline or someone's not factoring such a guideline into his all-things-considered practical judgments—need not constitute an adequate reason for anyone not to follow it.

It would appear that, similarly, it is not such a reason when the failure of "telling" numbers to follow one or several sound guidelines occurs in certain circumstances. It seems to me that one of these circumstances is this: the failure is widely recognized in the society as creating a need to strengthen the factors on which the extent of conformity depends, such as moral education, legal and other sanctions, and, last but not least, the malfunctioning of other parts of the social order (shown by widespread poverty, unemployment, social injustices, and so on), and this need is met by society's serious efforts to strengthen these factors.

However, even that may not be enough, as when the extent of other members' not doing their bit reaches such proportions or takes such forms that doing one's bit is transformed from being (at worst) merely unduly onerous to being dangerous: when not to kill another usually or very often is to risk being killed or maimed by him. In such a case, the social enterprise has deteriorated to such an extent that the climate of life it generates begins to resemble a Hobbesian state of nature. Then even members' sound all-things-considered practical judgments (including society-anchored reasons) cease to ground paramount practical reasons, and members are thrown back on interaction with one another in accordance with self-anchored reason.

No new considerations are introduced when the guidelines of an enterprise$_R$ require or forbid behavior by a single agent but the patient is constituted by a number of persons, for example, one that is violated by someone throwing a hand grenade into a restaurant full of diners, or one that pins responsibility on someone for the damage one of his blasting operations has inflicted on all those living nearby. Nor is it different when the agent is constituted by a number of people, as when three or more conspire to defraud one or a number of people. What remains the same, when the individual agent or patient is replaced by a collective one, is that what the relevant guideline now directs is *a single act* (whether the noninfliction or prevention of harm or the conferring of a benefit) to be performed by a collective agent intended to affect a collective patient.

An importantly new element is introduced, however, when the single act is replaced by a series of acts; when the impact (whether on individual or collective patients) which the guideline forbids or requires would be caused not by a single act, but only by a series of acts (whether of individual or collective agents). Suppose, for example, that no harm is done if my neighbor and his family walk across my lawn just once, or if the British fishing fleet fish in the Norwegian waters just on one day, but serious harm is done if the actions occur with a frequency above a certain threshold.[20] The problem is not significantly different if, as is the case in some of the examples often discussed (e.g., What if no one voted? or What if everyone spent an hour in the only accessible bathroom?), the agent is the same as or overlaps with the patient. For, in both types of case, the crucial question is the same: Does someone have adequate reason not to comply on account of her knowledge (or justified belief) that the proportion of noncomplying agents compounded by the frequency of their noncompliances add up to the threshold number? Or, in more familiar language, does that knowledge give her adequate, perhaps compelling, reason to be "a free rider"? Suppose Anne knows that the threshold number is 100 noncompliances and that there have been 150 during the relevant period. Then it may be claimed that her compliance will be contrary to reason, because gratuitous, because the damage has already been done, and because her compliance could no longer prevent it. Suppose, alternatively, that there have been only fifty noncompliances and that only another twenty could be made in the remaining time under consideration. Then, too, it may be said, her compliance will be contrary to reason, because gratuitous, since the damage can no longer be done even if her noncompliance occurred as one of the other still possible noncompliances. In these cases, it seems that the question, "What if everyone did the same?" loses its bite. For Anne can say in the first case that "the same" (walking across the lawn) has already been done by a sufficient number to make her behavior irrelevant, and in the second case that the same can no longer be done by a sufficient number to cause the harm, thus making her compliance unnecessary and so contrary to reason.

This argument draws solely on self-anchored reasons. The questioner considers only whether her "sacrifice"—compliance, not walking across the lawn—is a necessary and sufficient condition of success, avoiding the harm or conferring the benefit she has self-anchored reason to avoid or confer. However, the question, "What if everyone did the same?" with its (implied) complaint of contrariety to reason, does not draw solely on such reasons. It is often, perhaps primarily and properly, asked by, or on behalf of those who complied only or primarily because they thought it was

[20] I here borrow a number of ideas from David Lyons's insightful book *The Forms and Limits of Utilitarianism* (London: Oxford University Press, 1965), especially 62–118.

required by (society-anchored) reason to comply with this, as they believe, sound society-anchored guideline and in the expectation that others too are rational persons similarly motivated and so prepared to do their bit to bring about the desirable result which depends on everyone (or a sufficient number) doing that.

Clearly, this is not so in every case. If everyone were celibate, or had his dinner at the same time,[21] this would have undesirable consequences. Does this show that everyone has compelling reason to follow a guideline forbidding the doing of it? Surely not. There are enough who have no desire to be celibate, nor would not being celibate by some or even very many be contrary to their or anyone else's interest. Hence there is not only no need to ensure by one's own compliance that the threshold number of noncompliers will not be reached but also no unfairness in a laissez-faire arrangement under which people are free to follow self-anchored reasons. This is so because the natural distribution of desires is such that the undesirable case of everyone wanting to be celibate or having dinner at the same time is most unlikely to happen and there is therefore no need for the recognition of a society-anchored guideline forbidding celibacy and requiring different classes of people to have staggered dinner times.

But sometimes a desirable outcome (including the prevention of an undesirable one) can be reached only if a certain threshold number of people behave in a certain way they would not wish to behave in except because and insofar as such behavior contributes their fair share in what everyone must do if the desirable result is to be achieved. If 200 want to walk across the lawn but only 100 can do so without serious damage being done to it, then fairness would appear to require either that nobody walk across it or that they take turns or that they draw lots about who may do so, and so on. If an unspoiled lawn is a greater good than the general freedom for all to walk across it, and if all who want to cannot do so without the lawn getting badly worn, then the question, "What if everybody did the same?" gets a grip on those who walk across it. They have a completely satisfactory answer only if they can point to a fair procedure by which they but not others came to be exempted from the burden of walking around rather than across it.

It is, however, important to distinguish between a sound society-anchored guideline that has merely been thought of or stated by someone

---

[21] The second example is borrowed from Marcus Singer's *Generalization in Ethics* (New York: Knopf, 1961), 81–82, 151–52. But my treatment differs from his. See also Sidgwick, *ME*, 487.

and one that has actually been established in a given social order.* What is the relevance of this distinction here? That no one should drive his car to his work place downtown may be a sound society-anchored guideline, for not everyone can do so without the complete collapse of motor traffic in and out of the city. But clearly the knowledge or justified belief that, if everyone did drive his car to work downtown, this would have disastrous consequences, does not by itself suffice to generate a paramount reason not to do so. That reason is, however, generated if such a guideline is sound and is enacted as law or is generally recognized as another part of our mores. Suppose, then, that such a guideline has been enacted and that the proportion of commuters who do not drive their car downtown is well above the threshold, so that my not driving it downtown will be an unnecessary sacrifice. Does this mean that this gives me an adequate reason not to follow it? I think not. I would have adequate reason for this only if there were a fair subdivision of commuters into classes which have and others which do not have special exemptions from this rule and I belonged to a class thus exempted. The classes might be those who have even numbers on their plates and are allowed to drive downtown only on days with even numbers, and those with odd numbers on their plates only on days with odd numbers. Of course, it may be that any such modifications of the guideline and what it takes to ensure an adequate level of compliance is not worth its cost. In that case, the recognition in our mores of this guideline without exceptions would (if sound) ground a compelling paramount reason for everyone always to act in conformity with it.

I conclude that although the Enterprise$_R$ is utopian in the sense of being an ideal that can never be reached by any actual such enterprise, it is not useless for practical purposes. I have distinguished various dimensions along which actual enterprises$_R$ can fall short of Complete Success and have tried to indicate what sorts of flaws make what sorts of difference to the rationality of nevertheless treating its generally accepted guidelines as paramount reasons.

Section 4.   The Moral Enterprise

Is the moral enterprise different from or is it, as I believe, the same as the enterprise$_R$?[22] I hope that my account in the preceding section of the

---

[22] I shall follow the same conventions as for (the) enterprise(s)$_R$: "enterprise$_M$" for "moral enterprise," definite article for the type, indefinite article for (some) token(s), upper-case letter for (the) completely successful, ideal version(s), lower-case letter for (some) actual more or less imperfect version(s).

nature, structure, end, and function of the enterprise$_R$ has already inclined readers toward my identification of the "two," and that I need only remind them briefly of certain widely held convictions about the moral enterprise that, in my view, confirm my conception of it.

Concerning the first half of my task, which deals with the less contentious aspects of the enterprise$_M$—its nature and structure—I shall therefore merely remind readers of certain beliefs about morality which I take to be widely held. The support for my belief that they are, is not, admittedly, based on scientific evidence, but merely on my own (necessarily limited) acquaintance with other people's views, including those of my students, colleagues, and the publications of some moral philosophers. If I am right in my conclusion that these beliefs are indeed widely held, then that would be explained by their also conceiving of the enterprise$_M$ as having the same nature and structure as the enterprise$_R$. And if these beliefs imply that deviations in the nature and structure of particular enterprises$_M$, such as ours, are flaws in them, then their beliefs would also support (though not, of course, prove) my view that they conceive of the Nature and Structure of the Enterprise$_M$ to be the same as those of the Enterprise$_R$.

In the second half of my task, which deals with the end and the function of the Enterprise$_M$, I shall attempt to make it as plausible as I can that, if the nature and structure of the "two" Enterprises are the same, then their ends and functions also are.

4.1. The Nature of the Enterprise$_M$

It seems to me uncontroversial that, like the enterprise$_R$, the enterprise$_M$ is part of the social enterprise, at least in the sense that it is not a one-shot individual enterprise, like bringing in the harvest, and that it involves society at least to the extent of its having to see to it that every new generation is taught at least the rudiments of its morality: what morality requires of or recommends to all its members or all the members of the various classes into which it divides them; that satisfying these requirements and following these recommendations is a very important matter; that they can expect certain desirable things to happen or be done to those who satisfy the requirements and follow the recommendations, certain undesirable things to those who do not satisfy the requirements, and perhaps some desirable ones to those who follow the recommendations; and finally, that such requirements and recommendations may be formulated correctly or incorrectly, that getting them right is not an easy matter, that some other societies have got some or even most of them wrong, and that even their own society may not have got all of them right.

Of course, the belief that the various kinds of general moral directives, such as principles, rules, requirements, prohibitions, recommendations, and so on, can be got more or less right, and that there are criteria and tests of that, would not seem to be universally agreed (perhaps less agreed among moral philosophers than among laymen). But this opposing view does not now seem to be widely held and I think it rests on a misunderstanding. It will be recalled that my belief that one can get such general directives and their application to particular practical questions right or wrong does not rest on the fact that it is not linguistically odd to regard these general guidelines and the particular practical judgments one bases on them as capable of being either true or false, although this linguistic fact may have seemed to some strong reason to think that one can get these matters right or wrong. But I agree that this linguistic fact does give some support to this view, unless it is simply a mistake to accept the implication seemingly embedded in our language, that such general or particular normative judgments can be true or false, and I furthermore believe that this is not simply a mistake.

However, it will be recalled[23] that I do not take this fact to be the main reason on account of which one can get such normatives right or wrong. That there is this linguistic implication may be a good reason for thinking that this is possible, but it is not a necessary condition of its being so. For it would seem to be a linguistic accident that some of our moral judgments are expressible in normatives (and in other linguistic forms) that can be true or false. But I agree with the second part of what so-called "error theorists"[24] believe, who not only (wrongly) hold that such judgments cannot be true or false but also (in my view rightly) that the belief that such judgments can be true or false tempts one to believe (and some philosophers appear to have succumbed to this temptation) that they describe, truly or falsely, the features of a moral world which is supernatural, nonnatural, or at any rate different from our ordinary world with whose features we become acquainted through sense perception. I agree that the linguistic fact that (at least) some of our moral judgments can be true or false very naturally leads one to think that such judgments portray such a separate moral world but that there is no good reason to believe there is one. On my view, it will be recalled, the important reason why one can

²³ See above, chapter 6, p 220ff. and chapter 8, section 2.

²⁴ See J. L. Mackie, *Ethics: Inventing Right and Wrong* (London: Penguin, 1977), 15–49.

get these judgments right or wrong is not that they can be true or false
—for primarily they are not statements of how things are, but directives
telling us how to behave—but that they can be sound or unsound, that
is, that their being generally followed has certain good or bad consequences. Thus, getting such general directives right is accepting them
if general compliance with them is itself a good thing or has good consequences, and rejecting them otherwise. Getting them wrong is doing
the reverse.

Of course, this does not show that there could not be another
explanation of our belief that we can get these things right or wrong, one
which does not regard soundness as a property of them which they
possess if and only if they pass a criterion or test of soundness, but which
treats the ascription of soundness to them as merely the projection of the
speaker's liking of them. Against this rival explanation I here only suggest
that the best and main reason for its popularity is the belief—of whose
erroneousness I hope to have persuaded readers—that directives cannot
be the sort of thing one can get right or wrong because they cannot be true
or false, and that soundness/unsoundness cannot be characteristics of
them but only projections, varying from one person to another, of one's
like or dislike of the directives to which one ascribes soundness/
unsoundness.

This concludes my case for the claim that the nature of the "two"
enterprises is the same, a claim I shall now take for granted.

4.2. The Structure of the Enterprise$_M$

There would appear to be equally general agreement about the structure of
this enterprise. People appear to expect all others to solve their practical
problems in a way that does not violate moral requirements and preferably
(though not necessarily) also in a way that conforms to moral recommendations. And they appear also to believe that others (rightly) expect the
same of them, that no one is outside or above the moral norms that apply
to him. They also think that these requirements and recommendations are
based on very general principles which sometimes conflict with one's
desires and even with what would be in one's best long-range interest.
They also appear to believe that it would be a very good thing, not just for
them but for all the members of the enterprise, if that end were attained,
and that it cannot be fully attained unless all members or at least most of
them act in accordance with these moral principles.

That these views are widely held is supported by a number of things we regularly do and say which in turn are explained and justified by these widely held views. Thus people are always bemoaning the supposed general decline of moral standards and the increase of immorality, and they foresee disaster if the trend is not reversed. That we do and say these things is explained and justified by a widespread conviction already mentioned, namely, that the complete success of the enterprise$_M$, that is, the bringing about and maintaining of the state of affairs which it is its end to bring about and maintain, would be eminently desirable, and that it cannot be completely successful unless all the members "do their bit," that is, always correctly carry out their reflective and executive tasks (as I have called it), and they cannot do that unless the general directives on which they rely are sound and they correctly apply the relevant ones to the solution of the practical problem in hand.

I believe this suffices to show that, like that of an enterprise$_R$, the structure of an enterprise$_M$ is such that, in order for its end to be attained as completely as possible, all (or at least a sufficient number) of its members must, in all their actions, conform to their correct all-things-considered moral judgments, which requires that they take into account all the relevant facts and the relevant correct moral principles, and this in turn requires that not only the moral, but also the epistemic critics and reformers have done as good a job as possible, for the merit of their all-things-considered moral judgments depends not only on the sound- ness of the moral principles available for them to draw on, but also on what they take to be facts which depends on the soundness of the epistemic principles they have to rely on.

Again, like the general guidelines and the all-things-considered judg- ments of the Enterprise$_R$, those of the Enterprise$_M$ would appear to be regarded as paramount, that is, as defeating at least self-anchored reasons. That they are so regarded is confirmed by the difference in our attitude to those who have failed to follow a prudential and a moral guideline. When we discover that an acquaintance has failed in a self-interested enterprise, say, getting a driver's license or bringing in his harvest, we may be sorry for him or we may derive some satisfaction or malicious pleasure from this discovery. These feelings are quite different from the righteous indignation Lazarus presumably felt when he observed the doings of those whose doings violated the divine commandments (which Lazarus presumably regarded in the way we regard requirements of sound morality). And they are also quite different (I suppose) from Lazarus's rejoicings in the bosom of Abraham as he observes the torments of those suffering in hell for these earlier violations. We may perhaps think it cruel or at least hard-hearted of Lazarus to rejoice in their torments, but we would not find it strange or unnatural for him to do so, as we would if he rejoiced in the sorrow or unhappiness of his neighbor who had failed to get in his harvest or in obtaining a driver's license unless, of course, the neighbor had done unneighborly things on account of which he deserved to suffer.

This difference is further confirmed by what I take to be another widespread practice, found not only acceptable but desirable, not to say, indispensable, namely, the organization of social pressures, both forward-looking, that is, deterring, and backward-looking, that is, retributive or compensatory for "ill-gotten gains." We favor such social pressures or sanctions attached to failures to act according to sound all-things-considered moral judgments (especially, though not only, when the other-things-equal judgments on which they have relied have been incorporated in the society's law) but we do not favor them for failures to act according to sound prudential judgments. We would think it strange and unnatural for Lazarus to rejoice in even mild punishments administered, say, in purgatory to an acquaintance of his for having failed to do his regular exercises prescribed by his physician after surgery. Moral considerations thus appear to occupy, in our scheme of practical considerations, the same place as society-anchored reasons occupy in the Enterprise$_R$. Our conviction about the fittingness of social pressures in support of conformity with all-things-considered moral judgments but not with all-things-considered prudential judgments is fully explained if we think of the enterprise$_M$ as identical with the enterprise$_R$. For if we do that, then we must accept the following: (1) that sound all-things-considered moral judgments are *paramount* over what I have called self-anchored (including self-interested) reasons, and the practical judgments based on them; (2) that, therefore, some people are likely to be motivated to follow these rather than conflicting all-things-considered moral judgments even when they think them sound; (3) that complete success of the moral enterprise is, from every member's point of view, the best thing possible for all the members; and (4) that if success is to be ensured in all circumstances, all members must always follow their all-things-considered moral judgments rather than other conflicting practical ones. Thus, the facts about social pressure are explained by the belief in the general desirability of complete success and, its *dependence on* the success condition being satisfied, in the possibility or probability of a conflict of sound all-things-considered moral judgments with, and their paramountcy over, self-anchored practical ones, and in the resulting need to generate or reinforce motivation for conformity. The same sort of reasoning explains the already mentioned fact that so many people call for a revival of moral education and more effective methods of teaching.

The same assumption of the identity of the "two" enterprises also explains another already mentioned fact, namely, that we accept, as an important part of the moral enterprise, the general participation of its members in critical discussions of its precepts, and the recognition of the need for timely reform of recognizably unsound precepts in light of an increased understanding of human concerns, or for suitable adjustment when institutions are undergoing changes which render undesirable some of the effects on people's lives of the prevailing general practices which previously had been desirable.

This practice is explained and justified by our two most distinctive convictions about the moral enterprise, namely, that moral precepts can be sound or unsound, and that the desirability from every member's point of view of complete success in the moral enterprise depends on the soundness of people's all-things-considered moral judgments which, as I argued above,[25] depend on the satisfaction of the reflective task, the executive task, and the sound principles conditions which, in turn, include everyone's doing his bit.

And again, similarly, moral guidelines, like society-anchored ones would appear to be universal. As I have said before, by their "universality," I do not mean that they are binding on every member of a given moral enterprise, let alone on everyone everywhere at all times but, like laws, only on every member of the particular class of members of the relevant enterprise to whom they apply—some to parents, some to children, some to soldiers, some to the aged, and so on.

I can think of three reasons why moral guidelines are universal in this sense. The first and most important is that they have not been got right unless they are such that complete success is attained only if everyone follows them. Universality thus is a conceptually necessary design feature. The second reason is, fortunately, a desirable consequence of such universality. A moral enterprise is an important part of an "experiment in living," as J.S. Mill called it. The effect on the quality of life in a given social order by a change in a single guideline is more easily detected if the change in the guideline changes the behavior of all, or at any rate a significant number of, those to whom it applies. The parallels this creates to a scientific experiment are too obvious to need further elaboration.

The third reason is fairness. The burden which the paramountcy of moral guidelines imposes on those whom they may require to do what is not in accordance with their desire or their interest or their other

---

[25] See above, p. 237ff.

self-anchored reasons, should not be imposed unfairly. This requirement is more easily discharged when a guideline does not differentiate between the members of the class to whom it applies. Of course, this is only the first formal step in the effort of allocating these burdens fairly; the second and more difficult one is to devise a system of classification which is equitable, that is, not unfair simply in virtue of the differences, such as race, sex, age, religion, intelligence, education, wealth, skills, and so on, by which it distinguishes its various classes.[26]

4.3. The End and the Function of the Enterprise$_M$

As will shortly become apparent, it is best to continue our comparison between the "two" enterprises by attending simultaneously to both their ends and their functions. Is there, then, any evidence that casts light on whether or not their ends and functions are the same? Clearly, what we are talking about now is not the end or function of our morality or of some other particular one, but about what, ideally, is its end and its function, what it ought to be, in other words the end and function of the Enterprise$_M$.* Nevertheless, though all this be granted, there may still be more or less tenacious disagreement about the End. This, of course, depends on the specificity with which it is described, for the less specific the description, the more interpretations it will allow, and the more the underlying disagreements will be covered up. Indeed, an even more effective strategy for reducing controversy is not to give any direct description, at any level of specificity, of the state of affairs the production and maintenance of which would constitute attaining the end with various degrees of merit, but to rely instead merely on a statement of the conditions which such a state of affairs would have to meet, if producing and maintaining it at various levels of excellence is to count as attaining the end with various degrees of merit (or as achieving more or less complete success). Disagreements will then arise over whether the conditions are met. I have followed that strategy in regard to the end of the Enterprise$_R$, and I propose to do the same in regard to the end of the Enterprise$_M$.

First, though, a brief glance at the different ways in which the ends of different types of enterprise are determined. The ends of certain collective enterprises, such as the social enterprise and the enterprise of reason are not actual aims, not states of affairs consciously aimed at by the individu-

---

[26] I discuss equity and justice more fully below in chapter 8.

als whose individual enterprises they are, such as Smith's enterprise of getting a degree, or collective enterprises, such as Amnesty International or even General Motors, in which the participants may have quite different aims from one another and from the enterprise's primary aim which the participants at least accept as what *their* enterprise is designed to bring about and maintain. Rather, they are ideal ends, ends these enterprises ought to attain, not those they actually do. In some cases, the end is spelled out first and the structure is then designed with a view to enabling the enterprise to attain it, as in the case of a polar expedition or the production of a new computer by a firm that manufactures computers. In others, as in the case of bodily organs, the end can be inferred from their structure and from the way they function in the organism as a whole. There is a particularly tight connection between the structure and the end when the structure has parts the proper functioning of each of which is a necessary condition, and that of all of them is a jointly sufficient condition, of the whole system attaining its end.

The social and the moral enterprises lie somewhere in between. Normally, an existing social enterprise has not been designed and created by anyone with a certain structure in order that the proper functioning of its parts will bring about and maintain a certain state of affairs, which then counts as attaining the system's end. Even the Founding Fathers did not start from scratch, but they modified the existing structure in a great many ways, presumably with the intention that the proper functioning of the various parts of the new structure would bring about and maintain a state of affairs rather different from and superior to that which was brought about and maintained by the proper functioning of the parts of the old structure.

Suppose, then, to begin with, that the moral enterprise also reaches its end if and only if all its relevant parts perform their proper function. Suppose, furthermore, that the main "parts" are the guidelines and the members playing their various roles, and that the proper functioning of these main parts brings it about that the members are *able* and *willing* always to follow these guidelines even when they conflict with their self-anchored (including their self-interested) reasons. Of course, the proper functioning of the primary parts may in turn depend on the proper functioning of other subsidiary parts. Thus, the members' ability always to follow the guidelines may depend on the society's teaching and learning institutions, and the members' willingness always to do so, on the proper functioning of those parts of these teaching and learning institutions that have been designed to mold members' motivation, and on the various social pressures (such as the law and custom) which have come into, and have been sustained in, existence so as to compensate for the (probably unavoidable) inadequacies in the motivation-molding parts of the teaching and learning institutions. Some societies may fit this pattern. If so, their end can be said to be attained by the production and maintenance of whatever state of affairs is brought about and maintained by the proper functioning of these parts. I think societies at the premoral level of what I called "Pure Custom" may be said to have an end along these lines.

However, this sort of social order has no scope for certain roles generally associated with moral orders: the roles of moral critic and reformer, whose task it is to expose flaws in the currently accepted guidelines and to suggest corrections or improvements of them. But the way of determining the end of a social enterprise sketched in the preceding paragraph does not imply or even suggest a distinction between the soundness or unsoundness of its guidelines, let alone a criterion for that distinction. Thus, on the one hand, it has eliminated the most obvious path to such a criterion, namely, the aptness or inaptness of general compliance with them for bringing about the *proper* end. For if the ability and willingness of the members always to follow the guidelines, whatever they may be, attain what is sufficient to the enterprise's end, whatever the state of affairs that such universal compliance brings about, then we cannot, of course, base any distinction between sound and unsound guidelines on whether or not that universal compliance brings about that state of affairs. Nor does this model imply or suggest any other criterion either. We must therefore suitably modify the structure of our model social enterprise to allow the distinction between sound and unsound moral guidelines and for an acceptable criterion of that distinction.*

This problem would, of course, be solved if we could stipulate or assume that the Enterprise$_M$ has the same end as the Enterprise$_R$, simply on the ground that this would provide a criterion on which to base the distinction between the soundness and the unsoundness of moral guidelines and that it would provide a rational foundation for the moral enterprise. And perhaps this would be a satisfactory move if it were already established that the ideal moral enterprise is one that has or should have a rational foundation. But to postulate or assume it at this point would amount to begging the question here at issue. We need to find an independent reason for thinking that the end of these "two" enterprises is the same, namely, to bring about and maintain a state of affairs which is, from every member's self-anchored point of view, the best state of affairs that is possible for all of them and that, therefore, its sound guidelines are those with a content such that if every member is able and willing always to follow them, that state of affairs is brought about and maintained and that, therefore, it is in accordance with reason for every member of such an Enterprise$_M$ (all of whose members are able and willing always to follow its sound guidelines) always to follow them.

I think there is such an independent reason. Most people appear to think, with the Divine Command Theory, with Glaucon and Adeimantus, with Hobbes, with Kant, to mention only the most obvious, that the attainment of the end of the moral enterprise is a most important, if not the greatest good, and that it could not be that if doing one's bit in the collective effort to attain it were not in accordance with reason. That the question "*Why* be moral?" has, for so long, been so close to the heart of ethical thinking, attests to a widespread and deep conviction that there is a conceptual connection between the moral and the rational enterprises. For that question asks for an adequate, indeed compelling, reason why anyone and everyone should always follow the sound moral directives that apply to his case when he deliberates about what to do. If we interpret this question in the way in which, as I shall shortly attempt to show, it should be interpreted, then this amounts to adequate empirical evidence for the existence of a widely held firm belief about the nature of morality which warrants the identification of the ends of the "two" enterprises, and indeed of the enterprises themselves.

Of course, this widespread belief also is not about our own or any other particular morality, but about ideal morality, morality as it ought to be. If my account of the Enterprise$_R$ and its identity with the Enterprise$_M$ is sound, then it is always in accordance with reason for its members always to follow moral reason and never not to do so. And if my account of the relation between it and particular enterprises in the real world is also sound, then it need not be a pipedream to expect that, if such an enterprise$_M$ does attain its end at a level sufficiently close to Complete Success, it will in many identifiable cases be in accordance with reason to conform with its guidelines, and contrary to reason not to do so, even though the relevant guidelines may in fact be unsound and not all members may be doing their bit. And even if in some such cases, it may not be contrary to reason not to follow these guidelines, people may yet have adequate self-anchored reason to cultivate those preferences and desires that ground self-anchored reasons which recommend following even such unsound moral guidelines, for the good that would do other people and for the maintenance or enhancement of mutual goodwill.

That concludes my case for identifying the "two" Enterprises. Although this obviously would be an appropriate juncture at which to answer the question of why one should be moral, I think it will be easier to do so after a few other features of the moral enterprise have been further clarified.

Section 5.   Some Corollaries

Morality and Prudence.   If my account of the Enterprise$_M$ is on the right track, then morality is not a private matter. It is not solely our own business whether we do the moral thing or not. An effectively organized and socially supervised moral education of the young and the individually organized and administered specifically moral pressure and the socially mobilized (but only in the law socially administered) pressures of the mores are every member's business, for every member has a rational interest in the complete success of the moral enterprise, a success that depends on everyone doing his bit, and everyone's doing his bit depends (among other things) on an effective organization and administration of such moral education and social pressures.

Thus my account of the Enterprise$_M$ would tie in with our ordinary classification of practical reasons, according to which (very roughly speaking) prudential ones protect and promote the good of the agent, and moral ones that of other people. It also explains why we take it that, normally, it is solely people's own business—a private matter—whether or not they do what they have the best prudential (or other self-anchored) reason to do, and why we also think that putting such pressures on adults would be treating them like children—unjustifiable paternalism, meddling in their affairs—and why we do not think this about failures to comply with moral requirements.

Exactly why is this so on my account? Because each individual can achieve complete success in *her* (token of the) enterprise of self-anchored reason quite independently of anyone else's success in his. Since each individual's participation in (his society's token of) the enterprise of self-anchored reason takes off from what he is there and then able to do—whatever others did earlier or are doing now to enhance or diminish this ability—the success in every one of them is independent of the success in any other. This is quite different from someone's participation in some token of the moral enterprise, for the success and with it the rationality of each member's participation (doing his bit) depends not only on the soundness of the guidelines (as it does in the case of self-anchored reason) but also on what other members do. Thus every member of the same token moral enterprise has adequate reason to hope and work for all the members doing their bit, including their performance in the roles of critic and reformer, because complete success, for the attainment of which every member has adequate reason to do his bit, depends on every member doing his.

Relativism. This has an important corollary some "antirelativists" may wish to deny, namely, that an incompatibility between the moral precepts of the social moralities of two different moral orders does not show that one of them must be in error (nor of course does it imply either that there could not be considerable overlaps and similarities between them). My account is not relativistic in the sense that we cannot tell objectively whether a society or an individual has a morality; what the morality is, if it or he has one; and to what extent the morality is sound or unsound. But it is relativistic in the sense that what are sound moral guidelines in one moral order may be unsound in another.

Altruism. Here I should probably return to a question already examined before, namely, in exactly what way morality protects and promotes the good of others. As we noted, many believe that it prescribes altruism. Understood in the most natural way, that would seem to turn the moral enterprise into a self-contradictory individual one. For, like its opposite, "egoism," "altruism" refers to a certain sort of psychological makeup, though, of course, unlike egoism, it has a favorable moral connotation. Whereas egoism is the tendency to pursue one's own best interest *beyond the morally permissible*, altruism is the tendency to pursue other people's best interest *beyond the morally required*. Thus, for morality to require altruism it would require doing more than morality requires. Furthermore, such a requirement is unhelpful as a guideline to what is morally required since it presupposes an independent account of the morally required, which altruism supposedly transcends.

Could altruism simply mean promoting the good of others? If so, how is this recommendation or requirement related to promoting one's own? Must one never promote one's own? Is prudence always immoral? May one perhaps promote one's own good when and only when one could not promote that of another instead—or when one cannot do more good for others by refraining from promoting one's own or when one cannot do more good for others than one can do for oneself or only when it does not actually harm anyone else? Must one always promote other people's good as much as one can, in whatever way that affects one's own? Or need one promote it only as much as one can without harming oneself more than its promotion benefits others, or only as much as one can without harming oneself at all? Or should one then balance the promotion of other people's good against that of one's own, perhaps in a utilitarian way? I shall return to this last answer shortly. Many, if not all, of these solutions seem unduly harsh on oneself. And they seem undesirable when generalized, as presumably moral principles should be. For, by and large, people know better how to promote their own good than that of others, and it seems safer to let people promote their own good than to require others to promote it, except in special circumstances.

Impartiality. Similarly, on my account, loving our neighbors as we love ourselves, or the similar idea of impartiality between ourselves and others in all our interactions with them is not the most general and supreme moral principle. For surely it would sometimes be too demanding, at other times not demanding enough. It makes sense to expect parents to be impartial, for instance, in the ways they treat their own children, but surely not as between their own and other people's children. Nor does it seem right for parents always to weigh their own interests impartially against those of their children. Again, an employer should be impartial in dealing with job applicants, hiring solely on the basis of the applicants' qualifications. But should a job seeker be impartial in accepting job offers? Is there anything immoral about an African-American job applicant preferring a job offer from an African-American employer to a better offer from a white rival? Impartiality seems to be a moral requirement only in certain types of cases, not generally, and it does not seem to be the most general guiding principle underlying all moral precepts.

Similar doubts would seem appropriate about the supreme principle of some versions of so-called act utilitarianism, according to which everyone must always (at least other things equal) maximize the net sum of the good, whether happiness or utility or some other specification of it. The great attraction of these versions of utilitarianism would seem to be its ideal of objectivity or impartiality or nondiscrimination by anyone in any of his interactions with others, all being conceived as equal claimants— each to count for one, no more and no less—against one another, each to maximize the net sum of the good of all those affected by his action including himself. In my view, this does not adequately represent the society-relative, role-relative, coordination-dependent, cooperative nature of the moral enterprise. To be sure, impartiality in one's interaction with others has certain similarities with treating them in accordance with the best moral reason one has, but they seem to me superficial. I hope this will become more apparent as we go along.

Pairs of Moral Roles. To see exactly how moral reasons protect or promote "the good of other people," it will help to keep apart two important pairs of moral roles in interaction: (1) agent/patient and (2) self/other.

(1) Agent/Patient. Of course, in many cases, the same being (usually a person, though some animals are now also thought to be capable of being moral patients; I have not come across anyone who claims that some animals can be moral agents) will be agent and patient at the same time. If I wash my face or commit suicide, I am both washing and being washed, killing and being killed, simultaneously both an agent and a patient. If I lie to or accuse someone today, and am lied to or accused by someone tomorrow, I am an agent today, a patient tomorrow. However, whereas the role of agent is always assumed at will (if not always voluntarily or gladly), that of patient is often thrust upon one.

Much, perhaps most of our behavior is of a type that allows the same person, at least at different times, to be its agent or patient. It is with this sort of behavior that much of the moral enterprise is concerned. Such behavior by some agent can be beneficial or harmful to some patient. It is, you will agree, a platitude that moral reasons, being practical, can be acted on only by agents, that is, beings that can act for reasons. But that must not let us forget the fact that people may be as much concerned about these beneficial or harmful effects, whether on others or themselves, as they are about the actions themselves, and although practical reasons require or recommend us to perform or not to perform these actions, what makes them such reasons may be these effects implied by their proper characterizations.

Because of this possibly frequent change in people's role from agent to patient and back, every (normal adult) member of a moral order is at some times, relative to some patients, an agent, a "needed benefactor" or a "feared malefactor," at others a "needing beneficiary" or a "fearful victim." Sometimes people may behave as benefactors because of the need of the beneficiary, sometimes they will have other reasons, though they may then be pleased or annoyed by or indifferent to these "side effects," and sometimes they will fail to do these things because of or in spite of them. Conversely, people may behave as malefactors because of the expected suffering of the victim, or despite it, or they may be indifferent to it.

It is behavior of this sort which, when people hate or dislike or are indifferent to one another, can lead to suboptimal outcomes when they all follow self-anchored reasons. Hence such behavior is a paradigm candidate for the supersession of self-anchored by moral reasons. It is in such situations that moral reasons will protect or promote "the good" by preventing suboptimal outcomes. To accomplish this, they adjudicate between the self-anchored reasons that will either allow, require, or recommend to the agent to follow his dominant self-anchored reason and the patient to acquiesce in the adverse impact on her of that adjudication, or to forbid or counsel him not to follow that reason and her that she need or must not acquiesce in them, and perhaps recommend what remedial action she may or should take if he does not follow the moral adjudication; and there may be other possibilities we need not now consider.

What we do need to remind ourselves of is that, if the moral reason is an other-things-equal one, then in cases of this sort—I shall call them "one-way interactions"—the precept will always be the same, for example, not to kill, not to lie, not to harm, not to deceive, and so on, or to rescue those in peril, to feed the hungry, to love one's neighbor, and so on. This takes us to a second distinction that is not always kept apart from the first.

(2) Self/Others. Whereas, relative to the same type of action, one person can play both the role of agent and patient at the same time or at different times, he always plays the role of *self*, whether he is then an agent or patient, and very often, if perhaps not necessarily always, that of *other* in relation to certain persons, whether they are the agents or patients relative to that type of action. And while we can exchange the role of agent and patient ("Now I shall be the victor and you the defeated"), we cannot exchange the role of self and other ("Now you be self and I shall be other"). Neither of them is chosen, and both are relative to the point of view of a given person. Who is self and who is other depends on who is the speaker or the person surveying the scene.

Reversibility.   The agent-patient distinction is relied on in one of the most widely used accusations of moral wrongness, taking the form of a rhetorical question: "What if that were done to you?" It suggests that a principle governing one-way interactions must be acceptable to either role player. Rational acceptability from the agent's point of view is not enough; it must also be rationally acceptable from the patient's point of view. If no principle is acceptable from both points of view, in the sense that neither killing nor refraining from killing would be in accordance with the dominant self-anchored reasons both have, then we must see whether there is a cooperative arrangement that would remedy the suboptimality. It seems clear that general acceptance of "never to kill" as paramount would be an improvement over everyone always following whatever happen to be the dominant self-anchored reasons he has.

We may think of this popular way of exhibiting the moral inappropriateness of certain principles for guiding us in one-way interactions as simply applications of the Golden Rule. But we need not interpret them along the narrowly restricted lines of that rule, which makes the principle of interaction depend on the acceptability to the agent and the patient in the concrete case. If my account is sound, then the appropriate range of persons to whom the paramount principle must be acceptable are all the participants of an ideal moral enterprise. In the killing case, this will not be very difficult, since we may feel reasonably confident that the balance of everyone's self-anchored reasons will favor the protection of everyone's life against the being killed by others, over the protection of everyone's liberty to kill others when the latter is allowed, recommended, or required by the agent's dominant self-anchored reasons. This is, of course, perfectly compatible with modifications of the simple principle "never to kill any human being" by the incorporation of suitable exceptions.

I think we can improve the Golden Rule by incorporating this wider range of beings to whom a paramount principle or precept must be rationally acceptable if it is to be regarded as sound. The question we must ask about it then is not, "How would *you* like it if that were done to *you?*" but "Would every participant in the moral enterprise have an all-things-considered requiring and equally weighty self-anchored reason to recognize this precept as paramount?" that is, as a reason that required this sort of behavior of every participant of a certain class. Or, in shorthand, "Should we *in reason want* this behavior *of one another?*" "We" then stands for all the participants of an ideal moral enterprise, "want" stands for the whole range of intensity from "wish" to "demand,"[27] and "in reason" stands for the availability to every participant of an all-things-considered requiring and equally weighty self-anchored reason.

Symmetry/Asymmetry. This distinction concerns the question of whether moral prohibitions or requirements on certain agent-patient relations, such as killing and preventing harm, exclude or include self-self cases. Must we not kill ourselves? Must we prevent harm to ourselves in circumstances in which we must prevent it to others? Asymmetrists claim that the moral requirements applicable in cases in which the agent and the patient of a particular action are not the same person, do not hold when they are. On this view, there is no such thing as "*self*-victimization" and the moral requirement against killing humans does not apply to suicide. My conception of morality is asymmetrist. Moral philosophers and moral traditions disagree on this; some are ambivalent.

According to classical Utilitarianism, the basic moral question is what one must do to promote the greatest good of the greatest number; thus,

---

[27] For details on this, see the discussion of "levels of stringency" in chapter 8, pp. 300–302.

every moral agent must consider only the well-being of humanity, taken almost as a mass noun, and ignoring whose well-being or happiness, his own or that of others, is the result of this maximization, or how it satisfies or frustrates different people's claims on him to promote their well-being or happiness. Thus if, on a certain occasion by making oneself as happy as possible, one thereby achieves a greater overall happiness than by any other action open to one, then one must, morally speaking, make oneself as happy as possible, even if most people remain unhappy and even though they could be made happier than they would be as a result of such "impartial" maximization, simply by doing something else that would not make oneself quite as happy as maximization of happiness on this occasion requires.

Kant, in one of his formulations of the Categorical Imperative, also seems to reject the asymmetry condition: "Always act so that you treat humanity, *whether in your own person or another,* as an end and never merely as a means."[28] For Kant, the patient of any action (identified by its maxim) that is someone's duty, is any human being on whom that type of action happens to make some impact or other, irrespective of whether the agent who is the duty bearer is also the patient.* Mill seems ambivalent on asymmetry. His strong opposition to paternalism seems to put him in the camp of the asymmetrists, but his adherence to Bentham's formula of the maximization of happiness suggests he would support symmetry.

Although my account is asymmetrist, it does not rule out so-called "duties to oneself." There may be things, such as one's health or even one's contentment, that one has a duty to promote when, for one reason or another, one owes this to other people: one may cost one's fellow participants too much through loss of working days, hospitalization, medication, danger of infection, and so on, or one may be unbearable to live with, as a father, husband, or coworker. Nevertheless, the thrust is in the direction of asymmetry: discharging duties to oneself amounts to doing one's bit by others.

If my account is sound, then the moral (unlike the prudential or self-anchored) enterprise is a cooperative one in which every participant does his bit, and doing one's bit is designed in such a way that everyone's behavior is a fair contribution toward increasing other people's chances to lead a life as close as possible to their (internally unflawed) conception of a good life. This formulates, in somewhat greater detail than before, in exactly what ways the moral guidelines direct participants of a moral

---

[28] Kant, *Groundwork,* 96, 429. My emphasis.

enterprise to aim at what protects and promotes the good of other people, not their own.

Kant was rightly concerned (as were Plato, Hobbes, and Hume, among others) with a human tendency to derive an unfair double benefit from others doing their bit while not doing one's own, and he thought that the "universalizability" of one's maxim precluded this. I think my account of the moral enterprise improves on that of Kant's and of act utilitarians in two respects: the locus and the test of soundness. Both Kantians and act utilitarians are "individualists" in the sense that for them the locus of the test of soundness is the maxim or principle acted on by each individual on each occasion of choice. In this respect, my theory is closer to rule utilitarians in that it proposes two loci of assessment using different criteria of acceptability: the rule or maxim of individual choice, whose acceptability lies in its conformity to a sound moral precept, and the soundness of the moral precept itself which, as I said, lies in its recommending conduct which the members of the ideal moral enterprise should in reason want of one another.

The second difference lies in the criterion of soundness. Both forms of utilitarianism subscribe to some form of the principle of utility as a criterion of acceptability (though they apply it in different loci: act utilitarianism as a criterion and test of the rightness of particular actions and rule utilitarianism as a criterion and test of the soundness of a principle of action), whereas I accept the more complex criterion of (putting it roughly) the rationality of recognizing certain sorts of precepts as paramount. Kant, by contrast, employs the Categorical Imperative, a nonconsequentialist version of the principle of universalizability. That formula is supposed to enable us to select a maxim independently of any evaluation of the consequences of its universal adoption as a criterion of soundness; indeed, the establishment in this way of the moral bindingness of a maxim then obliges us to embrace whatever consequences an action on this maxim may bring. It is, unlike Rawls's, an unadulterated pure procedural criterion of soundness.

My own criterion of the soundness of the precepts (with which an individual's maxims of action must conform) is consequentialist in that it takes into account the impact of its universal adoption as such a criterion and of universal behavior in conformity with precepts that meet it. However, the criterion does not rank rival precepts by their capacity to maximize the net sum of the utilities of the members of the moral order, but one that imposes (in the way I explained) a requirement of equity on the way the rival rule candidates increase the members' chances to lead a good life. On my view—and here I believe I follow Rawls—the equity requirement is prior to the maximization requirement, for equity is a condition of every member having adequate reason to recognize the moral precepts as paramount. It should be clear by now that this ordering of the priorities is preferable because it does not bring it about that an increase in the rationality of the members—which is desirable on many grounds— imposes an additional strain on the acceptability of the precepts as paramount, and because it diminishes, as rationality increases, the need for suitable social pressures which are both inherently undesirable and costly. Finally, what is thus equitably maximized is not utility and not certain specific primary goods, but the chances of being able to lead a good life according to one's (internally unflawed) conception of such a life.

Section 6. The Moral Domain

We can now examine a question we set aside before, namely, what issues, matters, or questions are properly dealt with by a morality, and what, if any, by its mores or more specifically, its custom or its law, and which ones by more than one.

Both in describing the mores of a society and its morality, we spell out two things: what are the generally recognized guidelines we take to belong *to*, and which we take people to regard as belonging *in* these domains, and how the people subject to them actually behave. We can then distinguish between "first-level" and "second-level" guidelines, the former formulating how various classes of members are to behave in various circumstances, the latter how various classes of people are to react to conformity and nonconformity to the first-level ones.

We can call the first-level ones the "codes" of these domains: the code (rules) of custom, of law (the laws), and of morality (the moral principles, rules, and precepts). We may first learn these codes by example and suitable response to actual behavior rather than by explicit precept, as we may first learn the rules of chess by being shown and corrected when we make mistakes. Once these codes are spelled out, we can guide our behavior by them even in situations for which we have not previously learned (in this way) what is permissible, recommended, or required, and what impermissible.

These codes tell us what we need to know if we want to behave as they prohibit, permit, require, or recommend us to do and how to respond to those who behave or fail to behave in this way, or if we want to bring about or avoid those probable reactions by other members in which the second-level guidelines direct them to engage in response to our behavior. The society's moral code tells us what we need to know if we want to behave as the social morality directs us to, but it also in the same breath *purports* to tell us what *sound morality* directs. Thus what belongs in a morality are moral codes, that is, systems of directives that purport to give sound answers to moral questions. I shall say more about them in chapter 8.

But what are moral questions? My argument in the preceding sections leads to the conclusion that a question is a moral one if and only if it is one whose being generally answered in accordance with self-anchored reasons would have suboptimal results and which, therefore, should be answered on the basis of reasons which are paramount over self-anchored ones.* I argued, it will be recalled, that reasons are rightly so regarded if, in an ideal moral order, their generally being so regarded has optimal results, that is, if it results in the maintenance of a state of affairs which is, from every member's point of view, the best thing possible for all members. Hence, as I said, a sound answer to a moral question must be arrived at by a two-stage process: a search for all the relevant *sound* moral precepts (that is, other-things-equal general directives that are sound), and a *correct* compounding of them into an all-things-considered practical judgment. Correct moral performance also requires *corresponding* action, that is, action in conformity with that answer.

Moral codes, we said, are backed by the specifically moral pressures, those that consist in people morally judging one another, thereby trying to reinforce their disposition to choose correct (or weakening their disposition to choose incorrect) moral performances. We noted that such specifically moral pressures do not always sufficiently motivate everyone, hence incorporation of moral guidelines in custom or law with their more generally effective pressures is desirable when universal compliance is important and when it would suitably change the members' motivation without imposing costs that would detract from the success of the moral enterprise just as much as or more than nonincorporation.

Perhaps I should here reemphasize that not all moral questions are questions of what to do. Questions of what to be, what behavioral dispositions, character traits, habits or feelings to cultivate, and what attitudes to adopt, should be included for the same reason: that, like engaging in some types of behavior that is supported by self-anchored reasons, the general cultivation or adoption of some dispositions, character traits, and so on, that are supported by such reasons, may be suboptimal. Therefore, the question of whether or not to cultivate or adopt one of these "things" may also be a moral question, and one to which there may be sound or unsound moral answers.

I think action has, for some time now, occupied the limelight in ethics because, although we have a measure of control over all these things, we have the most direct control over them: they are things we can do or perform at will. *Nevertheless*, despite the great differences in the kind and degree of control we have over them, directive reasons apply to all of them, and so our performances in them can be judged from the point of view of reason.[29]

Where a social morality provides an answer to a practical question, an answer (whether the same or different) to that question may also be provided by its custom or its law. The answer's incorporation in its custom requires little if anything in the way of uniformity, specificity, and precision of the formulation of its content or of a formal procedure that establishes it as custom. Thus, questions about whom to tip and how much may be provided both by a society's morality and its custom, and the same differences of opinion about what and how much or how little is required or permitted can arise both about the society's morality and its custom. The case, as we noted, is rather different in the law. Where a society's morality contains some directives, say, about lying, all or some of these may also be incorporated in its custom and its law. But if these moral directives are to become law, they must first be subjected to certain formal incorporation procedures and their content must be formulated with a comparatively high degree of specificity and uniformity so that courts, when called upon, can determine with comparatively high consistency and predictability whether or not a person has acted lawfully.

Thus, there may be a certain overlap between morality on the one hand, and law and custom on the other. But whereas it will be comparatively easy to tell whether a certain form of behavior, say, abortion or robbery or breach of promise, is dealt with in a society's law, it may sometimes be quite difficult to say whether something like tipping, courtesy, or writing thank-you letters are regulated by a certain social morality or custom or both. For it may be hard to tell whether or not one can ask about the requirement, say, that one should tip waiters 15 percent, whether or not it is true or false that one should, and whether people generally respond to those who they know do not tip waiters 15 percent, in the ways in which they respond to violators of custom or of social

---

[29] See book 1, chapter 1, section 10, where I briefly discussed the case of belief which, though to some extent under our control is not normally regarded as belonging in the mores. However, a fuller discussion of belief is beyond the scope of this book.

morality, and the answers to these questions may point in different directions about whether these are regarded as matters of social morality or custom.*

Section 7.   Why Be Moral?

I now return to the question postponed at the end of section 4. On some philosophical accounts, such as Prichard's, the question has seemed senseless or illegitimate.** Some have puzzled about what sort of reason we could possibly give in our answer: it cannot be a moral one, for that would make the answer circular, but neither can it be a prudential one for, if one is moral for a prudential reason, one is prudent, not moral. And what other sort of reason could it be?

This would be a real problem if being moral were in important respects like, say, exercising, and the question "Why be moral?" were analogous to "Why exercise?" For then being moral would be an activity whose intrinsic desirability and whose effects vary enormously from one person to another, depending on her health, her age, her mode of life, and so on and whose nature is independent of the answer to the "Why?" question. Thus, in one case the answer to "why exercise?" may have to be, "for excellent reasons; I enjoy it and it is good for my health," and in another, "I don't; I have no reasons at all; I don't enjoy it and it is bad for my health" and so on, and neither answer would change one's idea of what constitutes exercising.

But those who ask "Why be moral?" would not be satisfied for long with this sort of answer. On their understanding of the question, the answer to it cannot be that one person may have excellent reasons to be moral while another has none at all, or that the same person may sometimes have excellent reasons to be moral, at other times none. If these were true, the question would not be about being moral, or not the right question about it, or the answer would not state the right sort of reason. For those who raise this question do not usually inquire into this or that individual or social morality. Their question presupposes a *universally true* positive answer to another question, namely, *whether* to be moral, and it requests a universally valid answer to why, for what reason, that answer is true, where that reason lies entirely *within* the ideal moral enterprise itself. If the answer to whether to be moral were to be negative, that would show, or at least constitute a very weighty reason to think, that the conception of morality from which that negative answer follows, must be mistaken. And if the answer is positive it must lie in the nature, structure, end, and function of the moral enterprise.

Thus, Glaucon and Adeimantus asked Socrates to prove to them that those who were moral were not fools or dupes, as Thrasymachus had claimed. They made clear that they expected a universally true *affirmative* answer to the question of whether to be moral, but that they took the appearance to the contrary to be very strong—after all, they thought they had built a strong case for thinking that the most profitable thing to do was (at best) to appear to be moral while taking advantage of every opportunity to profit from an immorality whose sanction one could evade—that they expected the answer to satisfy people like themselves who were determined to act in accordance with reason, and that they wanted to be given a detailed demonstration that the affirmative answer was a rationally sound one, thereby showing that everybody had adequate reason to be moral.

Glaucon and Adeimantus—and apparently there are many like them —are willing, indeed want, to be moral but not if it is a fools' game. Hence, in view of the strong case for thinking that only fools are always moral, rather than merely always giving the appearance of being so, they ask for a proof that it is always wise to be moral and never wise not to be. They hope and believe that there is something about the nature of morality that grounds such a reason.

My conception of the moral enterprise and that of practical reason can account for the wish of people of limited goodwill to want that question answered; that it can satisfy the demand for a morality that does not brand the moral person a fool or a dupe; that, indeed, it can account for and rationally justify the view that a sound affirmative answer is a necessary condition of the wisdom of being moral. Of course, as I granted, my conceptions of practical reason and morality can actually satisfy this demand only for ideal moral enterprises and those which, though falling short of the ideal, have only tolerable flaws.

When they first encounter Plato's "proofs" that the just man is happier than the unjust man, many students remain skeptical. Most want proofs with higher standards of rigor. But not all of them hope for a "positive" answer. Few doubt the possibility of conflict between morality and self-interest (at least in this world), but while some hope that such constraints on the pursuit of one's best interest somehow serve the common and so everyone's good, others hope, on the contrary, that these supposedly beneficial constraints are unnecessary or unacceptable, because they are fraudulent restrictions of their freedom. They hope for a proof that there is no good reason for anyone to be moral, that sometimes, probably quite often, it is not contrary to reason not to be moral, that only fools and dupes always are. But both groups purport to be sensible people who would always be moral if, but only if, that was in accordance with reason.

Perhaps (and it is of course my hope that) all this will be accepted as far as it goes. However, it may well be objected, at this point, that my answer to "Why be moral?" depends on an empirical assumption for which I have offered no evidence, let alone adequate evidence: that no one would have a better chance of leading a good life as they conceive it if they did not have to conform to the constraints imposed by the directives of the moral enterprise.

There seem to be three alternatives to life under a moral order: a life outside society, one in a society without mores, or one in a society with mores but without a morality. We can ignore the first because, even if we can give a clear sense to this alternative, still "a life outside society" would not seem possible for anyone now that the whole globe is covered without interstices by so-called nation states, or at any rate not for a sufficient number to be of great interest.

The second, some version of anarchism, rejects all or most of the mores of a society, retaining only such social enterprises as education and science, and perhaps art and religion. I say "perhaps" for two reasons. One is that the enterprise of art and that of religion may not be parts of the social enterprise but may be individual enterprises, like building a house or growing a rose garden, or they may be enterprises in voluntary association with others, like Amnesty International or Mothers Against Drunk Driving. The other is that one of them, namely, religion, might well be a part of a social enterprise and then constitute part of a society's mores.

An anarchist society so conceived (if it is conceivable) would not be what I called a social order, since it would have no mores, and so would not have anything recognized as society-anchored considerations or reasons. Thus, it would have only self-anchored practical considerations or reasons. Insofar as members had learned to judge their interaction in accordance with or contrary to reason, such interaction would be entirely "strategic."[30] But, as we have seen, such interaction, taken as a whole, would be suboptimal. Whether it necessarily is, would, I imagine, depend on two factors: one is whether the interagents know of ways in which to coordinate their behavior so as to avoid the suboptimalities resulting from noncoordination; the other is whether in such an anarchist society the circumstances are such as would make it, at least in so-called iterated PDs, rational for any of the interagents to initiate certain strategies (such as

---

[30] In the sense I take from Jon Elster. See *Ulysses and the Sirens*, 18.

those suggested by Axelrod, e.g., "tit for tat")[31] in order to make cooperation rational for all interagents and so avoid the suboptimalities resulting from noncooperation (or "defection," as it is often called, which is usually considered the dominant and so the only rational strategy, at least in two-person, one-shot PDs).

I am pessimistic about the possibility of such cooperative strategies in the sort of "social climate" that such anarchist societies (if indeed they are possible) might or probably would produce, or whether a sufficient number of people in such societies would be willing to take the risk of departing from the "safe," if suboptimal, strategy of defection, especially in multi-person PDs, which would be among the typical sorts of interaction in societies. In any case, such anarchist societies have not come about anywhere and, with the demise of the Soviet Union, even the hope for a classless society in which the state has withered away seems to have withered away, too. It seems we are stuck with the so-called "nation state" and perhaps should, at least in the absence of a functioning new world order, try to make the best of it.

The only alternative left would seem to be the third possibility, people living in typical societies with mores, and so with society-anchored considerations (though not reasons[32]) based on the precepts and rules of its customs and "laws" (though not laws in the morality-related sense discussed earlier[33]). If my line of reasoning about the moral enterprise was correct, then it is precisely in such societies that the need arises for tying the mores to practical reason and so to morality. For the uncritically accepted precepts of the mores are likely to be highly unsatisfactory, at least for some members of the society, because the ways in which they adjudicate conflicts of interest between different members tend to generate wildly divergent life prospects for different members. But one of the most important reasons for thinking that *everyone* should have the best self-anchored reason that everyone can have for regarding the moral guidelines as paramount, is that in a rational order the ability and willingness to

---

[31] See Edna Ullmann-Margalit, *The Emergence of Norms* (Oxford: Oxford University Press, 1977); also Robert Axelrod, *The Evolution of Cooperation* (New York: Basic Books, 1984).

[32] Since we are now considering societies in which the mores have not been linked, through the enterprise of morality, to the enterprise of practical reason, the considerations that people come to have through motivations based on the social pressures created by the societies' mores may not be suitably shaped by the requirements of practical reason, and so may not constitute practical reasons.

[33] I here ignore my own reasoning that ties "laws" to the existence of "law" and that to the existence of a social morality, hence I have "laws" in quotation marks.

be moral will be the greater the closer it comes to this ideal, even in the absence of severe social sanctions which otherwise are necessary but which have their own serious disadvantages and costs, as we saw in our discussion of Hobbes.

Grant me, then, that none of these three alternatives offers us a better chance of being able to lead a life that comes closer to the good life as we conceive it. But then the reason why members of The Enterprise$_M$ should be moral is that it offers them as good a chance as every member can have of leading a life as close as possible to a good life according to their (internally flawless) conception of it. And if the members of an imperfect enterprise$_M$ should be moral—and they should if that enterprise is sufficiently close to Complete Success—then the reason why they should is again the same: it is that being moral is what, in their moral order, offers them as good a chance as every member can have of leading a life that comes as close as possible to a good life according to their (internally flawless) conception of it.

Book Two

The Moral Order

PART TWO:
FROM THEORY
TO PRACTICE

CHAPTER EIGHT

The Design of Our Moral Code

Section 1. Introduction

In chapter 6, I argued that the mores of a society, which include its custom and its law, are the product of what might be called the regulative part of the social enterprise. It is the part which formulates society's will and impresses it on its members. I have construed that will as what members want of one another. The mores comprise the directives in which the society communicates its will to its members, their practice of complying with these directives, and their responses to other members' compliance and occasional noncompliance. I argued that the moral enterprise is an attempt to mold the mores so as to conform to the guidelines of the enterprise of practical reason and, therefore, to subject the directives of the mores to continual scrutiny and modification according to a criterion and test of rational acceptability or soundness. I expressed the thrust of that criterion and test in a single, very general, critical question about the accepted directives: whether what they direct is what we, the members of a certain moral order, should in reason want of one another. If these directives live up to this criterion and so are sound, and if all members follow them, then all members will "receive" from one another what they should in reason want of one another. In this ideal case, the resulting state of affairs will be the best thing that is possible for all of them. It will be a better thing for each than if each had tried to get what is best for him but, of course, it may and most probably will not be, for all of them, the best thing possible for each.

I stressed that the society's will may extend to things other than the appropriate types of conduct in a variety of situations; for instance, the cultivation of certain appropriate feelings, attitudes, character traits, habits, and so on, and the elimination of certain others. Such directives may, for instance, recommend the cultivation of self-discipline or courage or one's talents or even one's happiness on the grounds that being self-disciplined and courageous may, in certain situations that all members are likely to face occasionally, enable or encourage one to engage in the morally appropriate conduct. Or they may direct the cultivation of respect, love, or kindliness, not because it encourages or enables one to engage in certain morally required conduct but because it is these sentiments themselves (as manifested in certain forms of behavior) that we can in reason want or even demand of one another. However, to save space, I shall in this book consider mostly questions concerning conduct.

Bearing in mind the three main roles in the moral enterprise—agent, patient, and adjudicator—the three versions of the most general moral question are: what (as adjudicators) we may or should in reason judge to be due to one another; what (as patients) we should in reason receive from one another; and what (as agents) we should in reason do for, and refrain from doing to, one another. Obviously, none of these is a question it would be easy for members of a moral order to answer correctly without a great deal of help from society. A social morality and, to the extent they are geared to it, also the other parts of the mores provide what that society takes to be the appropriate premises from which each moral agent who is a member can by appropriate reasoning arrive at a judgment that answers his basic moral question for the case in hand. We can think of these premises as "our" moral code.

A moral code typically presents its directives simply as what is recommended or dictated to us by Morality, leaving open the question of whose dictates or recommendations they are. The Divine Command Theory represents them as coming from God. I have construed them as being what we should in reason want of one another with a certain appropriate degree of stringency, ranging from a mild recommendation to a peremptory demand, depending on the effect that general compliance or widespread noncompliance with the directive would have on the cooperative scheme of the social enterprise. Since a moral code's directives are necessarily addressed to moral agents, the part of the patient as beneficiary or victim is easily overlooked. But in my view, the rationality of the moral enterprise depends on a recognition of that role and its claims.

In this chapter, I want to examine the concepts our moral code uses in the directives that tell its members what kinds of things they are morally wanted to do, feel, adopt, cultivate, and so on, how important (or stringent) a particular such want is, and some indication of why certain things should be and are wanted with this or that degree of stringency. I shall devote some time to examining some of the terms we use in our moral code, terms such as *duty, obligation, right, responsibility, justice, and equity.**

Section 2. The Form and Status of Moral Precepts

However, it will be helpful if, before examining these moral concepts, I say something about the epistemic status of moral precepts and the linguistic forms (not to say guises) in which they are often clothed. We noted that they may be expressed in the form of "commandments," as in "thou shalt not kill"; or as Kantian "imperatives," as in "act so that . . ."; or as general normative statements, as in "one must never lie" or "one ought always to keep one's promises." What primarily interests us, of course, is not their grammatical form, but their epistemic status, and the former is not a reliable guide to the latter. Thus, the grammatical differences between "thou shalt not kill" and "one must never kill" do not imply that these two forms of words are not, in a particular case, used to formulate the same moral precept with the same epistemic status.

Moral precepts are what I call directives. As I use this term, it can stand for two things: a certain *use* of a sentence of any grammatical form suitable for being put to that use, or a *claim* that someone has made or might make with that use of some such sentence. Thus, "directive" is not, like "indicative" or "imperative," a purely grammatical term, but is, like "command" or "suggestion," a term that refers to a certain sort of use in which a certain type or range of types of sentence can be employed. Thus, although typically it is imperatives ("Uncork the wine, Tom") or gerundives ("Tom was to have uncorked the wine") that are used to formulate directives, other grammatical forms can also be used. Thus, the indicative, "Private Smith will report at headquarters at 08:00 A.M.," will be taken as a directive by Private Smith when he reads it in a communication received from his commanding officer. But it can also be used as a "descriptive" when Private Jones uses it to answer Private Baker's question when Smith will be at headquarters. However, certain sentences (say, "The sun will enter an eclipse at 10 P.M.") cannot be used as directives because no human agent can possibly comply or fail to comply with a remark made by them.

Thus, we can use one and the same expression in "different uses" (as descriptives or directives) and also (grammatically) different expressions (indicatives or imperatives or gerundives) in one and the same use (as a directive). The directive use* in which a person may intend his use of an expression is characterized by three features: (1) the expression must represent or depict a possible action by an agent somehow identified; (2) the point of offering this action representation or depiction is not, like that of a "descriptive," to enable the addressee or anyone else to have a correct representation of some aspect of the world, but is, rather, to spell out for him what behavior on his part would constitute *compliance with* the directive, namely, his performing the action represented in the remark; and (3) understanding that a sentence is or is intended to be used as a directive is to understand that the excellence peculiar to this use lies, not in the accordance between the way the world is and how the sentence represents it as being, hence not its having been complied with by "its subject" (the appropriate agent indicated in the directive), but rather in what makes it desirable for "its principal" (the issuer of the directive) to have issued it, and for "its subjects" (those to whom it applies) to be following it.

Thus, both descriptives and directives satisfy (1), for in both cases there may be accordance/nonaccordance between the aspect of the world the sentence purports to represent and the supposedly represented aspect of the world. However, whereas the chief excellence of claims made with descriptives lies in that accordance, that of directives has nothing to do with that. Thus, to claim that directives cannot be true or false is not to deny that their depictions of the part of the world they purport to depict may or may not, at the appropriate time, accord with that part, for directives may (or may not) be followed, in which case they do (or do not) at the appropriate time accord with what they purport to depict. If I follow the directive, "shut the door" (which depicts the world with the door shut, though, of course, as a result of my complying with the directive), then there is, at the appropriate time, accordance between the world as it is and as it is depicted in the directive. Nevertheless, that does not make the directive true rather than false because to say that would be to imply that this sort of accordance is an excellence, nonaccordance a defect, of that directive for, from the nature of directives, accordance and nonaccordance are evaluatively at most secondary.[1]

If the peculiar merit of claims made with directives lies in their being complied with, in their being "made true" by human endeavor, then the directives given to Eichman or the infamous Waffen SS would have been as excellent as directives can be. But, plainly, their excellence (if any) lies, rather, in their being supported by adequate reasons, both for giving and (especially) for complying with them.

---

[1] I said more about these problems in my paper "Reason and Experience," *Noûs* 7, no. 1 (March 1973): 56–67. I there acknowledge indebtedness to Professor Elizabeth Anscombe, while conceding that I may well have misunderstood and misrepresented her views. Both parts of this acknowledgment still apply here.

As I suggested, a great variety of expressions can be used as directives. Let us examine a few of the simplest and most straightforward. The cleaner's "What shall I do next?" is a directive question, his employer's answer, "Do the bathroom now" is a directive answer. We can agree that such a directive answer cannot be true or false, if I am right in thinking that being true (or false) is a merit (or defect) of descriptives, that is, claims purporting to depict certain parts of the world as they are at the time of claiming, whereas directives do not purport to do this; indeed, some, for example, "Please, shut the door" imply that the door is open at the time of the request.

We may even think of them as incapable of being sound/unsound, because it is not the sort for which we expect there to be good reason of the right sort for both the principal and the subject. The employer may have good or bad reasons of the right (self-anchored) kind, but we do not find the directive to be defective just because the subject does not have such a reason for complying. By contrast, a directive such as "Cleaners are to follow the instructions of their employer, within the scope of her authority" would seem to be capable of being sound/unsound, because both principals and subjects may or may not have adequate self-anchored reasons to accept that principle as one adjudicating in cases when the principal's and the subject's self-anchored reasons come into conflict. Even in this case, though, there is no question of truth/falsity, since this directive does not purport to say something that will enable the interlocutor to form true beliefs about the part of the world it depicts.

Consider, then, claims made with directives where the opposite may seem to be the case, for instance, "I advise you to give up smoking." Clearly it is or embeds a directive, "you, to give up smoking." And clearly, *as advice*, it can be sound/unsound. And equally clearly, though surely trivially, it can be true, indeed it can hardly be false: the three words, "I advise you," would almost always turn the directive into advice and so make it true that what I am doing is to advise you. But if by using the words "I advise you" I turn the directive into advice, does not my remark purport to be, and so imply that it is, sound advice? And if it implies that it is sound, does not that turn it into something that can be true/false? For may not this implication, that the advice is sound, be true/false? Is not this confirmed by the fact that if I now admit that my advice was unsound, I admit that (at best) it was a mistake to give that advice, that I must now withdraw it, that it would have been better if I had not given it, and the like? But does the fact that it was a mistake to make this remark imply that the remark I made was erroneous, false, contrary to fact? Or was my mistake merely another kind of defect, say, carelessness or recklessness? And does the fact that *I* imply by my remark that the advice is sound imply that *my remark* implies that the advice contained in it is sound and so that the remark itself is true/false? Or does *my* implying these things merely amount to "implicatures," to contextual implications, like the implication that one believes something which, as Moore noted, attaches to one's assertion of it? It seems to me that this is not a case in which the fact that a directive constitutes advice, the giving of which imposes certain epistemic responsibilities on the advice giver, turns his advice-giving remark itself into one that can be true or false. But the case is arguable and for my purposes, it makes no difference if it is only a borderline case.

In any case, it appears there are clear cases of what I shall call "pure" directives which cannot be true or false, although some of them can be sound/unsound. And we have examined one case, ("I advise you . . . etc.") which may or may not be a pure directive and so may not or may be true/false. Impure directives are those which, unlike pure ones, "embed," or make claims about, directives that are sound/unsound; and the latter imply that these embedded directives are sound rather than unsound, and therefore are true/false—true if the implication of soundness is true, false if it is not. Normative statements, such as "You ought to give up smoking" or "You really must pull yourself together," are such impure directives that can be true or false, for they are remarks about or embedding directives capable of being sound/unsound and implying that these directives are sound (rather than unsound). Their truth or falsity depends on whether or not the directives they are about or embed are sound as they imply. Moral normatives, such as, "One must respect other people's property," "One ought to give to the poor," "Killing is wrong," embed directives telling one to respect other people's property, to give to the poor, and not to kill, and to imply that these directives are sound, morally speaking, that is, that they come up to the criterion and pass the test of moral soundness.*

What distinguishes different types of moral normatives from one another are two things, the embedded type of sentence or use of sentence, and the modal terms employed. Not all normatives embed directives; "He ought to be there by now" may embed the descriptive, "He is there by now." Not all normatives employ the modal "ought"; some use "should," "must," "bound to," "obligatory," "wrong," and so on. The moral modals convey the weight of the moral reason implied to exist for the subject of the directive to comply with it; descriptive modals convey the weight of the cognitive reason implied to exist for the addressee to accept as true the embedded descriptive. "Must" implies the existence of requiring or conclusive reasons ("You must apply by December 31 or else lose your pension," "Another bus must come any minute now; look at the length of the line"); "ought" that of a significant balance of pros over cons ("You really ought to visit your mother; she is all alone and you are her only son," "We ought to hit a stream any moment now, if this map is any good"); and "should" that of a relatively weighty pro against a number of reasons that do not add up to much ("She should stop dyeing her hair that color; it makes her look like a tart," "It should crest in a few days now that the rain has stopped").

Turn now to another type of impure directives that can be true/false for a somewhat different reason: they embed a directive and imply a certain sort of institutional fact about it. Suppose the dean tells his secretary he wants to see Professor Smith and the secretary calls Professor Smith to tell him this. Suppose she says, "The dean wants to see you" or "You are to see the dean." Later, she tells the departmental secretary, "Remind Professor Smith, he is to see the dean." Her claim, "Smith *is* to see the Dean," can be true or false because it purports to state the institutional fact that Smith is under a conventionally binding requirement generated by an institutional authority to which he is subject, namely, the dean. If Smith had asked the dean to see him, the dean presumably would not be under such a conventionally binding requirement to do so, and so "The dean is to see Smith" (interpreted analogously) would be false, because it implies a certain sort of conventional fact when there isn't one.

By the Divine Command Theory, moral normatives are true/false because, if sound, they state or imply an institutional fact within the cosmic legal order, that the subjects of these divine directives are under orders that are conventionally binding on them the way laws are. On my view, too, moral precepts are true/false, but not because they state or imply an institutional fact within any institution. They are true/false because they imply an entirely different sort of fact, namely, that the directives they embed are sound.

Having said all this, I need to dispel the impression that I consider this of fundamental importance. What matters, morally speaking, is that moral principles, rules, and precepts, the directives intrinsic to the moral enterprise, may be sound or unsound, and that (if I am right) that soundness consists in their rational acceptability, and that the moral enterprise is a crucial part of the rational enterprise. The fact that moral precepts can be true/false is due merely to a peculiarity of our moral language: to the fact that we typically express them in normatives, that is, in statements embedding directives and implying that these directives are sound rather than unsound. But the moral enterprise would not be significantly inferior if we stated our moral precepts in pure directives* as long as we all realized that they are sound/unsound. In my view, that essential advance was made when societies left the stage of Pure Custom.

Section 3.   The Basic Terminology of Our Moral Code

The complexity of the moral enterprise with its several different roles, any of which has to be played by any member of it whenever he finds himself in the circumstances appropriate for playing it, requires a corresponding variety of moral guidelines. We need guidelines for the moral adviser or adjudicator who is called on by parties with conflicting interests to suggest a solution to their conflicts by applying these guidelines to answer such questions as what is due from whom to whom; for the moral critic or judge who is called on or volunteers to answer such questions as whether some particular person did or did not do what she was morally required to do and what is to be done by whom if she has failed; for the moral educators who must teach the young what is required of them when they find themselves in any of a wide range of circumstances and must try to inculcate in them adequate motivation to comply with these requirements even when they conflict with their inclinations or their self-anchored judgments; guidelines for all those who engage in that continuing adult education they may administer by applying the specifically moral pressures; guidelines for the moral reformers who are trying to improve accepted unsound ones; but above all, we need moral guidelines for moral agents at the time of action, for all the others refer to and build on these. I begin with them.

Given my account of the moral enterprise, what topics would we expect to find covered and what sorts of concepts employed in formulating them? If our basic question is what we should in reason want of one another, we may expect at least these five things of our moral code: (1) that it will identify certain types of behavior, such as killing human beings, and juxtapose each such type with its "opposite," thereby indicating a type of behavior in which we should in reason want one another to engage, and the opposite type in which we should want one another not to engage; (2) that these opposite ways of behaving will be selected on the ground that they affect in opposite ways each member's chances of being able to lead a life that comes as close to his (internally unflawed) conception of the good life as all members can get to theirs; (3) that it will divide the behavior of members into two other classes, one that consists of both the kinds distinguished in (1) and another which consists of types concerning which we and others should in reason be indifferent whether we engage in them or their opposites; (4) that it will formulate its precepts in terms that express the intensity of the want with which it would be rationally sound for us to want these things from one another; and, finally, (5) that the moral code will draw or enable us to draw a line of demarcation between those, failure to comply with which should be followed by the most intrusive, that is, the corrective social pressures, and those in regard to which analogous failures need not be met with these or any social pressures. As will become clear shortly, our moral code does all five of these things. This seems to me some confirmation that my account of the moral enterprise is on the right track.

(1) *The Morally Preferable.* Our code offers us certain action descriptions, say, killing, lying, doing someone a favor, having breakfast, and so on. Such action descriptions delineate a (minute) "universe of discourse," consisting of killing and not killing, lying and not lying, and so on. Each such universe of discourse will correspond to a pair of action descriptions that are mutually exclusive and jointly exhaustive of the possibilities, provided certain presuppositions are satisfied. What presuppositions? Those that are satisfied whenever someone is choosing between such opposites, say, killing Caesar or not killing him. They are not satisfied for all so-called "external" denials or negations. The fact that it is not the case that I killed Caesar is not the appropriate opposite of the fact that I killed Caesar. The fact that I could not have chosen to kill him refutes not only the claim that I killed him but also that I did not kill him, as here understood, that is, that I chose, decided, saw fit, or formed the intention not to kill when I had an opportunity, reason, and motive to do so.

Suppose I confront a choice between two alternatives, one of which I identify as a case of killing someone. Then I should, before my decision, examine whether the relevant universe of discourse (deciding to kill/ deciding not to kill) contains one alternative we should in reason want of one another. According to our morality, (deciding) to kill is wrong, (deciding) not to kill is not wrong. On my view, part of what this says is that deciding not to kill is *morally preferable* to deciding to kill. This fits in well with my interpretation of this claim: that we should in reason want of one another that, when we have this choice, we decide not to kill rather than to kill. As will be seen in the next few paragraphs, some other action descriptions will not result in a universe of discourse composed of this sort of pair.

(2) *The Areas of Moral Relevance.* Given our basic moral question— what we should in reason want of one another—and our belief about

which types of behavior favorably or unfavorably affect other people's life chances, we would expect the types of behavior selected by our moral code as morally relevant to be at least these three: what we should *do for*, and *not to*, one another, and in what sorts of cooperative schemes for common goals we should and should not *participate*. It seems to me obvious that these are the main areas our moral code selects as morally relevant.

(3) *The Morally Indifferent.*   We think of having breakfast, going for a walk, reading the newspaper, as neither morally preferable nor dispreferable to not doing these things. The universe of discourse picked out by the action description, "having breakfast," seems to us morally uninteresting because we believe that, morally speaking, from the moral point of view, it makes no difference whether or not we have breakfast. It may be better for us if we have breakfast than if we do not, but that is (normally) solely our business and no one else's. By contrast, their chances of leading a life closer to their ideal would be other people's business, not solely ours, but then these chances are not likely to be improved either by our having or by our not having breakfast. They therefore (normally) have no interest in our choices in this matter. Therefore neither of these choices is something we should, indeed could, in reason want of one another. Hence neither opposite is morally preferable to the other, hence this choice is not (normally) a moral matter at all. The universe of discourse this description of behavior defines is "morally nondifferentiating."

(4) *and* (5) *Degrees and Levels of Stringency.*   These two points are best discussed together because our moral terminology does not imply degrees but only "levels" of stringency. I noted that my account of the moral enterprise explains the need for suitable social pressures in support of the moral guidelines because what we want of one another may sometimes conflict with what we want for ourselves, but that getting what we want of one another is often more effective in getting us what we want for ourselves than is trying to get it by our own efforts, quite apart from the fact that in many cases what we may in reason want is the voluntary, perhaps eager, contribution by others. The greater the contribution other people's behavior would make, the greater the intensity with which we may in reason want it of one another, and the greater the likely reluctance of others to make it, the greater the need for more severe counteracting social pressures.

This aspect of what we should in reason want of one another is represented by another dimension of our moral code: the *stringency* of the moral precepts. What behavior is morally preferable to what, is indicated by the favorable or unfavorable moral "coloring" attached to the opposites created by our differentiating action descriptions themselves, as in "killing" and its opposite, "not killing" or (positively formulated) "letting live"; by contrast, what indicates how intensely we think we should in reason want the morally preferable behavior of one another, is the implication carried by each moral precept concerning the appropriateness of the *level of stringency* of what the precept tells us is morally preferable.

Our moral code can indicate one or other of two major such levels, which I shall call "optional" and "mandatory," corresponding to the two intensities, amounting to desires and demands, respectively, of what we in reason want of one another.

Claims, such as that some behavior is a duty, an obligation, or a demand of justice means both that it is morally preferable to its opposite, and that it is so at the mandatory level. Hence, in these cases, someone's choice of the morally dispreferable calls for the most intrusive, the corrective, (negative) social pressure, while a choice of the preferable at this level of stringency calls for no social pressure, positive or negative. That some behavior is beyond the call of duty or is supererogatory means that it is morally preferable to its opposite and that in such a case someone's choice of the morally preferable will (or may) call for positive (reinforcing) social pressure, whereas choice of the morally dispreferable does not call for any social pressure, positive or negative.

Thus some behavior may be morally preferable to its opposite, but only at the optional, not the mandatory level. Many think that doing someone a favor and giving to a deserving charity are morally preferable to their opposites but only with optional stringency. Doing these things is morally preferable to not doing them, but because the importance of getting these wants satisfied is not (they think) very great or the cost of it is very high, our demanding it of one another is not thought to be warranted. In such a case we say that, although giving to charity is not indifferent, because it is morally preferable to not giving, yet not giving (that is, doing the morally dispreferable) is morally *permissible*, and giving (that is, doing the morally preferable) is *not morally required*, not obligatory, not a duty.

The permissible is, of course, the contradictory of the impermissible, doing which is not doing the morally preferable at the mandatory level of stringency. The permissible includes the morally required (that is, the morally preferable at the mandatory stringency level), both the morally preferable and the morally dispreferable at the optional stringency level (that is, both the desirable and the undesirable), and the indifferent. Thus the indifferent is a subclass of the permissible.

We must now turn to the way our code divides the subject matter, the various types of behavior in the moral domain—as opposed to nonmoral behavior—which it characterizes as morally preferable or dispreferable to its opposites at one or other level of stringency. Our morality appears to work with a simple dichotomy between two domains, which I call "natural" (or "general") and "artificial" (or "institutional") morality, respectively. The former covers those situations in which moral agents face one another, not as players of institutional roles (other than the roles of the moral institution itself), and so not as role players with special role duties, like those of a mother, a teacher, an officer, an employee, and so on. The second covers situations in which people face one another as such institutional role players, exercising the rights and discharging the duties of their respective institutional roles. It is not implausible to think of natural morality as historically prior to artificial morality, since institutions comprising different roles seem to be latecomers in the evolution of social orders. In any case, they are considerably simpler and I shall begin with them.

Section 4.   Natural (or General) Morality

In modern societies people are members of a great many institutions and so play one or several of its roles, exercising its rights and discharging its duties. Even so they are not always "on duty" or "acting in their roles." A soldier on leave raping a woman he finds bathing in a stream, though occupying the role of a soldier, does not then actually play it; he is not performing one of his soldierly duties nor exercising one of his soldierly rights. It would be a trivialization of the idea of institutional role playing if we construed every action as the playing of some role or other, a bank robber robbing a bank, a jealous man killing his ex-wife's lover, a soldier raping a woman. Bank robber, jealous ex-husband, or rapist is not a recognized institutional role, however frequent the type of behavior, hence what these people do belongs in natural, not in artificial, morality.

4.1.   Natural Duties and Natural Wrongs

Consider again the precepts about killing; some belong to natural and some to artificial morality. Thus soldiers, executioners, police officers, security agents, and the like, are thought to have the narrowly circumscribed role right and role duty to kill certain classes of persons in certain circumstances, but when not playing their roles they are subject to the prohibition against killing from natural morality.

Is it a sound precept of natural morality? Should we in reason desire or demand of one another that we conform to this precept? Would its recognition as paramount pro tanto adequately increase one's chance of leading a fulfilling life? The answer would seem to be yes. It seems we would have such a chance if people could count on not being killed in any of those situations in which someone else has an opportunity and a motive to kill them, even though it also means that they, too, must refrain from killing others in just such situations. The gains each can hope for from being allowed to kill others would seem to be outweighed by the losses he must expect from others being allowed to kill him.

Of course, as I mentioned before, such differentiating action descriptions should not be taken as necessarily a complete and correct statement of the precept. They should be taken as holding only for "standard" situations which, like the boundary conditions of a scientific law, are at first known only vaguely if at all, but can gradually be stated more and more fully as we find evidence to show that the precept does not hold in certain situations which we then regard as deviating from standard. We have already noted such situations, for instance, self-defense, the just war, the executioner, and so on. In this way, we can, with greater experience of causal connections, acquire greater knowledge of the boundary conditions of the standard situation and of what we should in reason want of one another in various specific deviations from standard.

Thus, the precept—that, other things equal, killing someone is wrong; that it is, in other words, in the standard situation, morally dispreferable with mandatory stringency—amounts to a complex hypothesis: if this guideline becomes or remains part of our moral code and so continues to be generally regarded as paramount, then every member's chance of leading a life as close as possible to his conception of the good life will be greater than if the precept fails, or ceases, to be so recognized.

What if James thinks Joan's life will soon deteriorate significantly and that it would, as a whole, be a more fulfilling one if he killed her painlessly in her sleep and in such a way that it looks like an accident or suicide so that nobody has reason to fear that he will do the same to her when he thinks or knows that her life is on the verge of decline? Would this show that this is one of the deviations from the standard situation in which the precept does not hold? It is not if my account of the moral enterprise is correct; not if moral precepts are sound if and only if they direct us to do what we should in reason want of one another. For it seems clear that we should not in reason want one another to kill a person in this sort of situation. We do not *all* (if indeed any of us) have reason to want others to kill us when in their judgment (however sound it may be) we have reached a point in life beyond which we must expect decline, frustration, and disappointment. I think it a justified presumption, absent a strong case to the contrary, that a person's (internally unflawed) conception of a good life for herself includes being allowed to go on living unless she makes clear beyond any reasonable doubt that this is not so, that she now wishes to be killed.

There would then appear to be no need to prove that killing someone would be wrong even if in doing so we would not be inflicting harm on her or deprive her of something extremely valuable, or else that a person can be harmed or can suffer a loss even when she is no longer alive to suffer the harm or the loss, so that she can, by being killed, suffer in this way although she is not then alive to suffer it. Killing is wrong (that is, morally dispreferable at the mandatory stringency level) because it frustrates what we should in reason demand of one another, namely, to be (at least) allowed to live to the end of our natural life, unless we make clear that this is not what we want.

The moral asymmetry I mentioned between agent/patient and self/ other means that the moral precepts impose burdens on moral agents for the benefit of others that are patients. What justifies the imposition of such burdens is that the benefits are greater than the burdens, that every member stands to reap the benefits, that no one is required to shoulder the burdens while being barred from reaping the benefits, and that conformity of the precepts with the principle of equity ensures that everyone stands to gain as much as he can in reason want.

Who are the chief bearers of the moral burdens imposed by sound moral precepts? They are, of course, normal adult human beings. For they would appear to be the only ones (except perhaps precocious children) who can be moral agents. In view of what makes moral precepts sound, normal adults clearly are also the prime candidates for the role of moral beneficiaries. Still, there are other candidates. Our morality has extended that role to the senile, the severely handicapped, the mentally ill and retarded, to children and babies, and some want it extended to fetuses and the higher animals, even though it is clear that we cannot expect them to bear the full load of normal adults. With the possible exception of children, babies, and fetuses, who may eventually become normal adults, these other beneficiaries are in a sense moral "free riders," though not, of course, as is normally implied by this term, from an unjustifiable desire to avoid doing their bit and bearing their fair share of the collective burden, when they are perfectly able to do so. I shall not here examine the extremely difficult question of how we might justify the inclusion of various candidates for the role of beneficiary who are not moral agents.

Suppose it established then that the precept against killing is an other-things-equal directive against it with mandatory stringency. It says that killing is dispreferable to letting live; it states a moral wrong, something morally prohibited, something everyone must not do. Sometimes a distinction is drawn between positive and negative moral duties. If my account is sound, then, that distinction is less fundamental and important than is often thought.[2] For each duty attaches to the morally preferable half of a pair of opposites created by a differentiating action description. Sometimes either half can be expressed as the negation of the other: not killing as the opposite of killing, and not letting live as the opposite of letting live. Sometimes each half of this pair has a description of its own which does not explicitly reveal that one is the negation of the other, for example, killing and letting live. But sometimes one of these expressions is simpler, more frequently used, or for other reasons more conspicuous or salient, and then the moral precept will be formulated in terms of this action description irrespective of whether it refers to the morally preferable or the morally dispreferable half of the relevant pair of opposites. Thus, we more frequently say that killing is wrong than that letting live is a duty. If we want to express the moral precept in terms of "duty," then, since it must be ascribed to the morally preferable half, it has to be formulated either as the duty to let live or the duty not to kill; if we have a preference for putting it in terms of killing rather than letting live, then it will be a negative duty. But either formulation comes to the same thing. It seems largely a linguistic accident whether we have descriptions for both halves or only one half of such morally relevant opposites. Sometimes, as in the case of lying and telling the truth, the two descriptions are not exact opposites; not telling the truth is not necessarily lying. We then need two pairs of such opposites, each formed by one of the two independent descriptions and its negation. Thus, we have a duty to tell the truth and a duty not to lie, and these may be two different duties. But the duty to let live and the duty not to kill are only two formulations of the same duty.

Whether the relevant morally preferable alternative can be stated by an appropriate action description or requires the negation of one, a moral precept with mandatory stringency confronts moral agents, much as a law does, as something like a peremptory demand, a categorical imperative. It

_____

[2] For further details, see below, section 4.2.

makes the behavior it stamps as morally preferable with mandatory stringency a moral duty, something one morally must do. Noncompliance with such a precept would be a wrong or a failure to do one's duty. Thus to say that something is a duty is to say that it is the morally preferable half of a pair of opposites generated by a morally differentiating action description and with demandable stringency, while to say that it would be wrong—or a wrong—is to say that it is the dispreferable half of such a pair; to say that it was (a) wrong or a failure of duty is to say that it was an act that conformed to the dispreferable half of such a pair.

If this is right so far, then a natural wrong is also a *wronging of someone*, a doing someone (a) wrong. For all the morally differentiating behavior descriptions of natural morality impose their burdens for the sake of intended beneficiaries.[3] Thus, in the ideal moral enterprise, for each such wrong, each such failure in someone's duty, some intended beneficiary will not get his *due*, that is, the benefit due to him from the person on whom the guideline imposes the moral task that is his duty. In these cases, the intended beneficiary—and the others who have done their bit and accomplished the imposed task—have a justified grievance against the culprit. Such a grievance calls for redress; particular moralities should specify how this should be done and who must see to it that it is. The underlying assumption is that in a well-functioning moral order, people by and large discharge the moral duties laid upon them, so that (at least most) intended beneficiaries receive the benefits intended for them.

4.2.   *Types of Natural Duty*

It will be helpful if we clarify two distinctions between types of natural duty that we can find instantiated in our various moral precepts: that between preconditional and unpreconditional, and that between relational and nonrelational duties. As will be seen, these distinctions are sometimes misconstrued and such misconstruals are sometimes used to give (unwarranted) support to certain controversial substantive moral conclusions.

The basis of the first distinction is whether or not the duty arises out of what someone has done; a duty is preconditional if it does so arise, unpreconditional if it does not. Our so-called Good Samaritan duties are unpreconditional. If I pass a motorist lying injured by the roadside, then

---

[3] We shall see shortly (in section 5) to what extent this has to be modified for artificial morality.

(by our morality) I have a duty to help him just because he needs help, not because, for instance, he has done something for me in the past. But, if I help him, then (we think) he incurs an obligation of gratitude. That obligation is a preconditional duty, being conditional on his having received help. If I cause harm, then (by our morality) I incur an obligation to restore him to his former condition or suitably compensate him if restoration is impossible. That, too, is a preconditional duty.

This distinction seems to me to capture what is sound in the unsound distinction sometimes drawn between "universal" or "unconditional" duties, such as those against killing, lying, and harming others, which everyone is supposed to be under always and continuously, and "conditional" duties, which are supposed to arise only under certain conditions, such as Good Samaritan duties. The idea here is that only so-called *negative* duties, for instance, the duty not to kill, not to lie, and so on, are and can be universal or unconditional because they are omissions which "it takes no time to perform," and so can be continuously discharged.[4] If there were unconditional, universal positive duties, the argument goes, a person would be required to perform them continuously, without break, and therefore could not attend to much else, since most other doings would then be incompatible. Classical Utilitarianism is often thought to impose one single universal positive duty, to maximize utility, an impossibly onerous one, on all of us.

I myself think that certain versions of utilitarianism do indeed hold that morality imposes one such impossibly onerous duty, but what makes it so onerous is not that it is a positive duty, but that it is a universal unconditional one, interpreted in the sense just explained. The problem disappears when we interpret both the negative and positive universal duties in our moral code as unpreconditional rather than as unconditional ones.

Suppose a killer were to claim that we should take into account the billions of people he had not killed or the (literally) countless times when he had not killed anybody! Even if he insisted only on the thousands of people or times he did not kill when he was in a good position to do so, his case surely would not be much improved. For the occasions when he did or did not kill someone that count, are those when he did not or did let someone live, when he did not or did refrain from killing her, and the like.

---

[4] Charles Fried, for instance, says: "We can fail to assault an infinity of people every hour of the day. Indeed, we can fail to lie to them, fail to steal their property, and fail to supply their good names, all at the same time." (*Right and Wrong* [Cambridge, Mass.: Harvard University Press, 1978], 112.)

We have followed the precept against killing only if there was some identifiable person and occasion on which we could have killed her and had some inclination or motive or reason to kill her, but refrained from doing so.[5]

Thus, negative duties are in no better position to be unconditional in this sense than positive ones. We cannot continuously follow the precept against killing any more than the precept to give aid to injured motorists. And neither of these precepts in our moral code requires it of us. This is easily overlooked if one focuses on the fact that one has necessarily failed to comply with the relevant (negative) precept if one has (intentionally) killed someone at a given time, but not the relevant (positive) precept if one has not given aid to someone at a given time. But this difference is morally irrelevant since, in both cases, one would be failing to follow the relevant precept, if on an occasion for one to choose between killing and not killing or between not giving aid and giving aid, one picked the first, the morally disfavored alternative.

The second important but somewhat neglected distinction is between nonrelational and relational duties. The precepts that forbid killing and require giving aid to those in peril impose nonrelational duties because they impose these duties on every member of the moral order and for every potential beneficiary. By contrast, the duties of parents to their children, of the young to the aged, of the fit to the handicapped, impose relational duties, for in them either the duty subjects or the beneficiaries or both are members of specific classes. The most common, most complex, and most interesting cases of such relational duties occur in the domain of institutional morality: employees' duties to their employers, teachers' to their students, doctors' to their patients, and so on. In these institutional cases, the duty subjects often carry very onerous burdens, but there often is no difficulty in principle about justifying them, either because they have been assumed voluntarily or because there are comparable reciprocal services, often in the form of pay. In the case of natural duties of this sort, such justification must rely on our usual method, trying to answer the question whether we should in reason want of one another, that we carry these burdens and receive these benefits when we are members of these classes.

---

[5] It is important to bear in mind that in this context, a not doing of something, A, is a doing of not-A rather than a not doing of A. Not doing A includes being asleep, doing nothing, doing something else continents and eons away.

4.3. Intrinsic and Extrinsic Duties

So far we have considered situations in which one person, "the benefactor" (in a very broad sense) can either make another, "the beneficiary," better off, prevent him from becoming worse off, or refrain from making him worse off, or fail to do these things. Often, such "beneficent" actions also make the benefactor worse off, at least than he would be if, instead of following one or other of these "beneficent" precepts, he did not follow them but instead did what was then in his best interest.

Where such morally preferable types of behavior amount to duties and their opposites to wrongs, one can speak of intrinsic duties (or moral requirements) and intrinsic wrongs (or moral prohibitions) because, in an important sense, their requiredness or wrongness is not due to their consequences. Killing is intrinsically wrong provided that it is wrong even if it has no further morally undesirable consequences and that what it does, namely, terminating someone's life is, from its nature, morally dispreferable to its opposite, letting her live.

Conduct is extrinsically wrong if it is so only on account of its consequences or the frequency of its incidence. Shooting at a person is wrong for much the same reason as killing her, but it is not intrinsically wrong because the action description does not imply the infliction of the harm everyone knows will or is likely to happen as a consequence. A special case of this (which we already examined) are those types of action which have such undesirable consequences for certain patients only if the incidence of such behavior is high. They are the cases when we want to ask "What if everyone did the same?"

It may be thought* that such intrinsic natural duties and wrongs specified in our moral code are in no way dependent on or relative to the existence of our moral enterprise embedded in our social order, as are perhaps extrinsic ones, especially those based on the nonuniversalizability of certain types of behavior, or artificial ones, such as those depending on the institution of marriage and property. For, it may be said, surely everyone can see that killing is wrong, letting live a duty, and that its wrongness depends neither on the consequences of single acts (as does shooting at someone) nor on the frequency of its incidence (as does driving downtown). But this seems too swift. For there is a further factor on which the intrinsic wrongness of killing (and other natural wrongs and duties) depends: that the members of the moral order have some assurance that the sacrifices they may have to make for the good of others by following the generally recognized moral precepts are at least to some extent reciprocated by comparable ones made by other members. The fact that every single act of refraining from killing someone contributes the benefit to some beneficiary does not by itself ensure this further condition. To ensure it, two further conditions must be satisfied: that all recognize the same precepts as paramount and that the social order makes these precepts generally known and by education and social pressures motivates the members to follow the precepts.

Section 5.   Institutional (Artificial) Morality

General (natural) morality is the simplest, most easily formulated, historically earliest, most basic, and least contentious part of a morality. In a complex and advanced society, such as ours, it is, however, only a comparatively small part of it. The bigger part is our institutional morality. I begin my exposition of the main concepts of this part of our morality with an account of a modification of our natural morality by the addition of a very simple institutional role which I call the role of the principal.

5.1.   The Role of the Principal

The creation of this new role is an addition to the moral institution itself. In its simplest form, it is a device to enable the intended beneficiaries of a natural duty or the prohibition of a natural wrong to *release* the potential benefactor from his moral task. A loving son may wish to terminate his mother's agony in the final stages of cancer by administering a lethal dose of morphine. Natural morality provides no way for the mother to release her son from the moral requirement not to kill her. The mother may plead with him to end her suffering, but if he is morally upright and believes in the soundness of the precepts of our natural morality, then he must resist his desire to help her because killing her would be a grave natural wrong which, ex hypothesi, is all he has to go by.

Why not incorporate a suitable exception, as in the case of killing in self-defense, for instance, "except when someone is in the final stages of cancer and is suffering increasingly severe pain?" If that exception becomes generally recognized, then the son (or daughter, etc.) is morally required or morally free to kill or not to kill the mother. But this would seem to be unsatisfactory because it either requires the son to kill his mother even if she does not want to be killed, or else leaves the decision to him rather than to her.

If, however, we construe natural prohibitions and requirements as imposed on moral agents *for the sake of* some presumptive beneficiary, then in some circumstances a case can be made for enabling that potential beneficiary to refuse the benefit, especially if, in her considered opinion, it is not then worth having. We can accomplish this with the help of the role of "principal," that is, someone with "moral powers" to change by her say-so the natural moral relationship between herself and others. In the simplest case, the principal is the intended beneficiary and the moral power is simply the power to release the benefactor from his moral task. Once the role of the principal is recognized in a moral order, the point of the relevant precept is made explicit: the moral task has been imposed on moral agents for the sake of its potential beneficiary (or beneficiaries). Thus, if discharging that task does not confer a benefit on the intended beneficiary, the task is worse than pointless; it is a curse to the supposed beneficiary as well as to the benefactor.

The creation of the role of the principal disposes of this nightmare. It transforms natural wrongs and duties into wrongs and duties *to* the beneficiary/principal. They are now construed (not as commandments by some inflexible authority to some authority subject but) as moral bonds between the duty subject as normally wanted benefactor and the intended beneficiary who is the principal controlling the bond and who can, merely by his fiat, sever it, thereby releasing the duty bearer from his moral task and so eliminating the moral wrong of failing to execute that task.

With the introduction of A's duties and obligations *to* B, we have ipso facto introduced B's right against A, for they presuppose the same moral bond, now seen from the standpoint of the intended beneficiary/principal rather than that of the benefactor/duty subject.

Obligations to someone and rights against someone are things one can have because they have a life and value of their own, independently of the actions they require or permit. Unlike a natural duty, my obligation to Jones ceases to exist when I discharge it or when he releases me from it. Similarly, if Jones, the beneficiary/principal, has "waived" his right, that is, released me from the correlative obligation to act in a way forbidden by his right, then I have not violated that right.

The legal principle, "volenti non fit iniuria" is a recognition of the role of principal, but it is too broad. For it may not be desirable to construe the power of a principal to be unlimited. It may, for instance, be undesirable for people to have the power to "alienate" certain rights, say, to waive their right to life in exchange for a large sum of money.

The natural right to life thus goes beyond the natural prohibition of killing, in that it requires a moral institution with the role of "principal of a right and of its correlative duty," that is, the person who can release the duty subject from his duty. Without that power, someone's right to life would be close to, or would actually be, a duty to live: it would not merely "protect one morally" against attacks on one's life from others, but would also forbid one to ask for, and others to give, assistance in terminating one's life. This might be plausible if suicide were a natural intrinsic wrong, for then such a release from the duty not to kill would be an invitation to commit a natural intrinsic wrong. However, if my view of the moral enterprise is sound, then this is at least highly dubious, for it implies that we should in reason demand of one another that we not kill ourselves. But to what interest could we appeal? Of course, there may be special circumstances where we have such interests, as when suicide is a way of evading important duties, say, participating in the defense of a beleaguered city. Even then it would be hard to prove that we should in reason demand *that* much of one another. In any case, this would show only that what is intrinsically wrong is suicide to evade an important duty, not suicide as such. Hence suicide for other reasons, say, to avoid the suffering of terminal cancer, may not be intrinsically wrong.

5.2.   Institutionally Created Duties

We move still further away from natural morality when we reach those more complex roles, with their attached role tasks and role powers which are defined by a society's nonmoral institutions, such as the family, the business firm, the army, or the government. Where such institutions are morally acceptable or even desirable, their institutional role *tasks, empowerments,* and *titles* can be regarded as moral role *duties, powers,* and *rights.* Such role properties draw attention to another institutional factor, the "initiating" and "terminating" conditions: the person's coming or ceasing to play that particular institutional role with its characteristic conventional normative powers and tasks. A person has the duties and rights of a father, only when he has become and as long as he is a father, according to the conventional criteria of fatherhood.

Every normal moral agent has (much) the same natural duties and rights unless (this is sometimes disputed) there are, and he satisfies, special conditions under which such a moral agent is exempt from one or other of these duties, or he has in some way lost (e.g., "forfeited") one or other of these rights. By contrast, different normal moral agents may differ enormously in respect to the institutional duties and rights they have, for they may differ enormously in the extent to which they satisfy the various initiating and terminating conditions of these duties and rights.

We should distinguish moral role duties, powers, and rights—call them "moral role endowments"—from merely conventional (institutional) role tasks, empowerments, mandates, commissions, titles, permits, and licenses—call them "conventional role endowments." What is their relation to each other? The answer is that satisfying the initiating conditions of being a conventional role player and so having acquired the corresponding role endowments, *purports* also to satisfy the grounds that would justify the claim that such conventional role tasks amount to moral role duties and such conventional role titles to moral role rights and, more generally, that such conventional role endowments constitute moral ones. Of course, the ground on which these conventional role endowments constitute moral ones is again that we should in reason want of one another that our society have institutions with these roles and conventional role endowments based on these conventionally fixed initiating and terminating conditions.[6]

Unlike natural duties, institutional ones may not only be incurred, but also assumed or imposed. They are incurred if the conditions for occupying the status (which defines a corresponding role, e.g., motherhood) come to be satisfied. They are assumed if they are self-imposed, and they are imposed on oneself or another if someone has used a recognized procedure for imposing them, such as promising or legislating.

I need hardly add that it would be odd to apply these distinctions to wrongs. For just as natural wrongs are the nonperformance of natural duties, so institutional wrongs are the nonperformance of the corresponding artificial duties. Thus, while one can choose to assume or not to assume, and while those with the necessary authority can choose to impose or not to impose, a particular duty, things cannot come to be wrongs for us except through being failures to discharge a duty we have *come to have* in one of these ways. This is why we have duties but do not have wrongs. Wrongs are not incurred, assumed, or imposed because we do not come to have them in one or other of these ways. Wrongs are actions that are wrong, and their wrongness consists in the agent's failure to discharge a duty he has. Thus, whereas a contemplated action of a certain type *is* (not, would be) a duty, its opposite *would be* (not, is) wrong; *it* is a duty whether or not it is performed, its *opposite* would be wrong if it *were* performed. An action's being a duty does not depend on its being performed, an action's being wrong does; if *it* is not performed, *it* only would be wrong if it were.

For our purposes here, it is best to distinguish between assumed and

---

[6] I postpone to a later section a detailed discussion of one important subclass of such institutional duties often called "responsibilities." See below, section 6, Responsibility and Desert.

imposed statuses and roles. What sociologists call an "achieved status" is typically an assumed one, such as that of a physician, professor, senator, and the like. But what they call an "ascribed" status, one based on sex, age, position in the family, and class or caste (which in turn may be based on race) does not coincide with the class of imposed roles. Being a son, a slave, or an untouchable, is, but being a conscript, a eunuch, or a nun, is not an ascribed role though it need not be an achieved or assumed one either; it sometimes will be an imposed one.

If one's role is imposed, then one incurs one's role endowment including one's (supposed or real) role duties because one acquires them quite irrespective of whether one wants to play the role or not. In the case of nonimposed roles, one acquires them more or less willingly. The degree of willingness will vary from person to person: some beggars, unemployed persons, coal miners, prostitutes, and mothers appear to assume these roles much less willingly than others. Even so, they may assume them— and the role endowments that go with them—rather than face the alternatives, and perform them more willingly than they would if the roles were imposed. Role tasks and the corresponding duties can also be assumed within the role, as when a teacher volunteers to teach a certain class others dislike teaching, or when a lifeguard volunteers to take a Sunday shift no one else wants, although these are not duties assumed at the time they assumed the role of teacher or lifeguard.

Conventional role endowments and the corresponding purported moral role endowments fall under the general moral guideline of "my station and its duties": that it is our moral duty to perform our various role duties and respect other people's role rights. In most moral codes, the difference between purported and real moral role rights and duties is slurred over, but is of very great importance. Many of us are now well aware of how the design of many institutions and their roles is morally distorted by psychological forces such as racism, sexism, ethnic hatreds, and other prejudices, as well as the widespread unwillingness to remedy the injustices inflicted on the victims of these hatreds and prejudices when this involves giving up some of the gains made by the perpetrators or their innocent benefiting heirs.

In a sound institutional morality there must therefore be limits on what conventional role endowments can count as moral ones. In view of the conventional role endowments of institutions such as slavery, suttee, or untouchability, it should be clear to all that conventional role endowments are not necessarily moral ones. Since, on the other hand, it is desirable that there be institutions composed of roles with such conventional endowments generally accepted as moral ones, it seems to me that they should be regarded as creating a presumption that they are moral ones though that presumption should be recognized as rebuttable and must be rebutted before their moral soundness can be rightly denied. If the conventional endowments impose tasks the discharge of which would be the doing of something intrinsically wrong, then that would rebut this presumption, although further reasons may restore it. Practices such as female circumcision or the castration of those chosen to guard the sultan's harem or to sing in someone's choir seem to me to impose on those forced into these roles sacrifices we cannot in reason demand of one another; those required by their roles to carry out these mutilations would be required to do something intrinsically wrong and those made to undergo and acquiesce in them to be wronged. It would therefore require very strong arguments to restore this rebuttal of the presumption that such role tasks and burdens constitute moral duties.

However, these examples are not supposed to show that institutional role endowments cannot generate moral ones if they require the doing of a natural moral wrong. Defenders of such roles may be able to restore the rebutted presumptions that they do generate such moral endowments. Many think that the institution of criminal punishment and even the death penalty can be morally justified although they involve doing things (such as depriving people of their freedom or their life) which are intrinsic wrongs.

5.3. Obligations

Finally, I want to discuss an important subclass of institutional duties which I shall call "obligations." What is peculiar to them is that the institutions that generate them have only one role, that the content of the duties generated in this way is determined by the words used by the role player (rather than by the design of the institution), and that the aim of the institution is the generating of such tailor-made duties. Promising, contract making, and legislating are the most important of these institutions. In promising one obligates oneself, in legislating one obligates others. The most important thing that distinguishes an obligation from other kinds of assumed duty is that it is generated by one's saying something.

Promising generates a duty (of the sort I call an obligation) to keep the promise made. It is generated by a certain linguistic performance, such as "I promise to be home by seven," or some linguistic equivalent, such as,

"Sure, I'll be home by seven," or some nonlinguistic equivalent, such as, nodding in response to a question of the form, "Do you solemnly promise to do X?"; and its content, what one is obligated to do, is what one says one promises to do. Thus, what generates a promissory (moral) obligation is a certain linguistic (or equivalent) performance which constitutes a promise and the general (other-things-equal) moral precept to keep one's promises (at the mandatory level of stringency) which turns one's obligations into duties and promise breaking into wrongs.

It seems the moral precept would be empty in the absence of the institution or recognized practice of promise giving. Conversely, in the absence of that moral precept, the institution would merely turn a certain range of linguistic performances and their nonlinguistic equivalents into what is correctly called a promise, and certain actions into what are called keepings, and their opposites into what are called breakings, of it. But this would have no greater moral significance than the fact that certain linguistic performances constitute a sonnet or a contradiction in terms. And the same is true, mutatis mutandis, for legislation. What makes these practices morally important is that their linguistic outputs are thought to *be* morally binding, not just something correctly called that.

Clearly, the justification for the moral precept that makes the outputs of the institution of promising morally binding is much easier to give than that of the moral precept which makes the output of legislators morally binding. Although there are relatively few anarchists, we can all appreciate their distrust and fear of the state. By contrast there appear to be no detractors of the institution of promising (though some thinkers deplore what they regard as the excessive faith in the beneficial workings of contract) and if there were, we would find it hard to sympathize with their animus. I believe this to be so, at least in part, because we are much clearer that in making a promise we are not necessarily assuming an obligation than that in making a law legislators are not necessarily imposing one; and more importantly we are much clearer about when in making a promise we are and when we are not assuming an obligation than we are about when legislators in making a law do and when they do not impose one. Thus, most of us are clear that we have not assumed an obligation to the promisee to do so when, with a gun at our head, we have promised to hand over our money, or when we have freely promised someone that, for $10,000, we shall rob a bank. Giving a promise only gives rise to a presumption that the promisor has assumed the obligation to keep his promise. As in the case of other institutional duties, invalidating factors may prevent the promise from being the assumption of an obligation to keep it. At the same time, the existence of such invalidating factors constitutes exceptions to the moral precept, other things equal, that makes the keeping of one's promises a duty.

Invalidating factors are only one kind of defeating condition. Others arise in cases of so-called conflicts of duty, as when someone is in circumstances in which she cannot satisfy, at least not at the required time, everything that the promisee can in reason want of her on the grounds that it is something we should in reason want of one another. She may, for instance, be contractually required to deliver 10,000 rifles to a certain African customer at a certain date, and at the same time one hundred tanks to her own government. She may, however, come to realize some time before that date that, owing to strikes and the failure of some of her suppliers to deliver certain parts, she can fulfill only one of these contracts. She may think that her own government's claims on her have priority over that of her African customer. If she discovers at this point that there was an invalidating condition in the case of one of these contracts, then there would be no conflict of duty because that contract has turned out to have been "invalid ab initio" and so did not give rise to an obligation on her part to deliver. Thus what appeared to be, was not then and is not now such an obligation. The invalidating factor defeats, not indeed an obligation because there is none, but an obligation claim, the claim that she has an obligation to deliver. Sir David Ross's term, "prima facie duty"[7] would be most naturally taken to mean such a *merely apparent* obligation. An invalidating factor punctures that appearance; it exposes the apparent obligation as a *merely* apparent one. That, however, is clearly not what Sir David meant; he meant what is ordinarily called an obligation *other things equal*.

In other cases, where there are terminating or overruling factors, what is defeated are real obligations rather than merely obligation claims. When Smith releases Jones from the obligation to pay her $5, this terminates his (real) obligation to do so—it does not show that he never had that obligation. When Smith has two contractual obligations, only one of which she can discharge, then there is a genuine conflict of duties and she must determine which of them, if either, defeats the other. Supposing her obligation to her government is the more stringent one, then this obligation defeats the other one to her African customer, but that does not make it an illusory one. Although defeated, her obligation to her private customer is not without moral consequences. By her default, Smith incurs

---

[7] David Ross, *The Right and the Good* (London: Oxford University Press, 1930), 19–22.

a new obligation to her private customer which amounts either, simply, to performing at the earliest possible moment or, where warranted, to an additional obligation to compensate her customer for possible losses owing to the delay, or if later performance is impossible or unwanted, to paying damages for the losses incurred by the customer.

Section 6.   Responsibility and Desert

We must now examine a concept some have thought peripheral to morality[8] but which on my account is quite central. However, it does not seem to fit tidily into either natural (general) or artificial (institutional) morality and a coherent analysis of it is made more difficult by the variety of the contexts in which it is used. The concept I mean is that of responsibility.

What makes responsibility central by my account is, of course, the likelihood that people interacting with one another will at times have conflicting concerns and the consequent necessity in such situations for them to set aside, for their common good, their self-anchored reasons and to follow instead the moral reasons in conflict with them. Members will therefore come to have a rational interest in one another always following these paramount guidelines. If, as is widely assumed, self-anchored reasons tend strongly to motivate most if not all people, they will therefore also have a rational interest in their society having institutions designed to motivate members accordingly. One of these institutions is the society's mores that spell out these paramount guidelines and threaten appropriate negative social responses to their violation, and perhaps appropriate positive ones for conformity in certain cases in which conformity is, as we say, beyond the call of duty. This mutual interest in everyone's following these paramount reasons will be particularly acute in those types of case mentioned first, in which we should in reason *demand* of everyone that they do their bit. In those cases, it will then be desirable to subject people to the most intrusive social pressures for not discharging these tasks. But the interest will also be justified in those cases where we should in reason only desire that performance (rather than demand it) and where, therefore, we may have an interest in positively reinforcing any natural tendencies to act in a way that would carry out these moral tasks, perhaps by praise or by a reward.

---

[8] See David Ross, *The Foundation of Ethics* (London: Oxford University Press, 1939), 246–51.

However, before initiating these responses, we should in reason find out not only who has failed to follow these guidelines but also whether they have done so in circumstances in which these responses should actually be made. For when we look more closely at failures to carry out the tasks imposed by the moral precepts, we find that sometimes they occur under conditions in which we could not in reason demand compliance of one another. This may be so when, although the patients' benefits derived from agents' compliance would still outweigh the costs to the agents, these costs would be so high that they cannot in reason be demanded of anyone. By contrast it may not be so when, although these benefits would be outweighed by the costs, the agents can more easily afford the costs than the patients can afford the losses incurred through the agents' noncompliance. In the former type of case, we still should in reason want these tasks imposed by moral precepts but only at the optional level of stringency. It would not then be appropriate to respond with the most intrusive (the corrective) social pressures, but it might still be appropriate to positively reinforce the already existing motivation of those who have an opportunity to benefit particularly vulnerable or endangered persons, say, by praise or by a reward.

Questions such as these are raised when we ask whether someone and if so who is responsible for something. Where people's failures to do their moral duty are concerned, we shall want to ask whether these failures are culpable or justified or excusable or at least mitigated by circumstances or, to put it differently, whether or not the noncompliance *deserves* the (full measure of) the normally appropriate corrective sanctions. In the case of behavior that goes beyond the call of duty—supererogatory behavior— we shall want to know whether or not compliance deserves to be praised, commended, or rewarded. Let us then remind ourselves of a few important distinctions[9] that will help us get clearer about the various things that may be claimed when we ascribe to something the responsibility for something.

The most general idea presupposed by our practice of ascribing responsibility is that some things would in certain circumstances intervene in the natural course of events in ways that make that course thus deflected a more desirable one. The point of ascribing responsibility to something is

---

[9] See H. L. A. Hart, *Punishment and Responsibility* (New York: Oxford University Press, 1968), 210–30. Also see my articles on responsibility, including "Responsibility and Freedom," *Ethics and Society*, ed. Richard T. DeGeorge (Garden City, N.Y.: Anchor, 1966), 49–84 and "Moral and Legal Responsibility," *Medical Innovations and Bad Outcomes: Legal, Social and Ethical Responses*, ed. M. Siegler, S. Toulmin, F. E. Zimring, and K. F. Schaffner (Ann Arbor, Mich.: Health Administration Press, 1987), 101–29.

thereby to identify events, states of affairs, doings, material objects, or persons, that either have played or may play or have the ability to play an important causal or comparable role in deflecting events from their natural course in a desired and desirable direction.

The two most basic distinctions are (1) between the claim that something has the ability to play that role or that it has actually played it on a particular occasion, and (2) between the claim that the ability it has or has exercised is of one kind, namely, what I call "thing-responsibility" or of another kind, namely, what I call "agent-responsibility." Someone who ascribes responsibility for the car accident to the brakes or to a failure of the brakes (rather than bad visibility because of a thunderstorm or the sharp bend in the road), ascribes thing-responsibility to the brakes. The brakes are then said to be the decisive thing, and the failure of the brakes the decisive event, and either of them the decisive factor, that was operative in the coming or not coming about of a desirable or undesirable event or state of affairs. The factor to which such thing-responsibility is ascribed may be singled out for a variety of reasons: it is the most easily controlled (as in the case of the brakes), or it is abnormal (the bad visibility), and others. When one causal factor is an artifact with a function it has failed to perform (such as the brakes in our example), then this factor is an especially suitable candidate to whom to ascribe responsibility.[10]

The main point of the practice of ascribing the possession or exercise of either of these two types of ability is, in a sense, "forward looking": to ascribe the possession of the ability whose exercise would make the future better than it otherwise would be (e.g., to prevent harm that would otherwise be done or to make good things happen that would not happen otherwise); or to ascribe either an exercise or a failure to exercise that ability. However, the ascription of an actual exercise of that ability is, in a sense, "backward looking"; the "culprit" or "benefactor" is not identified until after the mishap or the benefaction has occurred, but the point of nailing responsibility to something is, of course, to do something about such failures to exercise the ability so that similar mishaps will in future be prevented, or to do something about its beneficial exercise in difficult circumstances so that it will in future be exercised again in these or other difficult circumstances. Although this harm is now done and so can no longer be prevented, knowing what *was* (not, *is*) responsible for it this time, may enable us to take steps to prevent it next time. We can repair the

---

[10] If I have understood him correctly, I here closely follow Joel Feinberg's illuminating article, "Sua Culpa."

brakes and, although we can as yet do nothing to prevent hurricanes or floods or earthquakes, we can build stronger houses or better dams or move to safer habitats. Ascribing thing-responsibility for something is thus quite similar to identifying its cause. It has, therefore, often been called "causal responsibility," but I think there are important differences between the two concepts, which we need not go into here, on account of which I do not follow this usage.[11]

There are many differences between thing- and agent-responsibility. The most important are bound up with the special abilities and powers of (rational and moral) agents: that agents can, if they want to, follow directives, that they can be motivated to do so in various ways, including the exertion of social pressures, that their failure to follow them may occur in circumstances in which it puts them at fault. Entities, such as brakes or even cats, cannot be agent-responsible, but only thing-responsible, because they cannot understand and follow directives; they therefore cannot be motivated to follow them if indeed they can be motivated at all. Some of them, such as brakes, can fail to perform their function and so can be faulty, but they cannot be at fault; the blame for the mishap can, therefore, be placed on them or their failures, but they cannot be (judged) blameworthy on account of their failures, and they cannot be culpable or deserve condemnation or punishment, or be liable to pay compensation.

There are various linguistic markers that tell us when someone ascribes thing-responsibility and when she ascribes agent-responsibility.[12] The brakes *were* (thing) responsible, the agent *is* (agent) responsible for the accident. Thing-responsibility cannot, agent-responsibility can sometimes, be *assumed*. As I noted, if something was thing-responsible for an occurrence, we can blame it for that, we can blame the occurrence on it, we can in some cases judge it faulty, but we cannot judge it to be blameworthy, at fault, or culpable. There is point in repairing the brakes, not in punishing them. Some philosophers have held that punishment is capable of producing in culprits something analogous to repair in faulty brakes, namely, reform or, as it is now usually called, rehabilitation, and some of them regard punishment as justifiable only if it tends to bring it about. Others, however, insist that punishing culprits is not at all like repairing brakes. There are ways of dealing with culprits that are similar to repairs or cures, such as treatment with drugs or brain surgery, but objectors say that

---

[11] I have said more about this in "Moral and Legal Responsibility," especially the section on "Causal Responsibility and Causation," 107–11.

[12] Here I follow Hare in *Punishment and Responsibility*, 214–15.

such "treatments" are warranted only when the agent's normal "response mechanism" has broken down, when he can no longer be motivated by threats, inducements, cajolings, persuasion, and rational argument.

These complexities in our practice of holding people agent-responsible have generated several senses in which we ascribe responsibility to them. The first major distinction (already mentioned) is that between "capacity" and "occurrent" responsibility. The former ascribes the combination of abilities and powers which, together, constitute the capacity whose possession makes a person capable of becoming agent-responsible in the various occurrent senses. People who lack this capacity, such as babies, the senile, the insane, and various other types of the mentally defective, cannot become occurrently responsible for anything they have done or failed to do. If a person lacks capacity responsibility, there is no point in investigating whether he has become occurrently responsible for something. For the whole enterprise of finding and holding people (occurrently agent-) responsible aims at influencing their motivation to do their duty, partly by the mere knowledge of and aversion to what is involved in being found and held thus responsible, and partly by the effect of having been found and held responsible for something one has done or failed to do. Of course, that still leaves open the possibility that such a "defective" human being may be found thing-responsible and treated in the appropriate way.

There are three main parts or phases of the practice of holding people (agent-) responsible. The investigation sets out from the occurrence of some unwelcome or (less frequently) a welcome event or state of affairs and suspicions, accusations, or gratitude directed at people who are thought responsible for it. I shall here ignore the cases dealing with the welcome development. The first phase (not necessarily in time) is one we have already talked about, the elimination of those who lack capacity responsibility; the second is the examination of whether any of the suspects had a duty not to do things that may be causally connected with the unwelcome occurrence or a duty actually to prevent it; the third is the examination of whether any of them has failed in one of his relevant duties and if so, whether and if so what social response should be made.

In the second part, the examination relies on the duties spelled out in the moral code. In this context, we must attend to an important type of duty which is also called "a responsibility"—I call it "task responsibility." We can say, truly or falsely, that one of a certain secretary's responsibilities (duties) is to secure and maintain adequate office supplies. Task responsibilities are a certain kind of complex duties, the kind that is created by an end-setting (often legal or administrative) general directive, such as,

". . . all departmental secretaries are responsible for office supplies." Their discharge is not simply the carrying out of explicit instructions of what to do, but involves a certain level of expertise, experience, organizational talent, foresight, planning, or initiative. What makes end-setting directives responsibilities is that their subjects have a duty to "see to it" that a certain event or state of affairs is brought about or prevented; he is not simply told what it is he must do, as he is in action-specifying directives, such as "The duty of a secretarial assistant is to stamp and mail the letters deposited in the 'outgoing' trays, to lock the office doors and the main gate before he leaves the premises each evening, and in general to carry out the instructions of the secretary." A responsible ("a three-ulcer") job is one with many difficult responsibilities at which one may have failed although one has tried to discharge them to the best of one's abilities. This does not, of course, mean that one can be responsible (in a backward-looking sense) only for failing to discharge one's responsibilities but not one's duties. On the contrary, one can be responsible in such a backward-looking sense only for a failure in one's duty of which one's (task) responsibilities are simply a subclass. What makes the "responsibility" for this kind of task interesting is that it strongly suggests the conceptual connection between failure of duty and (backward-looking) responsibility. It strongly suggests, though it does not entail, that one cannot be responsible for something untoward happening unless one had a duty to see to it—a task responsibility—that it not happen.

Thus, we may be responsible for one or other of two different kinds of thing, one comparatively simple, the other comparatively difficult. One is something for which there is a differentiating *action description,* such as killing someone or failing to come to someone's rescue, the other is something for which there is an *event* or *state-of-affairs description,* such as a child's not getting enough to eat or the office not having an adequate supply of pencils.*

Closely connected with the idea of (task) responsibility is that of *accountability.* As I construe it, it imposes on someone the task of giving to another a regular account of the way he is discharging his duties and his responsibilities for something. One sometimes hears the complaint that corporations do not discharge their social responsibilities (that is, their task responsibilities for certain social states of affairs, such as an unpolluted environment) and will not do so until they are made accountable to the government. Becoming accountable to someone is a little like being bound over or out on parole, close to converting the burden of proof from that of guilt to that of innocence, and shifting it from the accuser to the accused.

When it is established that someone has a relevant duty or task responsibility or that he is unable to give a satisfactory account of having done or discharged it, the second phase begins. The investigators must now attempt to make an adequate case for saying that one or other suspect has failed in his duty or responsibility. If a case is made against a suspect, then he is *answerable*. The same is true for an accountable person who has failed to give an adequate account. The accountable person can avoid answerability (in the matters for which he is accountable) by giving an adequate account but becomes answerable when he fails in this. Not all people with duties or responsibilities are also accountable; they may become answerable without having failed to give an adequate account, since giving an account was not required of them.

The answerable person must try to refute the case made against him. He must show that the evidence amassed to prove that he has violated a duty or failed to discharge a responsibility is inadequate. If he succeeds, the investigation stops and no social response is called for.

Failure to "answer" when one is answerable gives rise to a presumption of an unfavorable final outcome, *liability* for failure to do one's duty or discharge one's (task) responsibility. But this presumption can be rebutted by an exculpatory explanation, say, that he killed in self-defense or stole under duress. The former amounts to a justification, the latter to an excuse.[13] Exculpatory explanations are such that when they apply, we cannot in reason demand of one another that even those who have such an explanation of their failure to do their duty or discharge their responsibility should be held liable for this failure. When no such exculpatory explanations are available, the person who has failed to do his duty or discharge his responsibility is culpable and therefore liable.

Proof or disproof of a particular person's liability is the final aim of the enterprise of finding and holding people responsible. The various ways of derailing the train that runs from failure in one's duty or responsibility to liability are introduced in the more sophisticated versions of that enterprise because of the unnecessary, unprofitable, and unjustifiable hardships which their absence in so-called "strict liability" cases usually inflicts on those thus liable. There are, it would appear, a number of exceptions to this, especially in tort law, but we need not go into this here.

However, we should note that liability can mean two quite different

---

[13] For the distinction between justification and excuse, see, for example, J. L. Austin, "A Plea for Excuses," in *Proceedings of the Aristotelian Society, 1956–57*. Reprinted in J. L. Austin, *Philosophical Papers*, ed. J. O. Urmson and A. J. Warnock (Oxford: Oxford University Press, 1961), 123–52.

things, depending on the kind of duty and responsibility for whose nondischarge we are made liable. If the nondischarge consists in an act or a bringing about or a failure to prevent something, which is always something we should in reason want one another not to do, bring about, or fail to prevent, then agents should be made liable to the most intrusive, the corrective, social pressures, those intended to remotivate culprits so as not to want to continue engaging in his sort of duty-violating behavior. If, by contrast, it is something that is normally desirable but in exceptional circumstances inflicts some relatively minor and easily remediable harm, damage, or loss on the patient(s) while preventing serious and unremediable harm, damage, or loss to the agent(s), then agents need and should not be remotivated so as not to do these things again, hence their liability should be limited (at worst) to the restitution or repair of, and the compensation for, the losses, damage, and harm done. In these cases, the appropriate improvement in the situation lies not in a change in people's motivation, but in a guarantee that the disadvantaged patients be restored to their position prior to being disadvantaged.

At this point, I hope it has become sufficiently plausible to say, without adding further arguments, that "responsible" and "responsibility" are sometimes used to ascribe accountability, answerability, culpability, and liability. However, I think I should add a few words about the meaning of "*moral* responsibility," as opposed to other kinds, such as legal or customary.

There are at least three widely used senses of "moral responsibility." The first indicates one of the two possible outcomes, namely, culpability, of the particular step in the practice of finding and holding people responsible for something, at which they may be found culpable or not culpable. I think we understand the term "moral" here as an expression of the view that the moral (as opposed to the nonmoral) is the realm of the distinction between the moral and the immoral, and that that distinction is based on a complex mental element involving the knowledge that one has a moral duty or responsibility and that one lacks any moral justification or exoneration for failing to discharge it. Thus moral responsibility in this sense is naturally taken to be a sufficient and in some contexts also a necessary condition of liability, especially liability to condemnation and punishment. There does not seem to be an analogous sense of "legal responsibility," although in some jurisdictions criminal responsibility may require *means rea* (a guilty mind) and so something very close to moral responsibility in this sense.

In a different sense, "moral responsibility" means responsibility on moral grounds. In a parallel sense, "legal responsibility" means responsibility on legal grounds. There are, however, important differences between the sort of thing that is a moral and a legal ground, respectively. A legal ground always originates in a particular legal system, its identity usually clear in the context. When I speak of my legal responsibility for filing a tax return, I mean my task responsibility under the U.S. federal, Pennsylvania state, Allegheny county, and Pittsburgh city tax codes. "Moral responsibility" need imply nothing about the conventional origin of the requirement, but only that whatever that origin, the requirement itself is morally sound. What makes the ground of the responsibility a moral one is not a particular social origin or pedigree, but its ability to meet a criterion, or pass a test of moral soundness. In this sense "moral responsibility" may refer not only to task responsibility, but also to answerability and culpability. Thus, the first sense I distinguished, culpability, is simply a complex special case of the second. For the first case presupposes a moral ground for the supposedly violated duty or task responsibility as well as the absence of an adequate moral ground for that violation.

In a third sense, "moral responsibility" means a sanction that is appropriate for the violation of a moral duty or task responsibility. As we have seen, that can mean two quite different things. It can mean what I called the specifically moral sanction, that is, the communicating to someone of the moral judgment that she has culpably failed to discharge a moral duty or task responsibility, that is, has done so without there being an exculpatory explanation. Or it can mean a sanction peculiar to custom or law (such as ostracism and imprisonment, respectively) when that is morally justifiable or required. The contrasting legal sense is closely parallel except that, as we noted, there is no moral analogue to the peculiar sanctions of law and custom. To the extent that more generally effective sanctions than the specifically moral ones are appropriate in response to failure to discharge a moral duty or task responsibility, they must be the characteristic sanctions of law or custom. What makes the latter in certain cases moral sanctions is not, of course, that they are the peculiarly moral ones, but that in these cases they are morally required or justified in addition to the peculiarly moral ones.

Section 7.   Justice and Equity

I want to conclude this discussion of our moral code with an examination of two concepts, justice and equity—closely related both to each other and to the concept of responsibility—which, at least in my interpretation, provide further support for my conception of the moral enterprise.

7.1. *Justice*

I begin with justice which, I believe, has been misconstrued by several of the most influential moral philosophers of the past and present.[14] In trying to understand justice, it is tempting but, it appears, overhasty to begin by asking what it is and in what it consists. Most have taken it to be a virtue, perhaps the most important one, and to consist in something like a certain sort of behavioral disposition or disposition to choose. One of the oldest and most enduring accounts, attributed by Socrates (in Plato's *Republic*) to the poet Simonides, says that it consists in giving everyone his due. According to Aristotle, there is a general and a more specific sense of "justice." In the general sense, it refers to the whole of virtue (that is, character excellence) though only as far as relations to others are concerned (not, for instance, prudence), while in the more specific sense it refers to the appropriate mean between an excessive and an insufficient drive to increase one's share of the good things in life and decrease one's share of the bad. Hobbes also distinguishes between a general and a more specific sense, but takes the former to consist in the disposition to perform (or in the actual performance of) particular acts of complying with all "the Laws of Nature" (his version of the moral law), whereas in the more specific sense it consists in the disposition to perform (or in the actual performance of) particular acts of complying with the third Law of Nature, namely, to keep one's contracts. Hume regards it as the chief among what he calls the "artificial" virtues, the disposition to conform to the duties imposed by certain "conventions," the most important of which are property and promising. Kant says comparatively little about justice ("Gerechtigkeit") itself, but a lot about "Recht" (the moral core of Gerechtigkeit), a term often (somewhat misleadingly) translated as "duties of justice," possibly as a consequence of which Kant is often taken to have thought of these duties as the requirements of justice. Mill's account at least in one important respect resembles Kant's for he thinks of justice as tied to rights, as the virtue of being disposed to discharge all those of one's

---

[14] In this section, I borrow a number of points from my paper, "Justice and the Aims of Political Philosophy," *Ethics* 99, no. 4 (July 1989): section 7, 784–89, and from the first of my three "Perspectives Lectures" given at the University of Notre Dame in 1978.

duties (i.e., exactable utilitarian directives) that arise out of other people's rights against one.[15]

With Mill we return to a conception which, at its core, is close to that of Simonides: justice as giving everybody what is due to him from one.* However, Mill added three distinctive new details: the account of duty as a directive that "can" (that is, may or must) be "exacted," the specification of one's duties of justice as those that are correlative to other people's rights against one, and the utilitarian criterion of the soundness of practical directives and when they are duties or obligations, that is, "exactable."[16] Probably Kant's and Mill's views helped to popularize the conception of justice as a set of duties, namely, those one has to others because of the rights they have against one.

Two other conceptions with some support among contemporary philosophers must be added to our list. The first may be called "*formal justice*,"[17] by which I mean the virtue possessed by those who impartially and conscientiously discharge the role duties of their society's "major institutions," that is, those that "define men's rights and duties and influence their life prospects, what they can expect to be and how well they can hope to do."[18] This seems to me to capture one important element of the concept of justice. Those who think of justice as "treating equals equally and unequals unequally,"[19] may have in mind such impartial

---

[15] Plato, *Republic*, 8 [331e]; Aristotle, *Nicomachean Ethics*, 117–22 [1129a25–1131a5]; Hobbes, *Leviathan*, 215; Hume, *Treatise*, 477–84; Kant, *The Metaphysics of Morals*, tr. Mary Gregor (Cambridge: Cambridge University Press, 1991), introduction to the Doctrine of Right, section D, 57 (231); Mill, *Utilitarianism*, 246–47 [chapter 5, paragraph 15].

[16] As Hobbes conceives it, there can be no justice until there is "some coercive Power, to compel men," *Leviathan*, 202. For Kant, "There is connected with Right by the principle of contradiction an authorization to coerce someone who infringes upon it," *The Metaphysics of Morals*, 57 (231). For the relation between Right (Recht) and justice (Gerechtigkeit), see *The Metaphysics of Morals*, 50 (224) and 120 (305f.). And for Mill "Duty [in which is included justice] is a thing which may be *exacted* from a person, as one exacts a debt," *Utilitarianism*, 246 [chapter 5, paragraph 14].

[17] I borrow from John Rawls's *TJ* both this term and some but not all of its defining characteristics. The main differences are that on my account formal justice is an excellence of individuals and their actions whereas Rawls appears to think of it as an excellence of an "institution as realized and effectively and impartially administered . . ." (*TJ*, 55). The second is that, on my account, a person's or an action's being just does not imply that the society housing the institution whose role duties he impartially administers is what Rawls calls "well-ordered" (*TJ*, 56) meaning that it is "One effectively regulated by a shared conception of justice" (*TJ*, 56).

[18] Rawls, *TJ*, 7.

[19] For example, William K. Frankena, "Some Beliefs about Justice," *Lindley Lecture* (Lawrence: University of Kansas Press, 1966).

administration of the major institutions of a society. However, as Rawls says, following Sidgwick, "law and institutions may be equally executed and yet be unjust. Treating similar cases similarly is not a sufficient guarantee of *substantive* justice."[20]

The second of these conceptions conceives of justice as the excellence of societies or their basic institutions which is possessed by those that conform to a certain principle sometimes called "equity," to which I shall return in the next section (7.2).[21]

I think all these accounts misidentify the domain of justice. A world in which people have the virtues or discharge the various duties these authors believe to be the virtues and duties of justice would be an admirably, indeed perhaps miraculously, moral world because, for all that has been said, it might be one not only without injustice but also without justice, and that, if I am right, would (as will shortly become clearer) make its admirable morality (in the sense of compliance with moral requirements) truly astounding, to say the least. It seems to me that excessive self-advancement, breaking one's promise or contract, stealing, not discharging one's (Kantian) "duties of justice" or one's duties correlative to other people's rights is as certainly morally wrong as anything is, but it seems to me equally certain that it is not unjust, not unjust to anyone, not doing anyone an injustice, nor any other kind of injustice. And the opposite, surely, is not a case of being just, of dispensing or meting out justice to someone, of doing someone justice, nor any other kind of justice.

Suppose I have promised to pay you back on Wednesday the loan you made to me on Monday, and then I do not. Surely that was not an injustice to you or anyone else, I was not unjust to you, I did not do you an injustice; and if I had paid you on Wednesday, that would not have been a just act, a case of my being just, or just to you, or doing you justice. Saying this is not so much voicing a *moral* disagreement—for it is agreed that this sort of behavior is morally objectionable—but a disagreement about the kind of moral objectionability of which it is an instance. These accounts, it seems to me, have not hit on the particular and particularly important part of morality that is the domain of justice.

What, then, is that domain? I suggest it will be easier to locate our

[20] Rawls, *TJ*, 59. My italics.

[21] This conception closely resembles Rawls's notion of "formal justice," but still differs from it in that it does not require the society to be "well-ordered" (as Rawls's does), and that it does require (as Rawls's does not) that, to be formally just, institutions must conform to the principle of equity, not simply to any principle that is by and large accepted as a principle of justice.

quarry if, instead of asking what justice consists in, we start by exploring the various things of which we say that they are just or unjust. Surely, the paradigm case is judges and their judgments. What is it about them and various other roles, such as parents and teachers, that enables those that play them to be just or unjust in the performance of their role duties, whereas postal carriers, cooks, auto mechanics, designers, and the like can be conscientious, dutiful, responsible, or the opposite, but don't seem to have opportunities for being just or unjust in the performance of theirs?

Grant me, for the moment, this seemingly indisputable fact. What then is it about the role of judges and of the judgments which it is their central role duty to deliver, that makes their discharge of this role duty a just action and makes the judges on their account just? They are, of course, giving those they judge something that is due to them, but that can't be what makes their actions just, because when tailors or chefs or architects discharge their professional role duties thereby giving those to whom these things are due what is due to them, they are not just, nor are judges just when they give to the gas company, the cook, and the plumber what is due to them.

It seems clear that their giving those to whom these judgments are due, the giving of which is the discharge of their prime role duty, is doing something quite special: it is purporting to dispense or mete out justice. And, of course, they would not be fully discharging that duty if their judgments merely purported to, but did not actually, dispense justice.

What are the conditions that must be satisfied for something to be a dispensing of justice? Clearly, to be a judge, a person must have ex-officio authority to make such judgments and they must be binding on those to whom the judgment is given. Typically, such judgments are authoritative adjudications between claims of violations of rights and their denials, or conflicting claims and counterclaims, that have been brought to the court. Here we return to Simonides, for these judgments turn out to be authoritative "findings" of what, if anything, really was and what really is now, due to some of the claimants from certain others. Such judgments of courts are backed by the power of further institutions that are part of the institution of law and are designed to implement such court judgments. Lastly, such terms as "miscarriage of justice" make clear that what can purport to be a meting out of justice may in fact not be.

Thus, the fundamental question here is how judges, and how we, can tell what, if anything, is due from someone to someone else. Of course, in courts of law, judges have the law itself to fall back on. Even that is often quite difficult because courts must apply "the law." They must, in other words, apply the relevant general directives (statutes, recognized legal principles, the ratio decidendi of precedents, and the like) of which the law is composed, to particular more or less contentious cases before them. And they must do so when the relevant statutes, and so on, and what they have to say on the case in hand, may depend on what is the correct or best interpretation of the various candidates for what is relevant to the case in hand, with different judges plausibly interpreting them quite differently.[22]

However, the question is seen to be even more difficult when we stand back from or altogether leave the relatively determinate framework of the law. For the provisions of the law, even those of the relevant constitution, are not beyond moral challenge. We then have to tackle the question of whether the conventional role endowments (as I called them on p. 312ff) defined in our most basic institutions correctly or acceptably determine what is due from whom to whom and whether the relevant legal statutes, principles, and precedents should be accepted. I think this question then seeks some fundamental general principle(s) against which these general-ly accepted matters can be tested. I think there is such a principle and I have called it "equity." I postpone its discussion to the next section (7.2).

Granted that a judge, his behavior, and so on, are just if and only if he (correctly) discharges his primary role duty of dispensing justice, what is justice itself? It would seem that *it is the state of affairs that prevails* at a given time in a social order, or in the cosmos, as a result of the discharge of the primary role duties by the role players of the institution of dispensing justice. It is perfect justice if everyone in a society or in the world always receives justice and never injustice.* He receives justice if, every time there is disagreement about what is due to him from another or when someone fails to give him that due, the relevant justice-dispensing institution dispenses justice to him, that is, authoritatively and correctly declares what is or was due to him from that other, and those under the judge's authority charged with the task of implementing her findings, do so.

Injustice seems a little more complex than justice because it raises in a more acute form the questions we have so far neglected. Injustice occurs at a given time if at that time someone suffers an injustice at the hands of a role player in a justice-dispensing institution. But there are two main cases. One is that role player's failure even to act in a way that can purport to be a dispensing of justice, whereas the other is acting in a way that succeeds in

²² Here I follow the ideas on judicial interpretation expounded by Ronald Dworkin in *Taking Rights Seriously* (Cambridge, Mass.: Harvard University Press, 1977), especially chapters 4 and 5; *A Matter of Principle* (Cambridge, Mass.: Harvard University Press, 1985), 119–77; and *Law's Empire*.

purporting to dispense, but actually does not dispense justice. Now, if for someone to receive justice, the judge must satisfy both the condition of acting in a way that can purport to be, and the condition of actually being, a way of dispensing justice, then this raises the question whether someone's suffering an injustice also requires that both these conditions be satisfied or whether it is sufficient that either one be satisfied, perhaps with some additional conditions not yet mentioned, such as whether the judge failed to dispense justice knowingly, intentionally, or carelessly. I shall not examine these questions here. Nor shall I discuss whether the ideal of perfect justice is an unrealistically and unnecessarily demanding one, and, if so, what would be a more realistic but still adequate standard of acceptability.

Much the same can be said, mutatis mutandis, about the other roles I mentioned. Parents and teachers can be just or unjust because in their roles they are called upon to judge what is their children's or students' due, what they deserve or have a right to. However, unlike legal judges, teachers and parents must implement their judgments themselves. Parents and teachers do not have a police and prison system at their beck and call to carry out their judgments and one would hope that they do not often need it either. However, where it deems it necessary, the law "backs" their authority, that is, spells out in exactly what circumstances what parental or teachers' judgments, but also what failures in parental and teachers' role duties, it considers justiciable.

There is thus really a close connection between justice and giving people their due; indeed, there are two such connections. One is that dispensing justice is the primary role duty of the main role player in the justice-dispensing institutions, and it is her duty to those who have an institutional right to have justice dispensed to them. So in performing their role duty judges give those judged their due. The other is that in dispensing justice to those who have that right, the judge must declare what, if anything, is due from or to them from others under the judge's "jurisdiction" (analogically extending this term from the legal context to that of all justice-dispensing institutions). Thus, if my account of justice is on the right track, then although justice does not *consist in* giving everyone his due, a person can be just if he is a role player in a justice-dispensing institution; and in discharging his primary role duty he gives their due (i.e., dispenses justice) to those under his jurisdiction, and he can give them their due (i.e., dispense justice to them) only if he correctly declares what if anything is due from them to, or to them from, others.

This account draws attention to one of the reasons why we value justice so highly: our belief that our chances of getting what is due to us from others would be greatly reduced if we abolished the institutions whose role players make such authoritative judgements of what is due from whom to whom and get them implemented by subordinate institutions. If that were not so, then there would be no need for or point in having these—surely inherently undesirable—institutions.

If this is right, then we should perhaps add to Hume's list of the circumstances of justice,[23] also this (at least partly) psychological circumstance, that human beings are such that, in the absence of these institutions, people would very often disagree about what is due from whom to whom and would often, even when they agree, fail to give what is due from them to these others.*

If we accept this as an account of one, perhaps the most important, kind of justice, then we can see the close connection between it and responsibility. Both ideas presuppose the existence of the institution of bringing people to account. Both involve two main ideas: the monitoring of people's behavior with a view to determining whether or not they have discharged their duty to others and, if some have not, the possible imposition on them of new duties and their enforcement to restore "the moral equilibrium" which their failure to discharge their duty has disturbed. The institutions of dispensing justice focus on the authoritative determination of what was due from whom to whom, who if anyone has failed in discharging any of these duties, and, if someone has, what if anything is now due from whom to others. The institution of bringing people to account includes the identification of those (minors, morons, the insane, and the senile) who lack the psychological powers presupposed in bringing someone to account at all, and of those (the excusably ignorant, those under duress) who, though they have failed to discharge a duty and so have become answerable, have done so in conditions that constitute an exculpatory or extenuating explanation of their failure.

I conclude that one error common to the several conceptions of justice I listed would appear to be this: they all take it that the primary use of "being just" and of "justice" is as the name of a virtue that any moral agent can have. Supposing for the moment that ascribing justice to something and saying that it is just do not differ in important ways, we can isolate two mistakes: they overlooked that only certain role players and the discharge of their role duties can be just or unjust, and that the ascription of "justice" to these persons and their actions is a derivative use while the

---

[23] For Hume's account of the circumstances of justice, see *Treatise*, 495, and *Enquiries Concerning Human Understanding and Concerning the Principles of Morals*, ed. L. A. Selby-Bigge and P. H. Nidditch, 3rd ed. (Oxford: Oxford University Press, 1975), 183–92.

primary use occurs in "dispensing justice," which is the primary activity of certain role players charged with the task of authoritatively declaring what is due from whom to whom. What makes the former use derivative is that we value judges correctly discharging their main role duty of dispensing justice only because it is necessary and sufficient for what we value on its own account, namely, receiving justice.*

It is clear, however, that there is at least one other kind of justice which does not involve institutions that dispense justice. I have in mind those judgments we all make, in which we assess people's merits and demerits in respect of abilities and character, or their actual performances by various criteria and standards, including moral ones. We sometimes make these assessments simply because it gives us pleasure to do so, but also when others need to know about such merits and demerits of certain particular persons and we are in a good position to assess them. People's assessments of someone's merits and demerits over a large range of his abilities, character traits, performances, and achievements make up his reputation, and his life prospects may to a considerable extent depend on it. Communicating one's assessment of a person's abilities and so on to third parties thus may have important effects on these prospects. It would therefore seem a sound moral precept not to make and communicate to others such judgments when they are less or more favorable than is warranted by the relevant facts.** Thus, if someone judges a person's abilities, and so that person herself, as favorably as the facts warrant, that is, as she deserves, he does her justice and, of course, does not do her an injustice. Conversely, if he judges her less favorably or more unfavorably than she deserves, then he both fails to do her justice and does her an injustice. Doing someone (perfect) justice is (like perfection) an ideal limit notion, so anything falling short of it fails to do her justice and so does her an injustice. For, as in the case of perfection and imperfection, there is no logical space between justice and injustice. And, of course, nothing can be both doing someone justice and doing her an injustice by the same judgment. Hence these opposites appear to be contradictories.***

These cases of receiving justice/injustice through people's assessment of their abilities and so on differ in important respects from our first type, dispensing justice. In the first place, having a role duty to make such assessments is not a presupposition of their doing justice/injustice to those judged, as it is in the case of judges in law or parents and teachers. In the second place, in making such judgments, people do not, by means of them, authoritatively determine the merits or demerits they ascribe. Nor, in the third place, do such judgments authoritatively adjudicate between any competing claims although they may importantly enter into their settlement; if I write a testimonial for one of my students, I may do him (perfect) justice, yet those offering positions need not accept my assessment (grading) of my student as authoritatively fixing his place in their ranking of the candidates. In the fourth place, such judgments do not offer an opinion on, let alone authoritatively determine, what *rights* the judged have against those with whom they compete; they only advance an opinion and only on what "grade" they *deserve*. Nevertheless, in making such assessments, one is purporting to do the judged justice. In the fifth place, one can make such a judgment and in making it do the judged person justice although the making of such a judgment is not something due to the person judged. If the assessment is what she deserves, then the judgement does her justice, gives her her due, but the making of it need not have been something due to her from the judge. If I write a testimonial for one of my graduate students who is on the job market, then the writing of it was something that was due to her from me, but if I write for a colleague who has often pestered me for a recommendation, then I could have refused without violating a duty or an obligation. Thus, whereas, in the case of *dispensing* justice, I do so only if in my judgment I correctly and authoritatively determine what is due from one to another of the people judged and I thereby also do what is due from me to them. In the case of *doing* justice, making the judgment about someone may not be something that is due from me to her and I am doing her justice, not if I correctly and authoritatively determine what is due to or from her, from or to another, but if I assess her relevant merits or demerits in accordance with her desert (not her right).

The excellence of these (and similar types of) judgments (which make the only contribution anything can make to the coming about or prevailing of the state of affairs that constitutes justice in a society or in the world) consists in their doing justice to those they judge, that is, in their judging them according to their deserts, that is, according to what is warranted by the facts.*

Clearly moral "judges" (critics of people's moral performance) cannot *dispense* justice, for they cannot authoritatively determine what, if anything, is due from a given person to another in a case of dispute between them nor do they have at their disposal institutional machinery for implementing such determinations.[24] Indeed, the scope of moral judges'

---

[24] For a detailed account of "authority," see my "The Justification of Governmental Authority," lead paper in APA symposium entitled *Authority and Autonomy*, APA Eastern

judgments of what *is* due from whom to whom is limited to natural morality. For what is due from whom to whom in artificial morality is determined by the conventionally accepted definitions of institutional roles and their rights and duties. Thus, in this domain, moral judges can make judgments only of what *ought to be* due from whom to whom, that is, judgments on how these institutional roles ought to be defined.

What, then, is the connection between morality and justice? Well, in the first place, people can judge people's abilities, character traits, actions, and aims from the moral point of view and in doing so can do justice or injustice to those judged. In doing this, they help in bringing about, maintaining, or eroding that state of affairs which constitutes justice or injustice in a society or in the world.

In the second place, moral judges may offer their judgment or opinion on those matters in which legislators lay down in general what is due from persons falling under a certain classification in circumstances of a certain sort to persons under a certain classification, and what, if anything, is due from whom to whom if people in these classes do or do not give to others what is their due from them; and on those matters in which courts rule what, if anything, was due from a certain person to another at a certain time, whether that person has given the other what was his due from him, and if he has not, what, if anything, is now due from him to the other. Such moral judgments then are the moral judge's opinions on what the law (or custom), in general or in a particular case, morally ought to declare to be thus due from whom to whom.

At this point, it is important to bear in mind that, owing to the specific aims of the legal enterprise, there is only a limited isomorphism between the directives of morality and of law. Thus, it would not be desirable for the law to make all morally objectionable acts of lying and promise breaking justiciable again, disputes are brought to court in order to obtain an enforceable judgment without unreasonable delay, hence courts have considerable discretionary powers to cut short the potentially interminable efforts by both parties to strengthen their case, whereas moral controversies about the rights and wrongs of a particular case or about a general moral precept or principle are not under comparable time pressure from the need for implementation, hence moral controversies may go on interminably.

Division Meetings, December 1972. Published in *The Journal of Philosophy* 69 (1972): 700–715; and Joseph Raz, *The Authority of Law* (Oxford: Clarendon Press, 1979), chapter 1 and, by the same author, *The Morality of Freedom* (Oxford: Clarendon Press, 1986), chapters 2 and 3.

Nevertheless, despite these special aspects created by the institutional machinery of implementation and so absent from morality, many of the general issues (such as capital punishment, abortion, euthanasia, freedom of speech, product liability) and the particular cases on which moral judges may pronounce judgment need the backing of the appropriate parts of our mores. This motivates and justifies the continual efforts of improving our moral code and of applying it to particular cases in our moral thinking and controversies, for such efforts are, among other things, also attempts to help improve the directives of our mores, including our law, which are the only directives to which, rightly, our morality allows the most intrusive and supposedly effective social pressures (such as execution and imprisonment) to be applied.

To summarize. I have argued that (perfect) justice is the desirable state of affairs that results from everyone receiving something highly valued—receiving one's due, that is, what one has a right to or what one deserves—as the result of the (correct) performance by those who make certain judgments of what is one's due from others which help one get that due; and injustice is the state of affairs in which not everyone receives that valued thing. Thus, the primary use of "just" does not occur when someone, his behavior, his disposition to behave in a certain way, his character, or whatever, is said to be just, but when a society or the world is. "Justice" is not (except perhaps derivatively) the name of a *general* human virtue. Justice does not consist in doing, or having the disposition to do, a certain type of thing or in having a certain character trait, or in being in a certain state of mind or soul, but consists in the prevalence of a certain state of affairs in a society or the world. Thus the being just, the justice or justness, of people, their actions, behavior dispositions, characters, or whatever, is so only derivatively in somewhat the way the being healthy, the healthiness, of food is. The importance we attach to these things being just in this derivative sense derives from their relation to the prevalence of that state of affairs in our society and perhaps everywhere which is justice. What makes the prevalence of that state of affairs in a society, justice in it, is that people in it always receive justice, never injustice.

We can think in two ways of the two activities discussed so far, "dispensing justice" and "doing someone justice," which are most directly favorably relevant to justice. One is to treat the former as the full-fledged one, the latter as an extended case lacking certain features of the full-fledged one. Or we can think of the former as a special case with certain important additional features. For my purposes here, the first interpretation is more apposite because the judgments dispensing justice play a more central role in the moral enterprise than the judgments of merit. One reason for this is that they are from their nature tied to institutional machineries of implementation; the other is that both the judgments and the implementation are supposed to be guided by what I consider the central distributive principle of morality and practical reason, the principle I have (perhaps somewhat misleadingly) given the name of "equity."

7.2.   *Equity*

In the preceding section, I spoke of justice as something that may or may not prevail in a society (or in the world) and what is received by, because either dispensed or done to, those living in it. And conversely I spoke of greater or lesser injustice as what prevails when there are more or fewer instances of people not receiving justice and so suffering more or less injustice. I said that in both dispensing and doing justice to someone, one gives to that person or those persons something that is their due, though one does so in different ways. In dispensing justice, what is due from one to persons under one's jurisdiction is two things: the first is a judgment authoritatively adjudicating between the claims made against one another by particular such persons; the other is that this adjudication correctly state what, if anything, is due from these persons to one another. One can fail to dispense justice in two ways, thereby "inflicting" on another, that is, causing her to suffer an injustice: one can fail to make an authoritative judgment when it is one's duty to make one, and one can make such a judgment that misstates that due.

I need not now pursue the topic of doing someone justice, but I must say more about dispensing justice because in it the moral enterprise crucially connects with the legal. Moral judges cannot dispense justice because qua moral they lack the authority to determine what is due from people to one another and the power to implement their judgments. At the same time, legal judges are required to determine what is due to people from one another on the basis of the general directives of the law (recognized legal principles, statutes, precedents), which may yield judgments that conflict with the best interpretation of the social morality. Aristotle recognized this inevitable shortcoming of the law and dealt with it by distinguishing between justice as (roughly) the implementation of the law, and equity as (roughly) the dictates of morality. The conflict between justice and equity waxes or wanes as the institutional machinery for bringing the society's law in line with its morality improves or deteriorates. I recognize the need for some limits on judges' discretion in the application of the law (though there is a great deal of room for argument about just how these limits should be drawn[25]), but in my opinion the conceptual tension is minimized by construing justice so that it satisfies all the relevant demands on it. It seems to me that this is achieved by distinguishing between the requirements of the law, including those on a judge, and the requirements of justice, that is, what conditions a judgement must satisfy if it is to amount to dispensing justice. There may then be cases in which the judge, by making his judgment, has done his duty both as a judge and as a moral agent, if he takes everything into account including all the requirements of the law, and all those (of the relatively few) moral requirements on a judge that conflict with but are paramount over the law's requirements on him;[26] in such a case, he may have *done the right thing even if he has failed to dispense justice.* Thus we need not construe such cases as conflicts internal both to morality and to law, by distinguishing between the moral requirements of justice and those of equity and by setting up two parallel judicial systems, the courts of law and the courts of equity. We can allow, instead, that people's lives are better, taking everything into account if, having set up institutional machinery as effective as is desirable for bringing law into line with morality, we give the requirements of law a certain degree of independence from the requirements of morality, so that in a few cases it becomes *morally* acceptable, indeed required, for judges to apply the law without thereby dispensing justice.

I think this leaves conceptual space for the proper role of "equitableness" or (for brevity's sake) equity, as we can perhaps now call it without the likelihood of misleading anyone. As we have seen, what is due from whom to whom is "conventionally" determined by our social morality. In the case of natural morality, the determination is more or less uniform depending on where on the scale from monism to pluralism our social morality lies. Despite our high score for pluralism, there is plenty of uniformity left, say, in the region of killing, assaulting, injuring, lying,

<hr>

[25] On this topic, see the controversy between on the one hand, Hart, Neil MacCormick, and Joseph Raz, and on the other, Fuller, Richard Wasserstrom, and Dworkin (among others). See especially: Hart, *Concept of Law;* MacCormick, *Legal Reasoning and Legal Theory* (Oxford: Oxford University Press, 1978); Raz, *The Authority of Law;* Fuller, *Morality of Law;* Wasserstrom, *The Judicial Decision* (Stanford, Calif.: Stanford University Press, 1961); and Dworkin, *Taking Rights Seriously, A Matter of Principle,* and *Law's Empire.*

[26] Consider on this point the case of *Daniels and Daniels* v. *R. White and Sons* and Tarbard (4 All E.R. 258 [1938]), discussed in MacCormick, *Legal Reasoning and Legal Theory,* 19–52.

deceiving, etc. There is also a good deal of uniformity left in the design of our artificial morality, especially in the institutions of law, economics, and politics, while there is a great deal of pluralism, or perhaps rather uncertainty, about various institutions, such as those that regulate sexual and reproductive practices.

If my account of judges' activities of dispensing justice is correct, then they rely on what might be called second-hand versions of such conventional determinations, "second hand" in the sense that they are what at any given point in time have become— by a complex process of legislation and judicial decisions—recognized general legal directives on which judges must normally rely in their dispensings of justice. This process also incorporates the influence of the institutional machinery (if any) designed to bring the law into line with social morality, while the moral views of moral critics, reformers, and theorists in turn feed into that institutional machinery. As will be recalled, I argued that the basic principle that should underlie these modifications is what I call the principle of equity. I give it that name because, although it is often identified with justice, it is importantly different from the concept I elucidated in the preceding section. In any case, unlike "justice," "equity," by its etymological ties with "equality," suggests an egalitarian core. As I argued throughout this book, there is adequate reason for us to want our morality to pass a test of soundness and for that test to be at the same time a test of its being in accordance with reason for all of us to comply with its directives, even, and especially, when they conflict with those of our self-anchored reason. The principle has an egalitarian core because (as will be remembered) it requires that moral precepts, to be sound, be such that there is adequate reason for everyone to regard them as paramount over self-anchored ones, and that there are such reasons if and only if there are *equally good* self-anchored reasons and *as good as everyone can have*, for everyone so to regard them.

This principle, criterion, or test of equity also applies to dispensing justice. It does so by way of the content of the judgment judges must make, namely, what, if anything, is due from some under the judge's jurisdiction to others also under it. Since judges have to go by the conventional determination of what is thus due, they are not dispensing justice in doing their job unless the conventional determination of what is thus due conforms to the principle of equity. Of course, if there exists institutional machinery for bringing the society's law into line with its morality, then this will normally (but not necessarily) be the case. But how often these judgments will or will not conform to the principle of equity will depend partly on the moral critics', reformers', and theorists' appropriate understanding of and devotion to their task, and partly on the society's members' recognition of the importance of these roles. Therefore, the success of the moral enterprise does not depend solely on each participant's adequately performing his tasks as a moral agent. It also depends on a sufficient number adequately performing the tasks of the other roles of that enterprise including those of moral critic, reformer, and theorist, and of the members' taking note of their discussions and findings.

There are thus important differences between what, as I have argued, is ordinarily meant by "justice" and by "the principle of equity." One is that whereas justice (in the primary use of the word) is a certain desirable character of a state of affairs prevailing over a certain period in a society (or in the world), equity is a certain desirable character of the way in which a society conventionally lays down what is due from whom to whom, and the principle of equity states the condition that a way of doing this must satisfy if it is to have that desirable character. Thus, whereas equity (equitableness) is conformity of something with a principle, justice is what results from the performance of certain roles in accordance with the requirements specific to it, which I spelled out in the preceding section. Thus, if we can speak of the principles of justice at all, they include the principle of equity, but also the other requirements on the proper performance of the role of dispensing justice. A judge who fails to do what, if he did it, would be an act of purporting to dispense justice fails to satisfy one of these other requirements, but this does not imply that anything is failing to conform to the principle of equity. Even if the judge's declaration of what is due from one person to another relies on established legal principles and rules that do not conform to the principle of equity, that does not ipso facto amount to *his* failing to conform to that principle even indirectly since it may not be up to him to change the legal principles and rules; he may have to obey, even if they fail so to conform.

Thus, whereas the justice (or injustice) in a society comes from a judge's particular acts purporting to dispense justice (or from his failure even to engage in them), equity lies in, is a property of, some actual or envisaged way of conventionally determining what is due from whom to whom. Thus, we can explore in the abstract whether certain principles that govern hiring, or whether an actual or envisaged structure of the family is pro tanto equitable, but we have to look at a particular context before we can say whether the adoption of legislation requiring color blindness in hiring, or a requirement that a gainfully employed person pay his nonworking spouse a certain minimum wage for doing housework and looking after the children, would be making the prevailing state of affairs less unjust (or bringing it closer to justice).

Lastly, I want to stress that the principle of equity governs the whole of a morality, both its natural and institutional part. It applies not only to the society's basic institutional structure, but to the whole of its moral code.*

This concludes my discussion of some of the central concepts and terms we employ in making our moral judgments. I have, as far as possible, avoided commitments about what we ought to believe in any of these matters. In the next chapter I shall attempt to arrive at some conclusions about what would be sound answers to certain specific moral questions.

CHAPTER NINE
Applications

Section 1. The Moral Life

In this chapter, I want briefly to see what help my account of the moral enterprise, especially its attempt to show the appropriateness of a criterion and test of soundness, can give in answering substantive moral questions. To this end I shall take up a few questions of so-called casuistry. By this, I mean discussions of certain types of cases, either when stated in a very general way, as in whether killing is wrong or sexual abstinence a virtue, or when stated with somewhat greater specificity, as in whether it is wrong for a soldier in the army of a country fighting a just war to kill an enemy civilian he suspects of being a spy, or for a wife to refuse sexual congress with her husband because she does not want to risk conceiving again.

However, my first "case"—the morality of leading a moral life— would not normally be included in casuistry. For one thing, it is too general to be a "type of case." For another, it does not seem contentious enough to deserve discussion. The answer seems built into the very description of the type of case. As murder is the wrongful killing of a human being, so leading a moral life is leading a morally acceptable (perhaps required or meritorious) life. Nevertheless, in judging people's actions or their lives from the moral point of view, we need to ask whether what they did was murder and whether the life they have led so far and are now leading is a moral one. And for one reason or another people may themselves want to lead such a life, perhaps because of a liking for the things they understand that sort of life to involve, a wish to lead a life that deserves that title, a sense of duty, a strong feeling that their mother would have wanted them to do so, a belief that doing so is necessary for a worthwhile life, and so on. But then, as in the case of murder, it should—and usually will—have been made clear what sort of life constitutes a moral one. So there seems to be no special problem here. But there is a further question which it is not as easy to answer in the case of the moral life as it is in that of murder: exactly what moral precept is implied by this characterization of it when regarded as a type of case? In the case of murder, the answer is of course that it is wrong, but what is it in the case of the moral life? Is the moral life a duty, that is, morally preferable at the mandatory level of stringency? Or is it morally desirable or meritorious, that is, morally preferable at the optional level of stringency?

In asking what the moral life consists of, we may think of this question as analogous to asking what, say, the gardener's or the lawyer's or the teacher's life consists of; that it inquires into the criteria of relevance; that it requests a list of the sorts of things that are done or taken into account by those who lead this sort of life. But I think that would be a misconstrual of this question. For one thing, unlike a gardener's or lawyer's, it is not a way of life that we may or may not adopt depending on whether it appeals to us.[1] For another, leading a moral life contrasts with leading an immoral one and so implies the achievement of a certain level of excellence. This, too, calls for elucidation.

Both a moral agent and a moral critic must answer the question of what is involved in leading a moral life. We can assume that everyone who has learned what it is to be a moral agent also knows what it is to be a moral critic and, conversely, that those who have learned what it is to be a moral critic also know what it is to be a moral agent. And they also must have learned that, whether they want to or not, they must or ought to lead a moral rather than an immoral life. They can also be assumed to know that a life is a moral one if it meets, an immoral one if it fails to meet, a certain criterion and that the criterion a moral life must meet is conformity with the sound principles and precepts of the society's moral code.

However, there are two interpretations of what amounts to meeting this criterion. On one interpretation, both the moral agent and the moral critic must determine what behavior of the person in question (in the first case, her own behavior, in the second that of the person to be judged) would meet this criterion, that is, would conform to the relevant moral precept. On the other interpretation, the tasks of the moral agent and the moral critic diverge: the moral agent must formulate and execute decisions executing which would satisfy the criterion; by contrast, the moral critic must form (perhaps express) an opinion on whether the person to be judged has, on a particular occasion or in general, formulated and executed decisions that satisfy this criterion.

Each interpretation raises problems of its own and some problems are shared by them. Perhaps the most important common difficulty concerns

---

[1] Cf. Philippa Foot's description of the moral way of life as one subscribed to by volunteers. "Morality as a System of Hypothetical Imperatives," 167.

the extent to which someone's behavior must satisfy this criterion if her life is to amount to a moral one and the extent to which it must fail to satisfy it if it is to amount to an immoral one. Are "moral" and "immoral life" contraries, as "hot" and "cold" are? Or are they contradictories, like "dead" and "alive"? I construe them as contradictories, that is, as predicates which, given certain presuppositions, are mutually exclusive and jointly exhaustive. As I see it, no life can be both moral and immoral, nor can any be neither.

Where, then, is it most appropriate to locate the cut-off point between a moral and an immoral life? Is that point at the very top end of the scale running from perfection to ever-increasing imperfection, thus construing the moral life as a perfectly moral and any (less or more important) departure from it as a (less or more) immoral life? Or is that point best located somewhere below perfection on that same scale, so that both the morality (the being moral, the "moralness") and the immorality of lives are a matter of degree? If the latter, then there is still the question of whether or not there is an ideal limit to how moral a life can be or whether conceivably a person could always be leading a still more moral life than he is in fact leading, just as he conceivably could always be leading a still more immoral life than he currently is. I shall suppose, again without argument, that there is no ideal limit either to the degree of the morality or immorality of a life, but that there is a point below which a life would cease to be moral and above which it would cease to be immoral.

Finally, there may be difficulties in combining the various criteria into an overall ranking, just as there are for many other kinds of multicriterial grading, such as that of the size of a house or of the quality of a meal. But these difficulties in these hard cases do not militate against there being clear cases, just as the fact that it may be hard to say whether the Pinto is a worse car than the Hyundai, is compatible with its being crystal clear that the Mercedes is a better car than either.

Applying this to our first case—that of persons who want to lead a moral life because they know they ought—can we say to what, if any, degree of morality they must aspire if theirs is to be a moral life? Clearly it will not be enough if the life she leads is precisely as moral as she wanted it to be; it surely must be as moral as it ought to be and this means that it must satisfy the appropriate criterion to a sufficient degree. What is the appropriate cut-off point between the moral and the immoral life? How are we to fix the extent or degree of criteria satisfaction that is necessary and sufficient for a moral life? What is the appropriate aspiration level of the degree or extent of that satisfaction?

Some people think that we lead a moral life if we discharge all those of our duties which some philosophers (such as Kant and Mill) have called "perfect duties" even if we do not discharge "imperfect" ones. But others (for instance Kant) appear to have held that though we are not necessarily doing wrong on a particular occasion if we do not discharge an imperfect duty of ours, we would not be leading a moral life if we never discharged such duties. On the former view, a life amounts to a moral one provided only one gives every person what she has a right to, what is their due. Those who think of this sort of behavior as just, therefore, tend to think of the moral life as the life of justice. On the latter view, one's life amounts to a moral one only if one also discharges one's imperfect duties to others unless one has adequate reasons not to do so. There is some disagreement on what constitutes such adequate reasons, but it does seem generally agreed that one's own judgment of what are such reasons is not necessarily right. Thus, if a person in his whole life never discharges any imperfect duty to another, it must be supposed that he did not always have adequate reasons not to discharge such duties. In between these two different cutoff points lies the view that one's life is a moral one if one gives everyone what is their due which, however, includes not merely what they have a right to but also what they deserve without having a right to it.

One thing is not at issue between these two interpretations: that people who fail to discharge their imperfect duties, even if they never discharge any of them, do not on that account alone deserve to be punished. But those who favor the more demanding cutoff point do regard those who fail to satisfy the more demanding degree of satisfying the appropriate criterion and so to lead what they would judge to be an immoral life, as deserving moral disapproval and condemnation (though others, not being in a good position to judge the reasons why the judged have failed to discharge these imperfect duties, should be cautious in expressing their disapproval) and above all the pangs of conscience and guilt.

If, as I claimed earlier, the guiding question of the moral enterprise is what we, the members of a moral order, should in reason want of one another, then, as such members we are, in principle, each of us and all the time, the target of these wants. We know that we must satisfy some of these wants and ought to satisfy others to an extent that is indicated by the way in which we distinguish between what amounts to a moral and what to an immoral life, and by the degree of the morality or immorality of that life.

Our moral code purports to tell us what these wants are. Types of behavior it calls wrong, such as killing someone or lying to her, are, it appears, of the kind we have such reason to want one another not to engage in; those it calls duties, such as rescuing those in peril, are, it appears, of the kind we have such reason to want one another to engage in; and so on. Furthermore, as I also argued, if the aim of the moral enterprise is to be reached or at least to be approached as closely as possible, then all or as many as possible must lead the moral life, not merely in the sense of discharging the duties of moral agents, though that is, of course, essential, but also in the sense of doing our fair share in playing the other moral roles.

Which, if any, among the roles peculiar to the moral enterprise *must* members play and to what extent must they play them if the life they lead is to deserve the title "a moral life"? Clearly, the role of moral agent is the most plausible candidate. It is primarily as moral agents that we are targets of the wants we have compelling reason to address to one another. Small children, the senile, the insane, the incompetent are, for obvious reasons, not moral agents (though they are passive members, patients, recipients) and so are not such targets. And moral agents would appear to be so always, to be never "off moral duty." They must always be alert to what their moral code directs them to do (or more exactly, what "performances" it directs them to execute, that is, what motives, character traits, behavioral dispositions, tastes, and so on, to cultivate).

There appears to be agreement that if someone is a moral agent, she has led an immoral life to the extent that she fails to discharge any of her duties, that is, does the morally dispreferable at the mandatory level of stringency, even if the opposite, always doing what is morally preferable at that higher level of stringency, is not sufficient to make it a moral life. I shall not here attempt to discuss, let alone answer, the question of what would be the most sensible method to set the standard for ascribing "morality" (being moral, moralness) to a particular action or to a whole life. Although it would be tidier not to allow any immoral actions in such a life, it seems that we normally employ less demanding standards.

What about other moral roles? Consider, first, two very important ones—those of the moral learner and the moral teacher—about whose place in leading the moral life there is a good deal of unclarity. Aristotle thought that without a proper moral upbringing a person would not be able to recognize or to lead a virtuous life. Some contemporary psychologists, such as Piaget and Kohlberg,[2] appear to have thought that the

---

[2] Jean Piaget, *The Moral Judgment of the Child* (London: Kegan, Paul, Trench, Tubner, 1932); Lawrence Kohlberg, "Moral Stages and Motivation: The Cognitive-Developmental

normal experience of growing up in a family and normal interactions with others would provide for all or most of us an adequate upbringing to advance through the several stages of moral development ending in moral maturity. But Kohlberg, at any rate, appears to have concluded that not everybody reaches the highest (roughly, the Kantian, fully autonomous) stage of moral development and that more formal teaching might be necessary and would always be helpful for that final step. Kohlberg held, nevertheless, that the sequence of these stages is always the same in all cultures; for the young he studied in quite different societies, such as Turkey and Thailand, passed through the same stages in the same order as those in the United States. Of course, he did not mean that they all accepted the same moral precepts, but he thought they did reach the same very general attitudes and principles characteristic of our and their conception of the moral enterprise and of the basic distinctions between moral excellence and defect.

I think what Kohlberg meant by moral maturity included (but involved more than) a grasp of moral reasoning, that is, of the application of general moral precepts to particular cases, and at its higher stages the ability to subject the moral precepts first taken over from the moral environment to critical scrutiny and suitable modification. Perhaps that is all we can expect people to acquire through socialization which does not also expose the learners to explicit formal moral teaching, as is given in certain high schools or in university courses on ethical theory and applied ethics. But perhaps such ordinary socialization is sufficient for the young to become moral agents and so subject to moral directives.

Whatever the truth on this matter—and it surely would be important to become clearer about what exactly is necessary and sufficient for the young to become moral agents and so responsible at least for discharging their moral duties—it is clear that it cannot be the responsibility solely of the young themselves to become thus responsible. If simply growing up in a social order and becoming socialized in the process does not necessarily or even most of the time transform the little savages into civilized moral agents, and if it is important that as many as possible be thus transformed, then surely at least some of those who have become moral agents and who have seen the importance of all members being moral agents should do something about it. We usually put this responsibility on parents, clergy,

Approach," *Moral Development and Behavior*, ed. Thomas Lickona (New York: Holt, Reinhart, and Winston, 1976), 31–53; for a discussion of the moral development of women, and a critique of attempts—especially Kohlberg's—to fit women into models based on male development, see Carol Gilligan, *In a Different Voice* (Cambridge, Mass.: Harvard University Press, 1982).

and school teachers, though there is a great deal of disagreement about whether teachers should, and how they possibly can, conform their teaching to that of all the parents. This raises the extremely important and difficult question of exactly what are the duties of parents, clergy, and teachers in the field of moral teaching, and what tasks educational institutions should impose on their members.

In addition to these substantive questions about moral development and the role of moral education in it, we face a further question: what, if anything, must those comparatively few (including moral philosophers) who know what little can be said to be known in ethics and know the many different and conflicting things that are fervently believed, do by way of moral teaching if they are to be credited with leading a moral life? It seems to me that although the influence of the teaching profession, especially of those who teach the very young, is enormous, their performance should be assessed on the basis of their professional responsibility. They should be judged on the basis of the extent to which they have discharged the duties that membership in their profession has imposed on them. If their teaching role and their duties are badly designed, if what they have been taught in university schools of education or in teachers' training colleges is unsound, but if they perform up to the accepted standards of their profession, then they have done what can in reason be demanded of them. It seems to me that, at this point, the failure in moral education is not primarily moral failure, but failure through ignorance— ignorance of how to bring about certain results in the transformation of growing children, and ignorance of what results to bring about.

I think much the same is true about the roles of moral theorist and reformer. The aim of moral theory is to improve what moral teachers can teach their charges. Moral theorists give accounts of the moral enterprise, its aim and function, and on the basis of such accounts advance criteria of relevance and soundness for the assessment of rival moral precepts, principles, and rules. The hope of moral theorists has usually been to provide an account of the moral enterprise that does two things: first, to paint a recognizable picture of what we take ourselves to be doing when we engage in moral deliberation and decision, in our various ways of reacting to people's moral deliberating and deciding, and in moral teaching; and second, to extract from this descriptive account, including what counts as success or failure of the enterprise, criteria of relevance and soundness of precepts designed, if generally followed, to achieve success. (I have attempted to do this in chapters 6 and 7.)

There are, of course, fewer theorists than teachers, and their influence on moral agents is correspondingly smaller and more indirect. A fortiori, it seems clear that we cannot in reason expect everyone to devote a significant or indeed any part of his life to moral theorizing, hence that we should not think of someone's life as an immoral one simply on the ground that she has not played the role of moral theorist. For similar reasons, we should not expect more of a moral theorist than that she discharge the professional duties of her role.

But perhaps we can expect every moral agent to devote some thought to the questions professionally raised by moral theorists and to take some interest in their answers. However inadequate and controversial their efforts may be, every moral agent should, in my opinion, be exposed to enough teaching about the moral enterprise to understand both the importance and the difficulty of the subject matter and to have some qualms about whether he is devoting enough attention to the question of whether his is a moral or an immoral life and whether the moral code by which he conducts his life is sound. Perhaps someone's failure to do this should be counted as a choice of the dispreferable but merely at the optional level of stringency, and for this reason not as something that makes any particular failure a wrong and as turning the life of someone totally neglecting these matters into an immoral one.

Section 2.   Wrongful Death

There are many different sorts of things toward which we have favorable or unfavorable attitudes: things that happen to us—what befalls us, the mishaƒs and vicissitudes of life, such as an illness, an accident, the loss of a job or a friend, or the good things that come our way, an inheritance, the return of a valuable thing lost; the states of affairs in which we are more or less directly involved; the freedom, the prosperity, the security that prevails in the society in which we live, our having a job, our marriage, our being alive and well; what others do to and for us—the harm, damage, hurt they inflict on us, or the benefit, help, support, relief they confer on or give to us; the things others are willing to do with us or to let us do with them; the various cooperative activities, games, enterprises we engage in together or the various interactions they threaten us with and against which we have to take preventive measures; and perhaps others.

With regard to all of them, we can ask what attitudes we should in reason want our fellows to adopt, what responses to make (whether in anticipation or after the event), what insurance to take out against their happening or not happening, and what pressures society should organize for or against them. According to the account of the moral enterprise I have advanced, these occurrences and human activities may be proper moral matters if, but only, if we can ask these questions about them.

Where the things toward which we have favorable or unfavorable attitudes are human actions, activities, doings, conduct, or behavior, they are proper moral matters unless the appropriate action descriptions are truly nondifferentiating, for then morality is unconcerned about whether or not people do one thing or the opposite. Of course, in a given society, a given action description may be generally thought to be, and treated as, differentiating though it is not, or nondifferentiating, though it is differentiating. Most of us, I imagine, would now hold that so-called female circumcision is wrongly thought to be morally preferable to noncircumcision. Similarly, many of us, I imagine, would now think that male circumcision is nondifferentiating—neither having been circumcised nor not having been circumcised is morally preferable to the other. On this view, then, a social morality, according to which one or the other of these two conditions is generally thought morally preferable, is mistaken.

The matter is more complicated when what we have favorable or unfavorable attitudes toward are occurrences or states of affairs rather than actions. For then there must be a certain sort of relationship between that sort of occurrence or state of affairs and human behavior. Roughly, the relationship must be one of control over its occurrence or nonoccurrence. Thus, it is only if behavior so related to such an occurrence or state of affairs has a morally differentiating action description and so is itself a moral matter (a duty, a wrong, an act of supererogation, and so on), that the occurrence or state of affairs is also a moral matter.

It will, I think, be instructive if I illustrate this point by examining one of these occurrences that occupies an important place in most moral codes. I mean dying or death,[3] primarily of human beings, but secondarily also of some nonhuman animals. What turns this occurrence into a moral matter is that it can be brought about and prevented by human endeavor. We can deliberately, intentionally, recklessly, carelessly, accidentally, or unavoidably kill someone, or cause her death, or be its cause, or fail to prevent her death, refuse to save her life, or let her die. If none of these or similar relations holds between someone's death and someone's behavior (including that of the deceased, as in suicide), then her death is not a moral

---

[3] The opposite, life or being given life, is also a moral matter, though it is only recently, as a result of the so-called population explosion, that this moral matter has received any, but in my judgment still far less than adequate, attention. However, I must postpone the discussion of this controversial issue to another occasion.

matter, but at worst a regrettable occurrence which may cause grief to some and which some will rightly mourn.

However, this is only a necessary and not also a sufficient condition of a particular death being a moral matter, for instance, a *wrongful* death. It must be something which it was for someone a duty or an act of supererogation and so on, not to bring about or cause or be the cause of, and so on, deliberately, intentionally, knowingly, recklessly, carelessly, and so on, or something which it was for someone a duty or an act of supererogation to prevent or not to let happen, deliberately, intentionally, and so on. If it was such a duty, then dispensers of justice must rule that not to bring it about, or to prevent it, and so on, was due from the agent to the deceased and must find the agent guilty of this breach of duty and must hold him liable to the appropriate sanction for committing that breach, unless he has some exculpatory explanation for his behavior.

Thus, as we noted before in our discussion of responsibility, many of our morally differentiating action descriptions refer to behavior related in one or other of these ways to occurrences or states of affairs toward which we all of us normally are not indifferent, but have a positive or negative attitude. Our own and other people's death is an occurrence toward which we all normally have a negative attitude. Of course, as we also noted, there are exceptional circumstances in which some of us have a positive attitude toward such a death and there is good reason (at least in my view) to take this into account in how we morally judge someone, as when, for instance, he has killed another who has begged him to do so.

There are many importantly different relations between an agent's behavior and someone's death over whose occurrence or nonoccurrence that agent had a measure of control. Killing someone would appear to be the morally most important such relation. Let us, then, begin by asking whether killing someone is a morally differentiating or nondifferentiating action description, and, if the latter, how it differentiates.

To answer this, it will be recalled, we must first find its relevant opposite so that we can determine which, if either is, from the moral point of view, morally preferable. I have already emphasized that such opposites are not simply the external negations of each other. Thus, the opposite in the sense here in question of (1) "X killed Y at t" is not (2) "It is not the case that X killed Y at t." For (2) may be true even though X was in no position to cause Y's death at t, for instance if at t he was asleep or on another continent. But we must not construe the opposite of (1) as compatible with X's being in no position to cause Y's death, since opposites must be alternatives between which agents can choose.

However, opposites are alternatives which agents not merely can but must choose between, in the sense that if they choose at all, they must choose one or other, hence opposites must also always be each other's external negations. And since, as I just argued, it is not always the case that the external negation of what an agent can choose to do is its opposite, such an external negation must satisfy a further condition to be the opposite of what it negates. What might that condition be? It seems not implausible to think that it must be the sort of mental condition or state that turns the external condition into an action, for instance, that X deliberately, on purpose, intentionally, by choice, by mistake, reluctantly, and so on, did not kill Y.

But this would appear to be wrong. Suppose that X and Y are playing a game of chess in the latter's house and that X carried a gun and could have chosen to kill Y. Surely, in these circumstances, "X did not kill Y" is the opposite of "X killed Y," even if what he did at the time was entirely concerned with the game and never amounted to a choice or decision not to kill rather than to kill, to deliberateness or intentionality, or to resistance to some motive to kill, and so on. It seems sufficient that X had the choice between these alternatives which are external negations of each other.

This is not, of course, to deny that there are action descriptions—such as murdering, killing in self-defense, killing accidentally, and refraining from killing, taking care not to kill, letting the women and children live—which imply the opposites of killing and letting die, but imply additional, morally relevant aspects of these opposites. We need not here examine the complex question of what are the opposites of such more richly characterized alternatives.

Summing up, we can say that opposites in the sense relevant here are action descriptions which, relative to a given occasion, specify two mutually exclusive and jointly exhaustive ways of acting on that occasion. If such action descriptions are morally differentiating and so tell us which alternative is morally preferable and at what level of stringency, then we know which of these things we should—other things equal—choose to do when we have that choice.*

So, our next question is whether "killing a certain person" (as used in "X killed Y at t") is a differentiating action description and whether our moral code is sound in telling us that killing anyone is wrong, that is, (other things equal) morally dispreferable, at the mandatory level of stringency, to its opposite, not killing anyone. If our moral code is sound, then we can subsume our case of X having killed Y under the general precept that (other things equal) killing anyone is wrong and conclude that X's killing of Y was wrong (other things equal).**

By my account, answering this question about our moral code involves determining whether we can in reason demand of one another that whenever we have such a choice, we act as we would if we chose not to kill rather than as we would if we chose to kill. I put it in this roundabout way because what matters is how we act in a situation in which we *have* that choice, even if we do not actually have to *make* it because we have no hesitation, doubt, or uncertainty about how to act; if, in other words, we intentionally act in this way whether or not we have actually deliberated and made a choice to do so.

Well, then, can we in reason demand this of one another? If we can, then, it will be recalled, this requires that we, in our role as adjudicators between ourselves as potential agents (the would-be killers) and potential patients (the intended victims) find that everyone has self-anchored requiring reasons to accept the precept that killing anyone in general, and a given person in particular, is (other things equal) morally dispreferable, at the mandatory level of stringency, to not killing anyone in general and to not killing that person in particular.

Does everyone have such reason? Suppose, first, that—as seems reasonable—we all prefer to have (at least in our society) a climate of life in which it is safe to assume that people will not try to kill others whenever that is, or they take it to be, the best way to attain one of their aims in life. Suppose next, that—as also seems reasonable—an important, if not the most important, factor in determining a climate of life in a given geographical area is the mores of the society in whose territory that geographical area lies, and assume, further, that the society's morality is an important, perhaps the most important, influence on the content of the society's mores. Then this preference of ours for such a climate of life would be a sufficient self-anchored reason to yield the above conclusion about the moral dispreferability of killing over not killing. If that preference for that climate of life is also a sound as well as a very strong one (as it appears not to be in certain sections of the population of former Yugoslavia, Somalia, and even the United States) and if its being satisfied in his own case is of very great importance to everyone and if the danger of its often not being satisfied by others is great, then this would seem to be a sufficient reason for ascribing to that preferability the higher (mandatory) level of stringency and for its being supported, if possible, by the corrective sanctions justified at that level.

If this argument is sound, then the answer to our question ultimately hinges on very complex empirical facts about general human preferences and the ways in which people's efforts to satisfy their preferences, including the promotion of their interests, come into conflict with one another. As I claimed in the Introduction, this empirical question is of the greatest importance and raises the greatest difficulties for assessing the soundness of a morality, but unfortunately, this problem is beyond the scope of this book and my competence. However, as far as the precept against killing is concerned, the empirical beliefs on which, as I here argue, it is based, seem to be widely if not universally held in our society and they seem quite plausible as far as our everyday experience can tell us.

There are two obvious difficulties which we have already mentioned and briefly dealt with. The first concerns the case in which a person can save his own life only by killing another, the case of killing in self-defense (in a wide sense). The central and easiest example is that in which a person suffers a morally unjustified attack on her life and has no way of warding it off except by steps that risk, or are bound to cause, the attacker's death. This, then, is a case in which the interaction is likely to result in at least one death, the reaction of the initial patient's playing a major part in determining whose death. If we accept the general precept against killing and derive from it another against attempts to kill, then in the present case, we are dealing with behavior that is wrongful even if it is an unsuccessful attempt to kill, behavior that would presumably be even more seriously wrongful if it succeeded. In light of the grounds for the wrongness of killing and attempts to kill, the victim's trying to defend herself against a wrongful attack is not, as such, wrongful.*

Thus, when we compare the two lives, that of the attacker and that of the attacked, there seems no question about whose life deserves more to be preserved if both cannot be. It is only because of the attacker's attack that both cannot continue. Clearly, then, bystanders should help the attacked ward off the attacker, rather than help the attacker kill her. It seems clear, then, that we cannot in reason desire, let alone demand, of one another that we not defend ourselves against unjustified attacks even if such resistance risks or is bound to cause the death of the attacker. It also seems clear that we can in reason desire, perhaps even demand, of one another that we give assistance to those unjustifiably attacked in warding off their attackers, even if we thereby risk or ensure the death of the attacker, especially when such assistance costs us relatively little.

The reasoning in this case differs in one important respect from that employed in the simpler case discussed a few paragraphs earlier. There, no prior moral precepts or judgments had to be taken into account; our question there concerned the moral standing of a certain action and its opposite judged solely on their own comparative merits. In the present case, by contrast, we must construe someone's action as an intentional response to a type of behavior whose moral standing has already been determined on its own merits. This difference is important since it is because of it that the morality of self-defense, and of the defense of others, at the risk or even with the certainty, that one will thereby kill the attacker, must not be judged as if these were actions of a type that fall under the simple (unpreconditional) precept against killing. The morality of this response must, on the contrary, be seen as depending and indeed as based on the prior violation of that precept. It is because the attacker, by the attack that actually did, or was justifiably taken to, unjustifiably aim at the (intended) victim's death, has violated this very precept and so has not done his bit in the moral enterprise, that the simple (unpreconditional) precept against killing does not protect him against behavior that risks or even actually aims at his death (when it is, or is justifiably taken to be, the only way to ward off the attack).

Thus, the defense of an intended victim (whether by herself or another) against an unjustified attack on her, must not be judged simply by the number or the worth of (prized) lives threatened or extinguished by the attacker, as if the decisive issue were whether defending the intended victim saved more or more valuable lives than not defending her. Plainly, in this case there is or need be no difference in numbers; whether the victim is defended or not, one person does (or may well) get killed.

Admittedly, there is a sense in which the life of the intended victim may be said to be necessarily "more valuable" than that of the attacker; but this way of putting it is seriously misleading, for in order to assess which of these two lives is "more valuable," we do not have to find out what talents or virtues, and so on, either has or what contributions either has made; we only need to know who is the unprovoked attacker and who the intended victim. The difference between the two lives is less misleadingly rendered by saying, as we ordinarily do, that the attacker, in launching his unjustified attack, has failed to do his bit in the moral enterprise and thereby has forfeited (or in other ways lost or at least weakened or burdened) the protection given by the precept against killing, whereas the intended victim of an unjustified attack has not (at least in this matter) failed to do her bit in the moral enterprise and so is "innocent" and so has not lost the protection which a social morality should in reason give to every member of its moral order who has done his bit in the moral enterprise. The case of the attacker killed in the course of the defense of the victim, whether by herself or by one of her defenders, therefore falls outside the scope of the simple (unpreconditional) case.

Thus the opposites we are now considering are not X's killing Y and X's not killing Y, but Y's (or Z's) resisting X's trying to kill Y, and Y's (or Z's) not resisting X's trying to kill Y. Again, it seems to me that we can in reason desire of one another that, when we are bystanders, in circumstances from a pretty obvious range (say, similar to those of the bystanders in the case of Kitty Genovese[4]), we personally intervene so as to physically prevent the attacker from killing her; and that we can in reason demand of one another that we at least take immediate steps to alert the authorities (i.e., the police) whose institutional role duties include protecting members against such attacks. Much the same reasons that justify the simple precept against killing also justify this "higher-order (i.e., preconditional) precept" about coming to the aid of those under attack. In both cases, the aim is to protect members from dying a "wrongful death."

Of course, in these and other cases, the moral precepts justified in this way are to be understood as holding only other things being equal. The directives in them are sound only for the "normal" or "central" cases, and the exact range of the variables (in the present case, X, Y, and Z), for which the precept purports to hold, has not been spelled out. Further empirical investigation may reveal that the precepts cease to be sound when their range is extended beyond certain boundary lines.

To test this, it will be helpful to examine the case of suicide and assistance to suicide. It would appear that in the case in which X and Y, the killer and the killed, are the same person, these variables have crossed that boundary line beyond which the two precepts, the simple (unprecond-itional) and the higher order (preconditional), do not hold. Whereas we can in reason desire or even demand of one another that, other things equal, we not kill human beings, we cannot in reason demand or even desire this in those cases in which killer and killed are the same person. For the same reason, when the would-be killer and his "victim" are the same person, we cannot in reason demand or even desire of one another that we intervene personally so as to prevent the would-be killer from succeeding, or at least to alert the appropriate authorities of her efforts to do so. Of course, as J. S. Mill pointed out, we may sometimes justifiably stop a person from doing what she is planning to do if we have adequate reason to think she does not know that doing it will or is likely to bring about her death, but having warned her, we would no longer be justified in preventing her from doing it.

Similarly, while we cannot in reason desire, let alone demand of one another, that we help those who are planning to kill others, it seems we can in reason desire of one another, perhaps in certain central cases (say, family doctors, suitable relatives, and so on), demand of one another that we physically help those who, for adequate reasons, want to commit

---

[4] For the sad details of this case, see "The Night that 38 Stood By As a Life Was Lost," *New York Times* 133 (March 12, 1984), B1.

suicide but are no longer able to do so unaided, by themselves. For these reasons, then, whereas helping others to commit murder is morally dispreferable to not helping them do it, helping others who, for adequate reasons, wish to commit suicide, would seem to be morally preferable to not doing so. Similarly, whereas preventing others to commit murder would appear to be morally preferable to not preventing them, preventing others who, for adequate reasons, wish to commit suicide, would seem to be morally dispreferable to not preventing them.

Section 3.   Transplant

Consider, then, a relatively uncomplicated instance of a range of cases now often called Transplant,[5] about which there has been a great deal of illuminating controversy in recent years. A surgeon faces the following "doctor's dilemma." She can save the life of patient A(dam), who needs a new heart to survive, but only by replacing his heart with that of another patient, E(ve), who, however, will not agree to this transplant. Alternatively, she can save the life of E, who needs two kidneys to survive, by letting A die and then transplanting his kidneys into E. It would appear that, in the judgment of most people, the surgeon must not kill E to save the life of A, but may, indeed must, let A die, and then transplant his kidneys into E to save her life.

Why is this the morally best choice if she has these two alternatives from which to choose? A popular answer is this. Two lives are endangered in this case and either can be saved by a suitable organ transplant. We may assume that the surgeon has a duty to save both if she can, and a duty to save one or the other if she cannot save both. As things are, she can save either the heart or the kidney patient, but not both. She can save the former only by killing the latter against her will, whereas she can save the latter by letting the former die against his will. But killing someone against her will is morally worse than letting someone die against his will, and so she must let the heart patient die and transplant his kidneys to save the kidney patient. The solution reached by this argument seems sound and there seems to be something right in the claim (that killing is morally worse than letting die) offered to justify it but I think the soundness of this solution does not hinge on what is right about this claim. To make this

---

[5] For an excellent discussion of a whole range of these and other puzzling cases, see, for instance, Thomson, *The Realm of Rights*, 134–50.

clearer, let us take a closer look at the differences between killing and letting die and the relation between them.

3.1 Killing and Letting Live

As I understand these two concepts, they rest on our ideas of interference, preventing something and letting it happen, bringing something about and letting it not happen, and noninterference, intervention and nonintervention.[6] It presupposes a certain quite familiar way of looking at parts (or even the whole) of the universe, namely, as systems (or as a single system) with a "normal way of working," which consists in a series of conditionally predictable events, an important condition being the normal absence of interferences external to the system. (When we think of the whole universe as such a system, we tend to think of it as not subject to any interferences except possibly interventions, that is, intentional interferences, by the Deity, who is then conceived as external to the universe.) Examples are a pregnant woman's body under normal conditions undergoing a series of predictable changes from conception to giving birth, or a cancer-afflicted, or a drowning, person's (body) heading for death in a roughly predictable progression within a roughly predictable time. Or we look at them as systems which, under normal conditions and if they work normally, maintain themselves in a certain state. Examples are a person's body maintaining itself at a stable temperature or in a state of regular breathing.

Of course, the normal course of events in a system—say, the events constituting the revolution of the earth around the sun—must itself be conceived as "causally" ("physically") dependent on certain normally present external and internal conditions. Changes in these conditions, on which the normal "working" of the system "causally" depends, must

---

[6] The distinction has been drawn in various ways which it would take too long here to survey. I have learned much from the following: Jonathan Bennett, "Morality and Consequences," *The Tanner Lectures on Human Values*, vol. 2 (Salt Lake City, Utah: University of Utah Press, 1981), 45–116; Jonathan Glover, *Causing Death and Saving Lives* (New York: Penguin Books, 1977); Joel Feinberg, *Harm to Others* (New York: Oxford University Press, 1984), chapter 4.; Bonnie Steinbock, ed., *Killing and Letting Die* (Englewood Cliffs, N.J.: Prentice-Hall, 1980); *Matters of Life and Death*, 2nd ed., ed. Tom Regan (New York: Random House, 1980). I believe my own account is closest to that by Frances Myrna Kamm, "Harming, Not Aiding, and Positive Rights," *Philosophy and Public Affairs* 15, no. 1 (Winter 1986): 3–32, though she may not think it's close enough. Her most recent work (*Creation and Abortion* [New York: Oxford University Press, 1992]) appeared too late to be taken into account.

themselves be relatively rare. For otherwise it might be impossible to distinguish those external factors which cause those events in the system that are, or are the consequences of, interferences and so are deflections of events in the system from their normal course, from those that, though themselves causal factors in the coming about of events in the system, are nevertheless not interferences because they are among the conditions that must be satisfied if any course of events in the system is to count as its normal working. Hence they are not something that counts as an interference with that normal course; for that normal course of events in the system is the consequence of its normal working, is what happens in it in the absence of interferences. Interferences are necessarily "external to" the system, that is, events other than those that constitute its normal working or their consequences in the system and other than the relatively stable conditions on which that normal working "causally" depends.

In this case, too, we must draw a distinction between the external negation of the claim that something is an interference and its opposite. While the external negation of the claim "there was consistent hammering next door which interfered with my sleep" is "it is not the case that there was consistent hammering next door which interfered with my sleep," its opposite is "there was consistent hammering next door but it did not interfere with my sleep." We may usefully distinguish between events that are merely potential and those that are actual interferences. External negation of an interference claim can then be construed as denying the conjunction of two claims: that something (say, hammering next door) is both a potential and an actual interference with something (say, one's sleep); that such denials in other words affirm a disjunction, namely, that something (the hammering) either is not a potential or not an actual interference or is neither. By contrast, its opposite affirms that something (the hammering) is a potential interference, but denies that it is an actual one. Thus, the external denial of an interference claim differs from the opposite of such a claim, for the former can be true if the occurrence (say, a hammering) is neither a potential nor an actual interference, whereas the latter cannot be true unless it is one of these two.

Interferences and noninterferences may be human actions (such as someone's hammering next door) or other events (such as the knocking sound of an old-fashioned central heating system next door). Both of these are interferences if and only if they are not only potential but actual (effective potential) interferences, as when the hammering or the knocking next door wakes me up or prevents me from falling asleep. They are noninterferences if and only if they are potential but not actual interferences, as when hammering or the knocking next door does not wake me up or prevent me from falling asleep. And they are neither interferences nor noninterferences if and only if they are neither potential nor actual interferences, as when the hammering or the knocking occur, not next door, but at the other end of the city two miles away.

Interferences and noninterferences may also be intentional or unintentional. An interference is intentional if and only if it is an intentional human action (such as an intentional hammering) and it is intended to and does deflect events from their normal course (say, they wake me up or keep me from falling asleep). An interference is unintentional if either the human action is unintentional under that description (if—supposing this is possible—the hammering is unintentional) or the deflection of the events from their normal course is unintentional.

A noninterference is intentional if and only if it is an intentional action which is a noninterference, that is, the opposite of one that would be an interference, say, the person next door refraining from hammering so as not to wake me up. A noninterference is unintentional if and only if it is an action which is intentional under some description (say, a hammering), which is known to be a potential interference and hoped and expected to be, but which turns out not to be, an actual one, as when the hammering next door does not wake me up because I have taken a sleeping pill.

I shall speak of intentional interferences as interventions and of intentional noninterferences as noninterventions. Thus, as I use these terms, there are no unintentional interventions and noninterventions. A knocking noise in the central heating or a snore thus cannot be an intervention though it can be an unintentional interference, nor can dozing off while studying or a large comet's passing the earth without any impact be a nonintervention in the life on our planet, though it can be a *non*intentional (if hardly an *un*intentional) noninterference.

A killing may be an intervention or an unintentional interference, the latter when someone, for instance, accidentally kills another. Letting live, it seems to me, can only be a nonintervention (an intentional noninterference), a refraining from doing something (say, from shooting someone) which one thinks would be an interference. Hence killing and letting live are opposites (in my sense), provided only the agent knew he could, at that time, have chosen between these alternatives. Letting live is thus equivalent to not killing when that is the opposite of a killing (that is, a not killing by the same person, of the same organism, at the same time), provided only he knew he could have chosen between these alternatives at that time. Thus, although killing is not necessarily an intervention and letting live is, they can nevertheless be opposites, because they may, on one and the same occasion, be construable as interventions and noninterventions (intentional interferences and noninterferences), respectively. They must, of course, be so construable when we examine whether one of them is morally preferable and, if so, which one.

We should now examine a kind of "system" we have not so far considered explicitly: a normal adult human being. Such systems "function independently," that is, are able to maintain themselves in being, and normally do so, for what is sometimes called "the term of their natural life," with the possible exception of the senile end of it. Thus, we can think of childhood and senescence as two periods of dependence, during which we remain in existence only if someone else looks after us, that is, favorably intervenes in the course of our life, which would otherwise soon come to a premature end through starvation, sickness, or misadventure.

Of course, in addition to these two periods of dependence flanking our independent self-maintaining existence, there may be other more short-lived stretches during which various afflictions, such as illnesses, mortal dangers, or injuries, prevent us from coping with life alone, when assistance from others is necessary, or at least helpful, to survival.

As we noted before, events such as death and the onset of pain, or the recovery from an illness and the cessation of pain, are things we or others may be able to bring about or to prevent. We can speak of someone *having causal power over* a possible future event, such as someone's death, if and only if he can bring it about or prevent it at will (as we say), that is, if he but chooses to. Of course, if that were to occur in the normal course of events, then someone's power over it could be exercised only by preventing it, not by bringing it about. Contrariwise, if the event were not to occur in the normal course of events, then he could exercise his causal power over it only by bringing it about.

In whichever of these two ways people can exercise their causal power over a future event, they may or may not choose to do so. A woman who is pregnant and rightly expects the natural course of events to lead to her giving birth, may or may not choose to intervene in this course of events by having an abortion; a woman who, because of certain intervening factors, rightly expects her pregnancy to end in miscarriage, may or may not choose to exercise her causal power over that event by taking a drug designed to prevent the miscarriage. Thus, to use one's causal power over an event is to intervene in the natural course of events, whether to prevent an event that otherwise would occur or to bring about one that otherwise would not occur. Not to use or exercise one's causal power over an event is not to intervene in the natural course of events, whether in order to let an event happen that one could prevent, or to let an event not happen that one could bring about.

Some may construe a person's causing or being the cause of a future event as his exercising the causal power over that event. In human affairs, causing *E* and causing *not E* (e.g., causing an increase or a nonincrease in unemployment) often really are cases of persons intentionally or knowingly bringing about or preventing something, that is, cases of human intervention in what is, in some intuitively understandable sense, the "normal" course of events. Thus, a government agency's raising the rate of interest may be a case of its knowingly (if perhaps unhappily) causing, being the cause of, bringing about, an increase in unemployment.

However, not every case of causing or being the cause of something is an intervention, an intentional bringing about or prevention of it. If Jack kills himself because Jill has jilted him in a particularly cruel manner, she (or her jilting him) is the (ultimate or indirect) cause of his death, but, of course, she did not intentionally bring this about, let alone did she kill him (intentionally or even unintentionally); he himself did. At the same time, she was not indeed the immediate cause of his death, but the cause of his killing himself, and therefore the (ultimate or indirect) cause also of his death. Killing someone thus is not exactly the same as causing or being the cause of her death.

Neither is killing someone the same as intervening *so as to bring about her death*. If the boss of some organization hires a professional killer to kill a rival for the leadership position and the killer does so, then that boss has instigated the killing; he may well be the (ultimate) cause of his rival's death; and (unlike Jill) he has intervened in that rival's life so as to bring about that death, but he did not kill him—the professional killer did.

Thus, for *a person* to be someone's killer (the one who killed her), he must stand in a certain close relation to *what* killed her. If she was killed by an avalanche, the avalanche was what killed her and in such a case usually no one will have killed her because usually no one is related in this special way to the avalanche. If what killed her was her inhaling a lethal dose of poison gas, or a flowerpot falling on her head from a twentieth-story window box, or a car running over her, then someone killed her if he administered the lethal dose of the gas, threw the flowerpot from the window box, or ran the car over her; but no one killed her (even unintentionally) if the gas accidentally escaped from a chemistry lab, if the wind blew down the flowerpot, or if the car that killed her accidentally careered driverless down the hill where it had been parked.

Thus some deaths, for example, someone's dying of old age, are *not* "the result" or the "internal object," (as a jump is the result or internal object of someone jumping) of either *someone* or *something* killing her; others, as those in the last three examples in the preceding paragraph, are the result (or internal object) of *something* (e.g., an earthquake or an avalanche) killing her; and finally, some deaths, for example, those in the three earlier examples in that paragraph, are the result (or internal object) of *someone* killing her. The main distinction, in other words, is between those cases in which the event that is a death-causing intervention can be ascribed or imputed to a thing (e.g., a poison gas, a flowerpot, or a car) or a person (e.g., a poisoner, a pot thrower, or a driver) to which or to whom we can in important ways (related to thing and agent responsibility, respectively[7]) anchor these events and draw the appropriate normative conclusions from this anchoring; for example, that the thing or the person to which or to whom these events have been anchored in the appropriate ways, are to be held (thing or agent) responsible in the appropriate ways for their results.

This brings us to a crucial point in our moral inquiry. So far the terms employed to elucidate the distinction between killing and letting die— "the normal course of events," "intervention/nonintervention"; "having/ not having, exercising/not exercising, causal power"; "causing/being the cause of, some event"—were presented as having no moral implications, as being morally neutral; and where they involve opposites—for instance in the case of "intervention/nonintervention"—as morally nondifferentiating. Nothing was taken to be implied or presupposed about whether, in intervening or not intervening, exercising or not exercising one's causal power over an event, one ipso facto did or did not do something wrong, or something desirable, or discharged a duty, an obligation or a responsibility. We then tried to show, by independent arguments, under what conditions certain sorts of intervention in the normal course of events, (such as those that involved a certain exercise of causal power, or those that were the bringing about or the prevention of someone's death), were morally differentiating—the former morally dispreferable, the latter morally preferable. The question now arises whether the same considerations can show that the corresponding noninterventions, the corresponding nonexercises of this causal power, are correspondingly differentiating.

In Transplant, the case of which we gave a thumbnail sketch at the beginning of section 3, the physician may be construed as having a special professional (relational) duty to all his patients: to cure them of their illnesses, to prevent and, where that is impossible, to delay, their death, and, of course, the general (unpreconditional, nonrelational) duty not to kill anyone. Transplant seems to show that although the physician has both these duties, the duty not to kill is the stronger one, that a breach

[7] See above, chapter 8, section 6, pp. 318–26.

of it is morally worse than a breach of the duty not to let die, since, when she cannot discharge both, she must not kill A (who needs a good heart, possessed by E, and possess two good kidneys needed by E) and save the life of E (who needs two good kidneys possessed by A, and has a good heart, needed by A), but must let A die and save E.

The question, then, is whether the problem arises in this form only for physicians with their special professional duties, or whether we all have both these duties and whether they have the same relative "strengths" as they appear to have in the case of doctors. Presumably it is worse for a physician to kill one of his patients than a nonpatient, and worse to let a patient die than a nonpatient. May it not be that a layman does not have a duty at all not to let others die; that whereas the duty not to kill is a general (nonrelational and unpreconditional) duty, the duty not to let die is only a special (relational and/or preconditional) one? Furthermore, may it not be the case that it is merely supererogatory not to let die, and that it is for this reason that when one can (like the physician in Transplant) save only one of two endangered lives and must choose between saving A by a method that involves killing E, and saving E by a method that involves letting A die, one must choose the life one can save by a method that does not involve a breach of duty (killing E) but involves merely not doing (saving A) what it would be supererogatory to do (not letting A die) rather than the other way around, however much one might prefer to do the latter?

Some writers—convinced (in my view rightly) that much more ought to be done for the world's hungry and generally underprivileged than is done currently by affluent individuals and affluent countries—attempt to make their case, at least in part, by showing that letting people die *is just as bad morally speaking as killing* them. The maneuver seems similar to one often employed when people, to give greater moral force to their claim, maintain that they have a duty to themselves, for example, to take a vacation or move to a better-paying position, when the most they can give reasons for is that they have a right to do that or that they deserve it or even only that doing it would not be wrong. The strategy is to avoid facing the difficult question of whether letting die is as serious a moral lapse as killing or a lesser one (no one seems to think it is a more serious one). Instead it starts from the plausible premise that killing is a moral wrong and then argues that, since the reason why it is applies equally to letting die, it too must be a moral wrong, and so an equally serious moral lapse. This does not seem to follow since some wrongs (e.g., killing someone) seem more serious wrongs than others, say, lying, even when it is lying in an important matter. But it seems clear that the argument underlying this approach does not succeed even if this last point is mistaken. The argument goes something like this:

1. It is bad to kill someone whom one can avoid killing.
2. The reason why it is bad to kill anyone whom one can avoid killing is that it is bad to play a certain causal role in anyone's death.
3. But, in letting someone die, one is playing the same causal role in the death of that person as one would in killing him.
4. Therefore, it is bad to let someone die and, since it is bad for exactly the same reason, it is exactly as bad as it is to kill him.

The crucial premise is 3, for, if what I have said is at least on the right track, then one is not, by letting someone die, playing the same causal role in his death as by killing him. We can, of course, grant that, in both cases, the agent plays some causal role in the death of that person. We can say that one cannot kill a person or let him die unless, as we put it before, one "has causal power over his life and death." In killing someone, one uses that power to intervene in his life so as to bring about his death which, but for this or some other such intervention, would not have occurred. And in letting someone die one does not use that power to intervene so as to prevent his death which occurs unless one thus intervenes and no one else can or does. In both cases, the person would not have died unless one had played that causal role. But clearly, the causal role one plays is not exactly the same in the two cases. In one case *one intervenes* in a way that *brings about* a death which otherwise would not have occurred, while in the other *one does not intervene* in any way and so *does not prevent* a death already in the offing.

This argument thus clearly begs the question of whether or not there is a morally relevant difference between killing and letting die. For, as I argued in the preceding paragraph, there is a clear nonmoral difference between the causal role one plays in the two cases, and the argument is silent on whether this nonmoral difference makes a moral difference as well.

It will, I think, be instructive to examine an (at first sight) persuasive argument with a similar aim, advanced in an interesting and widely read article by John Harris.[8] The drowning man's death, he says, "*results from our failure*, whether we have a duty to save him or not. (We might have a

---

[8] John Harris, "The Marxist Conception of Violence," *Philosophy and Public Affairs* 3 (1974): 192–20. Reprinted in *Philosophical Issues in Law*, ed. Kenneth Kipnis (Englewood Cliffs, N.J.: Prentice-Hall, 1977), 136–58, especially 142.

duty to kill this particular man and discharge it by failing to save him.)* It is not the existence of the duty that makes the death of the [drowning] drunk *a consequence* of our failure to save him, rather it is the fact that unless we save him he will die that makes it our duty to save him." (My italics.)**

Harris's argument appears to go like this: (1) both killing and letting die is behavior which has death as a (causal) consequence; (2) there is a general duty not to kill because it is behavior whose causal consequence is death; (3) knowing whether someone's death was the (causal) consequence of someone's killing her or letting her die, does not presuppose knowing whether or not there is a general duty not to kill or not to let die;*** (4) therefore, there is also a general duty not to let die.

The first premise invites the comments already made about the differences between the causal roles an agent plays in killing and in letting die. We may grant that both in the case of killing and letting die, the agent "has causal power over a certain event" (as I put it), namely, the patient's death. But there is also an important difference: the killer has exercised that causal power over his victim's death so as to bring it about, whereas the one letting die has not exercised his causal power over his "victim's" death so as to prevent its occurrence. This leaves open the question whether the morally decisive factor is the shared causal element—the possession of the causal power—or the unshared one—the exercise of that power.

Because "[causal] consequence" is here ambiguous, Harris's claim that "the death of the drowning man [is] a [causal] consequence of our failure to save him" lacks the force required by his argument. If "[causal] consequence of" is taken to mean the same as "caused by," then it does not apply to cases of "letting die." The cause of the death of the drowning man who has been let to die sometimes may well be that he could not swim, or that he was sucked under by a riptide, or that he could not cope with the high waves, and so on. And one of these things may well be *the* cause, even if there was someone around who, in failing to save him, let him die. However when that person, on other grounds, had a duty to save him—say, he was a lifeguard—then perhaps his death can be said to have been a (causal) consequence of that person's (the lifeguard's) failure to save him, or that that failure was *the* cause of that death.

That the death is the causal consequence of the lifeguard's failure, and that the lifeguard's failure, and through it the lifeguard himself, is the cause of the death, does not mean that the death could not *also* be a causal consequence of the drowned man's inability to swim, and so on, or that these things could not also be the cause of that death. The correct answer to what was the cause will depend on the context in which we ask it: if we want to know who or what is (agent) responsible for the death, the more appropriate answer will be, "the lifeguard" or "the failure of the life-guard"; if we want to know what was (thing) responsible for the death, the riptide, and so on, will be more appropriate.

If these remarks are on the right track, then it seems beside the point to say, as Harris does, that "[i]t is not the existence of the duty that makes the death of the drowning man a consequence of our failure to save him, rather it is the fact that unless we save him he will die that makes it our duty to save him." For it may be true (I think it is) that what makes it *morally undesirable* (but not necessarily "our," i.e., a general, i.e., unprecondi-tional, nonrelational duty) that someone save him, is that unless some-one does he will die; and yet false, that it is not the existence of the duty that makes the drowning man a [causal] consequence of our failure to save him.

Thus, we can grant, at least for argument's sake, that what makes killing wrong is that it is behavior which has someone's death "as a [causal] consequence," but must reject the claim that letting someone die is also behavior that has someone's death as a [causal] consequence in that same strong sense of "[causal] consequence." It would appear, therefore, that the argument does not show that letting die must be morally wrong if killing is.

3.2.   *Moral Comparisons between Killing and Letting Die*

Returning now to our question of whether or not killing is morally worse than letting die, it seems we cannot avoid tackling head-on the question of whether there is a general (unpreconditional and nonrelational) duty (other things equal) not to let anyone die, just as there is such a duty not to kill anyone. For if there are these two duties of the same kind, as many believe, then, it seems, letting die is the same sort of moral lapse as killing: in both cases we are doing something that is morally dispreferable to its opposite at the mandatory level of stringency. If this is right, then, supposing "morally worse" means "being morally dispreferable to its opposite at the mandatory level of stringency," killing is not worse than letting die; they are both equally bad.

However, before we answer this question, we should get a certain objection out of the way. That objection says that the question cannot even be asked because, as formulated, it does not make sense. Killing can neither be worse nor not worse than letting die, because "is morally dispreferable" is used to evaluate only choices between opposites in the sense explained above, but "killing" and "letting die" are not opposites in that sense. The opposite of "killing a person" (an intervention) is (when negatively formulated) "not killing that person" or (when positively formulated) "letting that person live" (a nonintervention in both formulations). The opposite of "letting die" or (negatively formulated), "not preventing death" (both clearly *noninterventions*) is "preventing death," or (negatively formulated) "not letting die" (both clearly *interventions*). Thus killing and letting die are not opposites in the relevant sense since, although mutually exclusive, they are not jointly exhaustive of a person's choices: one may neither kill nor let die on a particular occasion, as is normally the case throughout a family breakfast. But then we cannot sensibly ask which opposite, killing or letting die, is worse.

Worse still, it might appear, at first sight that, opposites or not, killing and letting die are related in a way that precludes the very possibility of anyone ever having an opportunity to choose between them. For, as we have seen, killing someone and letting her die are, respectively, interventions and noninterventions in a person's life which amount, respectively, to the bringing about and the prevention of her death. But the conditions under which these particular interventions and noninterventions are possible seem to be mutually exclusive. Just as the conditions for opening and closing a window cannot simultaneously be satisfied—one can open a window only if it is closed and close it only if it is open, and it cannot both be open and closed at the same time—so the conditions for bringing about and preventing someone's death would appear to be mutually exclusive, since one cannot intervene in a person's life to bring about her death if that death were to occur anyway, even without that intervention, and one cannot intervene in that person's life to prevent her death unless her life were to continue anyway, even without that intervention, but it cannot be the case at any particular time both that her life would continue and that her death would occur, anyway, even without such intervention.

This appearance is deceptive, however, for it depends on an indefensibly narrow conception of the time when we can have the opportunity to choose between killing someone and letting her die. For on that conception one would have an opportunity to kill her only at a time prior to her death, since of course the moment of her death or afterwards would be too late for killing her; but since one could not fail to intervene to prevent something (her death) at a time when it (her death) would not happen anyway, without any intervention, one could have an opportunity to let her die only at the moment of her death, that is, at the time of her death, but then one's intervention would not only not be needed but nothing would count as one. I cannot let you die in January if, without any intervention to kill you, you will not die until February.

But surely this is absurd, for both killing and preventing death (which is what one is failing to do when one lets someone die) are things that take time; thus killing a person, which ends with his death, involves "a process" that begins earlier—a lot earlier in the case of shooting someone with an arrow, not much earlier in the case of shooting someone point-blank with a rifle. Hence it is possible for a person to kill someone and to let her die only during a certain period prior to her death which begins and ends at certain specific points in time. It begins at a point before which it is not the case that she would die at a later point anyway, that is, would die unless someone were able, and were, to do something that would prevent her death, and ends at a point prior to her death after which no one is any longer able to prevent her death. It is during this period that someone has both an opportunity to kill her and to let her die, and so can have an opportunity to choose between these actions.

The objector may allow this, but reject the conclusion on the ground that the time prior to the death during which one can *no longer* kill a person (or let her live) is the same as that during which one cannot *yet* let a person die (or prevent her death). But it is simply false that these two times necessarily coincide. The processes involved in these two interventions (or noninterventions) in killing (or letting live) and preventing death (or letting die) may be very different from one another and may take different lengths of time. Surely, a successful attempt to rescue someone (to prevent his death) could have ended prior to the time at which his death would have occurred if no one had rescued him. Any of several actually unsuccessful attempts prior to the successful one might have been successful and then would have occurred earlier than would his death if he had been let die.

Thus, surely, a more generous conception of these times, such as the one we ordinarily have, would be more appropriate. But then, on such a broader conception, one can have an opportunity to choose between killing someone and letting her die. In that broader sense, we can (that is, have the opportunity to) let someone die only if there is in her life a point in time when she will die "soon" unless we can take certain steps that will prevent her death, and a later point after which we can no longer take such steps. Before the earlier and after the later point one (conceptually) cannot let her die because one (conceptually) cannot then choose to do the opposite, prevent her death. For, as we have seen, one cannot choose an action of any type unless one can also choose one of the opposite type.* But that is precisely the position one is in before the earlier and after the later point. For, of course, prior to the earlier point one (conceptually) cannot intervene to prevent her death since her life would continue anyway, and after the later point one (physically) cannot intervene to prevent her death because there is no effective way of doing so.

On this ordinary construal of the time when we have an opportunity to let someone die, we necessarily also have an opportunity to prevent his death and we may, but do not necessarily, have an opportunity to kill him. We must have an opportunity to save him for otherwise nothing would count as our having (chosen to) let him die. But we may not then also have an opportunity to kill him; we may be close enough to throw him a rope but not close enough to hold him under. When I choose not to give to famine relief, I may know that I thereby choose to let some starving child or other die, but I do not then necessarily have an opportunity to choose between not killing *that* child and killing him, or even between not killing and killing some child or other.

Under these conditions, there may then be (in terms of these action descriptions) four alternatives, two pairs of opposites, for us to choose from: killing, not killing, letting die, and not letting die. If we think of our situation in terms of certain other action descriptions, then there are only three: intervening to bring about death (killing), intervening to prevent death (not letting die), and not intervening either to bring about or to prevent death (neither killing nor preventing death). In terms of yet other action descriptions, there are two: acting in a way whose consequence in the circumstances will be either that a certain person will die "soon" or that he will continue to live (well) beyond that time. The number of choices we have thus depends on how we pick out the alternatives. If we are interested only in whether or not that person remains alive to the moment beyond which he can no longer be rescued by us, then our nonintervention will amount to both our letting him live and our letting him die. If other things are taken into account, this may not be so, for there may be others who would rescue him even if we did not; in that case, our not killing him would not also amount to our letting him die, and its consequences may be indistinguishable from those of our preventing his death.

The upshot of this long and somewhat tortuous examination of the objection that we can never have a choice between killing and letting die (not preventing death) because they have incompatible presuppositions is this. On the most plausible conception of the conditions under which one can have the opportunity to kill someone and the opportunity to let her die, one *can* have both these opportunities at the same time and then can choose between them. Thus, the objection fails and we can therefore return to our main question. Even if we accept this refutation of the objection, the choice one then has would not be one between opposites.

Hence the grounds for thinking that killing is worse than letting die could not be simply that killing is morally dispreferable at the mandatory level of stringency to letting die, as it is to not killing. But since it is plausible to think that we sometimes have a choice between killing and letting die, the question remains whether or not there is both a general unpreconditional and nonrelational duty not to kill and not to let die. For if there is such a duty, then it seems that killing need not be worse than letting die; but if there is not, then killing would seem necessarily to be worse than letting die. We have already given reason to think that there is such a duty not to kill and we have rejected an attempt to show that there must be a parallel duty not to let die on the mistaken grounds that the basis for the duty not to kill equally supports the duty not to let die. Let us then try to tackle this question head-on, as we did in the case of killing and its opposite, not killing (or, what normally comes to the same thing, letting live).

3.3.   Another Kind of Moral Comparison between Killing and Letting Die

In the preceding subsection, I argued that there is a use of "morally worse" which occurs in moral judgments of particular actions that are open to an agent on a particular occasion and that are related to each other as opposites in the sense explained. In such judgments, the criterion of one action being morally worse than the other is that it is morally dispreferable to it. I then argued that, in morally comparing killing and letting die, we cannot judge on the basis of this criterion because they are not opposites in the sense in question and so can be neither morally preferable nor dispreferable in that sense, or on the basis of a criterion that is applicable only when we judge choices between opposites. Nevertheless, as I argued, one sometimes must choose between killing someone and letting someone die, as in Transplant, and sometimes one has a choice between these alternatives and others as well. An example would be the tragic case of a certain Mrs. Bouvia, a quadriplegic, entirely dependent on others even for the simplest and most personal activities, in pain, and unable to find any sense in continuing to live, in the manner in which her severe disabilities forced her.[9] As many readers will know, she asked that the unwanted artificial feeding be discontinued and that she be allowed to die, but this was refused on the grounds that it is morally wrong to let someone die whom one can keep alive. Mrs. Bouvia might well have asked

---

[9] For a description of this case, see "Right to Die—Does Anyone Have It?" *U.S. News and World Report* 95 (December 19, 1983): 11.

(although she actually has not) to be killed rather than be force-fed or starved to death, but the hospital would surely have refused that too, on the grounds that killing is even worse than letting die, especially for those who have taken the Hippocratic Oath.

Today, some hospitals and physicians appear to be prepared (under certain safeguards against abuse) to grant the wish of a patient, such as Mrs. Bouvia, to be allowed to starve to death. However, even today, in many countries their laws, or their physicians and hospitals, would deny such a patient's wish to be killed, or to be assisted in committing suicide, however clearly and rationally she might manage to express it, usually on the grounds that for anyone, but especially physicians and hospitals, to kill is morally worse than to let die.

It would appear, then, that there must be, for certain contexts, another appropriate criterion (or sense) of "morally worse." For, surely, when people are in a situation in which they must or can choose between killing and letting die, it is a perfectly sensible question to ask whether it is morally indifferent which they choose, or whether choosing one is morally worse than choosing the other and, if so, which one is. However, before turning to an account of the criterion (or sense) of "worse" in that question, it will help to get clearer about another question expressible in the same words, which arises in an importantly different sort of context.

We are in that other context when we want to know things such as whether what Jack did when he killed Jill was morally worse than what he (or someone else, say, Art) did when he let Beth die. In these cases, what is evaluated is not a single choice, one in which someone or other on a certain occasion chose between killing a certain person and letting her die, but two choices: one in which a particular person (Jack or Art or whoever) chose between killing another person (whether Beth or Jill or whomever) and not killing her, and a second one in which a particular person (Jack or whoever) chose between letting another person (Jill or whomever) die and not letting her die. In this sort of context, we are not asking whether, when we have a choice, or have to choose, between killing someone and letting her die, the morally preferable choice is killing her *or* letting her die, or whether they are equally bad; what we are now asking is whether if, in choosing between killing and not killing, someone chooses killing, he has made a morally worse choice than if, in choosing between letting die and not letting die, he (or someone else) chooses letting die. The question is whether in both cases the chooser is choosing the morally dispreferable alternative and, if so, whether the former choice (killing rather than not killing) is morally worse, less bad, or neither than the latter choice (letting die rather than not letting die).

This more complex question clearly has two parts. The first part is whether the two alternatives in these two pairs of opposites are morally indifferent in one or both of these pairs, or whether one is morally dispreferable to the other in one or both pairs, and if so, which is dispreferable. The second part is whether, supposing there is a preferable and a dispreferable alternative in both of these two choices, one or both are equally bad or good or whether one of the dispreferable ones is morally worse or less good, and, if so, which of the morally dispreferable ones is the morally less good or the morally worse.

It is important to note two things about this question that are easily overlooked. The first thing is that "Is killing morally worse than letting die?" is quite naturally interpreted as a specific version of the second part of this complex question. The second thing is that, when so interpreted, this question presupposes a certain answer to its first part, namely, that in both pairs of opposites, one of them is preferable to the other (rather than indifferent, that is, neither preferable nor dispreferable), and that killing (in preference to not killing) and letting die (in preference to not letting die) are the dispreferable choices.

If we grant this supposition (that killing and letting die are the dispreferable alternative choices in the two pairs of opposites open to the chooser), then there remains a further question, namely, whether both of these dispreferable choices, killing and letting die, are equally bad or whether one of them is the morally worse one, and if so, which one. Clearly, that further question could quite naturally be expressed in the words, "Is killing worse than letting die?"*

In this interpretation, "Is killing worse than letting die?" is elliptical for "Is X's killing of V at tm, which is morally dispreferable to X's not killing V at tm, morally dispreferable to Y's letting W die at tn, which is morally dispreferable to Y's not letting W die at tn?" This question is completely general and answers to it can be construed as (rival) other-things-equal guidelines for making particular moral judgments about the actual behavior of at most any two particular agents (because, of course, X and Y are variables standing for possibly but not necessarily different persons), at most any two particular patients, and at most any two particular times (circumstances). Since these guidelines are especially general, they must abstract from the peculiarities of particular agents, particular patients, and the morally relevant circumstances and conditions prevailing at particular times.

The judgments based on this guideline are about the moral merit and demerit of agents who have already made or would make such choices of the dispreferable ones among the four opposites open to them. They are, therefore, only judgments, other things equal, which may have to be modified in light of the peculiarities of the case in hand. I shall shortly turn to this matter. At this point, I want to draw attention to the fact that such judgments are about different choices possibly by and about different people. They are judgments such as that it was or would be morally worse for Jack to kill Jill than for Art to let Beth die. These comparative moral judgments thus might not have been suitable for guiding the hospital in the case of Mrs. Bouvia, since neither Jack nor Art need have a choice between killing their victim and letting her die. For, as we have seen, one may be in a situation in which one can choose between letting die and not letting die but not between killing and not killing, hence not between killing and letting die, or in a situation in which one can choose between killing and not killing, but not between letting die or not letting die, hence not between killing and letting die. Nevertheless, in the limit case—same agent, same patient, same time—the fact (if it is a fact) that killing is worse than letting die would be a general guideline not only for judgments of choices already made but also for judgments about what choice to make. Thus, in the case of Mrs. Bouvia, it seems we should agree with the hospital that if and because killing is worse, other things equal, than letting die, we must, other things equal, neither kill Mrs. Bouvia nor let her die and that, if for some reason we *must* choose between the two, we would be, other things equal, doing something even worse if we killed her than if we let her die. Again, in the case of Transplant, we should agree that the physician who cannot discharge his duty to save the life of both his heart and his kidney patient but *must* choose between killing one or letting one die, should choose to let one die rather than kill one. Note, though, that this is not a limit case, in the sense just explained, for although there are two methods by which the physician can save the life of one of his patients (but none to save both), in choosing between the two methods to save one life, he is also choosing a different life to save. Hence, while the agent is the same, the patient and the time are not. Thus the difference in method—killing and letting die—is not the only difference between the two cases that may be morally relevant. We would still have to show that these differences are morally irrelevant. I shall return to these points in the next section.

Bearing in mind the meaning of the question we are examining, can we offer a reason for the conviction that killing is morally worse than letting die, that those who kill someone do something that is, other things equal, morally worse than those who let someone die? Let us, in particular, bear in mind that this conviction is not incompatible with the conviction that not letting die is the morally preferable opposite of letting die. Indeed, as I tried to show above, to believe that killing is worse than letting die *implies* that both killing and letting die are morally bad, other things equal. To say that letting die, though bad, is not as bad as killing, may be to say only that its badness does not warrant the same severe moral response as the badness of killing. We can perhaps put this by saying that we do not have a general unpreconditional, nonrelational *duty* not to let die.

Is there any reason to support this view? It seems clear that deaths that could have been prevented by someone are, in themselves and other things equal, undesirable, just as undesirable as those that come by way of a killing. On the face of it, then, it would seem a sensible social aim to reduce to an insignificant minimal percentage of all actual deaths, those that go with killings and those that go with instances of letting die. Could we all in reason want of one another that we follow guidelines, at the highest (mandatory) level of stringency, for the attaining of both these ideal aims? Is there any reason to reject the view that there is a general (unpreconditional, nonrelational) duty, other things equal, both not to kill and not to let die? Might it be the case that, although the loss suffered through these two kinds of death is the same, the nature of the moral failure of the agents involved in them is generally different, and that therefore killings are worse than instances of letting die?

My thesis is that there is such a general duty against killing but not against letting die. There are several reasons for accepting this view. One is simply this: no conflict is generated by the supposition that all of us who have an opportunity to kill Jones must, other things equal, not do so because there is a general (unpreconditional, nonrelational) duty not to kill anyone and so not to kill Jones. By contrast, such a conflict will often arise and there will be mutual interference and waste of effort, if it is generally believed that there is such a duty not to let die and if everybody attempted to discharge it; that is, if everybody who has an opportunity to let Jones die, attempted to prevent his death. As I argued before, the difference is obvious: if Jones is to survive, everybody who has an opportunity to kill him, *must not* do so, and there is no problem with everybody not doing it. By contrast, for Jones to survive, it is neither necessary nor desirable for everyone who has a choice between letting him die and preventing his death to (at least try to) choose the latter. This difference seems to me to amount to a sufficient reason for thinking that while there is a general (unpreconditional, nonrelational) duty not to kill, there is no such duty not to let die.

This difference amounts to such a reason on account of the great variety of causal or quasi causal relations that hold between a person's death or nondeath and someone's bringing it about or preventing it. We need not now examine the question of whether or not the complexities of killing are greater than those of letting die, for whether or not they are makes no difference to how we must answer our main question about killing and letting die. For the greater the complexity and cost of killing someone, the weightier the nonmoral reason for not killing him; by contrast, the greater the complexity and cost of preventing someone's death, the weightier the nonmoral reason for letting him die. Thus, if we ask whether we can in reason want of one another that we not kill anyone, then, whatever the complexity and cost of killing someone, the answer is in the affirmative. For in the "worst" case, when killing is most complex and most expensive, we have the best nonmoral and a sufficient moral reason not to kill; and in the "best" case, when killing is least complex and least expensive, we have no nonmoral reason not to kill but the same (sufficient) moral reason not to kill. Thus in all cases, from the best to the worst, there is adequate reason to hold that there is a general duty against killing.

The situation is quite different with letting die. Here the self-regarding reasons work in the opposite direction from that for killing. In the best, the least complex and expensive case, as in throwing a rope to the drowning man, the moral reason against letting him die would appear to be sufficient; we surely can in reason demand (not merely desire) this of one another. But as the complexity and the cost increase, there will arrive a point at which we can no longer in reason demand of one another that we not let die.

Our morality recognizes and accommodates these differences. Whereas it affirms a general duty not to kill, it does not affirm such a duty not to let die. Instead, we find a subdivision into various classes of cases, depending on what is thought the fairest and most efficient way of getting the ideal of minimizing the incidence of deaths due to killing and letting die. The main apportioning of the burden of preventing death is divided between three major classes of case: those in which there is a general (unpreconditional, nonrelational) duty to prevent death, those in which there is a special (relational) duty to do so, and those in which preventing death is not a duty at all, whether general or special, but is merely desirable, that is, morally preferable to its opposite (letting die) only at the lower (the optional) level of stringency.

Given the important modifications in our negative moral judgment of letting die as the complexity and costliness of preventing death increase, it should not come as a surprise that our society deals with preventing death by a combination of measures and by different moral judgments and responses. In one type of case, rescuing those in danger, it imposes a general duty not to let die. In others, it imposes on certain classes of people special (relational) duties to prevent the death of certain other classes of people, for example, on parents to "look after and care for" their children. In yet other cases, it ensures or encourages the existence of certain institutions, such as medical schools, hospitals, and health insurance companies, so that people can secure for themselves, at more or less reasonable costs, those services by experts that provide the best chance that those best able to prevent avoidable deaths will in fact do so. Lastly, it fosters a moral climate in which preventing death, even where it is not a duty, is encouraged as meritorious.

It will, I hope, be helpful if I illustrate these different social techniques for ensuring the saving of life and these different moral assessments of saving and failing to save life by describing four different types of cases. The first, that of "Good Samaritan" interventions, is one in which there are no social or other institutional role duties of saving life, but a general (unpreconditional and nonrelational) duty to rescue those in danger. The people to be rescued are competent persons, that is, those capable of looking after themselves, (unlike, e.g., infants, the senile, or the severely disabled) who are only temporarily incapable of doing so, such as the drowning, the injured, or those held captive. Rescuing them is getting them out of the condition that threatens their life or liberty or some other great good, such as bodily integrity or freedom from pain, and keeping them going until they can manage by themselves again. All moral agents are subject to this duty, but it is, like most or all duties, an other-things-equal one. Other things are, of course, not equal if one is not in a position to undertake the rescue. If there is more than one person who is in a position to rescue the one in danger, then, unless more than one is needed to effect the rescue and since it is undesirable for unnecessary would-be rescuers to get in each others' way, it is reasonable to conceive of the subjects of this general duty as being only those among the people able and in a position to perform the rescue who are in the best position to do so. A good case can also be made for saying that, even if someone is the only one in a position to undertake the rescue, he has no duty to undertake it if it will be very costly to him, as when the rescue involves a serious risk of life or major injury or exorbitant cost to the rescuer.

Clearly, the details of the conditions under which one does not have the duty to rescue are not crystal clear, even at the level of stating them, let alone when trying to determine whether they are satisfied in an actual case. It is, therefore, in general desirable if a society provides, for frequently recurring situations of danger, expert rescuers, whether volunteers or paid professionals, who are "on duty" in certain dangerous places at certain times. On some dangerous beaches, there are lifeguards who keep watch on swimmers and come to their aid when necessary. On a beach where there is such a lifeguard, it is he (or she) alone who has the duty to rescue swimmers in trouble. On such a beach, others have the duty only in exceptional circumstances, as when some swimmer gets into trouble while the lifeguard is busy rescuing another.

It is, however, virtually certain that expert lifesavers cannot be trained for all situations of danger and that, even if it were possible, it would be too expensive. In fact, the availability of such experts is likely to remain the exception and so the duty to rescue is likely to remain a general one, the cases where there are expert lifesavers counting as exceptions when the general duty is superseded by the special one.

The second type of case in which there is a serious need for death preventers and more generally help providers is that of *the incompetents*, such as children, the senile, the sick, or the insane. Not letting such a person die involves much more than is involved in rescuing him. For these are people who cannot lead an independent life—their continued existence depends on their being taken care of and looked after for more or less extended periods of time. In these cases, most every society defines the classes of people whom it regards as needing such care and, depending on the importance it attaches to these people getting the care they need, on how it believes the care is best provided and on the resources available to it, it generates institutions determining who will be looked after by whom and in what way.

Not letting any of these people die will primarily be, as it is with lifeguards, a special duty of the relevant role players. In our society it is parents who look after their own children, doctors and hospitals who look after their patients, adult children (or more and more frequently, nursing homes and hospices) who look after their aged parents (or the paying or payed-for aged), and so on. What makes it morally wrong to let such people die by not adequately looking after them is not that it is the violation of a general duty not to let die, but that it is the neglect of a special protective role duty not to look after a person to whom, as to the corresponding role player of protégé, one has that duty. It is only in exceptional cases[10] of this type that one would not be meddling in other people's business if one were to attempt to prevent the death of such a protected role player, and in very exceptional cases that it would be wrong

---

[10] See *Jones* v. *United States*, 308 F. 2d. 307 (U.S. Ct. of Appeals, 1962); excerpted in Kenneth Kipnis, *Philosophical Issues in Law* (Englewood Cliffs, N.J.: Prentice-Hall, 1977), 101–5.

for one not to make the attempt. Normally, one would be meddling, as one would if one attempted to save a drowning swimmer's life on a beach patrolled by lifeguards.

The third type of case is that in which a person is being *kept alive artificially*. This type of situation is similar to the preceding one, except that the question of whether to prolong such a life is desirable, is not exceptional but normal. We take it for granted that rescuing people in danger or looking after the temporarily incompetent, such as children and the sick, or those who have at least a chance of recovering their competence, such as the insane, is a good and desirable thing because the life we save is one which the person values and wants to continue. But when it comes to keeping people artificially alive, especially when, as in the notorious case of Karen Quinlan,[11] their so-called quality of life is reduced to zero, the question of whether to save such a life becomes acute. For if the life of such people is not worth living, then presumably it is not desirable to keep them alive, and so it would presumably not be wrong or even undesirable (other things equal) to let them die, perhaps even undesirable or wrong to keep them alive.

The fourth case is that of saving the lives of those who, though competent, are *in danger of dying for lack of the necessities of life*. In this case, it is surely reasonable to assume that, normally, they would want to have and use these necessities and use them rather than die. Thus, it would seem that such indigent people would have at least a weak claim, other things equal, against those of their fellows who have ample supplies of these necessities, to help them over their difficulties. This case is similar to that of rescue, but it differs in that there is no clear limit to the need. The factors on account of which they are now indigent may continue indefinitely to keep them so and so also their claim against the affluent.

This raises considerable difficulties about how this vague claim against the affluent is to be translated into specific contributions, whether they are construed as duties or desiderata. How much of his own resources must or ought any individual provide for the needs of others to whom he does not stand in any special relationship of responsibility, such as parent, relative, friend, or fellow citizen? What more should he do than give "something" to those whose needs he has come to know about through normal personal experience and which he can meet by personal help? What organizations should a society create to take care of needs which could not or would not be adequately met by such conscientious individual atten-

---

[11] For a description of this case see Tabitha M. Powledge and Peter Steinfels, "Following the News on Karen Quinlan," *Hastings Center Report* 5 (December 1975), 5ff.

tion? What must or ought a person do when his society does not generate the necessary organizations and institutions which it ought to set up to meet such needs? How should a society, especially a very affluent one, deal with the claims of its own indigent members when they are in competition with similar but more urgent claims of members of other societies?

These are extremely important and difficult moral questions which go beyond the scope of this investigation. I mention them only because they seem to me to show, perhaps beyond reasonable doubt, that in this fourth type of case even more than in the second and third, letting die is not morally wrong, not the breach of a general (unpreconditional and nonrelational) duty, but is, as such, only undesirable, though in many instances very seriously so. One reason for saying this is that, in this last case, we are even less able to state clearly what a person must do to discharge his duty. But since duty (and wrong) imply the highest level of stringency (being mandatory), which in turn implies the justifiability of coercive social intervention when someone fails to do his duty, we cannot justifiably consider something a duty concerning which it is never possible to say whether a person has or has not done it.*

If this is right, then there is no clear single answer to the question of whether there is or is not a duty not to let die. For although there is a general (unpreconditional, nonrelational) duty not to let die in certain classes of cases, for instance, that of rescuing, in other cases there is only a special (relational) duty to prevent death or no duty at all, but only a desideratum, a moral preferability at the optional level of stringency. Thus, we may perhaps accept the claim that killing is worse than letting die, but only in the sense that, other things equal, we cannot say anything as strong against letting die as we can against killing. For, killing as such is wrong, other things equal, whereas letting die as such is only either wrong or undesirable, other things equal. I conclude that these facts justify us in saying that (in one sense) killing is morally worse than letting die.

3.4. Judging Particular Cases

I now suppose it granted that my argument was adequate to show that there is at least one generally understood sense of "morally worse" in which we want to raise the question whether killing is morally worse than letting die and to which the answer is in the affirmative. In other words, I now take it for granted without further argument that the two uses I distinguished for each of the two expressions "morally worse" and "morally dispreferable" had only slightly different senses in the following two sets, (A) and (B), of parallel interrogatives in which I considered them: (A)(1) "Is killing morally worse than not killing?"; (2) "Is letting die morally worse than not letting die?"; (3) "Is killing morally worse than letting die?"; (4) "Is not killing worse than not letting die?"; (B)(5) through (8) are the same as in (A)(1) through (4) except that "morally worse" is replaced by "morally dispreferable."

The slight difference between "morally worse" and "morally dispreferable," I assume, is simply that the former does, whereas the latter does not, presuppose that both comparanda are morally bad. In my view, this means, however, that whereas (1) through (3) and (5) through (8) have an affirmative answer, (4) is a question that does not arise since a presupposition of something being morally worse than something else is not satisfied, so answers to it are either false or have no truth value, whereas this is not true for the analogous question (8). Since the common view that both killing and letting die are, as such, other things equal, morally bad rather than morally good or indifferent, and since we sometimes have a choice between killing and letting die, the question whether killing is worse than letting die does appear to make good sense and, for reasons I gave, appears to require an affirmative answer.

I also take for granted a second, more important, conclusion. Although (apart from the minor difference I noted in the preceding paragraph) the expressions "morally worse" and "morally dispreferable" mean the same in all these questions, the criterion on the basis of which they are answered are not the same in all of them. For whereas in (1), (2), (5), and (6), the comparanda are pairs of opposites, so that the chooser must select one but cannot select both of them, in the other questions, that is, (3), (4), (7), and (8), the choices to be morally evaluated are not between alternatives each of which is the opposite of the other, but between alternatives each of which is one side from a different pair of opposites. Because of the peculiarities of killing and letting die, whenever a person in what I called the limit case has a choice between them, he must also have a choice between them and their opposites, hence the best choice need not be either killing or letting die; in fact, since both not killing and preventing death are, as such, other things equal, morally preferable to either killing or letting die, letting die, though morally preferable to killing, is never, as such, other things equal, the morally best choice. Although, therefore, we must conclude that at the most general level of judgment, killing is (as such, other things equal) morally worse than letting die, we must also conclude that, at that level of generality, letting die is never what we ought to choose, since we then always have a morally better choice, to prevent death.

But, of course, such general conclusions are seldom what we must be satisfied with. We often know a lot more about the particular situation of someone. Return, then, for a moment to Transplant, in which our conclusion that letting die never is the best solution appears not to hold. It seems, on the contrary, that the physician must let the heart patient die and use his kidneys to save the kidney patient. But, of course, in this case, we know that the best alternative, to save the lives of both patients, is impossible; the physician has to decide which patient's life to save. It may therefore be concluded that, since the method of saving one involves killing whereas the method for saving the other involves letting die and, since letting die is morally preferable to killing, the best choice open to the physician is to let die.

It may be objected that this solution is objectionable because it treats the heart patient as merely a means to benefit the kidney patient; she lets the former die in order to save the latter. But it is not hard to see that this would be a misdescription of that case, though it would be an accurate one if another suitable heart had been available to save the former's life and she let him die to use his kidneys to save the latter.

It may, however, be doubted whether the reason I gave for thinking that killing is worse than letting die applies in this case. For, by my thesis, what makes killing worse than letting die is that whereas the former is as such, other things equal, morally dispreferable at the mandatory, the latter is so only at the optional level of stringency. But while this may be so at the highest level of generality, we have enough information in this case to abandon that level. For the physician has a special, professional (relational) duty to his patients, not merely not to kill them, but also to prevent their death. Thus, the fact that there is no general (nonrelational) duty not to let die is not a relevant reason in this case for thinking it morally preferable for the doctor to let die rather than to kill. Our intuitions seem to be that there is something about killing and letting die themselves, quite apart from whether one has or does not have a duty not to engage in these types of acts, that makes the former morally worse than the latter.

The question is a difficult one and I am not confident that my answer provides the whole story, but I think it is at least an important part of it. My answer involves two points.

The first could be put in two different ways. One is to say that a general (unconditional and nonrelational) duty has a greater defeating force than a special (relational) duty. The other is to say that the combination of a general and a special duty not to do something has a greater defeating force than such a special duty by itself. But the physician has both a general and a special duty not to kill, and only a special duty not to let die.

Hence, on either interpretation, for her to kill one of her patients is morally worse than for her to let one of them die.

We may have doubts about this general claim about the relation between general and special duties, but this is too big a topic to take up here. It must suffice to allude to the way in which the duties we can assume at will by promising or those that can be imposed on us at will by legislation, are generally thought to lie within the broader domain mapped out by general duties. Thus, it appears to be generally accepted (I think rightly) that we cannot assume a duty to kill someone by promising to do so. We may think that this gives analogical support to my thesis about the relation between general and special duties.

This leads me to the second point in support of my thesis about why killing is morally worse than letting die even for those who have both a duty not to kill and not to let die. There is something right and something wrong in our intuitions, as I have stated them two paragraphs ago. What is right is this: killing is worse than letting die not merely because we have a general duty, other things equal, not to kill, and not such a general duty not to let die. What is wrong is this: as I stated it, our intuition locates that ground in the difference between the natures of these actions themselves. It seems to me, however, that the ground lies in the undesirable consequences of the general acceptance of the view that killing is not worse than letting die in those cases in which one has a special (relational) duty not to let die, as a physician has toward her patients. For one's trust in one's physicians would be most undesirably undetermined if one was taught and came to believe that they regarded killing their patients for spare parts for other patients even without the owners' consent as, at worst, morally on a par with letting patients die when no suitable (already donated) spare parts are available. This consequence would probably be serious enough to warrant the claim that it would be morally worse for a physician to kill a patient to harvest his organs to save the life of another patient than to let a patient die for lack of an organ to transplant.

We can now go back to the case of Mrs. Bouvia. The hospital authorities knew they had a choice between killing her, letting her live (that is, not intervening to save her life, which is tantamount to letting her die), letting her die, and preventing her death. They prevented her death, which, other things equal, was the morally most preferable alternative. However, they had more information than that they had these four choices. They knew also that she wanted, for good medical and personal reasons, to end her life and so did not want to be kept alive by being fed artificially. Does this additional information make a moral difference which changes what is the morally most preferable choice for the hospital officials?

Let us set aside economic, legal, political, and religious considerations such as that, if they made a certain decision, the hospital would or might well be boycotted by certain political and religious groups, including perhaps some of their own medical and administrative staff, that the decision is or might be held to be against the law and that the hospital would face prolonged and costly lawsuits, and that in the end the hospital would or might well lose so much money that it would go out of business. I am not here denying that the supreme consideration should be maintaining the hospital's ability to carry on or that this is not a moral consideration; I am merely proposing to examine the case solely on its intrinsic moral merits, to the extent that we can isolate them from considering also its extrinsic ones.

Does this information show that her life is not a desirable one, in the sense of being one which should be continued, even if she expresses the wish to terminate it? I have argued elsewhere in greater detail[12] that a life is not a desirable one if (though not only if) it is not one worth living, and that it should be considered not worth living if the person finds it so, and there is no reason to think that she is not in a position to judge this matter rationally. Given her situation, there seems to me adequate reason to think that her judgment was rational. If anyone's life can, at a given point, fail to be worth living, hers would seem to satisfy this condition. One can doubt it only if one is convinced on general metaphysical or religious grounds that no life, however bad, can deserve that characterization. Only a miracle could improve her condition at all, let alone sufficiently to be found worth living by her or anyone. Everything points in the direction that, as she gets older, her condition will continue to get worse.

If this is correct, then this makes keeping her alive which is, other things equal, the morally most preferable choice, into a morally dispreferable one. Whereas, in the case of the drowning man, letting him die or killing him is not the morally most preferable choice, but saving his life is, because his life can be assumed to be one that is at least worth living, in the case of Mrs. Bouvia the most preferable alternatives are letting her die or killing her, for her life is not worth living and she wants it to end, probably to have it terminated.

Some will grant all this, but still maintain that killing is worse than letting die and that, therefore, she can only be let die, not killed. But we have already seen that the reasons that lead to the judgment that, other things equal, killing is worse than letting die, does not translate into killing

---

[12] See my "Threats of Futility: Is Life Worth Living?," *Free Inquiry* 8 (Summer 1988): 47–52.

is worse than letting die, all things considered. When we move from the former to the latter, we must take into account the available information about the particular instance of this general type. If we are agreed that the morally desirable thing is her early death, then the main point that should be decisive is the character of the two ways which lead to that death. But in this particular instance, what stands out as the main difference between killing and letting die is the brutal inhumanity involved in letting die as opposed to killing. In view of that inhumanity, and the availability of quick, painless, and dignified ways of terminating her life, it seems clear that this sort of killing is morally preferable to letting her starve. Of course, there are other ways of letting her die. She could be sedated to the point of unconsciousness and allowed to fade away in her sleep. If these are the alternatives, then it seems difficult to be sure of which is morally preferable. I can see no strong moral objection to either.

Once it is granted that Mrs. Bouvia's life is not a desirable one because she finds it not worth living and there is every reason to think it will not get any better, either killing her or letting her die are morally preferable to preventing her death. The moral choice between killing her and letting her die—supposing that she has asked for either—will depend on the comparative merits of the methods available.

3.5.   *Morally Wrong—Absolutely; Other Things Equal; All Things Considered*

One reason why people exaggerate the importance of the truth that killing is worse than letting die is that they wrongly regard it not as a judgment, other things equal, but as an absolute one. That means that all we need to know when making a particular moral choice between two or more alternatives is that one is an act of killing, the other one of letting die, and that no further information can make a difference to which act we ought to choose.

Most people now believe that there are only few if indeed any sound absolute moral judgments, for example, it is wrong intentionally to kill an innocent human being, or it is wrong to torture a baby for fun.[13] I am not convinced that there are any nontrivial such judgments, but I am convinced that there are many moral judgments that are not absolute. I think the judgment that killing is worse than letting die is not absolute, but is true only other things equal. In other words, information relevant to the

---

[13] Thomson, *The Realm of Rights*, chapter 1, especially 18–20.

case in hand may overturn it. I have argued that in the case of Mrs. Bouvia, the judgment is overturned. And even in Transplant, the final judgment that killing a patient would be morally worse than letting one die is not a straightforward application of the general truth to this particular case. To arrive at the conclusion, we need to take into account the special facts of the case, for example, that both are patients of the same physician who therefore has both a professional (relational) duty not to kill and to save the lives of his patients.

I suspect that one of the reasons why so many people arrive at what I regard as mistaken moral judgments in such cases is that they think that killing is absolutely wrong while letting die is wrong but not absolutely so. If one believes that, then one is quite likely to believe also that whenever one has a choice between killing and letting die, one must always choose letting die, never killing. I want very briefly to run through some cases in which this seems clearly false.

Consider then a few cases in which one can save the lives of some by killing others. Let us begin by reminding ourselves of a notorious and relatively uncontroversial one which I have already examined briefly. Kitty Genovese was raped and killed. If anyone of the many in the neighborhood who passively watched this had come to her assistance and found that to defend her he had to kill the assailant, our morality would say, I am sure, that it would be better (morally preferable) for him to kill the assailant, thereby saving Kitty, than to let the assailant live, thereby letting Kitty die. Thus, the additional information, that this was a case of killing an assailant in defense of the assailed who would (or in all probability would) be killed unless the defender warded off the assailant, possibly or certainly killing him, rebuts the presumption that if one has to choose between killing and letting die, one must choose letting die, into the all-things-considered judgment that it is morally preferable (though not necessarily a duty) not to let the assailed die even if that requires killing the assailant. In this case, of course, one does not, as in the case of Mrs. Bouvia, choose between killing one person and letting her die, but (as in Transplant) between killing one person and letting another die. The judgment here rests on the fact that the danger to one person is one-sidedly and unjustifiably created by a second and can be avoided only by the killing of the second.

Take now a more difficult case in which that danger was not created by the one killed. Suppose a lifeboat in which there are three has enough supplies only for two. Suppose all three would die if no rescuers appeared within seven days and the supplies were shared among all. Let us agree for

388   BOOK TWO: PART TWO: FROM THEORY TO PRACTICE

argument's sake that it is morally permissible, other things equal, for all to agree to share the supplies equally and so to take the risk of all dying. Could they also agree to draw lots on which of them should die so that the other two would have a better chance of surviving? It seems a case can be made for this on the following grounds. One is that it seems better that two should live than that all three should die, and that the selection of the victim by lot is fair. (The case would be different if the group were asked to determine, by majority vote, who should be sacrificed.) The other is that, although there is no one who one-sidedly and unjustifiably caused the threat to their lives originally, they all, equally, contribute to that threat now by their equal consumption of the available supplies; if one of them stopped eating or drinking, the others' chances would be increased.

This becomes significant if the three are not unanimous about what should be done. The difficult question, then, is whether a majority vote (2:1) can justifiably bind all three to either of the following two solutions: (1) sharing equally and waiting for rescue to arrive, at the risk of death for all, or (2) drawing lots about who should be excluded from supplies; in this second case, there is also the question of whether they can legitimately agree on whether the person who has lost the draw should be allowed or forced to starve to death or commit suicide, as he chooses, or whether he should be killed, even against his will. In the case, as so far described, there would seem to be no good reason that would justify killing the loser, and one very strong reason not to: that there is always a chance of rescue. However, a good case can perhaps be made for saying that a majority vote would constitute a binding decision about whether to divide the food equally or to exclude one. But the acceptability of the latter majority decision would appear to depend on the choice and availability of a fair method for selecting the "victim," such as drawing lots, rather than itself a majority vote, since unfair biases may intrude, as when one is strongly disliked by the other two.

If this is sound and if a decision is made to divide food and drink unequally and draw lots on who shall be the "victim," it seems clear that a decision to let the victim die is necessarily morally preferable to a decision to kill him if there is a realistic chance that a ship will turn up before the victim starves to death.

I want to conclude this discussion by a few tentative remarks about the infamous, troubling, and especially difficult case of *Regina* v. *Dudley and Stephens.*[14] I want to do this, not because the case is difficult—there are

---

[14] Queens Bench Division 1884 14 Q.B.D. 273.

many other equally difficult cases that would not have served my purpose—but because its kind of difficulty seems to me ethically instructive. In this case, there was a reason to kill a particular one out of three in a lifeboat: he was sick and unlikely to survive even in the case of an early rescue, so he was the obvious choice to provide more food and drink for the other two. Perhaps, in such a situation, a case can be made for the view that a majority (rather than unanimous) vote on *whether* one of the three should be excluded from sharing in the available food and drink constituted a *morally permissible* collective choice procedure, that is, one that is not morally dispreferable, at the mandatory level of stringency, to not adopting this or any such choice procedure—though presumably not the morally most preferable one. For I can see no reason why such a procedure should be regarded as morally binding on any participant, least of all on the one who has been chosen to be the excluded "victim." The procedure becomes more questionable still if the decision of who is to be the victim is also made by majority vote rather than by a unanimous one or by drawing lots. If, in the circumstances, this is a morally permissible collective decision procedure, though perhaps one that does not obligate those whose behavior (as agents and patients) it directs, then it would be morally permissible for the two healthy ones to vote to withhold food and drink from the sick (and perhaps dying) third one; here it is unclear whether this is a case of killing or letting die. If that is morally permissible, then if the victim dies either from his sickness or from lack of nourishment, or a combination of these factors, it would, for reasons similar to those advanced in the Bouvia case, also seem morally permissible for the others to kill him in a quicker and more humane way than by starving him to death against his will. Lastly, if all this is morally permissible, then it may also be permissible for the two healthy ones to eat his body and drink his blood, since not to do so would waste precious nourishment on which their survival may depend, for the sake of which they voted not to share the scarce supplies with him in the first place.

Situations such as that faced by Dudley and Stephens must be regarded as exceptional,* even if they are not as rare as one might hope them to be. It seems to me that in them we reach not only the limits of human endurance but also the limits of morality. As the Court in this case remarked, even though what Dudley and Stephens did (they killed the third man and ate his body and drank his blood) was not permissible under British law, they surely had a powerful excuse. Perhaps not many could say with justified conviction that in these circumstances they would have judged and acted as the law required. I believe the core requirements of morality deal with matters concerning which most men could honestly say that they would have seen clearly what was morally required and either would have satisfied these requirements or that, if they had not, they would have lacked a good excuse. This seems to me a case in which people not only cannot see clearly what is morally required or desirable, but in which morality loses its grip. The reason why people cannot see clearly what is morally required is that there is nothing that can soundly be said to be so required or even recommended; there is no guideline which is sound, none that is truly paramount over self-anchored reasons. We are thrown back on self-anchored ones.

Of course, if I am right, this does not mean that reason then requires us to do what is most advantageous to us. We may well think that we would prefer to die rather than exclude one of the survivors from the available supply to food and drink, let alone kill him or let him die to eat his flesh and drink his blood. And if we feel like that, then our self-anchored reason—which is now supreme—tells us to do just that.

But if I am right, what tells us this is the voice of self-anchored, not of moral, reason. Our disapproval of and horror at what these shipwrecked people did would seem to be "natural" revulsion which many of us may well feel, but not moral condemnation. I do not think that this conclusion exposes a deep flaw in my moral theory. For it seems to me that certain practical matters are not open to solutions that pass the test of moral soundness. The case seems to me ethically instructive because it reminds us of the possibility that there are such limits to moral reason and suggests that we have here reached a point on the boundary line.

NOTES

CHAPTER ONE: THE CONCEPT OF REASON

*Note to p. 27. I intend the word "rational" in "rational justification," to cancel the moral overtones of justification. English, unfortunately, has only the one word, "justification," where some languages have two. Thus, German has "Rechtfertigung," which is a moral term, and "Begruendung," which is not. If I act "aus guten Gruenden" (for good reasons), then my behavior is not necessarily "gerechtfertigt," (morally) justified, but it is "begruendet," (rationally) grounded or justified. But unlike the German "begruendet," "rationally grounded" lacks clear meaning, so with some misgivings I make do with the established "rational justification."

*Note to p. 30. It may be argued (see Henry David Aiken, "An Interpretation of Hume's Theory of the Place of Reason in Ethics and Politics," *Ethics* 90, no. 1 [October 1979]: 66–80) that Hume was concerned, not indeed to deny the importance of raising evaluative questions about one's ends, but rather to replace the then current conception of reason by a wider and more satisfactory one. According to such a wider conception, "the general rules of morality, . . . represent, in accordance with familiar usage, a form of reason. This usage, he [i.e., Hume] adds, will be easily understood, 'if we consider what we formerly said concerning that reason, which is able to oppose our passion; and which we have found to be nothing but a general calm determination of the

passions, founded on some distant view or reflection' (p. 583)."
(Aiken, p. 72. Aiken's page reference is to Hume's *Treatise*.)

Hume does indeed allow in the *Treatise* that actions (and
presumably choices, ends, and preferences) may be called reasonable (and presumably rational) but only in an "abusive" way
of speaking, that is, by a misuse of language, "which philosophy
will scarcely allow of," namely, when they are ("obliquely")
caused by reasonable beliefs of the agent about matters of fact or
matters of right, or when they cause such reasonable beliefs.
Strictly speaking, in themselves, nonobliquely, they cannot, in
Hume's opinion be in accordance with or contrary to reason.
(Selby-Bigge, *A Treatise of Human Nature*, book 3, part 1, section 1,
p. 459.) In other places he makes similar points, but almost
always adds that this wide sense of "reason" is the "vulgar" and
philosophically unacceptable sense. (For other relevant passages,
see, e.g., Selby-Bigge, *Treatise*, 419, 536, 583.) But of course, as so
often, Hume may, here too, have spoken tongue-in-cheek.

Hume thus appears to have thought we possessed two quite
different kinds of powers, one enabling us to enlarge our
knowledge of facts, the other concerned with our attitudes and
emotions toward these facts, and that it was confusing and
confused to think of these two powers as one and the same and
call them both, reason. Where certain ends and preferences are
unsatisfactory, it is not because they are contrary to reason in the
proper sense but because they are contrary to some other mental
capacity, which may be called "reflection," and construed as a
certain development of the calm passions. Hume thus appears
content to confine reason to the theoretical realm, to deny any
conceptual connection between reason and human good, and to
grant it a merely subordinate and still essentially theoretical
function in practice. My interpretation of Hume's account of
reason was greatly modified over the years by discussions with
Annette Baier, but I fear not sufficiently to meet with her
complete agreement.

CHAPTER TWO: THE FORM OF DIRECTIVE REASONS

*Note to p. 66.   Keeping in mind the differences between these three contexts
also dissolves the old "paradox of subjective duty," as it has
often been called. It is generated by the question of whether we
ought to do what is our "objective" or what is our "subjective"
duty, what really is our duty or what we believe, rightly or

wrongly, is our duty. (See W. D. Ross, *Foundations of Ethics* [Oxford: Clarendon Press, 1939], 148–56.) Since this question can be asked either in a context of deliberation or justification, it requires different answers in these two contexts. In the former what we want to know is, of course, our objective duty. If, as often happens, we get it wrong, then we have not done what we ought to have done, but, switching now to the context of justification, it may be that we could not have been expected to know what we ought to have done; we then want to know whether there is an exculpatory or an inculpatory explanation of our having got it wrong. Thus to get off the hook in a justificatory context, it is not enough that we did our subjective duty, what we believed was our duty, for instance to kill Jews because, as Nazis, we believed it our duty to do so. We need an exculpatory explanation of why we were wrong. It is only in the explanatory context that whatever we believed to be our duty (not what really was or what we had adequate reason to think was our duty) was the reason we had, was the reason for which we acted. Here our subjective duty is the explanatory reason, but it is not a correct answer to our initial question. The paradox arises only because we think, wrongly, that the question of our culpability hinges solely on the meaning of the question of whether or not we did what we ought to have done, whereas it hinges also on the appropriate context in which the meaning of that question is ascertained.

*Note to p. 66. However, we should note that, whereas its very meaning ties "warranted assertibility" to the context of justification, neither "there being a reason" nor "having a reason" is tied to merely one of these three contexts. Both apply in all three but only in the deliberative contexts do they come to the same thing. (For a slightly different view, see Russell Grice, who distinguishes between "having reason" and "there being reason" in a context-neutral way. On his account, one has reason if and only if there is reason and one knows there is, and there is reason for one, even if only an omniscient being could know there is.) Whether a person acted in accordance with reason is normally asked in the context of justification and then it usually asks whether he had an adequate reason only in the sense appropriate for that context. However, on some occasions, the questioner might instead be inquiring into whether he acted in accordance with the best reason *there was*. If so, the answer may be that he did not act in accordance with reason even though he acted in accordance with the best reason *he had*.

CHAPTER THREE: PRACTICAL REASONS AND MOTIVES

*Note to p. 95. This distinction bears on the question of what we can (and could) do if we but choose (or chose) to and thereby on the problem of free will. Clearly if there is nothing we can do at will because we would not have even a will let alone a free will if all the things we did were reflex actions, because then it would not only be difficult but impossible to act differently if one but chose.

*Note to p. 107. My distinction between what someone ideally and what he actually wants is similar to Bosanquet's between someone's real and his actual will. I prefer "ideal" to "real" to make it clearer that the will I am talking about is not necessarily anyone's actual will and because, unlike Bosanquet, I am not purporting to give an account of Rousseau's distinction between the General Will and the Will of All. For the reference to Bosanquet see footnote 13 in this chapter.

CHAPTER FOUR: THE GROUND OF PRACTICAL REASONS

*Note to p. 121. Sidgwick was quite contemptuous of Kant for resorting to such a postulate: "I am so far from feeling bound to believe for purposes of practice what I see no ground for holding as a speculative truth, that I cannot even conceive the state of mind which these words seem to describe, except as a momentary half-wilful irrationality, committed in a violent access of philosophic despair." (Henry Sidgwick, *The Methods of Ethics*, 7th ed. [London: Macmillan, 1907], p. 507, n. 3.) But Sidgwick thought that the existence of such a God would be a solution to his problem. He seems not to have thought it strange that such a benevolent God should be prepared, if that was necessary for the coextensiveness of the two principles, to reward those who choose to follow practical reasons based on the universal good rather than following those based on their own good, while punishing those who make the opposite choice. Why should a God of whom, presumably, he conceives as perfectly rational discriminate between these two classes of people, neither of whom, according to Sidgwick, acts contrary to reason?

*Note to p. 129. Thus, what I mean by self-anchored practical reasons are not the precepts of reason Hobbes called Laws of Nature, which he thought people could know in a State of Nature. Hobbes distinguished between two kinds of such laws, those "dictating Peace, for a means of the conservation of men in multitudes" and those forbidding "other things tending to the destruction of particular men; as Drunkenness, and all other parts of Intemperance"

(*Leviathan,* chapter 15). Hobbes thinks that for his inquiry, "The Doctrine of Civill Society" (ibid.), only the former are pertinent. For my present inquiry only the latter are. For self-anchored reasons are based on guidelines following which is a good thing from the point of view of self-anchored reason irrespective of whether others do likewise. The opposite is true for the first kind of rational guidelines, the kind of which Hobbes lists nineteen in chapter 15 of *Leviathan*. I shall return to this matter in chapter 5 and in Book Two.

*Note to p. 131. There is a further difficulty I can only sketch here. Even when the fact that a knife's becoming sharper than it was would make it a better knife, it is not clear whether that fact is a reason other things equal for anyone or everyone to sharpen it. For in such a case it is hard or impossible to distinguish between "prima facie" and "other things equal" reasons, that is, between wrongly (whether justifiably or unjustifiably) thinking that this fact is a reason for someone to sharpen that knife, and rightly thinking that this fact is a reason for someone to sharpen it, even though, all things considered, it may not be. Or putting it another way, it is hard or impossible to distinguish between two kinds of fact: those facts (e.g., that the knife belongs to someone else, that the person has easy access to other sharper knives, that he does not want to do anything for which he needs a sharp knife, that he is mistaken in thinking that he needs a sharp knife for doing what he wants to do) may well show that the supposed reason is not a reason at all and those other facts (if indeed there are any) which, unbeknownst to the person (but through no fault of his) may well rebut the presumption that this fact is such a reason for him.

*Note to p. 139. Perhaps Bishop Butler was right in thinking that it would be better if the desire for one's good were strong enough to hold these passions in check. And perhaps being adequately informed, in Sidgwick's sense, would bring us all closer to Enlightened Egoism. However, this is a question of contingent empirical fact; it is not, as Sidgwick's definition wrongly implies, necessarily so. For doing whatever one most desires to do whenever one is adequately informed, is not necessarily what is for one's own good.

There are several types of people sometimes wrongly identified with the Principled Egoist, that is, a person who does (or has adopted the principle of doing) what and only what is for her good. In particular, as we saw, the Principled Egoist is not to be identified with the type, defined by Sidgwick, who does what he really wants—call him the "self-realizer." We can for now ignore what little differences there are between him and "the expected-utility maximizer" of game theory. Both should be distinguished from the person who takes no interest at all in other people's interest, sometimes called "economic man"; we might call him "the wholly self-regarding person." And all three should be distinguished from the person who has only self-referring desires, call him "the wholly self-centered person." Unlike the wholly self-regarding person who may desire to talk to or play with others—of course, without caring how that affects their interests—the self-centered person does not desire to do anything that involves other people. However, he need not be a narcissist but in fact may fiercely hate himself, perhaps because he cannot socialize or get involved with other people or take an interest in their interests.

It may seem that a self-realizer can never act spontaneously. Admittedly, he may have desires to act spontaneously under certain conditions, which remain unaffected by adequate information. In that case, he would, as a self-realizer, have to set out to seek adequate information about the consequences of acting spontaneously under these conditions. Thus, he subjects himself to information which might undermine his desire to act spontaneously in them. He cannot, for the sake of spontaneity, resist information, say, about AIDS although that information could ruin his spontaneity in the bathhouse. Thus, the self-realizer can have only adequately informed, circumspect, prudent spontaneity. This may not satisfy the spontaneity buff who not only values spontaneity more than safety, but regards even a general check on the safety of spontaneity in certain circumstances as a contradiction in terms. It is not clear to me, however, that such prudent spontaneity would be a contradiction in terms, though it might be undesirable where unchecked spontaneity is more important than safety.

We can, if we want to, distinguish yet another type, the Strict Egoist. She is close to but in one respect different from the Enlightened Egoist, for though, like him, she takes an interest in and even caters to some interests of some other people, she does so only if doing so does not conflict with her own good or, where it does, only if she can be quite sure that this will be for her good in the long run. Thus, the Strict Egoist favors her own good over that of others when the two conflict on a particular occasion and when acting for the good of another would or might be a genuine sacrifice. The Enlightened Egoist, by contrast, is prepared to take some risks in particular cases, as long as, overall, the cases in which he acts for the good of others are of a sort that promises to more than compensates for the sacrifices, at least in the long run. Still, like the Strict Egoist, he never makes what he knows to be a genuine, uncompensated sacrifice.

The purely self-regarding person does not have to watch his other-regarding desires since he has none; the Strict Egoist, by contrast, may have some and then must watch them lest they get out of hand. She must organize her self-regarding and other-regarding desires under the supreme principle of acting solely for her own overall good. Sidgwick's self-realizer and game theory's expected-utility maximizer do not have a supreme organizing principle, which might require them to act contrary to a dominant inclination, for they simply follow their adequately informed inclination or preference. All they need to do to improve over the natural balancing out of their inclinations or preferences on the basis of the relative strengths of these behavioral dispositions is to resist the inclination to act before being adequately informed. As we have noted before, this is not only a difficult but, as Sidgwick and others since have conceived of it, an impossible task. One could make it more manageable if, instead of maximizing, one were satisfied with Herbert Simon's "satisficing." For the satisficer limits his search for information in light of the costs and benefits the information is likely to bring, and of course the costs and benefits of working out the costs and benefits of generating this information, and perhaps the costs and benefits of that, until the costs of gaining the information can be expected to outweigh its benefits. We can ignore this question here.

*Note to p. 142. At this point, I ignore the possibility of an afterlife because although, perhaps, it makes sense to assume it possible, I think we do not know or even have any inkling about what it is like, so that it is hard to see how we can have reason to take such matters into account in deciding how in general to lead our life here or what to do next.

*Note to p. 144. By someone's own point of view I do not, of course, have in mind the sense in which everyone *necessarily* has his own point of view, however internally flawed and unstable it may be; call that his *actual* point of view. What I mean is, rather, *a type* of point of view that is without internal flaws and concerning which a person may wonder whether or not to adopt it and which in the end he may not adopt. Of course, none of this makes sense for one's actual point of view.

CHAPTER FIVE: SOCIETY-ANCHORED REASONS

*Note to p. 168. Failure to distinguish between, on the one hand, rationality in the capacity and ability senses, and on the other, in the evaluative and normative senses, would help to conceal this difficulty with acquiring this knowledge. For there is, of course, no such problem with the first two senses. For a more detailed discussion of such a failure, see my article "Rationality, Reason, and the Good," in *Morality, Reason, and the Good*, ed. David Copp and David Zimmerman (Totowa, N.J.: Rowman & Allanheld, 1985), 193–211, especially 196–99.

**Note to p. 168. Absent any clear answer to this question, one's actual risk proneness or risk aversion will have to do.

*Note to p. 171. At the same time, the fact that, in two-person PD situations, acting on the principle of prudence does not produce the best possible outcome for both or for each does not imply that acting on the principle of prudence is not, nevertheless, the best possible response available to each. Unfortunately, we often can envisage greatly improved situations without there being any known ways of getting from the present unsatisfactory situation to the envisaged improved one. The maintenance of a social order prevents the development of something like a Hobbesian State of Nature which probably would be worse than even a poor social state of affairs. The creation and continuous improvement of a moral order (see book 2) further improves the conditions created by a social order. But that alone, as Parfit (cited in footnote 11 in this chapter, p 165) convincingly argues, does not prevent the cropping up of new PD situations created by our morality. Perhaps it is often possible to eliminate such undesirable suboptimalities by generating suitable modifications of our moral precepts and rules to defeat or replace the currently accepted guidelines for these PD situations. But until we have such generally recognized paramount rules, adhering to the jointly suboptimal rules may well be, from the point of view of an optimizer, preferable to following a rule that would give everyone better outcomes *if everyone followed it*, but would give the one or the few unilaterally following it the worst possible outcome, which can range from the bearably unpleasant to the disastrous.

**Note to p. 171. Hobbes thought that people in a State of Nature could set up a social order by mutual agreement and thus suitably transform PD situations. But he also thought that all who lived in societies had excellent reason to maintain that social state so as to prevent a return to the State of Nature with its many PD situations. It is not, of course, plausible to think, along Hobbesian lines, of the State of Nature as one in which people interacted with one another without the benefit and constraints of any sort of social order. It is difficult, perhaps impossible, to conceive of a presocial state in which individuals are sufficiently sophisticated to pass on from generation to generation a common language and culture including practical guidelines they *regard as reasons*. To make sense of a State of Nature in which people are able to regard certain facts as practical reasons for doing something, such as concluding a social contract, we must think of it as at least a former social state in which only what we called "self-anchored independent reasons" were recognized and are still remembered. Such a State of Nature resembles Hobbes's in the most important respect: it is governed by what Hobbes called the Right of Nature. The primary guidelines of reason provided by such a society tell each member what he must or can do to make the best reply to whatever others will be doing. In such a State of Nature, the role of society is that sketched in chapter 4, governed by our simplifying supposition.

*Note to p. 173. Hobbes himself is aware of the first point. As he sees it, reason (through the second law of nature; see *Leviathan*, chapter 14) requires people to set aside their own interest whenever, *if others are willing to do likewise,* all fare better than if each persisted in seeking his own good irrespective of how it affects others. We may construe Hobbes's individuals as engaging only reluctantly in strategic reasoning, in always making their best reply whatever others may be doing and in whatever way it affects them. They would prefer to set aside the pursuit of their own uncooperatively pursued best interest whenever (as in PD) they would fare better by doing so where others do likewise. They are willing to give up the chance of doing even better for themselves by making their best reply, but only when others are also willing to give up that chance. The only reason they reluctantly continue to make their best reply is that in a State of Nature they cannot count on others doing the cooperative thing. This departure from Principled Rational Egoism into Principled Limited Rational Egoism is not exactly an increase in altruism since it may be motivated simply by the belief that such a change of attitude *on a reciprocal base* is the only chance or the best hope of *doing better for oneself,* but not a concern for other people's well-being.

*Note to p. 174. This is not the same problem as Arrow's famous paradox, which arises in the context of constructing a so-called social preference function out of the members' individual preference functions. But there is a similarity: the paradox arises only for certain individual preference profiles. In this case, too, an undesirable result could be avoided if people simply had different preferences. For a more detailed discussion of these questions, see Kenneth Arrow, *Social Choice and Individual Values* (New York: John Wiley & Sons, Inc., 1951), and Jerome Rothenberg, *The Measurement of Social Welfare* (Englewood Cliffs, N.J.: Prentice-Hall, Inc., 1961), especially chapter 11.

*Note to p. 175. There is a second suggestion in Sen's paper. Sen says that it would be "a moral exercise" (Sen, 64) to attempt to shift one's SD preferences from SF to AG (for a definition of these terms, see p. 178f) and if one succeeded one would have reached a condition one would regard as morally superior (Sen, 61, 63, 64). Now if there is to be no conflict between individual rationality and morality, then presumably it would also have to be rational to attempt to bring about a general shift of this sort. With this I can agree. But Sen seems also to imply that it would be rational for people who have SF preferences to act *as if* they had AG preferences for "if people behave *as if* they have these modified preferences (AG or OR preferences in our example) they end up being better off even in terms of their unmodified preferences (PD preferences)" (66). If I am right, this could, however, be true only if one knew or had adequate reason to believe that the others would act likewise. But in real-life situations, that assurance would seem to be possible only through suitable sanctioning of the coordinative guidelines. Such sanctioning is the more necessary since, as we have seen, if a given person with SF preferences has the assurance that others "will do the right thing," then it would be irrational for him "to do the right thing." This conclusion could be avoided only if his own assurance that others would do the right thing somehow depended on their having *a comparable assurance* that he, too, would do the right thing himself. But how can this be accomplished except by such sanctions? Admittedly, it is thus a very important fact that universal behavior of a type such that it would be socially optimal for people who have AG preferences and know this about one another and know that they know, would also be individually optimal and so individually rational for them. But that fact does not make it individually rational to act in this same way for people who actually have SF preferences, who know this of one another and know that they know, even though they also know that they *would* all do better *if* they *all* acted in that way. Thus, this suggestion, if indeed Sen intends it, also fails. As R. B. Brandt saw, some versions of Ideal Moral Code Utilitarianism are exposed to this difficulty. From the fact that, if we all stopped using our cars to drive downtown, we would all be better off, it does not follow that it would be contrary to reason (or wrong) for anyone to use his car in this way. (For a fuller discussion, see R. B. Brandt, "Some Merits of One Form of Rule Utilitarianism," in *Utilitarianism. John Stuart Mill*, ed. Samuel Gorvitz (Indianapolis, Ind.: Bobbs-Merrill Company, Inc., 1971), 324–44.

CHAPTER SIX: THE SOCIAL AND THE MORAL ORDER

*Note to p. 211. It is worth noting that once such terms for distinguishing different ways of judging various parts of the mores emerge in a language, there also emerges the possibility of critically examining the ways in which we distinguish these ways of judging these parts of the mores. We may come to doubt whether a given person correctly distinguishes between what *is* the customary, the legal, the moral, the religious, etc. way of judging certain attitudes, actions, directives, or persons, and the relations between these ways of judging. Discussions, say, of the immorality of certain sexual orientations may raise this doubt.

*Note to p. 214. I use the term "individual" rather than "personal," although in my view both individual and social moralities typically are those of Individuals in Strawson's sense of this term. "Personal morality" too strongly suggests two inappropriate senses here: "idiosyncratic morality" and "morality of, or concerning, a person rather than an action or society." To avoid confusion, I use upper-case letters for Strawsonian Individuals.

**Note to p. 214. Of course, there are also important differences, at least linguistic ones, between the two concepts. However, some of these may give an impression of greater divergence than is actually the case. Thus, there is no analogue from the concept of reason for the term, "a morality," and its plural, "moralities." We lack the expression "a rationality" (or something equivalent) to refer to a society's conception, theory, or code, of what is according, what contrary to reason. Of course, despite this lack of a name for it, a society may still have something that is such a conception, theory, or code. Perhaps what some philosophers have called "common sense" is exactly that: all the things which we, in this society, believe to be rational or in accordance with reason. If this is right, then the absence of a term ("a rationality" analogous to "a morality") for what a person or a society regards as rationally required of someone might incline us to exaggerate the differences between the structures of the two concepts.

Note, in this connection, that we do have a moral analogue of the term "Reason," with an upper-case letter, so to speak, as in "She often acts contrary to Reason," which in my view should be interpreted as "contrary to the balance of the (primarily practical) reasons she has"; and we similarly speak of acting contrary to Morality, also as it were with an upper-case letter, which, again, in my view should be interpreted as "contrary to the balance of the (primarily moral) reasons one has" (for a more detailed discussion, see section 5 of this chapter). Thus, both "Morality" and "Reason" appear to have been coined (perhaps by philosophers) to give support to the objectivity of the (balance of) our rational and moral directives by portraying it as stemming from a single entity, a quasi-person who communicates linguistically formulated directives to us, either orally (the voice of Reason or of Morality) or in writing that we all can read (written on the hearts of man). Plainly, "morality," too, has an evaluative and a tendency sense. Its opposite is "immorality" which, in the context of deliberation, involves only the evaluative, in that of justification also the dispositional, sense of "moral/immoral" and "according/contrary to morality." Thus, the deliberator can judge actions open to him to be both according/contrary to reason and to morality, while the critic can judge both actions and agents rational/irrational and moral/immoral. The deliberator's judgments are analogous to those of legality (i.e., that an action actually conforms or would conform with the law); the deliberator asks either whether at that point there is, among the actions open to him, one that morality requires or forbids, or whether the particular thing he is hoping to do conforms with morality. The status of the critic's judgments is analogous to those of warranted assertibility (i.e., that at the time someone made the assertion, he was warranted in making it); for justifications of agents are based on whether they raised the deliberative question, answered it with adequate care, and acted as permitted by their answer, while justifications of actions are based on whether their agents acted as a justified agent would have. When I deliberate about whether it would be immoral, wrong *for* me, to marry Jane, I cannot of course be in reason expected to take into account those facts (e.g., that she is my long-lost sister) which I could not then know even if I had taken all the steps I could have been expected to take, and which, when discovered later, show, in the context of justification, that it was wrong *for* me to do so but, in view of my justified ignorance, not immoral, not wrong *of* me. What I now know, in the justificatory context, shows that I was right in thinking that marrying her would not be immoral, not wrong *of* me, but that I was mistaken in thinking that it was not wrong *for* me to do so.

Perhaps, we sometimes also ascribe morality, as we ascribe rationality, in the capacity and ability senses. We may want to speak of chickens or squirrels as nonmoral beings, and of babies as premoral, as not yet fully moral beings. But, if I may anticipate a little, in my view, this would not serve any useful purpose, since morality in these two senses is not distinct from rationality. If I am right, the *capacity* for being moral is the same as that for being rational, and even a normal adult's *ability* to be moral does not go beyond full rationality (as I called it in part 1). What makes being moral different from being rational is not that the two presuppose distinct capacities and abilities—perhaps a special moral sense or special moral emotions—but merely that acting immorally is acting contrary to what one (rightly or wrongly) takes, or what one should but does not take, to be the weightiest moral reasons; whereas acting irrationally is acting contrary to what one (rightly or wrongly) takes, or what one should but does not take, to be the balance of reasons in a particularly flagrant way, which (as I argued in part 1) may not always be the case when one acts contrary to the weightiest moral reasons.

*Note to p. 217. I am putting this tentatively because at this point I still have to rely on intuitions based on our morality. As I develop my theory it will become clearer on what this intuition rests. I shall argue that it is not inconceivable that abortion should (other things equal) be morally wrong in New Jersey but not in New York, but that it would be very highly improbable. For the grounds on which the difference rests would have to be relevant differences in social conditions, such as the inability of many couples to procreate and the failure of all other methods of birth control to prevent dangerous overpopulation, and it would seem very highly improbable that one of these conditions could prevail in New Jersey and the other in New York.

**Note to p. 217. At the same time, this does not mean that a society's morality, even one as pluralistic as ours, does not have an agreed core. For it may well be true that, in the absence of such an agreed core of its morality with a certain society-neutral content, that society could not have survived, as Hart has suggested about a society's law. For references, see footnote 3, p. 201.

***Note to p. 217. Perhaps in a legal order, such as ours, in which judicial review plays an important role in determining what the law is, there are cases in which a long-accepted and acted-on law is declared unconstitutional by judicial review but in which this declaration does not have this "retroactive" force.

*Note to p. 218. As the abortion controversy shows, it is often unclear whether that hope has been finally dashed and if so what should then be done to prevent the reasoned disagreement from degenerating into open conflict and the use of force. A fuller discussion of this important and difficult problem is beyond the scope of this book.

**Note to p. 218. Rousseau and Kant tried to push the idea of the subjects' participation in making the law to which they are subject to the limit at which, in Rousseau's words, "everyone is subject only to himself." I think that, when taken to this limit, this idea is incoherent. When we think about what we want, we find that, because our propensities often conflict, we need to establish priorities among them and so rein in some of them if we are not to suffer even greater harm or miss out on even greater good. We may or may not be able to impose that discipline on ourselves, but we do realize that we may not and probably will not establish a harmony among all our existing propensities: some of them will have to be frustrated, if not by ourselves, then by society. One of the important problems is to distinguish between those that society may frustrate and those it may not.

***Note to p. 218. It should be clear from these remarks that, by "a social morality," I do not mean either a "concurrent" or a "conventional" morality, in Dworkin's interesting terminology. "A community displays a concurrent morality when its members are agreed in asserting the same, or much the same, normative rule, but they do not count the fact of that agreement as an essential part of their grounds for asserting that rule. It displays a conventional rule when they do." (Ronald Dworkin, *Taking Rights Seriously* [Cambridge, Mass.: Harvard University Press, 1967], 53.) What I have in mind is neither, because both these kinds of social morality presuppose that (all or most of) its members are agreed in asserting the same or much the same normative rule, whereas I do not require this presupposition. That would be so even if "agreed in asserting the same normative rule" is interpreted so loosely that their *happening* to subscribe to the same general moral directives would suffice. For by "a social morality" I mean "the" morality composed of the personal moralities its members come to have; that includes those moral orders in which its members strongly disagree on some moral issues. Nor does my conception of a social morality either require or forbid that (at least or not even) part of the grounds on which the society's members subscribe to some of its directives be that all subscribe, that is, that they would not subscribe to them if some, many, most, or all others did not also subscribe. My conception does not exclude those social orders as having a social morality in which none or only some, but not all of the members of a moral order subscribe to general directives such as "never to violate the moral rules of property *if and only if* the rule is generally accepted, generally followed, and adequately enforced."

*Note to p. 219. Consider certain similarities with the concept of freedom. There, too, we can distinguish between individual and social freedom, and we can think of the shape or the contours of social freedom as determined by the varying extent of the (individual) freedom of the society's members. It is this shape of social freedom that Hobbes had in mind when he spoke of "the liberty of subjects" as "those things which in regulating their actions the sovereign has pretermitted" (*Leviathan*, chapter 21). But, of course, he notoriously ignored or treated quite inadequately the question of the ideal or proper "shape" of individual and social freedom.

CHAPTER SEVEN: THE MORAL ENTERPRISE

*Note to p. 227. The legal model to some extent encourages this conflation of sin and wrong, for it seems we do wrong when, for instance, we break the speed limit even when we do not hit and so wrong anyone. What makes it wrong, it might seem, is not the harm we do, but the violation of the law. But that raises anew the question, "What is it that makes the law binding on its subjects?" At some point, this line of justification must come to an end. Justification of *every* lower law by conformity with a higher must give rise to a vicious regress. The two versions of the Divine Command Theory I shall discuss here appear to recognize this point for they give different answers to the question of why we are bound by the Divine Commandments. The simpler version implies that the moral distinctions between morally good and bad, right and wrong, and so on, are created by the fiat of the supreme legislator, just as our legal distinction between the lawful and the unlawful is created by the fiat of the earthy legislators. Essentially we are bound by them because our salvation depends on obedience to them. The second in essence says that we must obey God's commandments because God loves us, because he knows best what is good and what is bad for us and so commands us to do what is good, forbids us to do what is bad for us, and because therefore obedience is for our good, disobedience is to our detriment.

**Note to p. 227. However, it is not clear to me how one might support this position. Foot, for instance, believes that what morality is and what it requires of us is discovered by an empirical examination of the everyday concept of morality. This, she says will yield "starting points fixed by the concept of morality. We might call them 'definitional criteria of good and evil,' so long as it is clear that they belong to the concept of morality—to *the* definition and not to some definition which a man can choose for himself. What we say about such definitional criteria will be objectively true or false." (Philippa Foot, "Morality and Art," reprinted in *Philosophy As It Is*, ed. Ted Honderich and Myles Burnyeat, [Penguin Books, 1979], 14.) Like Harsanyi, she thinks that these objectively true criteria of what is morally required do not necessarily provide us with reasons, let alone defeating reasons, to do what is so required. For practical rationality consists in doing what

will satisfy one's desires or preferences, hence a person has
reason to do what morality requires only if he already desires to
pursue the aims which are, by such an objective definition, the
aims of morality. As I mentioned, she thinks of those who respect
the precepts of morality as "volunteers banded together to fight
for liberty and justice and against inhumanity and oppression"
("Morality as a System of Hypothetical Imperatives," for references, see above, Introduction, footnote 10) or whatever other
aim(s) may turn out really to be the aims of our everyday morality.
On this view, it seems, neither morality nor reason is the ultimate
justifier; the former is society relative, the latter person relative, so
they seem incommensurable. An amoralist or an antimoralist
need not be making any sort of mistake. It seems to follow that
social pressure to conform to the requirements of morality (that is,
the morality of one's society) interferes with the amoralist's (and
presumably also the antimoralist's) freedom no less than would
such pressure to change his ways simply because his style of life
displeases those who control the social machinery of repression.

Postscript, October 1993. In fairness to Professor Foot, I
should add that, a short time ago, I heard her read a paper at a
philosophy conference in Vienna, sponsored by "The New
Vienna Circle," in which she explicitly repudiated the views here
quoted from "Morality as a System of Hypothetical Imperatives"
and, it seemed to me, by implication though not explicitly, also
those quoted here from "Morality and Art." But her paper was
long and deep, a condensation of a book-length project and a
good deal of it remained obscure to me. Thus, even if I am right in
thinking that she has now abandoned her earlier views—and I
may well have misunderstood just how much of them she has
abandoned—these earlier views seem to me sufficiently interesting and influential to warrant their being included at this point.

*Note to p. 236. Jacob Marschak (see footnote 11) usefully distinguishes three
kinds of collective enterprises: "foundations," "teams," and
"coalitions." A team, he says, comes into and remains in
existence solely for the purpose of attaining an end common to
all members. A coalition, by contrast, is a group of persons
having a variety of ends, only some of which are shared though
all are mutually tolerated. It is so organized that their mutually
coordinated activities no longer hinder but actually promote the
attainment of their respective ends. Finally, a foundation is
organized to achieve a given purpose, which is the purpose of
some members but not of all; those who join a foundation do so
not because their aim is the aim of the foundation but because

they are rewarded for their efforts to achieve the foundation's purpose.

Thus, John Sr.'s business would be a foundation if he hired an assistant, but a team if he made his son a partner rather than bequeathing the shop to him; and the farmers bringing in their harvest could become a coalition if they agreed to help one another bring in their harvest at the different times their crops ripen.

Note to p. 236. When I here speak of "the" social enterprise, I usually mean a *type* of (collective) enterprise, rather than one of its *tokens* (instances, specimens); when I mean a token, I usually speak of "a" social enterprise. At this point, the discussion is mainly about the type, not this or that token. I speak of "The" or "An" "Enterprise" (with upper-case letters) when I refer to a type of enterprise that embodies a certain (already specified) ideal or to one of its tokens.

*Note to p. 237.** We can distinguish three kinds of end a particular society (i.e., a particular social enterprise) may have come to have and pursue. One is the kind concerned to achieve certain life prospects for certain classes of members of the society (e.g., men, the old, the wellborn, soldiers, and so on). Attaining this end is bringing it about that these classes of people do have the desired life prospects. Plainly this first kind of success is not all that (at least some of) the members may expect the social enterprise to accomplish.

The second kind of end (analogous to the society's international law or international agreements, that is, the provisions of its national law regulating interactions of its nationals with those of other societies) is concerned to ensure that its pursuit of the first kind of end have or do not have certain effects on the members of the societies that are its neighbors or its allies or its enemies, and so on. International organizations, such as the League of Nations and the United Nations, and international agreements establishing military, political, and economic rules (such as NATO, OPEC, NAFTA, EU, and GATT) or international legal provisions, such as those governing the extradition of criminals or the laws of war, are attempts to give voice to the "patients" (usually victims) of the pursuit of the (collectively determined) ends of the social enterprises of the big bullies among the "collective individuals" who compose the so-called "family of nations."

Finally, the third kind, such as the annexation of territory, the overthrow of the government of a neighboring country, the eradication of communism, or the triumph of Islam, comprises ends which are perceived by all, or by a significant proportion, of its members as "in the national interest" or for other reasons desirable from the point of view of every member or of a significant proportion of all members. I am here concerned only with the first kind of end.

*Note to p. 239. I have, for simplicity's sake, used the word "critic" to mean someone who unfavorably assesses a member's performance on the basis of the way in which he has played the roles of An Enterprise, and the word "reformer" to mean a critic of an enterprise$_R$ who finds fault with it. It probably would have been less misleading, but more complicated, if I had used a more general term, such as "critical examiner," the class to which both "critic" and "reformer" (in my senses) belong, and restricted the term "reformer" to the subclass of critical examiners who critically examine an enterprise$_R$ with a view to improving it and maintaining its strengths, and the term "critic" to another subclass which is concerned with assessing a particular individual's particular performance in one of the particular roles of an enterprise$_R$, irrespective of whether the assessment is positive or negative.

*Note to p. 242. To the extent that luck plays a role in morality (as some philosophers, such as Bernard Williams ["Moral Luck," in *Moral Luck*] and Thomas Nagel ["Moral Luck," in *Mortal Questions* (New York: Cambridge University Press, 1979)] have claimed), there seem to be two quite different ways in which luck can intrude. One is good or bad luck in the course of trying to attain an end particular moral agents are required by their role in the moral enterprise to try to attain. Some may find it easier, others more difficult, yet others (because of unforeseeable and insuperable obstacles) impossible to attain that same end. I take it that we would want to say that Complete Success had not been achieved when these factors of good and bad luck were not taken into account in determining what the moral enterprise requires of particular agents. It may well be true that these matters cannot always be adequately taken into account and that, therefore, Complete Success, by this very demanding standard, cannot be achieved. We shall see that there are matters other than luck that pose similar difficulties, and we shall have to examine what this means for our moral practice. At this point, it must suffice to say that we have many ideals, say, the eradication of illiteracy, crime, and disease, which it would seem to be impossible to achieve completely, but which it is nevertheless desirable to pursue and come as close to as is possible. For the moment, I shall simply assume that that makes sense also about the ideal of complete success in the moral enterprise. For further details see below, section 3.6 in this chapter.

*Note to p. 243. "Must" here means two things. One is that the reason they have is a requiring one. The other is that it is or would be rightly backed by a corrective social pressure. For earlier discussions of this question, see Introduction, p. 18, and Book One, chapter 2, section 2.3.

*Note to p. 244. The satisfaction of the first and second conditions together amounts to the correct discharge by all the members of what I earlier called their "reflective and executive tasks" (see above, p. 9). The satisfaction of the third condition turns a social order into something like Rawls's "well-ordered society," (see Rawls, *TJ*, 4f), except that it requires the general acceptance not only of a single conception of justice, but of a single conception of the whole of morality and that this conception be sound. The satisfaction of the second condition parallels Rawls's notion of "strict compliance" (see Rawls, *TJ*, 8), but is even more demanding (and so further removed from the real world), since again it implies not only strict compliance with the requirements of the generally accepted conception of justice but with all moral requirements and that these requirements be not merely generally accepted but also sound, a condition which is unlikely to be satisfied often, if ever.

*Note to p. 253. I should perhaps point out that, even if the practical impossibility of achieving Complete Success exposed a flaw in ICT, it would not be exactly the same as that in DCT. DCT can prove that, *if* its factual claims are true, then everyone has requiring reason always to follow the Divine Commandments, but it can offer no empricial evidence in support of its factual claims. By contrast, the (supposed) flaw in ICT is its inability to prove, independently of an enterprise$_R$'s closeness to Complete Success$_R$, that its members have requiring reason always to follow its guidelines. However, since ICT can appeal to the empirical evidence of a causal connection between the behavior of the members of an enterprise$_R$ and the quality of the resulting lives, it may be able to provide, if not proof, at least adequate reasons for thinking, that an enterprise$_R$ has reached a certain degree of closeness to Complete Success$_R$, and that this may be sufficient reason to think that its members have compelling reason always to follow its guidelines rather than their self-anchored ones, or at any rate that they have such reason in respect to certain of its guidelines, and if that closeness is not sufficient to amount to such a reason, an indication of how much closer they must get to have such a reason. Thus, while the fact that an enterprise$_R$ at a certain time is not Completely Successful$_R$ is a reason for its members to work for its change in the direction of Complete Success$_R$, the extent to which it falls short at that time may not be such as to give them adequate reason not to follow its relevant guidelines.

*Note to p. 254.   There is an important complication I must ignore here: that it may be necessary, in testing the soundness of a given guideline, to take into account other guidelines to see whether the unsoundness of one cancels or aggravates the undesirable effects of the unsoundness of another. Thus, it is sometimes argued that the traditionally overburdened role of women in the family is lightened, perhaps counterbalanced, by the overburdened role of men in national defense. This sort of concatenation probably occurs most frequently between guidelines spelling out role rights and role duties, but I assume without argument that the soundness of some guidelines can be determined individually, without taking others into account.

*Note to p. 256.   To simplify matters, I assume that this proportion of members fails to conform, and so on, not because they know or justifiably believe that others, too, fail to conform, but for other reasons, mainly their knowledge or justifiable belief about the unsoundness of some of the recognized guidelines or about the more or less serious malperformance of their cognitive and/or executive tasks by a larger or smaller proportion of the members.

*Note to p. 258.   Of course, one might want to put the same point less paradoxically by saying that certain guidelines require a certain specifiable type of behavior of everyone, but only under certain conditions, for example, that no one else has already done it. In such a case those who do not engage in that behavior when these conditions are not satisfied, not only do not fail to do their bit but also do not fail to conform to the guideline. Thus, the benefit-requiring guideline is of this sort, the harm-prohibiting one is not. But while this is less paradoxical and in essence true, it conceals the important facts on account of which these two guidelines are thus different.

*Note to p. 262.   Hobbes seems to have something like society- and self-anchored guidelines in mind in his distinction between two kinds of laws of nature discussed above (see *Note to p. 129). And he seems to have in mind something like my distinction between merely formulated directives thought suitable for being society-anchored guidelines and actually established ones, when he says "These dictates of reason men used to call by the name of laws, but improperly, for they are but conclusions or theorems concerning what conduces to the conservation and defense of themselves, whereas law, properly, is the word of him that *by right has command over others*. But yet if we consider the same theorems as delivered in the word of God, that *by right commands all things*, then they are properly called laws." (*Leviathan*, chapter 15, 132. My emphases.) It seems, then, that we can think of the laws of nature in these two ways: (1) as theorems which satisfy three conditions: human beings (a) concerned about "the conservation of multitudes," (b) intending them to be enacted in a social order such that its lawgiver will be most likely to enact just such laws, and (c) would, if they used their reason, come up with correct formulations of them; and also (2) as enactments of just such laws by just such a legislator in just such a social order.

*Note to p. 269. If it is objected that The Enterprise$_M$ is bound to be as practically useless as The Enterprise$_R$, I would have to agree, but in response I would suggest the procedure, sketched above in section 3.6 of this chapter, for determining what difference its various flaws make to the rationality of its members' continuation to do their bit.

*Note to p. 271. It may now be objected that my way of introducing the distinction between sound and unsound guidelines prejudges what is at issue between deontologists and teleologists in favor of the latter. For that distinction need not be based on the suitability or unsuitability of compliance with these guidelines for bringing about and maintaining one sort of state of affairs rather than another. One could instead base it on the procedure by which the guidelines came to be generally recognized. One could rely on "pure procedural" soundness, to adopt Rawls's idea and term (Rawls, *TJ*, 120). The character of the state of affairs brought about by general compliance would then be irrelevant.

This objection seems to me well taken. To meet it would require a much longer treatment than I can here give it. I can make only one brief ad hominem point of whose inadequacy I am well aware. It is that it seems to me impossible to describe a procedure for arriving at moral guidelines which could persuade us of their bindingness on all of us irrespective of the character of the state of affairs produced and maintained by universal compliance with them. Rawls seems well aware of this, for his principles of justice are principles of the distribution of primary goods whose definition connects them with people's conception of the good life for themselves (Rawls, *TJ*, section 15).

*Note to p. 279. Of course, what makes an action someone's duty is not the fact that an action based on this maxim would make this sort of impact on others, but the fact that this maxim would pass Kant's Categorical Imperative while a contradictory one would not. Perhaps I have misrepresented Kant. For although, when he turns to specifics (see Immanuel Kant, *Metaphysics of Morals*, tr. Mary Gregor [New York: Cambridge University Press, 1991]), he affirms two apparent asymmetries, namely, that we have a duty to make *others* happy, *but not ourselves,* and we have a duty to try to perfect *ourselves, but not others,* these claims may not involve an acknowledgment of asymmetry, for they may simply be an application of his view that we cannot but aim and try to make *ourselves, but not others* happy, and that we can perfect *ourselves, but not others,* hence cannot have a duty to perfect them, either.

*Note to p. 282. Mutatis mutandis, the same also holds for moral issues and problems, which I construe as two subclasses of moral questions. The former (such as whether abortion is wrong) are those on which members embrace strong opposing views, each side having what seem to them powerful supporting reasons. Moral problems are questions which for some people are problematic, that is, questions concerning which the reasons for and against a certain answer seem equally weighty to *them.* A moral issue may not be a moral problem for a particular or any person. For many anti- and pro-abortionists, the central moral question of whether abortion is wrong does not seem to be a moral problem. For them the only problem is how their opponents can be caught up in this error or this wickedness.

*Note to p. 284. Although the point is important, I cannot here expatiate on the serious mistake that can flow from misclassifying certain questions as moral or nonmoral ones, and giving answers to the former that purport to be sound moral ones and answers to the latter that purport to be sound religious or self-anchored ones. Thus, it seems to me that sexual orientation is not, as such, intrinsically, a moral question, any more than celibacy, even though it may be true that if, let us say, all were homosexual or celibate, this might well be disastrous for the future of the race. The reason would seem to be that the number who are homosexual or celibate is much too small to have that effect, and that the explanation of its being that small is not that a large number of heterosexuals and procreators are such from a sense of duty rather than from inclination. By contrast, the question of the rationality of the use of scarce resources by the affluent industrial powers may not be, or be only, a question of self-interest, but also or only a moral question. The matter is somewhat controversial, for in the first place it is not generally agreed that the consumption of these resources at that level by all societies would be disastrous for humans and other living things, and because those who are not now consuming them at that level are failing to do so not from disinclination, let alone a sense of duty, but from inability. The relevant question, then, is not whether the developed nations are something like free riders but whether they are preventing the underdeveloped nations from acquiring the relevant ability or failing to help them acquire it and whether either of these things would be wrong.

Note to p. 284. Prichard thought "Why be moral?" was, among other things, a request to show why it was a mistake to think that being moral sometimes was contrary to one's best interest. He, by contrast, thought that the requirements of morality sometimes did conflict with one's best interest and that the question was therefore illegitimate. From the fact that, throughout its history, moral philosophy took "Why be moral?" to be one of its central problems, he inferred that it has rested on a mistake. He thought the mistake lay in wrongly assuming that all people acted only from self-interested motives, and that once the mistake was brought to light the wish to ask the question would vanish. In my view, Prichard may well have been right in ascribing this mistake to Plato and other philosophers, but I do not think that the discovery of this mistake by Plato and others shows "Why be moral?" to be an illegitimate question.

CHAPTER EIGHT: THE DESIGN OF OUR MORAL CODE

*Note to p. 292. Other cultures may not use terms that are the exact or even near equivalents to ours. This is more obvious when the cultures are very different, for instance ours and that of the Navajos, the Chinese, or even the ancient Greeks, as when we cannot do much better than translate Plato's *dikaiosyne* or Aristotle's *eudaimonia* by our *justice* and *happiness*. Because of Plato's and Aristotle's enormous influence on our moral thinking, such assumptions of synonymy have even led some into misconstruing not merely their terms but also our own. Such misunderstandings can occur even for contemporary European cultures. Thus, contrary to widespread belief, the English "ought" and the German "sollen" do not mean exactly the same. Kant's idea of the Categorical Imperative is more naturally formulated with "sollen" than with "ought." Conversely, imperativalist analyses of "ought" may seem more persuasive if one has studied and understood Kant in German and thinks that "ought" and "sollen" are synonyms. In fact, "sollen" is much closer to "shall" than to "ought." "Du sollst nicht toeten" is, I think, better rendered as "Thou shalt not kill" than by "You ought not to kill." Conversely, "He ought to give up smoking" can no more be translated into "Er soll das Rauchen aufgeben" than it can be rendered as "He shall give up smoking." Although, like "ought," neither "shall" nor "sollen" can be used to give direct orders, both can be used, unlike "ought," to express a resolve to see to it that someone, whether oneself or others, is successful in doing, getting, or retaining something, for example, "They shall overcome," "You shall have it," "He shall not pass": as "Sie sollen siegen," "Du sollst es haben," "Er soll hier nicht durchkommen." However—and that may partly explain the mistaken assimilation —"sollen" can be used to transmit orders without backing them. "Du sollst ihn abholen," is best translated as "You are (supposed) to pick him up," not "You shall pick him up," except perhaps in the sense of "You shall have the opportunity of picking him up (if you want to)," when it is not the transmission of an order but of a permission or a promise. "Ought," which, unlike "sollen," simply does not have any "pure directive" use (as imperatives are typically used, despite the popularity of some imperativalist analyses), is therefore a term much better suited for capturing the rational element in morality than "sollen," which does conjure up Moses coming down from the mountain and transmitting the Divine Commandments received there, the way a sergeant transmits orders given by a lieutenant to the troops under the latter's command.

*Note to p. 293.   It will not have escaped the reader that I am here using each of the expressions, "a use of a word" and "a directive" in two different senses, each sense of the first of these expressions tied closely to one of the two senses of the other expression. I shall give the same name to these corresponding senses of the two expressions. In the first, call it the "committal," sense, "a use" means someone's making of an assertion or claim or something similar with a word or an expression, that is, someone's using of words in a way that puts his credit on the line as a linguistic performer; the contrast is with a nonuse of this sort, such as a mere "mention." In the second, call it the "interpretive" sense, "a use of a word or expression" is a certain interpretation of it that is appropriate when it is used in the committal sense in certain circumstances; it is one of several possible such interpretations of it depending on the context. "A directive," in the analogous committal sense comes into existence if a certain word or expression (say, the sentence, "The procession will enter the town hall at 10 A.M.") is intended in a directive use (in the interpretive sense of "use"). I shall not examine in detail under precisely what conditions someone's use of a sentence with a directive use (in the interpretive sense) brings into being a directive in the committal sense of "use," as when the sergeant bellows the command, "Right turn!"

*Note to p. 296.   It may perhaps be thought that such normative claims are false if they do not pass this test but that they are not true just because they pass it, because from the fact that p implies q it follows that if q is false, p is false but not that p is true if q is true. However, this is so only for ps and qs that could be true or false even if no implication relation held between them. For in that case p is not necessarily false if q is false, but it would be true or false. Directives which do not stand in implication relations to propositions that can be true or false are not themselves true or false. Only normatives which are directives that stand in such relationships to propositions that can be true or false can themselves be true or false; they derive their capacity to be true or false from the truth or falsity of the propositions they imply. Thus, the implication contained in these normatives amounts to an equivalence. If the falsity of what they imply to be true implies their own falsity, then the truth of what they imply to be true implies their own truth, for otherwise we would have to allow that they can be false but not true, since nothing else could show them to be true.

*Note to p. 297. That they are directives does not necessarily turn moral precepts into "prescriptions," in the sense made famous by Hare (see R. M. Hare, *The Language of Morals* [New York: Oxford University Press, 1964], chapters 1 and 2, especially 163f. and 176ff.; also *Freedom and Reason* [New York: Oxford University Press, 1965], chapter 5). If I understand him correctly, Hare's prescriptives are a subclass of my directives, namely, those that satisfy two further defining characteristics on top of my three. These additional characteristics bring them closer to commands than my directives do. One is, (4) the speaker *purports to want* the addressee to satisfy the directive; the other is (5) if the addressee "accepts" (i.e., commits himself to carry out) the directive, then he must be *resolved to comply* with it.

It is clear, I hope, that (4) is not plausible. Telling someone what he should do does not necessarily also tell him to do it or purport to tell him that one wants him to do it or ipso facto express that want. It may merely inform him of what it is best for him to do.

It will perhaps be objected that at least the most important normatives, those expressed with the word "ought," are prescriptives. For would it not be absurd, indeed, self-contradictory to say "You ought to leave now, but please stay a little longer"? Of course, the remark is (linguistically) odd, but not, I think self-contradictory. The oddness can be avoided by a small addition that could not possibly dispose of a self-contradiction: "I *know* that you ought to go now, but please stay a little longer." The oddness is better explained as an inconsistent Gricean "implicature" rather than an implication, for with the above addition the remark no longer "implicates" that she wants the addressee to go now, she merely acknowledges that a sound directive to that effect applies to him but she pleads with him to ignore it. But if the oddness had been due to an implication, the addition could not have been eliminated by this addition.

Criterion (5) also seems to me implausible. Surely, the acceptance of a moral precept is not analogous to the "Aye, aye, Sir" of a private receiving orders from his commanding officer (Hare's example). Even if it were, it might still amount to no more than an acknowledgment that the command has been heard and understood. It may, of course, amount to the subject's now being committed, in the sense of obligated, to carry it out, but not necessarily in the sense of being resolved to do so.

But is accepting a moral precept really like accepting an order? In the case of moral precepts (and other normatives), the subject confronts two disparate parts, the directive and the implication of its soundness. He may acknowledge understanding it without accepting either part, or accepting one part only, or accepting both. Some of the most interesting and difficult questions, those of weakness of will, arise for cases in which one accepts the soundness of the directive but is not resolved to comply with it.

*Note to p. 309. Hume might have thought this, if he had wished to extend his distinction between natural and artificial virtues to duties and wrongs about which he said so much less than about virtues.

*Note to p. 323. Admittedly, in the second case we have the general action descriptions, "failing to bring about . . ." or "failing to see to it that . . . " and "letting it come about that . . ." or "failing to prevent . . . ," but a specification of what these actions are requires the specification of the relevant events or states of affairs. And there is another difference. In the second case, we have discharged or failed to discharge our responsibility depending on whether the required event occurs or the required state of affairs prevails. By contrast, in the first case, we have discharged or failed to discharge our responsibility depending on whether we have done our duty, that is, acted as required by the relevant precept, irrespective of whether or not the state of affairs prevails for whose sake the duty is imposed; we have done our duty not to kill, if we have not killed anyone, and so have not on this account become responsible (in a backward-looking sense), however many people die (though we may have become responsible in that backward-looking sense for some of these deaths because, in addition to the duty not to kill, we also had the task responsibility "for some people's lives," that is, to prevent their death); conversely, we have failed to discharge our duty to drive below the speed limit, if we drive above, even though we do not injure or kill anyone and even though that speed limit was imposed to prevent such mishaps.

*Note to p. 328. In an illuminating and rightly influential article, from which I have greatly benefitted ("Noncomparative Justice," *Philosophical Review* 83, no. 3 [July 1974]), Joel Feinberg appears to endorse Simonides's general conception of justice, for he says, "in all cases, of course, justice *consists in giving a person his due* (p. 298; my italics). But although this formula may state a necessary condition of something being just—we shall shortly see that and why it does—the examples I give in the text (p. 328f) at least strongly suggest that giving a person his due is not what justice consists in, not what makes something just.

*Note to p. 331. In his paper, "Noncomparative Justice," Feinberg examines the notion of cosmic justice/injustice, but lists only two senses, that done *by* and that done *to* the cosmos. These senses at least strongly suggest a conception of the cosmos as something like a person which would not be generally acceptable. I here use another sense of "cosmic" and "societal" justice/injustice, that done or received *in* a social order or in the cosmos. For there to be cosmic justice/injustice in my sense, the cosmos itself need not be a moral agent or a moral order; it is enough that there be one or several moral orders in it with the appropriate institutions of dispensing justice, and that members of these moral orders receive only justice and no injustice through these institutions.

*Note to p. 333. As I said before, this belief of ours is highly plausible. Indeed, a state of affairs in which people always agree on what is due from them to another and vice versa, and always give everyone their due without such institutions would strike us as close to miraculous, more astonishing than Marx's withering away of the state and of the concept of justice. For the desirability and the point of such institutions and of justice need not vanish even if and when one day we move from a realm of necessity (scarcity) to a realm of freedom (plenty). Such a move would, of course, remove one of the major causes of conflict, but there would be plenty left: obscenity and pornography, the use of drugs and other stimulants, racism and ethnic cleansing, pollution through increased consumption of energy and commodities by increasing populations, sexual and other kinds of harassment, rape, sexual and other kinds of jealousy, and many more. It seems to me quite implausible to expect that, simply as a consequence of a general increase in affluence, the need for an enforceable determination of what is due from whom to whom will vanish.

*Note to p. 334. I here want very tentatively to offer a suggestion about a difference between "justice" and "justness" that may strike some as quite implausible or worse. Note first that there are certain adjectives, such as "healthy," "true," or "happy," that have a primary and several derivative senses, and where the noun (if there is only one) or one of the nouns (if there is more than one) may be a derivative from only the primary sense. Health is a state of a living thing, hence "he is healthy" is a primary use, but "healthy food," "healthy complexion," "healthy appetite," and so on are derivative, for "the health of food," and so on makes no sense; we have to speak of the "healthiness" of these things if we want to use a noun. Truth is a property of a statement, hence "what he said is true" is a primary use, but "a true friend" or "a true die," are derivative, for "the truth of a friend" and so on makes no sense; we have to speak of the "trueness" of these things if we must use a noun. "Happiness" is a mental state, hence "she is happy now" is a primary use, "happy life," "happy coincidence," "happy outcome" are derivative, for "the happiness of the coincidence" and so on makes no sense; this is easily overlooked because there is no word, say, "happyness," to contrast with "happiness" as "health" contrasts with "healthiness" or "truth" with "trueness," to alert us to what is the primary sense and what are derivative ones.

It seems to me that "just" and "unjust" also have primary and derivative senses, that we could reserve "justice" and "injustice" for the primary sense of "just" and "unjust," "justness" and "unjustness" for their derivative senses. If "just action" and "just judge" are only derivative uses of "just," and if "justice" is a noun like "health" or "truth," then "justice" is not the name of a virtue (if that is taken, as it usually is, to be the name of a character trait), just as health is not a property or state of healthy food and truth is not a property or state of a true friend. To avoid misleading people about what justice is, we should then speak of the "justness" of judges and their acts rather than of their justice. Of course, in view of the frequency of expressions such as "the proverbial justice of Solomon," it would be worse than pedantic to insist that it should be "proverbial justness." So perhaps we have to say that "justice" is the noun derived both from the primary and the derivative uses of "just." Nevertheless, if I am right about what is the primary use of "just," it remains true that the widespread conviction that justice is one of the most important human virtues, if not the most important, has misled many, not only Simonides, about what justice in the primary sense is and consists in.

**Note to p. 334. Feinberg, in the article "Noncomparative Justice," divides injustices into three classes—I have already commented on his first two—the third being "those that wrong their victims *by means of false derogatory judgments about them*" (pp. 297–98; my italics).

The class I have in mind is much broader than Feinberg's, for it includes assessments to the effect that the person does or does not possess certain abilities (such as skills, know-how, experience, and so on), or traits (such as ambition, gaucheness, shyness, undue optimism) and that he has or has not to his credit or debit certain performances or achievements (such as military service, publications, community service, and so on); not having these, though in some way negative, need not therefore be derogatory.

***Note to p. 334. Two linguistic facts seem to militate against this. Suppose, first, he judges her more favorably or less unfavorably than she deserves. Then he neither fails to do her justice nor does he do her an injustice nor does she suffer an injustice through his judgment. He does indeed fail to give her her *exact* due, but does not give her less than it. Thus doing someone justice (and doing her an injustice) are coextensive with giving her no less (giving her less) than her exact due, but not necessarily with giving (not giving) her her due, for the latter may be thought ambiguous as between including and excluding giving her *more* than her due; we may think of giving her more than her exact due as neither giving nor not giving her her due. So while, on one interpretation, there is a logical space between giving and not giving someone her due— because on that reading giving her more than her due is neither— this does not show that there is a logical space between doing someone justice and doing her an injustice by one and the same judgment. For though in giving her more than her exact due one may neither give nor not give her her due, one is not thereby doing her an injustice and so does not fail to do her justice and so is doing her justice.

But now suppose, second, that he judges her as unfavorably as she deserves, he then gives her her exact due and so his assessment should be a case of doing her justice. But I think many would regard it as odd to use that expression to characterize this assessment as *doing her justice*, even though he does not fail to do her justice nor does he do her an injustice nor does she suffer (or receive) injustice through his assessment. We have four choices: to deny that there is anything odd about this use of "doing someone justice"; to accept that it is odd, but to deny that it affects the truth of the remark and so to accept the view that these two expressions are contradictories; to accept that it is odd and therefore not to use "doing her justice" in this case, while allowing that she receives justice; and finally to admit that the two expressions are not contradictories. I incline to the third alternative, but I do not think the issue is important for my purposes here.

*Note to p. 335.   I here depart to some extent from Feinberg's view by making judgment central to all cases of justice.

*Note to p. 342.   Although I have learned more from, and been influenced more by, John Rawls than by any other contemporary moral philosopher and although there are not many important issues on which I strongly disagree with him and although this is hardly the place in which to start a detailed comparison of our views, what I have just now said about justice and equity may seem to express a disagreement on Rawls's central thesis, and so I probably should add a few words of clarification.

One difference between this book and Rawls's great masterpiece, *A Theory of Justice* (apart, of course, from the difference in quality) is that, as he has recently made clear, his approach is primarily political while mine is primarily ethical. However, since my main aim is to unearth the social roots of reason and morality, I have placed considerable emphasis on some of the social factors involved in the moral enterprise, but I have tried to abstract from the purely political ones, in the rough and narrow sense in which politics is the "game" politicians play in their professional roles, while others don't play it at all or only in their spare time. (For a few further comments on this difference, see the paper referred to in footnote 19, this chapter.)

I suspect, in the second place, that my account of rationality, reasonableness, cognitive, practical, and moral reasons, the "faculty" of reason itself, and reasoning may diverge from Rawls's account in minor or possibly even major ways. But I am not sufficiently clear about his account (or mine, for that matter) to put these differences briefly and clearly. Perhaps, if one day my account is firmly resisted or warmly embraced by someone, she will clarify the significant differences; if it is entirely ignored, then the effort would not seem worth making anyway.

Admittedly, on the topic on which Rawls has made the greatest contribution, there are indeed some differences between us, though not primarily in practically important areas. Perhaps some philosophers will concede that what I call "justice" elucidates one of the many senses of that term; some may even allow that it is an important and wrongly neglected sense. But many would probably insist that what I call "equity" is simply another now widely employed use of "justice." Be that as it may, I want to emphasize that I see little philosophical importance in whether or not the words "justice" and "equity" are often or most naturally or ordinarily used in the ways I outlined. I have tried to clarify that use for two reasons. One is that it elucidates an important legal practice and its overlap with morality. The other is that it provides some indirect and (to me) welcome support for my account of the moral enterprise and its relation to the society's mores.

At the same time, the way I distinguish between justice and equity may have some substantively important implications. For the reasons given in the text, it seems to me that this distinction cannot be captured simply by defining "justice" in such a way that one of its senses, say, "social justice" means what I mean by "equity." Such a definition would not do this job because Rawls's social justice is a virtue of what he calls the basic structure which, if I have not completely misunderstood him, is confined to the institutional structure of a society and so does not contain the part of the mores and of the morality that deals with noninstitutional matters, such as killing, lying, raping, and so on. Thus, it seems, Rawls would not merely not hold that killing, lying, and so on are injustices, or unjust actions, or that people who engage in such actions are unjust on that account or commit injustices, but would deny that the precepts forbidding such behavior are part of a basic social structure which is just on account of including it. If I am right in this, then, according to Rawls, this part of the mores and the social morality is not governed by the principle(s) of social justice, but, in my view, it is governed by the principle of equity. If this view of equity is tenable, then that principle would unify morality in an important way, whereas Rawls's conception of justice and its principles would appear to have no analogue to my conception of equity and its principle. Perhaps I am mistaken on this last point. Perhaps at least Rawls's first principle, that of freedom, could be interpreted so as to include these matters. It is a question I have unfortunately not had time to explore.

There are two related difficult and (at any rate in my mind) ill-articulated issues on which Rawls and I may well differ. The first is connected with his apparent move in the direction of moral relativism. He now seems to want to say that Justice as Fairness may be justifiable only to those who already embrace the ideals of human beings as free and equal. I, too, embrace a form of relativism, but I am unclear about whether or not it is the same as Rawls's. My view is a form of moral relativism in the sense that I think of the subject matter of the moral enterprise (the type) as varying to some extent from one (token) moral enterprise to another, because each such (token) moral enterprise aims at improving the mores of the society in which it is located.

But on my view, the principle on the basis of which the effort to improve the relevant mores is made, is the same principle for all, namely, the principle of equity. To the extent that the principle of equity implies acceptance of the conception of human beings as free and equal, these two ideals are not affected by my concession to relativism. However, if they are independent ideals that belong to the society's culture and so will vary from culture to culture, then they are affected by my relativism. It seems plausible to me that the principle of equity does require the acceptance of the ideal of equality but that the case for freedom may be less clear.

The second point concerns the possibility of a reductive account of the moral enterprise. It seems that Rawls might well reject that possibility. In any case he does not embrace such an account himself. In setting up the framework for the choice of the principles of justice, he does not attempt to provide a purely nonmoral starting point so that there can be a derivation of a moral conception of justice from a purely nonmoral starting point by a method that has no moral commitments. Since he entertains the possibility of a similar derivation of other moral concepts, such as that of rightness, he may well think that reductive derivations are not possible. In that case, there would be a disagreement between us, since I have tried to give an account of the moral enterprise as an important part of the rational enterprise without reliance on any prior specifically moral commitments.

CHAPTER NINE: APPLICATIONS

*Note to p. 353. This need not be taken to imply that when we can do something, we can do its opposite, in the sense here explicated. If I am locked in my room and do not know that I am, then I (conceptually) can intentionally form the intention to stay in the room, though I then may well not be (physically) able to do the opposite, that is, leave the room. Can I (conceptually) choose to stay in the room only if I (conceptually) can choose to leave it, and in these circumstances can I (conceptually) choose to leave it? Would anything count as such a choice? It seems that if I knew I was locked in, nothing would count as such a choice. But it seems to follow from this that in these circumstances I (conceptually) cannot make this choice, that anything I do can at most count as mistakenly thinking that I am making it. If this is sound, then in these circumstances I (conceptually) cannot intentionally leave the room or choose to leave it, but at most I can mistakenly think that I am doing this or have done it. But if I (conceptually) cannot make this choice, then I do not have the choice between leaving and not leaving the locked room and so in these circumstances I do not have the opportunity to make the choice having which is a presupposition of choosing to act in either of these opposite ways. I can willingly or gladly stay, but I (conceptually) cannot make the decision or choice to stay rather than to leave (or to leave rather than to stay), although I can take myself to have made this decision or choice.

**Note to p. 353. Perhaps this point can be made less ambiguous if it is put this way: there is no one it is not wrong to kill, that is, no one of whom it is not true that killing him is, other things equal, morally dispreferable, at the higher (mandatory) level of stringency, to not killing him.

*Note to p. 355. Indeed, resistance may be judged morally preferable to nonresistance—though perhaps only at the optional level of stringency—because acquiescence may be thought to encourage such attacks, resistance to discourage it. The moral preferability of resistance becomes still more persuasive in the case of killing in defense of another, because the life saved is not that of the person saving it but that of another. Hence it is a case of discharging the duty to rescue, not merely one of exercising the right to preserve one's own life which, because self-promotive, may be thought suspect: surely, no one would have condemned Kitty Genovese either for warding off her attacker even if that had led to his death, or for failing to offer any resistance, and many have condemned the many onlookers for their inactivity. Turning the other cheek may be thought preferable, especially in cases such as unprovoked insults which are seldom fatal. But such cases raise difficult empirical questions about the long-range consequences of retaliation, forgiveness, or punishment, which again take the issue beyond the scope of this book.

*Note to p. 367. This point may, at first sight, seem compelling, but it begs the central question. If there is an important moral difference between killing and letting die, then we may not have discharged our duty to kill someone if we have let her die. In some jurisdictions, a criminal sentenced to die receives medical treatment necessary to keep him alive so that he can eventually be executed. In such a case, the authorities would not have discharged their duty to kill him if they had let him die. It is only in those cases in which one's duty is to see to it that someone dies by a certain time, that is, does not remain alive beyond that time, that we can discharge our duty by either killing him or letting him die. Thus, the duty we can discharge by either killing a person or letting her die is not the duty to kill her, but the duty to see to it that she is dead by a certain time. Conversely, the duty not to kill anyone is not the same as the duty to see to it that no one dies whose life one could save. Hence if the duty not to kill is not the same duty as that not to let die, then the real issue, whether we have both a duty not to kill and a duty not to let die, is left open, even if we agree that what makes it our duty not to kill anybody is that killing someone is doing something which results in her being dead.

**Note to p. 367. I have slightly reformulated the nerve of Harris's argument to bypass a trivial objection to the effect that B's death could not be the causal consequence or result of A's failure to save him or prevent his death, but only a conceptual result or consequence of it since, unless B dies, A has not failed to save B's life or to prevent his death or let him die. A's failure to save B or prevent his death can no more be the cause of B's death than A's killing B can be its cause, and for the same reason, B's death cannot be the causal consequence or effect of A's failure. Sound or unsound, this objection is trivial, for it can be bypassed by simply replacing "killing" with a suitable specification of it, such as "stabbing." Clearly, A's stabbing B can be the cause of B's death and in that case amount to A's killing B. Thus, the reason that A's killing B cannot be the cause of B's death is not that killing is not constituted by something, such as stabbing, which is the cause, but that it does not specify the cause independently of the effect. To say that killing is the cause is like saying that *something* that is the cause is the cause. For the same reason, B's death cannot be the causal consequence of A's killing B. Similarly, although (perhaps) A's failure to prevent B's death cannot be the cause of that death nor the death its causal consequence, A's failure to throw B a rope is not conceptually precluded from being the cause of B's death, nor the death from being its causal consequence.

***Note to p. 367. I impose a double-barreled constraint on Harris's argument because without it, the argument cannot get off the ground. His argument commits Harris to two claims: (1) what makes it a duty for A to save B's life is the fact that unless he does so, B will die; and (2) B's death is the (causal) consequence of A's failure to save B, even if A does not have a duty to save B. I take (2) to be implied by Harris's claim that "[it] is not the existence of the duty that makes the death of the drowning [drunk] a consequence of our failure to save him, rather it is the fact that unless we save him he will die that makes it our duty to save him."

The constraint is that A must *know* that unless he saves B, B will die. Otherwise, (1) would entail that any A who can save the life of any B who will die unless A does so, has a duty to do so, irrespective of whether he *knows* that he can save B's life and that B will die unless he does. But in that case, the "even if . . ."

clause of (2) would always be counterfactual, for then these two facts alone, whether known to A or not, make it A's duty to save B's life. But then we could never test Harris's claim that B's death is the (causal) consequence of A's failure to save him rather than of his failure to discharge his duty to save him, since these two cases could never be separated from each other. I assume, therefore, that Harris would agree that, even if B would die if A did not save him and that A could save B, A does not have a duty to save B, unless A knows that B will die unless A saves him and that A can do so. With this constraint, it makes sense to say that it can be found out whether B's death was the causal consequence of A's failure to save B even when A had lacked the knowledge which is a condition of his having a duty to save B.

Note to p. 374. It should be clear by now that, strictly (pedantically) speaking, "Is killing worse than letting die?" presupposes the moral dispreferability of both killing (to not killing) and letting die (to not letting die). If "killing" is morally dispreferable to not killing, but "letting die" is morally nondifferentiating, and so neither it nor its opposite is morally preferable to the other, then "Is killing *worse than* letting die?" does not arise. Asking it in that case would be like asking whether iced tea is less hot (or is colder) than boiling water, or whether boiling water is less cold (or hotter) than iced tea. Since boiling water is not cold, it cannot be less cold than something that is cold, and so on, for the other comparisons. "Colder" and "less cold" are used to state comparisons between things that are cold, and similarly "hotter" and "less hot" for things that are hot. If we want to state such comparisons between things that are hot and things that are cold, we should use comparative terms, such as "higher/lower temperature," which operate on both sides of the dividing line between hot and cold. "Morally worse" and "morally better" are comparative terms which, like "colder" and "hotter," operate only on one side of the relevant divide, in this case between "morally good" and "morally bad."

To avoid the above presupposition, we could use the term "morally preferable," which, like "temperature," operates on both sides of the relevant divide, but then in this context we do not, of course, use it, as we did earlier, to evaluate choices a single individual has at a given time, between opposites in my special sense. In the present context it would also evaluate choices by different individuals on different occasions about quite different matters, as when we ask whether it was morally worse (or morally dispreferable), say, for Cain to kill Abel or for Judas to betray Jesus for thirty pieces of silver.

Note to p. 381. It therefore seems to me that the traditional term "imperfect duty," for something about which it is impossible to say objectively whether a person has discharged it, is an unfortunate choice, to put it mildly.

*Note to p. 389. Professor Anscombe has made the perceptive point that philosophers who calmly ask what should be done in such situations reveal a lack of moral sensitivity or worse. It seems to me, however, that one can ask these questions calmly, that is, in a rational frame of mind even when one is deeply moved and troubled by the thought of people in such situations. Reflecting about such cases when we are not under the emotional pressures experienced in them may help us find the right moral answers or realize that the problems lie outside the moral domain. This might enable us at least to know what decision to make when we have to make one in a hurry or under considerable duress, and that should help us *do* what we know to be the right or at least the least unsatisfactory thing, even if it does not, in the end, under the stress of the circumstances, move us to do it.

BIBLIOGRAPHY OF PUBLICATIONS CITED

Alchurrón, Carlos E., and Eugenio Bulygin. *Normative Systems.* Vienna: Springer-Verlag, 1971.

Aquinas, Saint Thomas. *Summa Theologica,* excerpted in *The Political Ideas of St. Thomas Aquinas.* Ed. Dino Bigongiari. New York: Hafner, 1953.

Aristotle. *Nicomachean Ethics.* Ed. Terence Irwin. Indianapolis, Ind.: Hackett Publishing Co., 1985.

Arrow, Kenneth. *Social Choice and Individual Values.* New York: John Wiley & Sons, Inc., 1951.

Austin, John. *The Province of Jurisprudence Determined Etc.* Ed. H. L. A. Hart. London: Weidenfeld and Nicolson, 1954.

Austin, John L. "A Plea for Excuses." In *Proceedings of the Aristotelian Society* (1956–7). Reprinted in J. L. Austin, *Philosophical Papers,* ed. J. O. Urmson and A. J. Warnock, 123–52 (Oxford University Press, 1961).

———. *How to Do Things With Words.* London: Oxford University Press, 1962.

Axelrod, Robert. *The Evolution of Cooperation.* New York: Basic Books, 1984.

Baier, Kurt. "Action and Agent." *Monist* 49, no. 2 (April 1965): 183–95.

———. "Moral Obligation." *American Philosophical Quarterly* 3 (July 1966):1–17.

———. "Responsibility and Freedom." In *Ethics and Society,* ed. Richard T. DeGeorge, 49–84. Garden City, N.Y.: Anchor, 1966.

———. "Value and Fact." In Kiefer and Munitz, eds., 1968, 93–121.

———. "The Justification of Governmental Authority." Lead paper in APA symposium entitled *Authority and Autonomy,* APA Eastern Division Meetings, December 1972. Published in *Journal of Philosophy* 69 (1972): 700–15.

―――. "Reason and Experience." *Noûs* 7, no. 1 (March 1973):56–67.

―――. "Rationality and Morality," with a reply by Sen. *Erkenntnis* 11 (1977):197–223.

―――. "The Social Source of Reason." Presidential Address, APA Eastern Division, 1977. Published in *Proceedings and Addresses of the American Philosophical Association* 51, no. 6 (August 1978):707–33.

―――. "Maximization and the Good Life." In *Akten des 5. Internationalen Wittgenstein Symposiums, 25. Bis 31. August,* 1980, 33–42. Vienna: Hölder-Pichler-Tempsky, 1981.

―――. "Rationality, Reason, and the Good." In Copp and Zimmerman, eds., 1985, 193–211.

―――. "Moral and Legal Responsibility." In Siegler, Toulmin, Zimring, and Schaffner, eds., 1987, 101–29.

―――. "Threats of Futility: Is Life Worth Living?" *Free Inquiry* 8 (Summer 1988):47–52.

―――. "Rationality, Value, and Preference." *Social Philosophy and Policy* 5 (1988):17–45.

―――. "Autarchy, Reason and Commitment." *Ethics* 100, no. 1 (1989):93–107.

―――. "Preference and the Good of Man." In Schilpp and Hahn, eds., 1989, 233–70.

―――. "Justice and the Aims of Political Philosophy." *Ethics* 99, no. 4 (July 1989):771–90.

―――. "Egoism." In Singer, ed., 1992, 197–204.

―――. "Review of Thomson." *Dialogue* 33 (1994):1–13.

Barry, Brian. "Exit, Voice, and Loyalty." *British Journal of Political Science* 4 (1974). Reprinted in Brian Barry, *Democracy and Power,* Essays in Political Theory 1, chapter 7, 187–221 (Oxford: Clarendon Press, 1991).

Belnap, Nuel, and Michael Perloff. "Seeing to it That: a Canonical Form for Agentives." *Theoria* 54 (1988):175–99.

Bennett, Jonathan. "Morality and Consequences." *The Tanner Lectures on Human Values,* vol. 2. Salt Lake City, Utah: University of Utah Press, 1981.

Bentham, Jeremy. *A Fragment on Government.* Ed. J. H. Burns and H. L. A. Hart. Cambridge, UK: Cambridge University Press, 1988.

Bosanquet, Bernard. *The Philosophical Theory of the State.* 4th ed. London: Macmillan, 1923.

Brandt, R. B. "Some Merits of One From of Rule Utilitarianism." In Gorovitz, ed., 1971, 324–44.

Braybrooke, David. "The Insoluble Problem of the Social Contract." *Dialogue* 15 (March 1976):3–37.

Broad, Charlie D. *Five Types of Ethical Theory*. London: Kegan Paul, 1944.

Butler, Joseph. *The Works of Joseph Butler*. Vol. 2. Ed. W. E. Gladstone. London: Oxford Press, 1897.

Castañeda, Hector-Neri, and George Nakhnikian, eds. *Morality and the Language of Conduct*. Detroit, Mich.: Wayne State University Press, 1963.

Chisholm, Roderick M. "Freedom and Action." In Lehrer, ed., 1966, 11–44.

Clifford, W. K. "The Ethics of Belief." In Stephen and Pollock eds., 1947.

Collingwood, Robin G. *An Essay on Metaphysics*. Oxford: Clarendon Press, 1940.

Copp, D., and D. Zimmerman, eds. *Morality, Reason and Truth: New Essays on the Foundations of Ethics*. Totowa, N.J.: Rowman and Allanheld, 1985.

Dancy, Jonathan. *Moral Reasons*. Oxford: Blackwell, 1993.

Darwall, Stephen. *Impartial Reason*. Ithaca, N.Y.: Cornell University Press, 1983.

Darwall, Stephen, Allan Gibbard, and Peter Railton. "Toward *Fin de siècle* Ethics: Some Trends." *Philosophical Review* 101, no. 1 (January 1992):115–89.

Davidson, Donald. "Actions, Reasons and Causes." *Journal of Philosophy* 60, no. 23 (November 1963):685–700. Reprinted in *Essays on Actions and Events*, 3–19 (London: Oxford University Press, 1980).

Dworkin, Ronald. *A Matter of Principle*. Cambridge, Mass.: Harvard University Press, 1985.

———. *Law's Empire*. Cambridge, Mass.: Belknap Press of Harvard University Press, 1986.

———. *Taking Rights Seriously*. Cambridge, Mass.: Harvard University Press, 1977.

Elster, Jon. *Ulysses and the Sirens: Studies in Rationality and Irrationality*. Cambridge, UK, and New York: Cambridge University Press, 1979.

Falk, David. "'Ought' and Motivation." *Proceedings of The Aristotelian Society* 48 (1947–48). Reprinted in Falk, ed., 1986, 21–41.

———. "Morality, Self, and Others." In Castañeda and Nakhnikian, eds., 1963, 25–68.

———, ed. *Ought, Reasons, and Morality: The Collected Papers of W. D. Falk*. Ithaca, N.Y.: Cornell University Press, 1986.

Feinberg, Joel. "Sua Culpa." *Doing and Deserving*. Princeton, N.J.: Princeton University Press, 1970.

———. "The Nature and Value of Rights." *Journal of Value Inquiry* 4 (Winter 1970):243–57.

———. *The Moral Limits of the Criminal Law*. Vol. 1, *Harm to Others*. New York: Oxford University Press, 1984.

———. "Noncomparative Justice." *Philosophical Review* 83 (July 1974):297–338.

Finnis, John. *Natural Law and Natural Rights*. Oxford: Oxford University Press, 1980.

Foot, Philippa. "Morality as a System of Hypothetical Imperatives." *Philosophical*

Review 81 (1972). Reprinted in *Virtues and Vices,* 157–67 (Berkeley, Calif.: University of California Press, 1978.)

————. "Morality and Art." Reprinted in *Philosophy As It Is,* ed. Ted Honderich and Myles Burnyeat, 14 (New York: Penguin Books, 1979.)

Frankena, William K. "Obligation and Motivation in Recent Moral Philosophy." In Melden, ed., 1958.

————. "Some Beliefs About Justice." *Lindley Lecture.* Lawrence: University of Kansas Press, 1966.

————. "Three Questions About Morality." *Monist* (January 1980).

Fried, Charles. *Right and Wrong.* Cambridge, Mass.: Harvard University Press, 1978.

Fuller, Lon L. *The Morality of Law.* New Haven, Conn.: Yale University Press, 1969.

Gasking, Douglas. "Causation and Recipes." *Mind* 64 (October 1955):479–87.

Gauthier, David. *Morals by Agreement.* Oxford: Oxford University Press, 1986.

Gilligan, Carol. *In a Different Voice.* Cambridge, Mass.: Harvard University Press, 1982.

Glover, Jonathan. *Causing Death and Saving Lives.* New York: Penguin Books, 1977.

Goodall, Jane. *The Chimpanzees of Gombe.* Cambridge, Mass.: Harvard University Press, 1986.

Gorovitz, Samuel, ed. *Utilitarianism. John Stuart Mill.* Indianapolis: Bobbs-Merrill Company, Inc., 1971.

Green, Thomas H. *Prolegomena to Ethics.* 5th ed. Ed. A. C. Bradley. London: Oxford University Press, 1906.

Greenwalt, Kent. *Conflicts of Law and Morality.* New York: Oxford University Press, 1989.

Grice, Russell. *The Grounds of Moral Judgment.* London: Cambridge University Press, 1967.

Hampton, Jean. *Hobbes and the Social Contract Tradition.* Cambridge, UK: Cambridge University Press, 1986.

Hare, Richard M. "Review of Stephen Toulmin's *The Place of Reason in Ethics.*" *Philosophical Quarterly* (1951):372.

————. *The Language of Morals.* Oxford: Oxford University Press, 1952.

————. *Freedom and Reason.* New York: Oxford University Press, 1965.

Harris, John. "The Marxist Conception of Violence." *Philosophy and Public Affairs* 3 (1974):192–220. Reprinted in *Philosophical Issues in Law,* ed. Kenneth Kipnis, 136–58 (Englewood Cliffs, N.J.: Prentice-Hall, 1977).

Harsanyi, John. "Ethics in Terms of Hypothetical Imperatives." *Mind* 67 (July 1958):305–16. Reprinted in *Essays on Ethics, Social Behavior, and Scientific Explanation,* 24–36 (Dordrecht, Holland: D. Reidel, 1976); also in *Rational Behavior and Bargaining Equilibrium in Games and Social Situations* (Cambridge: Cambridge University Press, 1976).

Hart, Herbert L. A. *The Concept of Law.* Oxford: Oxford University Press, 1961.

———. *Punishment and Responsibility.* New York: Oxford University Press, 1968.

Hirschman, Albert O. *Exit, Voice, and Loyalty. Responses to Decline in Firms, Organizations, and States.* Cambridge, Mass.: Harvard University Press, 1970.

Hobbes, Thomas. *Leviathan.* New York: Penguin Books, 1951, 1984.

Hume, David. *Enquiries Concerning Human Understanding and Concerning the Principles of Morals.* Ed. L. A. Selby-Bigge and P. H. Nidditch. 3rd ed. Oxford: Oxford University Press, 1975.

———. *A Treatise of Human Nature.* Ed. L. A. Selby-Bigge and P. H. Nidditch. 2nd ed. Oxford: Oxford University Press, 1978.

Joseph, H. W. B. "Plato's Republic: The Nature of the Soul." *Essays in Ancient and Modern Philosophy,* 52–53. Freeport, N.Y.: Books for Libraries, 1971.

Kadish, Mortimer R., and Sanford H. *Discretion to Disobey: A Study of Lawful Departure from Legal Rules* in the *University of Pennsylvania Law Review* 124 (1975):577–80.

Kagan, Shelly. *The Limits of Morality.* Oxford: Oxford University Press, 1989.

Kamm, Frances Myrna. "Harming, Not Aiding, and Positive Rights." *Philosophy and Public Affairs* 15, no. 1 (Winter 1986):3–32.

———. *Creation and Abortion.* New York: Oxford University Press, 1992.

Kant, Immanuel. *Groundwork of the Metaphysics of Morals.* Trans. H. J. Paton. London: Hutchinson University Library, 1948.

———. *The Metaphysics of Morals.* Trans. Mary Gregor. Cambridge, UK: Cambridge University Press, 1991.

Kiefer, Howard, and Milton K. Munitz, eds. *Contemporary Philosophic Thought.* Vol. 4, *Ethical and Social Justice.* Albany, N.Y.: State University of New York Press, 1968, 1970.

Kipnis, Kenneth. *Philosophical Issues in Law.* Englewood Cliffs, N.J.: Prentice-Hall, 1977.

Kohlberg, Lawrence. "Moral Stages and Motivation: The Cognitive-Developmental Approach." In Lickona, ed., 1976, 31–53.

Körner, Stephan, ed. *Practical Reason.* New Haven, Conn.: Yale University Press, 1974.

Kraut, Richard. *Aristotle on the Human Good.* Princeton, N.J.: Princeton University Press, 1989.

Lehrer, Keith, ed. *Freedom and Determinism.* New York: Random House, 1966.

Lickona, Thomas, ed. *Moral Development and Behavior.* New York: Holt, Reinhart, and Winston, 1976.

Lyons, David. *The Forms and Limits of Utilitarianism.* London: Oxford University Press, 1965.

MacCormick, Neil. *Legal Reasoning and Legal Theory.* Oxford: Oxford University Press, 1978.

MacIntyre, Alasdair. *Whose Justice? Which Rationality?* Notre Dame, Ind.: University of Notre Dame Press, 1988.

Mackie, J. L. *Ethics. Inventing Right and Wrong.* London: Penguin, 1977.

———. *Hume's Moral Theory.* London: Routledge and Kegan Paul, 1980.

Marschak, Jacob. "Towards an Economic Theory of Organization and Information." In Thrall, Coombs, and Davis, eds., 1954.

Melden, A. I. ed. *Essays in Moral Philosophy.* Seattle, Wash.: University of Washington Press, 1958.

Mill, J. S. *Utilitarianism* in *Utilitarianism, Essays on Ethics, Religion, and Society: Collected Works of John Stuart Mill.* Vol. 10. Ed. J. M. Robson. Toronto: University of Toronto Press, 1969.

Moore, George E. "A Reply to My Critics." In Schilpp, ed., 1968.

———. *Principia Ethica.* Cambridge, UK: Cambridge University Press, 1903.

Nagel, Thomas. *The Possibility of Altruism.* Princeton, N.J.: Princeton University Press, 1970.

———. *The View from Nowhere.* New York: Oxford University Press, 1986.

Parfit, Derek. "Prudence, Morality, and the Prisoner's Dilemma." *Proceedings of the British Academy* 65, 539–64. London: Oxford University Press, 1979.

———. "Prudence, Rationality and Prisoner's Dilemma." The Henriette Hertz Trust Lecture. London: British Academy, 1981.

———. *Reasons and Persons.* London: Oxford University Press, 1984.

Piaget, Jean. *The Moral Judgment of the Child.* London: Kegan, Paul, Trench, Tubner, 1932.

Plato. "Euthyphro." *The Trial and Death of Socrates,* 12–14 [10a–11b]. Trans. G. M. A. Grube. Indianapolis, Ind.: Hackett, 1975.

———. *Republic.* Trans. Francis MacDonald Cornford. Oxford: Oxford University Press, 1941.

Popper, Karl R. *Conjectures and Refutations.* London: Routledge and Kegan Paul, 1963.

Powledge, Tabitha M., and Peter Steinfels. "Following the News on Karen Quinlan." *Hastings Center Report* 5 (December 1975):506–28.

Prichard, Harold A. "Does Moral Philosophy Rest on a Mistake?" *Mind* 21 (1912). Reprinted in H. A. Prichard, *Moral Obligation,* ed. W. D. Ross, 1–17. (Oxford: Clarendon Press, 1949); also reprinted in *Readings in Ethical Theory,* 2nd ed., ed. Wilfrid Sellars and John Hospers (Englewood Cliffs, N.J.: Prentice-Hall, 1970).

Rawls, John. *A Theory of Justice.* Cambridge, Mass.: Harvard University Press, 1971.

Raz, Joseph. *Practical Reasons and Norms.* London: Hutchinson University Library, 1975.

———. *The Authority of Law.* Oxford: Clarendon Press, 1979.

———. *The Morality of Freedom.* Oxford: Clarendon Press, 1986.

Regan, Tom, ed. *Matters of Life and Death*. 2nd ed. New York: Random House, 1980.

Rescher, Nicholas, and Kurt Baier, eds. *Values and the Future*. London: The Free Press/Collier-Macmillan, Ltd., 1969.

Ross, Sir David. *The Foundations of Ethics*. London: Oxford University Press, 1939.

———. *The Right and the Good*. London: Oxford University Press, 1930.

Rothenberg, Jerome. *The Measurement of Social Welfare*. Englewood Cliffs, N.J.: Prentice-Hall, Inc., 1961.

Ryle, Gilbert. *The Concept of Mind*. London: Hutchinson's University Library, 1949.

Sanders, Steven, and David R. Cheney, eds. *The Meaning of Life*. Englewood Cliffs, N.J.: Prentice-Hall, 1980.

Schilpp, Paul A., ed. *The Philosophy of G. E. Moore*. 3rd ed. Vol. 4, The Library of Living Philosophers. La Salle, Ill.: Open Court, 1968.

Schilpp, Paul A., and Lewis E. Hahn, eds. *The Philosophy of Georg Henrik von Wright*. Vol. 19, The Library of Living Philosophers. La Salle, Ill.: Open Court, 1989.

Schneewind, Jerome B. *Sidgwick's Ethics and Victorian Moral Philosophy*. Oxford: Clarendon Press, 1977.

Schopenhauer, Arthur. "On the Vanity of Existence." In Sanders and Cheney, eds., 1980.

Sen, Amartya. "Behaviour and the Concept of Preferences." *Economica* 11 (1973):241–59.

———. "Choice, Orderings, and Morality," along with J. W. N. Watkin's reply "Self-Interest and Morality" and Sen's rejoinder. In Körner, ed., 1974, 54–82.

Sidgwick, Henry. *The Methods of Ethics*. 7th ed. London: Macmillan, 1907.

Siegler, Mark, Stephen Toulmin, Franklin E. Zimring, and Kenneth F. Schaffner, eds. *Medical Innovations and Bad Outcomes: Legal, Social and Ethical Responses*. Ann Arbor, Mich.: Health Administration Press, 1987.

Simon, Herbert A. *Reason in Human Affairs*. Stanford, Calif.: Stanford University Press, 1983.

Singer, Marcus. *Generalization in Ethics*. New York: Knopf, 1961.

Singer, Peter, ed. *A Companion to Ethics*. Oxford: Blackwell, 1992.

———. "Bandit and Friends." *New York Review of Books* (April 9, 1992):10–11.

Smith, M. B. E. "Is There a Prima Facie Obligation to Obey the Law?" *Yale Law Journal* 82, no. 5 (April 1973):950–76.

Soper, Philip. *A Theory of Law*. Cambridge, Mass.: Harvard University Press, 1984.

Steinbock, Bonnie, ed. *Killing and Letting Die*. Englewood Cliffs, N.J.: Prentice-Hall, 1980.

Stephen, Leslie, and Sir Frederick Pollock, eds. *The Ethics of Belief and Other Essays*. London: Watts, 1947.

Sterba, James. "Justifying Morality: The Right and the Wrong Way." In Thomas, ed., 1987, 45–69.

Strawson, Peter F. *Individuals*. London: Methuen & Co., Ltd., 1959.

Thomas, Laurence. *Living Morally: A Psychology of Moral Character*. Philadelphia: Temple University Press, 1989.

————, ed. *Festschrift in Honor of Kurt Baier*. *Synthese* 72, nos. 1–2 (1987).

Thomson, Judith Jarvis. *The Realm of Rights*. Cambridge, Mass.: Harvard University Press, 1990.

Thrall, R. M., C. H. Coombs, and R. L. Davis, eds. *Decision Processes*. New York: John Wiley and Sons, 1954.

Toulmin, Stephen. *The Place of Reason in Ethics*. London: Cambridge University Press, 1950.

Turnbull, Colin. *The Mountain People*. New York: Simon and Schuster, 1972.

Ullmann-Margalit, Edna. *The Emergence of Norms*. Oxford: Oxford University Press, 1977.

Urmson, J. O. *The Emotive Theory of Ethics*. London: Hutchinson, 1968.

Warnock, Geoffrey J. *The Object of Morality*. London: Methuen, 1971.

Wasserstrom, Richard. *The Judicial Decision*. Stanford, Calif.: Stanford University Press, 1961.

Williams, Bernard. "Internal and External Reasons." Reprinted in *Moral Luck*, ed. Bernard Williams, Essay 8, 101–13. Cambridge, UK: Cambridge University Press, 1981.

————. *Ethics and the Limits of Philosophy*. Cambridge, Mass.: Harvard University Press, 1985.

INDEX